Violent Modernities

Violent Modernities

Cultural Lives of Law in the New India

Oishik Sircar

OXFORD
UNIVERSITY PRESS

OXFORD
UNIVERSITY PRESS

Oxford University Press is a department of the University of Oxford.
It furthers the University's objective of excellence in research, scholarship,
and education by publishing worldwide. Oxford is a registered trademark of
Oxford University Press in the UK and in certain other countries.

Published in India by
Oxford University Press
22 Workspace, 2nd Floor, 1/22 Asaf Ali Road, New Delhi 110 002, India

First Edition published in 2021

ISBN-13 (print edition): 978-0-19-012792-3
ISBN-10 (print edition): 0-19-012792-9

ISBN-13 (eBook): 978-0-19-099214-9
ISBN-10 (eBook): 0-19-099214-X

Typeset in Adobe Garamond Pro 11/13
by The Graphics Solution, New Delhi 110 092
Printed in India by Rakmo Press Pvt. Ltd.

For D,
fierce and tender

That life is complicated is a fact of great analytic importance. Law too often seeks to avoid this truth by making up its own breed of narrower, simpler, but hypnotically powerful rhetorical truths.

—Patricia J. Williams, *The Alchemy of Race and Rights: Diary of a Law Professor* (1992)

It has long been my belief that law is the most disabling or estranged of professions. Such at least is its most radical danger: it inculcates a fear which finds its most prominent expression in the closure of the legal mind, in the lawyers' belief in a norm or rule which speaks as 'the law'.

—Peter Goodrich, *Law in the Courts of Love: Literature and Other Minor Jurisprudences* (1996)

Go back to uni, study the law. Accept the law, even when it's unjust.

—Kamila Shamsie, *Home Fire (2017)*

Contents

Figures

Foreword

Hanif Kureishi's short story, 'My Son the Fanatic', tells the story of a Pakistani immigrant, Parvez, and his son, Ali. Parvez invests decades in his work as a taxi driver to create a life sustained by ambitions and hopes for his son's modern British future—marked for him by the twinned ethe of tolerance and assimilation. Imagine how unnerved he is then when he finds that as he grows up, Ali pivots towards orthodox Islam: Turning from his accountancy exam to mosque devotions, rejecting his cricket bat for a prayer mat, dismissing his father's celebration of secular moral tolerance for an authoritative ethical compass, turning from material rewards to religious discipline, rejecting the promise of assimilation into 'modernity' for the promise of spiritual fulfilment in the afterlife, deriding his father's debts to white Britain, to instead embrace visions of worlding beyond those of the West. Parvez, the mild-mannered tolerant liberal, becomes incensed at his son's rejection of those very promises of modernity that provided scaffolding for his immigrant dream. He beats up his son till Ali is on the floor, kicked, punched, and virtually insensible. Through bloodied lips, Ali has the final word: 'So who is the fanatic now?'

The imbrications of the discourses and institutions of modernity and violence have been pivotal to colonial and post-colonial histories. This imbrication is a central dimension of our current moment from the domestic and micro-political (such as in Kureishi's short story), to the global and macro-political (consider the war in Afghanistan). Oishik Sircar's remarkable book illuminates these tangles of modernity and violence with sophistication, originality, and insight. *Violent Modernities* is anchored in contemporary India and that historical context is central to the political struggles Oishik is invested in, and the analytical arguments he advances. Indeed, vigilant about the risks of universalizing his critical interventions, he insists that the work is not conceived as 'atemporal and portable'. This work invites us into grappling with the specific histories and geographies of contemporary India and shines a light onto the braiding of the 'rule of law' and violence in this pivotal moment in Indian debates about modernity and its futures. However, I began with a story of modern Britain and its promises to underscore how the theoretical portals Oishik opens up have a wider purchase. That grappling with debates grounded in the specific histories and geographies of contemporary India have much to teach us about how violence inhabits discourses and institutions of modernity, including the 'rule of law', in other spaces and places.

Central to the entanglements of 'violent modernity' that are the focus of this book, is the terrain of law, its institutionalization and its imagination. The book speaks of how laws get constituted through processes that have far-reaching local impacts, while emerging from transnational processes of professionalization of legal knowledge. 'Global Economic Constitutionalism' and 'New Legal Order' are examples of these travelling knowledge regimes that Oishik describes (drawing on Jasbir K. Puar) as 'history vanishing' frameworks. They build on long-standing investments in notions of the 'rule of law' that have emerged as distinctive features of how modernity has come to be defined by dominant institutions and political cultures in India. This work tells us how law and cultures of legality interpolate modern citizenship through what Oishik identifies as 'spectacles of emancipation' that seduce faith and compliance through the mirage of law as a conduit for justice, or even as itself a metonym of justice.

The striking achievement of the 'spectacles of emancipation' that this story lays bare is that liberal legality and majoritarian violence have moved forward as co-travelers in shaping the contours of modern citizenship from courtroom battles to cinematic dramas. Thus, while the Special Investigation Team exonerated Narendra Modi for his role in the orchestration of the anti-Muslim pogrom in Gujarat, giving him a 'clean chit' carrying the imprimatur of supreme legality, cinematic representations of the afterlives of Gujarat in cultural memory represent and rationalize the constitution and 'state-making' practices that were the pre-histories of the pogrom. Through analysis of the Best Bakery massacre and the Bollywood film *Dev*, Oishik shows how a space is made for Islamophobic violence that is represented in both law and cinema as ever present but with no one responsible—indeed, it emerges as compatible with the 'secularism, legalism and developmentalism of the New Indian State'. Naturalized and aestheticized as a necessary backdrop for the nation, the film allows anti-Muslim violence to be remembered anew in ways that re-inscribe national mythologies of heritage and heroes, reconciliation and redemption, tolerant Hindu majorities and ever outsider Muslim minorities. Oishik describes a 'jurisprudential–aesthetic' narrative compact that carries subliminal cinematic cues (about Hindi–English as the national–universal for instance) that work alongside constitutional inheritances to shape conditions of legibility for modern political subjectivity in ways that exclude and marginalize minorities. The analysis powerfully portrays the mythic lives of law—offering nuanced portrayals of the hyperbolically visible and audible jurisprudential orientations of Bollywood on the big screen, but also with an eye acutely alert to the nuances of affect in a film's reception, attentive to the work of 'minor jurisprudence' in the cinemagoer's aesthetic consumption.

Critical legal theorists who speak of the social construction of law have developed a body of work on the development of institutions and traditions of judicial interpretation; equally, there has been work on the relationship between social movements and legal developments. This book takes these conversations further into the realm of cultural production and connects the dots between institutions tasked with the administration of justice (including social services), social movements making justice claims (for instance, around sex work in one instance, and sexual rights in another) and the interpolation of the juridical in realms such as film (documentaries to advertisements). For instance, in the case of children of sex workers, the analysis (co-authored with Debolina Dutta) offers a compelling critique of how dominant humanitarian tropes of 'rescue' deny children's agency and the complexity of their familial and social relations. It is an argument that deconstructs the affective structure of compassion in this domain, and how it facilitates violence and abuse against these same communities precisely by advancing narratives in their name.

The complexity of the multiple lives of law and its disciplinary technologies that Oishik describes is that these dynamics worked differently for social movements seeking institutional legibility for the sexually marginalized in struggles for the decriminalizing of adult, consensual, and private sex. Here, the driving trope of liberal modernity was not humanitarian compassion but the mythos of equal rights, and how it has been invoked and deployed in ways that domesticated the subversive thrust of queer politics. Oishik's argument in this discussion deconstructs the affective structure of inclusion into neoliberal, market-friendly modernity, and how it presses depoliticization and individualization onto queer communities precisely by advancing narratives in their name for the redemption of 'New India' and new markets. In both these cases, Oishik is not just an observer but an activist and his reading of these domains also situates his own creative interventions and solidarities in these struggles (including, he says, in performing 'stuckness', following Lauren Berlant). Thus, these are not arguments for abandoning activism but for doing it differently by wrestling with intersecting structures and identities to stay with the fraught political challenges of thinking collaboratively with social movements about how to advance justice claims but refuse 'homonationalism' and interrupt neoliberal citizenship.

This a book of dazzling erudition—Oishik is in conversation not only with other legal scholars in India and elsewhere, but also with the theorizing of legal modernity in a range of other disciplines from literary theory to postcolonial studies to anthropology to queer theory. Masterfully drawing attention to and analyzing the assemblage of mnemohistories in the formation of a national consciousness driven by the juridical unconscious, this work offers a remarkable tour de force journey through battles over the life of the law, showing the co-constitutive intimacy of constitutional and cultural domains. Yet, what is most striking is the insistent self-reflexive situating of these conversations in his own role in academia and social movements with particular political investments. The discussion of his feminism and the vexed entanglements of those commitments, from the personal to the professional to the political, offers but one example of what is a running sub-narrative that is a dialogic companion to every argument in the book.

In other words, the book's erudition and multiple interdisciplinary conversations are not channeled into the disinterested pursuit of critique as enlightenment, but a constant questioning of the theorist as activist, and the activist as theorist. In fact, one may situate the notion of enlightenment here as akin to the notion of critique that Foucault articulates in 'What is Enlightenment?' Foucault argues that Kant's essay should not be understood as a celebration of the knowledge regimes associated with the historical moment of enlightenment but as an interrogation of that moment—or indeed, a critical interrogation of the moment one is in. Such an interrogation is a constant companion to Oishik's analysis—an alter ego, pushing at every analytical move, grappling with hard questions about the relation of text and context at each turn, relentlessly holding itself to account. In this sense, in this book that gives expression to the responsibilities of critique alongside the hope embedded in struggle, Oishik may be a worthy inheritor of Upendra Baxi's mantle and his simultaneously inspiring and discomforting presence in a wounded world.

In the Kureishi short story that I began with, Ali criticizes his father's investment in Britain's promises, asking 'Papa, how can you love something that hates you?' Parvez does not answer the question but perhaps the story of Parvez's love is that he had to fight against the hate of injustice to create the space for his life; that fight engendered the investment that Ali terms love. Oishik's critique of the law and the injustices it has wrought in the name of justice, also loves wrestling the law for the space that justice struggles demand. This comes through in the aesthetics and rhythms of this beautifully written book that was such a pleasure to read. I lean on James Baldwin here who speaks of love as 'a battle; love is a war'—but love is also, as he says in another passage, 'a state of being, or a state of grace … in the tough and universal sense of quest and daring and growth.' *Violent Modernities* in chapter after chapter, can be seen to be just that, an expression of love as a brawl with law for space—the space to invoke, listen to and perform law differently in a quest marked by grace and daring.

Vasuki Nesiah
Professor of Practice
Gallatin School of Individualized Study
New York University

Acknowledgements

> A book is not an isolated being: it is a relationship, an axis of innumerable relationships.
>
> — Jorge Luis Borges, *Labyrinths*(1962)

The essays collected in this book document my scholarly and activist journeys through the labyrinths of the learnings and failings of my politics over a period of a decade. I would like to thank those whose influences have played a foundational role in both strengthening and questioning the praxes of my proclivities and predilections over these years.

Ravi Nair, for initiating me into the world of human rights activism and research. Ranabir Samaddar, for making me realize that activism is fortified through theorizing. Hutokshi Doctor, for training me to never underestimate the intelligence of readers and for cautioning me against my love for jargons. Sharmila Rege, for showing me the joys of bringing together teaching and writing for social justice. Rustom Bharucha, for demonstrating through his writing and thinking how to read politics into aesthetics and vice versa. Ratna Kapur, for lending me a feminist language to work through my double-binds. Brenda Cossman, for pushing me to think of the worth of critique as scholarly practice. Shaun McVeigh, for provoking me to think of conduct as different from critique. Jasbir Puar, for enlivening theory as life practice.

Sundhya Pahuja, for impressing on me the political worth of scholarly conventions. Dianne Otto, for keeping alive the flame of activism in scholarship. Peter Rush, for showing me why style matters for scholarship. Joan Nestle, for insisting on the political necessity of pleasure and poetry. Jennifer Nedelsky, for emphasizing how material conditions of gendered work are intrinsic to the politics of scholarship and activism. Janet Halley, for urging me to never flinch if I want to take a break. Ritu Birla, for teaching me history as process, not event. Flavia Agnes, for keeping alive a faith in law's promises in dark times. Upendra Baxi, for practicing a scholarly life that brings alive the struggles of keeping faith in law's promises and learning from law's betrayals.

Friends, mentors, comrades, colleagues, and collaborators whose lives, work, and generosity have materially, gastronomically, emotionally, and intellectually sustained and nurtured me in ways that might be completely unknown to them: Adil Hasan Khan, Trina Nileena Banerjee, Sakyadeb Choudhury, Shayanti Sinha, Deepti Mohan, Saptarshi Mandal, Rohini Sen, Rajshree Chandra, Claire Opperman, Anirban Ghosh, Garga Chatterjee, Shilpi Bhattacharya, Dipika Jain, Samia Khatun, Carolina Ruiz Austria, Alivia Dey, Ann Genovese, Sara Dehm, Luis Eslava, Rose Parfitt, Vik Kanwar, Julia Dehm, James Parker, Cait Storr, Dolly Kikon, Yasmin Tambiah, Sally Engle Merry, Kalpana Kannabiran, Saumya Uma, Bina Fernandez, Jaya Sagade, Maria Elander, Bikram Jeet Batra, Farrah Ahmed, Mohsin Alam Bhat, Mohsin Raza Khan, Albeena Shakil, Rahul Rao, Nikita Dhawan, Meenakshi Gopinath, Swati Bhatt, Agyatmitra Shantanu Mehra, Ruchira Goswami, Arun Sagar, Arpita Gupta, Rajgopal Saikumar, Priya Gupta, Sneha Gole, Anagha Tambe, Sannoy Das, Danish Sheikh, Prabhakar Singh, Maddy Clarke, Sagar Sanyal, Aashita Dawer, Ankita Gandhi, Sanskriti Sanghi, Max Steuer and Anish Vanaik.

My students at Jindal Global Law School who have humoured and tolerated my ideas in the Jurisprudence, and Violence, Memory, and Justice courses—some of which were built on the essays in this book and some which contributed to the essays. Thanks to Shivangi Sud, Uday Vir Garg, Amshuman Dasarathy, Rhea Malik, Aishwarya Koralath, Medha Kolanu, Sanjana Hooda, and Rohan Talwar for your research assistance. Pallavi Mal, Muskaan Ahuja, Ishani Mookherjee, and Shubhalakshmi Bhattacharya, for your assistance with teaching. Rishabh Bajoria, Siddharth Saxena, Ayushi Saraogi, Dikshit Sarma Bhagabati, Malini Chidambaram, Neeta Maria Stephen, Katyayani

Suhrud, and Amala Dasarathy for your provocations in the classroom. I am immensely grateful to each one of you for your efforts, engagement, and unremunerated labor. You have been my closest readers and most thoughtful interlocutors. You are the motivation behind bringing this book out. If I have an imagined ideal reader in mind, it is a young student at an Indian law school like you. Thank you for teaching me about how to make the politics of law relevant and accessible for tomorrow's critical lawyers.

A range of organizations and institutions supported the writing of the essays at various times for over a decade without whose intellectual, financial, and infrastructural support I could have possibly never written. Thanks to: Mahanirban Calcutta Research Group, Krantijyoti Savitribai Phule Women's Studies Centre at the University of Pune, West Bengal National University of Juridical Sciences, Child Rights and You, Centre for the Study of Developing Societies, Public Service Broadcasting Trust, Centre for Studies in Social Sciences Calcutta, Johannesburg Workshop on Theory and Criticism at the University of Witwatersrand, Australia India Institute at the University of Melbourne, Institute for Global Law and Policy at Harvard Law School, Institute for International Law and the Humanities at Melbourne Law School, and the Jindal Global Law School (JGLS). Among these, I spent the most amount of time in Melbourne and JGLS, Sonipat and I am especially thankful to these institutions. I would like to particularly thank C. Raj Kumar, my dean at JGLS for fostering a culture of critical interdisciplinary legal research that has been most generative for me. JGLS has always been a location of contradictions for me—one with which I have a relationship of uneasy affinity. That is what has also made it one of the most provocatively productive spaces to inhabit as a critical legal academic in the New India.

I would like to acknowledge that the writing done at the Melbourne Law School was carried out on the lands of the Wurundjeri People of the Kulin Nation who have not ceded their sovereignty. I pay my respects to their elders, past, present, and emerging. This acknowledgement is necessary because even as a temporary migrant to the settler colonial state of Australia, I was the beneficiary of colonialism's loots that allowed me to pursue my doctoral studies there.

Every expression of gratitude will fall short for Vasuki Nesiah's incisive and generous foreword to the book. Thank you for writing it so beautifully. Vasuki has been a constant figure of encouragement and support for several years. I continue to learn new lessons about scholarly humility, collegiality, and care from her writings and teaching. It is a very special feeling to have the essays prefaced by her words (written under the very difficult circumstances of the COVID-19 lockdown in New York City).

I am so excited about this book featuring a cover image designed by Siddhartha Dutta. I cannot thank him enough for lending an unusual aesthetic intensity to an ordinary photograph that I had taken many years back. I have for long admired his creative imagination as a visualizer and it is an honour to have his work on the cover.

Irrespective of their interest in what I research on and write about as an academic, my family members have remained an unconditional source of love, overenthusiasm, and distraction. I'd especially like to acknowledge the presence in my life of my parents, Anjan and Anjana, my mother-in-law, Pratima, my aunts, Swapna, Roma, Ratna, Manjula, uncles, Amal, Partha, Tapan, and Pradip, my siblings, Ishika and Shayak, their partners, Sayak and Aashima respectively, my little nephew Ricco, my cousins, Sreya, Kanishka, Tisha, and Ayan, and the indelible memories of my grandparents, Bani, Prafulla, Santosh, Dolly, Krishna Narayan, my uncles, Alok and Ranjan, and my father-in-law, Ajit.

Since much before the ten-year period through which the essays in this book were researched, written and published, I have been living a life of immense joy, exhilarating frivolity, and deep reflection with D. She has been my teacher in how to live an ethical life that takes the quotidian and the relational seriously. She continues to exemplarily live out both the possibilities and perils of 'the personal is political'. Her sarcasm keeps my academic vanity in check and her love provides a *lihaaf* of comfort and care that I cannot live without. She is my fiercest critic and my most intellectually stimulating collaborator. I am proud to be able to feature one of our collaborative works in this book. To D—on her fortieth birthday—I dedicate this book as a gift to celebrate our life together as partners in politics, profanities, and vulnerabilities.

Special thanks to the former and current team at Oxford University Press who helped with bringing the book to fruition: Manish Kumar,

Barun Sarkar, Moutushi Mukherjee, Mousumi Bera, Marianne Paul and Paulami Sengupta. I also thank the two anonymous reviewers whose very supportive feedback helped with sharpening some key arguments

———

I thank the editors of the journals and books where the essays were first published for giving me writing space and to the publishers for the permission to republish them as part of this book. Thanks are also due to the peer reviewers who had commented on the articles and chapters for their considered reading and feedback.

Chapter 1 was published as 'Spectacles of Emancipation: Reading Rights Differently in India's Legal Discourse,' *Osgoode Hall Law Journal* 14: 3 (2012) 527–573. Chapter 2 (co-authored with Debolina Dutta) was published in parts as 'Beyond Compassion: Children of Sex Workers in Kolkata's Sonagachi', *Childhood: A Journal of Global Child Research* 18: 3 (2011), 333–349 and 'Notes on Unlearning: Our Feminisms, Their Childhoods', in Rachel Rosen and Katherine Twamley (eds) *Feminism and the Politics of Childhood: Friends or Foes?*, London: UCL Press (2018) 75–81. Chapter 3 was published as 'Bollywood's Law: Collective Memory and Cinematic Justice in the New India', *No Foundations: An Interdisciplinary Journal of Law and Justice* 12 (2015) 94–135. Chapter 4 was published as 'New Queer Politics in the New India: Notes on Stuckness and Failure in a Negative Moment', *Unbound: Harvard Journal of the Legal Left* XI (2017) 1–36. Chapter 5 was published in parts as 'The Silence of Gulbarg: Some Inadequate Images', *Human Rights Defender* 25: 1 (2016) 24–28 and 'Gujarat 2002: Refracted Memories, Inadequate Images', in Satvinder S. Juss (Ed.) *Human Rights in India*, London: Routledge (2019) 125–151. Chapter 6 was published as 'Professor of Pathos: Upendra Baxi's Minor Jurisprudence', *Jindal Global Law Review* 9: 1 (2018) 203–222. Chapter 7 was published in parts as 'Doing and Undoing Feminism: A Jurisdictional Journey', *Economic and Political Weekly* L: 12 (2015) 44–47 and 'Doing and Undoing Feminism: A Jurisdictional Journey', in Romit Chowdhury and Zaid Al Baset (eds) *Men and Feminism in India*, New Delhi: Routledge (2018) 73–100.

Preface

Negative Spaces

> The relationship between law and violence is paradoxically structured: law is the opposite of violence, since legal forms of decision-making disrupt the spell of violence generating more violence. At the same time, law is itself a kind of violence; because it imposes a judgment that determines its 'subject' like a curse.
>
> — Christophe Menke, 'Law and Violence' (2010: 1)

> [L]aw as a unified entity can only be reconciled with its contradictory existences if we see it as myth.
>
> — Peter Fitzpatrick, *The Mythology of Modern Law* (2002: 1)

That law and violence share an antithetical relationship in modernity is a virtuous cliché.[1] Violence—both exceptional and ordinary—is commonsensically considered the other of law.[2] It is axiomatic to value lawfulness as progressive and lawlessness as primitive.[3] A condition of lawlessness is understood to produce violence. A fetishistic desire for the rule of law and human rights (Kerruish 1992: 99), particularly in the postcolony (Comaroff & Comaroff 2006), is pursued as a means of resisting and repairing the violence of lawlessness. Unless, lawlessness is desired by law itself (couched in the language of exceptionalism) to achieve the promise of a greater common good (Hussain 2006; Agamben 2005; Roy 2019: 25–75).

In *Violent Modernities: Cultural Lives of Law in the New India*, I locate law and violence in a negative space—'the recessive areas that we are unaccustomed to seeing but that are every bit as important for the representation of the reality at hand' (Daly 2003: 771)—where they are not adversaries but allies. The seven essays[4] that follow constitute a bricolage[5] that speaks to select 'critical events' (Das 1995) in contemporary India to offer explorations of the paradoxical relationships between law and violence. Each essay tells a story about the relationship between law and violence not as one of animosity, but of deep intimacy, where one symbiotically feeds off the other (Cover 1995: 203–8). Instead of casting law as the heroic Hercules that slays the hydra-headed demon of violence (Flood & Grindon 2014: 7–9),[6] the essays unsettle and blur this relationship—not to claim that there are no differences between law and violence, or to favour violence over law, but to interrogate the terms on which such differences are founded, sustained, and reified. I foreground the political and ethical stakes involved for a critical legal praxis in considering either law or violence as hermetically sealed, Manichean categories of good and bad.

Modern law's mythology—founded on the ideas of parliamentary democracy, constitutionalism, state secularism, social development, economic growth, techno-scientific advancements, and justice—is what popularly makes postcolonial India a modern and liberal nation-state. That law carries the potential to be violent or unjust is not outside of the liberal imagination. Law in this imagination is a public good that entitles citizens to rights, limits the state's totalitarian tendencies, and criminalizes those who threaten the polity and the people through their speech or deeds. However, a liberal critique of modern law is mostly concerned with the nation-state's inability to guarantee access to or strengthen justice-delivery mechanisms, with the nation-state's acts of overreach into the arena of individual rights like privacy and property, and with the nation-state's demonstration of 'softness' towards thoughts and actions of those considered 'anti-national'. Such a critique is interested in expanding or limiting law for the enhancement and flourishing of the lives of individual citizens (Cole & Craiutu 2018). Of course, who qualifies as the citizen deserving of protection from harm by the law has historical roots in liberalism's violent exclusions of those considered to be in their 'nonage' (Mehta 1999; Kapur 2005). For 'dealing with barbarians', wrote John Stuart Mill in *On Liberty*, 'despotism is a legitimate mode of government [...] provided the end be their improvement' (2002: 8).

The essays in this book question this commonsensical wisdom of the liberal critique to understand law not as the slayer of violence, but as its conduit. What would justice look and feel like if law, as the path to it, is one that authorizes violence—spectacularly and stealthily—in the name of justice? The book engages in a reading of law's relationship with violence to offer an insight into the cultural imaginaries of justice in the New India—one marked by the combined rise of neoliberalism and Hindutva (Desai 2004; Gopalakrishnan 2006: 2,803–13; Nanda 2009; Teltumbde 2018), which, 'far from being antagonistic forces [are] actually lovers performing an elaborate ritual of seduction and coquetry that could sometimes be misread as hostility' (Roy 2019: xvii).[7]

Law, as matter and metaphor, has been at the heart of the contestations over cultural politics in India today—be it in the struggles for social justice, for holding the state accountable for mass crimes, demanding sexual autonomy for queer people, calibrating experiences of suffering, or the pedagogical practices of citizen-making in the university. The essays step out of the regular venues of legal activity to focus on reading a set of cultural sites—literary texts, Bollywood cinema, documentary films, social media posts, photographs, advertising, and the university—where the law's promise of emancipation and the performance of violence live a life of intimate paradoxes.

Researched and written between 2008 and 2018, the essays speak to the time of their writing to provide an at once theoretical, activist, and self-reflexive critique of select critical events that have animated the cultural lives of law in the New India.[8] I understand culture as the terrain on which legal knowledge is produced that is not solely attached to the sources of modern 'positivist' state law—courts, judgements, or legislations. While I engage with these sources, the essays are primarily interested in understanding what happens to the meanings produced by these sources when they enter the negative space of culture, or one of 'shared meanings' that are in flux and fossilized at the same time (Hall 2009: 1).

If you read the essays in the order that they appear in the book, it will become apparent as to how they are tied together by a political and disciplinary commitment, that is, to engage in a reading of culture from the vantage point of jurisprudence in order to understand the relationship between law and violence. However, the essays can also be read independently of each other, or in an order that the reader deems fit; in either case, the commitment will still be evident. To make the reading experience enabling for both the continuous and discontinuous reader, each chapter mentions the year and place of writing with a line offering the context in which the essay was written.

It is also for this reason that the keywords that make up the title of the book—law, violence, modernity, culture, New India—are not coherently theorized. For the sake of some preliminary and contingent clarity, I will hazard an attempt at holding these to a bare minimum of an expression over which each of the essays will add layers of meaning. What I offer here in brief are not definitions, but indications of the nature of their use in the essays to follow.

Law: When used with the capital 'L' is mostly state-sanctioned modern law, understood in the nature of legislations and judgements, authorized (enacted or passed) by parliaments and courts in a secular democracy like India; or international law emanating from the United Nations (UN). These 'Laws' are posited in documents like the Constitution of India or international conventions/treaties, and they command obedience through a combination of custom, civility, routine, shame, deification, obligation, and fear.

law: When the 'l' is in lower case, the term refers to the polysemic imaginations of law, emanating from sources like literature, film, popular culture, rumour, that are not considered sources of legitimate legal knowledge. The scriptural and visual languages that make up this universe of imaginations comprises, among others, metaphors, images, sounds, objects, and emotions. When used with the small 'l', law also has an ethical dimension to it, where judgement and justice are understood not as purely hermeneutic/cognitive activities, but also as sensory and affective ones (Davies 2017).

I don't indicatively use the upper- and lower-case versions through the essays. These are just indicative of the two ways I use the word 'law', and on many occasions, both apply to the same situation where I am undecided/indeterminate about holding the meaning to only one. I invite the reader to participate in this figuring-out process with me.

Violence: These are deeds and words (even when unconscious and unintended) that have the capacity to produce suffering and vulnerability (fear and risk) and whose impacts on life (both humans and non-humans) can be corporeal, psychic, structural, intergenerational, ritualistic, anaesthetic. The law, when it claims to resist or undo violence and its causes and consequences, must first categorize it as a violation by naming a right. In effect, many forms of violence do not qualify as such in the eyes of the law if they do not correspond with the recognized and protected right in question. Often, in the name of justice, law embalms violence and violent regimes to preserve a higher order of institutions, structures, and humans. Memories of violence don't die—their traces live on through trauma. Trauma is recorded on bodies, in documents, and in inherited minds that live on after the bodies are no more. Experiences of violence do not have any universal currency. Trauma and suffering are lived differently by different peoples at different times and places. The law's recognition of what qualifies as violation results in a hierarchized calibration of forms of suffering.

Modernity: This is a progression away from primitivity. It is an idea that is both temporal and aesthetic. Enlightenment thought, or what can be called liberalism, is the modern idea of modernity. It carries a 'history vanishing' (Puar 2007: xix) and eventocratic quality (Kalyan 2020) that gets applied to interpret the contemporary by marking certain events as the epochal beginning of a time period or a thought movement. Modernity promotes the values of liberty, secularity, rationality, individualism, and contractualism, among others, and uses these to establish its temporal and aesthetic distance from its dichotomous other, called tradition, and located mostly in the non-West, in the spiritual, the magical, in and on non-white bodies. While the liberal idea of modernity has been historically used to justify colonialism (and its vicissitudes in capitalism and imperialism), it has also been used by the colonized to authorize their own versions of modernity. Thus, postcolonialism as a body of critical thought was born out of modernity to unsettle the modernity–tradition dichotomy.

Modernity is also nativist, not only universalist. Proponents of the Hindu caste system use its putative ancient foundations to declare it to be timeless and pure, and thus modern. The caste hierarchy considers those at the top of it to be modern compared to those below. To try to move up the caste hierarchy by emulating the practices of the upper castes is understood sometimes by those below (even if it might be a myth) to be a move towards modernity. A similar argument is advanced by capitalism to justify its seductions. Similar to caste, the other structure of hierarchy that does not offer any incentives for becoming modern is patriarchy. However, feminism as a modern counter to patriarchy sometimes embraces the promises of liberalism to promote a move up the gender hierarchy where being modern is equated with a training in the sartorial and labouring masculinities in the public (never in lieu of femininities though). This has historically advantaged only some women and queers, but carries major popular currency in law-reform initiatives.

Modern law promotes the liberal values of democracy, freedoms, due process, secularism, and rationality. It provided the opportunity to split the state and religion and to ostensibly lend the state more secular authority to make rules that would govern the lives of people. It made the state the (almost) irreplaceable system of political organization. Modern violence, genealogically, was understood as a move away from the phantasmagoric violence of religious sovereign power on the treasonous human's body. It produced an appreciation for the humanization of violence where routine replaced torture (Foucault 2012). In the wake of Guantanamo Bay, Abu Ghraib, Manus Island, Papa II, Khairlanji, Gujarat 2002, and the ongoing and unending public lynching of Dalits and Muslims in India, such a move is coming full circle. Modernity is multitudinous. It cures and it kills. It cares by maiming (Puar 2017).

Culture: Raymond Williams, in his classic work *Keywords: A Vocabulary of Culture and Society*, wrote: 'Culture is one of the two or three most complicated words in the English language' (1988: 87). Understandably, I am ill-equipped to offer even a tentatively adequate indication. So I borrow an extract from Williams himself. This is what he calls the 'social definition' of culture: 'in which culture is a description of a particular way of life which expresses certain meanings and values not only in art and learning but also in institutions and ordinary behaviour. The analysis of culture from such a definition is the clarification of the meanings and values implicit and explicit in particular ways of life, a 'particular culture" (Williams 2001: 57). In the case of both modern international and municipal laws, culture is deployed in the context of relativism. Institutions of modern law promote certain cultures and civilizations and work towards abolishing, censoring, or criminalizing others. Most of this work—which oftentimes takes violent forms—is carried out under the liberal guise of reform, development, and progress.

New India: Shapeshifting. Promising and pathetic. Precarious and perverse. It is a 'war machine' (remember Salwa Judum and Ikhwan, for starters):

> Polymorphous and diffuse organizations, war machines are characterized by their capacity for metamorphosis. Their relation to space is mobile [...] The state may, of its own doing, transform itself into a war machine [...] A war machine combines a plurality of functions. It has the features of a political organization and a mercantile company. It operates through capture and depredations (Mbembe 2003: 32).

This is the 'infrastructure of impunity' (Roy 2017). What's *new* about this India?

Here, then, is a sneak peek into the topics of the essays to pique your interest. The seven chapters are arranged in two parts. In a spin on a classic feminist slogan, Sara Ahmed has written 'The Personal is Theoretical': 'Theory itself is often assumed to be abstract: something is more theoretical the more abstract it is, the more it is abstracted from everyday life. To abstract is to drag away, detach, pull away, or divert. We might then have to drag theory back, to bring theory back to life' (Ahmed 2017: 10).

I offer a reverse spin on Ahmed. Part I is called '... the Theoretical ...' and Part II, in continuation, is called '... is Personal ...'. This is an acknowledgement of the direction of my journey (and that of the sequence of the essays)—which begins with theory, and opens up to the personal. In this, theory offers a frame to curate the personal, but the personal spills over and spoils the frame, thus helping me to encounter failure and see the finitude of theory. The personal, however, doesn't trump theory or the other way around—their relationship is both dialectical and dialogic. The ellipses indicate a 'joyous wandering' between and across fractures, asymmetries, slowness, entanglements, and repetitions (Derrida 1978: 294; Toner 2015).

Chapter 1 ('Spectacles of Emancipation: Reading Rights Differently' [2012]) is an essay that complicates the relationship between rights and the idea of emancipation to offer an expansive critique of liberal faith in constitutionalism. I demonstrate how the promise of emancipation in the Constitution of India can be a spectacle that blinds justice seekers from its violent dimensions. Just in case you decide to begin at the beginning, this essay sets up the political and methodological orientations for what is to follow in the rest of the book. So, Chapter 2 ('Beyond Compassion: Children of Sex Workers and the Politics of Suffering', co-authored with Debolina Dutta [2011]) continues to use the metaphor of the spectacle to look at how liberal human rights work contributes to producing hierarchies of suffering and regimes of compassion that depoliticize citizenship claims made by children of sex workers in Kolkata's Sonagachi red-light area. Chapter 3 ('Bollywood's Law: Cinema, Justice, and Collective Memory' [2015]) engages the question of memory to understand the relationship between law and violence by reading a filmic representation of the 2002 anti-Muslim pogrom in Gujarat. In doing so, I offer a critique of how cinema reifies a narrative of memory in which secular law triumphs over religious violence, and thus leaves unquestioned the role of secular law in enabling the violence in the first place. The triumphs and tribulations of the legal battle against Section 377 of the Indian Penal Code (IPC) that criminalized the lives of India's queer people are the subject of Chapter 4 ('New Queer Politics: Notes of Failure and Stuckness in a Negative Moment' [2017]). By studying a range of popular cultural artefacts, this essay offers an account of the troubling turns that the queer movement's engagement with law has taken in the wake of neoliberalism and Hindu fundamentalism. Chapter 5 ('The Silence of Gulberg: Refracted Memories, Inadequate Images' [2018]) is an autobiographical account of an ethical crisis that I confronted as a researcher when I returned to Ahmedabad 10 years after the 2002 pogrom to survey the public remnants of violence. Combining text and images produced by me, the essay struggles with working through the interpretive dilemmas of witnessing and memorializing mass violence by 'outsiders' like me who were not the targets of the violence in the first place.

With the two concluding chapters, I enter the space of the university that I inhabit on an everyday basis. These two chapters are also an account of my personal negotiations in teaching leftist law in a capitalist university, and a partial acknowledgement of my feminist inheritances as a legal academic. In Chapter 6 ('Professor of Pathos: Upendra Baxi's Minor Jurisprudence' [2018]), I do a reparative reading of law professor Baxi's minor works to emphasize the ethical responsibilities incumbent upon the critical legal scholar in times that are marked by the perverse coexistence of acute precarity and spectacular affluence. In closing, Chapter 7 ('The Conduct of Critique: Jurisdictional Account of a Feminist Journey' [2018]) takes another autobiographical turn where I think through the ethics of what it means for me to be a male feminist legal scholar inside the neoliberal university. This essay is a self-reflexive account that gestures towards a practice of feminist jurisprudence that takes responsibility to acknowledge failure. My analysis invites a consideration of a legal critique that embraces the idea of failure as a productive way of thinking about its practice of responsibility.

Gestures and Tendencies

> Since subject position is everything in my analysis of the law, you deserve to know that it's a bad morning. I am very depressed. It always takes a while to sort out what's wrong, but it usually starts with some kind of perfectly irrational thought such as: I *hate* being a lawyer.
>
> — Patricia J. Williams, *The Alchemy of Race and Rights* (1992: 3, emphasis in original)

This was never meant to be a book. The essays were written without any prior sense of them mutating into bound form with a material beginning and an end. After writing and publishing them at different times and places, I felt that I was able to hear some keynotes resonating through the pieces. While this has allowed me to claim authorship of a rhythm that ties the notes together, I have also had misgivings about whether I was forcing captivity on them within a neat composition. What you will encounter, thus, are essays that are working through negotiations between the paradoxes of fragmentation and cohesion, indeterminacy and coherence, glee and caution. These negotiations pertain not only to my own experience of attempting to collate the essays into a chapterized sequence for the book, but more significantly, to the thematic whole of the book itself and its parts in the chapters.

The period of research and writing the essays is bookended by the defeat of the erstwhile National Democratic Alliance (NDA) government headed by the Hindu nationalist Bharatiya Janata Party (BJP) in 2004, and the return of the BJP in 2014 with a full majority marking an unprecedented presence and spread of Hindutva consciousness in both the private and public lives of India. The intervening years through which the United Progressive Alliance (UPA) ruled, headed by the Indian National Congress (INC), presented the possibility of some secular social justice promises being fulfilled, only to be massacred by a full-blown neoliberal assault (a state–corporation–military complex) on the poor, and the fledgling emergence of neoliberalism's favourite minority in India's urban queers. The current BJP government has done well to capitalize on the meticulous anti-poor groundwork done by the UPA, and has produced its own toxic concoction that sophisticatedly and perversely fuses neoliberalism and Hindutva.

Through this decade-long period of researching and writing, I have also been teaching and studying across three continents. I am formally trained in Indian law, and have subsequently acquired jurisprudential training in Canada and Australia. Methodologically, I write from the interstices of a disciplinary location that continues to be challenged and enriched through these travels and learnings both within and beyond the postcolony (Arif 2015: 53). My postcolonial legal and aesthetic sensibilities keep me on alert regarding both the possibilities and limitations of the theoretical bricolage that I have put together. A part of this sensibility consists of the practice of responsibility towards the place, the peoples, and the texts I am writing about, as well as towards the multi-jurisdictional disciplinary locations that I am writing from. The book, therefore, demonstrates a mongrel heuristic that works through the oppositional and shared epistemologies that I have inherited (Kapur 1999: 353; Genovese 2013: 41).

The analyses that each of the essays present are limited to events and instances that are specific to their time of writing. I have purposefully desisted from updating the essays with current developments because I do not want to propose that my critique is atemporal and portable.

This is a methodological and political decision that wishes to avoid the arrogance of suggesting that the theoretical frames and positions of critique that I draw on and deploy carry universal explanatory valence—they do not. However, I do think that the datedness of my analyses offers a contemporary pre-history of the current forms of modern violence and its relationship to law in the New India—particularly those that have transpired since the BJP's return to power in the 2019 general elections.[9]

Each essay offers two things simultaneously: a partial report on how the political ambience of the time impacted the cultural relationship between law and violence, focusing on 'snapshots and flashpoints' (Puar 2017: xix); and a semi-autobiographical account of my relationship with the discipline of law as a legal academic and a lapsed human rights activist. Through the period of writing I experienced a stepping away from full-time human rights work, to stretches of unemployment and freelancing to becoming a full-time academic in possibly India's first neoliberal private research university. These transitions were repeatedly punctuated by several personal tragedies—especially of losing some of my most dearest people.

If the essays are read in their order of appearance, one will be able to identify a shifting ethos in the tone of my writing: from coherence to indeterminacy to undecidability; from reform to resistance to responsibility. These shifts are elliptical. The proportions of the tonal characteristics just mentioned are not consistent, but they move in the aforementioned directions. In the first chapter, I offer a Marxist critique of rights—and present such critique as a coherent political position. The second essay instils doubt in the universal good attached to the idea of compassion in human rights work—this marks the turn towards indeterminacy that in a sense coincides with my own ethical dilemmas as a scholar-activist at that time. The third essay returns me to a less certain coherent politics—however, instead of a completely structural analysis of the Gujarat pogrom, I merge the structural with the sensory. This is what might be called a contingent structuralism, rather than a paranoid one (Kennedy 2001: 1,173–7). The fourth essay demonstrates a coming together of coherence, indeterminacy, and undecidability in understanding the emerging dynamics of a new queer politics, which demands decriminalization of sodomy and embraces capitalism at the same time. This is also where I speak of failure—of legal activism and legal interpretation. This offers the cue for the next section, in which the three essays take on a semi-autobiographical mode of writing about these shifting affects in thinking through my scholarly inheritances and what role they play in shaping my research and pedagogy as a jurisprudent and feminist legal scholar.

My authorial voice also shifts between being dispassionate and intimate. There are a few occasions where my doctrinal training in law gets the better of me, and there are those instances where my critical legal sensibilities struggle with the way I use the 'I' narrative—authoritatively or tentatively; clinically or experientially; egotistically or with passivity. As a legal academic, my relation to law is one that echoes Patricia Williams's epigraph earlier. Irrationality is an affect that I take seriously when thinking about the law (Bortolotti 2014)—the irrationalities of the law's violence, the irrationalities of lawless violence that the law tries to censor, my own hermeneutic irrationalities that carry the potential of committing interpretive violence and countering the law's rationalization of its own violence.

To be depressed and hateful are passionate emotions that sit uneasily with the decorum of modern law (Bandes 2012; Nussbaum 2013) but are befitting for the period that I have inhabited and have written about. Thus, the repeated resort to the polemical and the poetic in the essays when the analytical frame becomes inadequate—which is quite often. In a similar vein, experiences of hopelessness, slowness, and failure recur. All of these are presented in varied filtered forms through all the six essays. These shifts in tone and voice speak to the mood of the period/issue/incident/event/experience I was writing about. The abiding mood through the book is complicitous, foreboding, and suspicious of both selves and others. If there is a place for a normative hope, it is in the acknowledgement of failure and my, and our, contradictory inheritances—wherever we wish to locate our political and personal selves on the leftist, feminist, queer, anti-caste, anti-race, decolonial, secular, crip spectrum. There are faint traces of humour—but never pronounced. This, I regret.

The essays collectively demonstrate the workings of a philosophical–methodological tendency that combines description and critique aimed at 'mak[ing] visible precisely what is visible, that is to say, to show that which is so close, which is so immediate, which is so intimately linked to us, that because of that we do not perceive it' (Foucault 1994: 540; Orford 2012: 609). This tendency, thus, does not claim to reveal anything new about the New India. Instead, it draws the reader into slowly paying attention to the overlooked ordinariness of negative spaces. My allusion to the newness of an India is not a discovery, but the acknowledgement of a complicitous continuum between law and violence.

The book is written in the form of a bricolage of descriptive refractions that have animated my practices of *queerfeministmarxistpostcolonial* critique and activism both inside and outside the legal academy over the last decade, especially through a period where I have had to negotiate and come to terms with the contradictions of my own politics and the complicities that have contaminated any claim to purity (Sircar 2013). They carry tinges of the experiential,[10] but are not written as such. Which explains my use of the expression 'refraction', instead of reflection. Reflection has the possibility of being a self-contained engagement; on the other hand, refraction is a project with the potential to destabilize and bend our disciplined contours of thought. Refraction doesn't necessarily suggest a 'moving away' from issues at stake, but a critical engagement that confronts not one, but competing truths that give rise to the affective paradoxes of failure and stuckness (Jay 2003: 2; Sircar 2011: 182). I approach this refractive practice of *queerfeministmarxistpostcolonial* critique from what Paul Cilliers would call a 'modest position'—one that acknowledges the 'limitations of our understanding of this world' (2005: 5). This is not a position of relativism, but a 'counter-position' (Van Marle 2013: 109–22) to 'arrogant self-assurance' (Cilliers 2005: 260) that engages with complexity without any predetermined technocratic objective of problem-solving.

Drawing on the interdisciplinary insights of postmodern jurisprudence, feminist legal theory, cultural studies, memory studies, queer theory, and postcolonial theory, *Violent Modernities* argues that legal imagination in India does not only emanate from courtrooms, legislations, and judgements, but is lived in the practices of ordinary disobediences and everyday failures, in the cultural chronicles of life in literature, cinema, art, and the practices of pedagogy. It is only when law can be re-imagined as such that the violence at the foundations of modern state law can be unsettled, even if momentarily. To engage in this project of re-imagination, thus, becomes the responsibility for those who wish to think with and about law, with criticality and care.

Caveat lector: '... the preface harbors a lie'[11]

This preface was written *after* the writing of the rest of the chapters in the book. It was 'a retrospective exercise, an afterthought expressed with the benefit of hindsight' (Chaudhuri 2013: 62). Its positioning at the beginning of the book is a conceit for a promise of hope that can only fail because the consequence of the promise has already been exhausted. This preface is thus a statement of hopelessness and failure.

To an often-asked question by many colleagues 'what do you work on?' I would have a facile response: 'my work is hopelessly theoretical'. This was originally constructed as a self-deprecating gesture, an awkward way to avoid trying too hard to explain why what I do will be of interest to them or of consequence to the world at large. Some of this awkwardness came from my own suspicions about my *queerfeministmarxistpostcolonial* orientation as mere posturing without a commitment to progressive transformation. I used to be a human rights activist, working in the trenches, as it were, and then took a decision to become an academic and lodge myself inside the comfortable precints of the neoliberal academy where I could engage in radicalspeak even as I lived a relatively secured and slow life of reading, teaching (and occasionally writing) in the company of ideas and my students. It was as if I was betraying Marx's final call in 'Theses on Feuerbach': 'The philosophers have only interpreted the world, in various ways; the point is to change it' (Marx 1978: 145). Over time I have come to appreciate how my unease with the response can itself be a conceit. To be hopelessly theoretical might in fact be the practice of an ethics of failure and finitude.

In these times in the New India—where the state 'skilfully combines both the *rule of law* and *reign of terror* into the hegemonic tasks and apparatuses of governance' (Baxi 1991: 185, emphasis in original)—I have come to understand theory as a 'dangerous aid... a [necessary] prosthesis' for being and living (Cixous 1997: 4). '[Theory] is dangerous,' writes Margaret Davies 'because it risks the calcification of its objects, but it is an aid because without it we cannot understand these objects' (Davies 2002: 22–23). Like the preface lends shelter to a lie, theory extends hospitality to hopelessness and failure. Without theory our lives would be reduced to algorithms, metrics, and anthropocentrisms (as if it already isn't)—and hopelessness and failure would be hindrances to human progress to be tamed or caged like an animal, annihilated like a disease, or exploited or conquered like nature (by law, neoliberalism, and technoscience) rather than being conditions of fracture, decay, regeneration and vulnerability that we live with, care for, and die in.

I do not mean this as resigning to fate or to valorize theory, but as the task of accounting for hopelessness in my practices of reading, teaching, and writing. These practices would appear to be insignificant in comparison to revolutionary forms of mass mobilizations, but as the chapters in what follow will demonstrate, I see these as a commitment to an 'ordinary ethics' (Das 2012: 133) of reparative critique (Sedgwick 2003: 123) that does not romanticize transformation as a normative aspiration of all politics. This commitment allows me to acknowledge the limitations and violence in practices of interpretation, while remaining acutely cognizant that the teleological progression from interpretation to change need not be the only point of philosophizing and theorizing.

What if the negative space that theory opens up can be a 'healing place' (hooks 1991: 2) for the shared failures and vulnerabilities that an ethos of 'associated living' (Ambedkar 1979: 57) demands of us? How might we live in theory—especially in the current phase of death and devastation in the New India? By 'grieving for the lives lost… [to] not fade from the struggles of the present but re-channel that grief into struggles worthy of those lost lives' (Nesiah 2005). Such scholarly conduct, as Vasuki Nesiah reminds us powerfully 'is not a passive or therapeutic grief about past tragedies, but an active, discordant challenge to present crisis' (ibid.). *Violent Modernities* inadequately tries to keep the challenge alive.

A luta continua? Certainly. *A vitória é certa*? I doubt.

Notes

1. As borne out by the work of someone like Steven Pinker (2011, 2018). For an Indian instantiation, see Mukherjee (2018).

2. As Satish Deshpande writes: 'Common sense is a vitally important social institution because it supplies the cement that holds up the social structure… Common sense is pre-judice in the strict sense—it is "always already" in place and hard at work long before we make any conscious judgments' (2004: 2).
3. For a counter to this logocentric axiom, see Derrida (1992).
4. I have chosen to characterize the chapters as essays purposefully. As Brian Dillon writes: 'The essay is diverse and several—it teems. But of course it also *tries*—and gives up […] But here arises a conflict inside the essay as form: it aspires to express the quintessence or crux of its matter, thus to a sort of polish and integrity and it wants at the same time to insist that its purview is partial, that being incomplete is a value in itself for it better reflects the brave and curious but faltering nature of the writing mind' (Dillon 2017: 17–18; emphasis in original).
5. '[I]f one calls bricolage the necessity of borrowing one's concept from the text of a heritage which is more or less coherent or ruined, it must be said that every discourse is bricoleur' (Derrida 1972: 255).
6. This Greek myth, via the legal theorist Ronald Dworkin, has become a key metaphor for understanding the process of principle-based adjudication by the superhuman judge in the figure of Hercules, to arrive at the 'one right answer' when confronted with hydra-headed 'hard cases'. The myth has been read as a representation of European masculinity colonizing Oriental femininity. See Barnett (1998: 103–10).
7. In the field of Indian legal scholarship, Upendra Baxi's *The Future of Human Rights* (2002) and Ratna Kapur's *Erotic Justice: Law and the New Politics of Postcolonialism* (2005) can be considered to be this book's scholarly predecessors which have contributed to critical legal theory in India from within the discipline of law. More recently, Kalpana Kannabiran's *Tools of Justice: Non-discrimination and the Indian Constitution* (2012) has offered a sociological critique of law, focusing particularly on questions of identity and rights within the constitutional framework. The edited volumes *Crime Through Time* (Rao & Dube 2013), *Violence Studies* (Kannabiran 2016) and *Rethinking Law and Violence* (Vashist & Sood 2020) have engaged with the relationship between law and violence in India, but mostly from disciplinary perspectives outside of law.
8. Following Margaret Davies, I understand critique as 'a detailed analysis of the foundations of the way we understand the things we think about, whatever they are. Critique is useful and necessary to all forms of theory, because it exposes the assumptions we make as being not natural or neutral but, rather, associated with our particular position in

the world. Critique can therefore enable us to understand, at least, that our own view is partial' (Davies 2017: 207).

9. Consider, among others, the abrogation of Article 370 and 35A of the Constitution of India legalising India's military occupation of Kashmir; the Citizenship Amendment Act (CAA) combined with the Supreme Court's judgment in the Babri Masjid case, that strengthen the government's commitment towards turning India into a Hindu Rashtra; the amendment of the the already draconian Unlawful Activites Prevention Act, 2004 (brought in by the Congress government) that now enables individuals to be legally declared as 'terrorists'—which in a sense follows the media trials that declared them as 'urban naxals'; the Transgender Person's (Protection of Rights) Act that denies trans people the right to self-determination. Paralelly, we have seen the invocation of police powers to unleash brutal violence against young students excercising their right to protest against the CAA, the surveillance and arrests of human rights lawyers and activists on the accusation of being 'anti-national'. The putative silverlinings in the Sabrimala judgment, the abolition and criminalisation of Triple Talaq, the reading down of Sec. 377 to decriminalize sodomy, and the hanging of the accused in the Jyoti Singh Pandey gang rape and murder, speak to perverse forms of neoliberal Hindutva populism that use a sophisticated concoction of rights and revenge to celebrate our democracy. The only rehabilitative gesture that I can think of is the Delhi Hight Court's judgment in the Hashimpura massacre case, which was followed by Justice Muralidhar's reprimand of the Delhi Police for failing to file FIRs in the wake of the North East Delhi riots—only leading to his summary transfer to the Punjab and Haryana High Court in Chandigargh.
10. I do not privilege experience, or disavow it, and remain attentive to the relationship between experience and practice of theorizing. See Joan Scott (1991: 773–97); Guru and Sarukkai (2012); Oksala (2014: 388–403).
11. Spivak (1997: x).

List of Abbreviations

Preface

United Nations (UN)
Indian Penal Code (IPC)
National Democratic Alliance (NDA)
Bharatiya Janata Party (BJP)
United Progressive Alliance (UPA)
Indian National Congress (INC)

Chapter 1

Fundamental rights (FR)
Global economic constitutionalism (GEC)
Aligarh Muslim University (AMU)
Union Carbide Corporation (UCC)
Right to Education Act (RTE)
New Legal Order (NLO)
Armed Forces Special Powers Act (AFSPA)
Supreme Court (SC)
public interest litigations (PIL) social action litigations (SAL)
Teach India (TI)
Oxford University Press (OUP)

Special Police Officers (SPOs)

Chapter 2

Amra Padatik (AP)
Durbar Mahila Samanwaya Committee (DMSC)
Nanhi Kali (NK)
New York Times (NYT)
Immoral Traffic Prevention Act, 1956 (ITPA)
Restore International (RI)
Child Welfare Committee (CWC)
Probation officer (PO)
Indira Gandhi National Open University (IGNOU)

Chapter 3

Central Board of Film Certification (CBFC)
Kai Po Che (KPC)
first information reports (FIR)
chief minister (CM)

Chapter 4

National Legal Services Authority (NALSA)
Rashtriya Swayamsevak Sangh (RSS)
Christopher Street Day (CSD)
Queers Against Israeli Apartheid (QuAIA)
All-India Muslim Law Board (AIMLB)

Chapter 5

Vishwa Hindu Parishad (VHP)

Chapter 7

Krantijyoti Savitribai Phule Women's Studies Centre (KSPWSC)
Jindal Global Law School (JGLS)

PART I

... THE THEORETICAL ...

1

Spectacles of Emancipation

Reading Rights Differently*

Ustad Mangu's Faith and Fate

> The new constitution is going to be like boiling hot water is to bugs who suck the blood of the poor.
>
> —Ustad Mangu (Manto 2008: 209)

Mangu the *tongawala* (horse-cart driver) is the protagonist in Saadat Hasan Manto's short story 'The New Constitution' (Manto 2008: 206–15). The story is set in 1935 in Lahore, in what was then the undivided Indian subcontinent. The satirical provocations in this humorous story are an apt preface to concerns that I wish to share and explore in this chapter. Because of his ability to wax eloquent on anything under the sun, Mangu was endearingly given the salutary

* Written through 2010–12 in Delhi and Sonipat; in the wake of 'Operation Green Hunt', and 60 years of the Constitution of India. I dedicate this essay to Professor Ranabir Samaddar for the faith he has reposed in me through all these years. I have learned enormously from his critical generosity and remain inspired by his commitment to not let the ephemerality of culture trump the materiality of politics.

title of Ustad (the Great One) by his fellow tongawalas. Ustad Mangu hated the British. Once, after getting into an argument with a drunken *gora* (white man) who was abusing him, he told one of his friends:

> I am sick and tired of these offshoots of monkeys.... Every time I look at their blighted faces, my blood begins to boil in my veins. We need a new law to get rid of these people. Only that can revive us, I swear on your life (Manto 2008: 207–8).

Ustad Mangu's faith in the imaginary power of law to end colonial oppression and resist the colonizer was strengthened when he heard two of his passengers talk about the Government of India Act, 1935—the precursor to the Constitution of India (Constitution)—to be passed on 1 April, which was only a few days away. The news about the new constitution elated Ustad Mangu—he just could not control his excitement and wanted to get back to his tonga stand as soon as possible and share it with his friends:

> He was very happy. A delightful cool settled over his heart when he thought of how the new constitution would send these white mice [he always called them by that name] scurrying back into their holes for all times to come (Manto 2008: 209).

As 1 April approached, he overheard good and bad things about the new constitution from his passengers, but his belief in its transformative potential remained unshaken:

> The new constitution ... appeared to him to be something bright and full of promise. The only thing he could compare the new constitution with was the splendid brass and gilt fittings he had purchased after careful examination a couple of years ago... When the fittings were new, the nickel-headed nails would shimmer and where brass had been worked into the fittings it shone like gold. On the basis of that analogy ... it was essential that the new constitution should shine and glow (Manto 2008: 210).

On 1 April, Ustad Mangu woke up early and took his tonga out for business with an irrepressible thrill in his demeansour. He decorated his horse's head with a new plume to celebrate the birth of the new constitution. He tried to spot newness in everything he saw. However, except for the new plume made of colourful feathers, everything looked old. He was not disappointed and told himself that as the day progressed things would look different.

Sometime later, he heard someone call out to him. Mangu turned around to find that it was the same gora he once had an argument with. A feeling of intense hatred grew in his heart and he wanted to go away without responding to his call. But he controlled his anger and turned his tonga around—he did not want to miss the fare, and he had no reason to fear the British on 1 April. He stopped the tonga, gave the gora a defiant look, and, emboldened by the promise of liberation that the new constitution would usher, quoted five rupees for the trip. Without intending to get into a confrontation with Ustad Mangu, the gora raised his cane and instructed him to move so that he could board the tonga. In this gesture, the cane touched Mangu's thigh a few times. In response, Mangu landed a powerful blow on the gora's chin. The gora was taken by utter surprise but could not do anything to save himself. Mangu kept at his blows and screamed:

> 'The same cockiness even on April 1! Well, sonny boy, it is our Raj now!' A crowd gathered and he declared to them: 'Those days are gone, friends, when they ruled the roost. There is a new constitution now, fellows, a new constitution.'

Two policemen emerged from the crowd, rescued the gora, and took Ustad Mangu away to the police station. The closing lines of the story are telling:

> All along the way, and even inside the station, he kept screaming, 'New constitution, new constitution!' but nobody paid any attention to him. 'New constitution, new constitution! What rubbish are you talking? It's the same old constitution.' And he was locked up.

Ustad Mangu's faith and fate sets up the metaphor of what I call 'spectacles of emancipation', which is the gap between the vision of emancipation that the law promises and the reality of violence that the law performs. Faith in the law emerges from two sources: one is the lived experience of knowing that the law *delivers* justice; the other is the perception of the law *as* justice (Sircar 2009:210). This chapter will attempt to disrupt the linear, progressive equation that holds that more laws equals more rights equals more justice. This is an equation that has informed and been informed by the working of fundamental rights (FR) jurisprudence and law reform, the enactment of legislation to guarantee socio-economic rights, and many of the strategies of social movement activism in India. My goal is not to disparage or dismiss the law. That would be both an exercise in futility—given the hope that people's struggles rest in the law—and intellectually dishonest, given my own contingent belief in the ability of the law to at least deliver a semblance of justice. Rather, I aim to better understand how the spectacles of law's emancipatory potential are accompanied by an anaesthetization of the subaltern's resistance through the deployment of governmental tactics that discipline conduct, not using overt coercion but by cajoling consent with the promise of welfare.

Ustad Mangu's comparison of the new constitution to the glittering nickel-and-brass fittings on his tonga that would shine and glow was the spectacularized image of what the new law promised to deliver. His unshakeable belief operated as a psychological anaesthetic, preventing him from understanding that the Government of India Act, 1935 was actually an 'imperial event' (Muldoon 2009: 3), which, by merely permitting limited self-government to Indians at the local and provincial levels, guaranteed no rights to colonized subjects. Without a bill of rights, the new constitution allowed the British government to take back total control whenever the need arose. But the impact of this anaesthesia did not last long, and bolstered by the strength of the new law, Ustad Mangu exercised a corporeal act of rebellion. The consequence was incarceration and a banal reminder that despite the new constitution, nothing had changed.

This story is an important 'lesson in the discrepancy between subaltern struggles and bourgeoisie aspirations' (Mufti 2000: 21). The constitution's birth served as the aspirational markers for civilization, sovereignty, and the rule of law for the nationalist Indian elite. But for the subaltern, it was a blinding spectacle. As Aamir Mufti puts it in his reading of the short story:

> ... Manto highlights the differing relationships between the subaltern and the bourgeoisie nationalists to colonial political 'reform'. Half understanding [or blinded by] the nationalist interpretation of

> the law, the subaltern is willing to act and claim the new dignity and status ['citizen'] he thinks it is promising him, only to be roundly disabused by that illusion (Mufti 2000: 22).

In postcolonial India the narrative of the law's relationship with the subaltern remains as fraught with contradictions as it was during Mangu's time. Manto's story sets up a pithy challenge to the spectacularization of constitutionalism—the rule of law, development, democracy—as the panacea not only for injustices, but also for the so-called unreasonable demands of 'unruly' populations who conduct their engagement with the state on their own terms, and not on the civic–legal terms that the state demands. The constitution ends up serving a pacifying, depoliticizing role in achieving the promise of emancipation.

In the course of this chapter I will provide concrete examples to illustrate how the constitutional framework that is used to claim and gain guarantees to FR is being compromised through the use of the very same constitution and the courts. The poor place faith in the law to deliver them from injustice, and the law holds them captive while they are without rights. The cruelty of this experience is aptly captured in the term Pharmakon. The Derridian reading of this expression, first introduced by Plato, means medicine that is cure and poison at the same time (Derrida 1981: 95). And that is what makes negotiations with the law's spectacular promises of justice both an unsettling and exasperating experience for the subaltern.

Faith in the spectacle of legal justice and the resultant fate of the 'rightsless' bears cruelly disproportionate outcomes. Using spectacles to represent emancipation and justice is a necessary tactic of liberal statecraft and market craft, both of which operate through a seamless intersection of managerial and militarized agendas. This tactic makes us believe in the benevolence of the state towards citizens, in the commitment of the state to national security, in the ideals of constitutionalism and the rule of law, and, of course, in human rights. It bolsters our faith in the constitution and the judiciary as the ultimate source, giver, arbiter, and interpreter of rights and makes us look at law as the primary legitimizing discourse concerning rights and emancipation. Spectacles of constitutionalism work as a process of mobilizing and sustaining what Upendra Baxi calls the 'will to stateness', which is a 'totalizing formation' in which legal recognition of communities and rights postures as the *telos* of justice-seeking enterprises within liberalism. In doing so, spectacles of constitutionalism put constitutional law on a hallowed pedestal worshipped by the state, the market, and citizens alike (Baxi 2002: 32).

The themes of promise and performance of law as an emancipatory tool on the one hand, and the law as a tool of domination on the other, have been explored in the Indian context in great depth by many scholars across disciplines. This essay does not rehearse those arguments, and does not claim to make any path-breaking revelations on that front. Rather, I attempt to identify some of the emancipatory incantations at work in contemporary India. In so doing, I show how the ways in which the law's spectacle works to maintain the rightsless citizens' continuous faith in the state (and now the market)—even as they are under attack from the state and the market and are left disappointed by the constitution's promises of emancipation.

Commenting on this 'double vision', and what I would call a double bind, of the law's position in Indian society, Marc Galanter wrote in a 1983 essay:

> India is a society in which law [in the conventional sense of authoritative general rules propounded by official agencies] is called upon to play a major role in maintaining order, effectuating social control, implementing deliberate change, and adjusting the accompanying strains and tensions... In its adherence to legal forms and loyalty to legal procedures, India is quite unusual among third world countries. Upon closer observation, this reliance upon and loyalty to law turns out to be more ambiguous than it first appears. In place of the image of India as a *Rechtsstaat*, we might substitute a double vision in which law in India is at once elaborated but attenuated, pervasive but precarious (1983: 9, emphasis in original).

In the New India, this double vision contingently persists. But the image of India as a *Rechtsstaat* has not subsided—rather, it has only strengthened. In contradistinction to Galanter's observation, which was made close to three decades ago, the idea of the rule of law in India today is elaborate and pervasive, where the state in a mode of legislative overdrive projects new laws and law reform as primary forms of good governance. What have become attenuated and precarious are the entitlements and lives of the marginalized.

The advent of the politically organized liberalization of the economy in 1991, and the accompanying privatization of the socio-political practices of statecraft and citizenship, have given emancipation a whole new meaning in which promises of emancipation do not remain the privileged preserve of the state and the constitution alone. The ostensible power to create and determine access to 'human rights' is being championed as rigorously, if not more, by the market, and we are all invited to participate. In a traditional *Rechtsstaat* polity, governmental power is limited by the law and by the constitution—in the *Rechtsstaat's* post-1991 avatar in India, power is further limited by the market. The abrogation of state accountability is accompanied by the propagation of increasing state withdrawal, and this state of affairs is thought to be most conducive for the flourishing of liberal ideals of emancipation. It is useful to quote Baxi at length in this context:

> What is new … about contemporary economic globalization is that it encases the Indian constitution within the emergent paradigm of *global economic constitutionalism*. This paradigm creates many-sided impacts, principal among which is the transformations of notions of accountability/ responsibility. The Indian state … is placed in a situation where internationally assumed [or imposed] obligations to facilitate the flows of global capital, trade and investment command a degree of priority over the order of constitutional obligations owed to Indian citizens and peoples. The three Ds of economic rationalism [deregulation, disinvestment, and denationalization], for example, favour many development policies that threaten, and at times nullify, achievements of rights and justice discourse (2002: 41, emphasis added).

I would actually go a step further than Baxi to contend that the three Ds of economic rationalism operate as spectacles that blind us into believing that they strengthen the rights and justice discourse rather than nullifying it. Global economic constitutionalism (GEC)—the practice of constitutionalism using the logic of neoliberalism[1]—operates as a history-vanishing moment or as what David Kazanjian, in a different context, refers to as 'flashpoints': 'a centripetal turbulence of illumination so powerful that it may blind the past even as it spotlights the present and lights up the future' (Kazanjian, cited in Puar 2007: xviii). This history-vanishing moment blinds us to the contested and insurgent origins of our Constitution and the cultures of dissent that have shaped our constitutional character. The pre-independence anti-colonial struggles and the post-independence struggles by subaltern populations are considered aberrations in public memory and are not counted as contributions to the making of India's constitutional democracy.[2] As this chapter tries to show, the celebratory march of the nation from a colonized country to a neoliberal power that is responding commendably to the global demands of economic restructuring is the only narrative of history that the courts have been responding to.

In other words, the logic of GEC, to invoke Susan George, 'gives the impression that all people from all regions of the globe are somehow caught up in a single movement, an all embracing phenomenon and are all marching towards some future Promised Land' (2003: 16). The image of this future Promised Land, as I argue, is scripted by the liberal rights discourse of the Indian constitution and the courts as one that is secular, nationalist, heterosexual, meritorious, multicultural, and market-friendly; it is one that will effectively remedy inequality, subordination, exclusion, and annihilation. As a history-vanishing moment, this works to depoliticize histories of struggles that upset the neatness with which the celebratory and linear narratives of the journey from repression to emancipation operate in India's post-liberalization legal and judicial discourse.[3]

My signification of these phenomena through the expression 'spectacle' is borrowed from the work of French situationist, Guy Debord. In his influential book, *The Society of the Spectacle*, Debord refers to 'spectacle' as the accumulation of capital to the point of collapse, where capital itself becomes an image (Debord 1983). In this chapter, I argue that the idea of emancipation has become a spectacle—a site of accumulation and commodification (Katz 2005: 5). I will illustrate how 'products' (in this case judgements or laws that promise emancipation for rights-less peoples) are forms of spectacle that ensure their sustenance as landmark precedents, without doing much to dismantle the structural causes of rightslessness. Spectacles can ascribe excess value to the law or judgement in question.

Akin to Debord's idea of 'commodity fetishism'—in this case judgement or legislation fetishism—spectacles seduce people into believing that judgements are cultural markers of legitimate recognition of injustice for the disenfranchised. Spectacles effected through ostensibly emancipatory judgements or laws are a tactic through which people's struggles against injustices are pacified and depoliticized.

The chapter explores some ideas about how the miscegenation between the state and the market creates technologies through which the *Rechtsstaat* image of India is produced, consumed, and sustained. The chapter also highlights the ways in which assemblages and deployment of the liberal language of legal rights creates spectacles that make the rights-less believe in the state—and then, inescapably, in the market—to 'deliver' them their economized share of emancipation.

The temporal register for this chapter is restricted to the years between 2000 and 2010, wherein I make brief references to a select set of judgements, legislations, activist strategies, and privatized representations of emancipation to further my argument about how these operate as spectacles that have the ability to discipline the ways in which we memorialize justice. The truncated timeline and sources have been selected to signify a dense period in the history of contemporary India, one in which 'critical events' (Das 1995) have collided and converged, giving the polity a unique hybridity that has sophisticatedly blurred the line between state and market. It is necessary to note that this blurring has not diluted the position of power that the state or the market wield; however, when critically examined, it exposes the intimate ways in which they collude to simultaneously promise emancipation and maintain monopoly over violence. This essay makes a modest attempt at mapping the contours of this disciplinary tactic, which operates as the leitmotif of democratic and juridical governance in India today.

Glimpses of the Spectacular Present

Before I get into the thick of conceptually unpacking the arguments, it is necessary to get a glimpse into some of the contemporary manifestations of the Mangu experience in postcolonial India. The illustrations that I share below are merely indicative of the trend I am trying to identify.

1. Imagine that Ustad Mangu is a homosexual in a post-section 377 scenario who,[4] drawing strength from the Delhi High Court's judgement in the Naz Foundation (*Naz Foundation vs Government of NCT of Delhi and Others*, 2009) case that decriminalized sodomy, openly declared his sexual orientation. He would surely not escape societal stigma attached to sexual minorities, which continues to be legitimized through the operation of the legal excess in constructing a public culture of homophobia that Section 377 of the IPC, 1860 has embedded in our socio-political and cultural consciousness.[5] The state can and does continue to use a plethora of other laws, including the Police Act, the Railways Act, and public nuisance laws, among others, to target the sexually marginalized. The case of Dr. Ramchandra Siras from the Aligarh Muslim University (AMU)—who was secretly filmed in an act of consensual sex with another adult man in the confines of his residence and whose employment was then terminated by the university authorities—is a rude reminder of the fact that nothing has changed, despite the judgement. A cruel consequence of this incident was that Siras was found dead under mysterious circumstances a few days after the Allahabad High Court ordered AMU to reinstate his appointment (Sarkar 2010).
2. If we substitute Ustad Mangu with Binayak Sen, Arun Fereira, Kopa Kunjam, Soni Sori, Seema Azad or Syed Mohammed Kazmi[6]—just a few of the many human rights defenders in India who were or are in jail because of their alleged anti-national activities—we realize the limitations inherent in the constitutional guarantees of freedom of speech, due process, and the right to life and liberty. It does not take much state strength to keep individuals incarcerated despite flimsy evidence or to subject them to torture in the name of extraordinariness under special security laws (such as the Chhattisgarh Vishesh Jan Suraksha Adhiniyam, 2005). Such laws effect a return to Emergency-like conditions in present-day 'shining' India and establish a normalized order of 'Gulag constitutionalism' that 'represents dissent as treason' (Baxi 2002: 31).
3. The fate of several victim-survivors of the Union Carbide Corporation (UCC) gas leak in Bhopal in 1984 has been sealed not only by the cross-generational devastation that the leak

unleashed, but also by the victim-survivors' committed attempt to place faith in the judiciary to bring them justice. This has resulted in many activists, including women and children, being arrested and brutally beaten by the police (BBC 2002). Immediately after the tragedy took place in 1984, in a pathetic show of paternalism, the state unilaterally decided to act as *parens patriae* for all victims, which, in effect, was an attempt to mask and escape accountability for its own collusion in the event. To save itself from being made tortiously liable in US courts by the many American personal injury lawyers who flew in after the leak, the state, in its capacity as *parens patriae*, passed the Bhopal Gas Leak Disaster (Processing of Claims) Act, 1985 to take over and pursue the claims of the victims in and outside India, ostensibly because the victims would not be able to do so. Non-state human rights groups and the victims themselves lost all legal standing to claim compensation. While this move seemed as if the state was taking its obligations to remedy the violations faced by its citizens seriously, in effect, this enabled the state to escape liability by taking on the persona of the victim. The constitutionality of the law was challenged, but it was upheld by the SC (*Charan Lal Sahu vs Union of India*, 1990). The spectacle that this benevolent posturing created overshadowed the state's two-pronged plan to allow Warren Anderson, CEO and chairman of UCC at the time of the disaster, safe passage out of India, and to save itself from being targeted by mass compensation lawsuits. The case moved to the United States in 1986, but it was dismissed on the ground of *forum non conveniens*. This dismissal worked well for UCC because it meant that the case had to be tried in India where the law of compensation for industrial disasters and corporate crimes was not well developed (Hanna et al 2005; Galanter 2002: 172–86; Fortun 2001). The so-called settlement of 1989 was another spectacle that was aimed at effecting a closure to the issue of compensation. The latest travesty—taking the form of a judgement issued on 7 June 2010, which criminally convicted some of the accused of Union Carbide India Limited—pays mere lip service to the cause of justice and reparation for which the people of Bhopal have been struggling for over 25 years now (Nundy 2010).

4. The impunity with which urban evictions continue in big cities in the name of beautification, cleanliness, development, and now security (especially in the wake of events like the 2010 Commonwealth Games in New Delhi) is another instance of the abrogation of rights by the state at the demand of market actors (Mishra et al 2012) and of a modern-day Mangu-like experience. This is occurring despite the right to shelter and livelihood for the homeless being a recognized as a constitutional right in the Olga Tellis (*Olga Tellis and Others vs Bombay Municipal Corporation and Others*, 1986) judgement. The courts, showing more concern for the rights of privileged citizens to drive on roads sanitized of beggars and the homeless, have unapologetically suffocated the expansive and pro-human rights interpretations given to the right to life and liberty under Article 21 through a progressive history of judicial activism. The violence unleashed by anti-poor judgements like *Almitra H. Patel and another vs Union of India*, 2000 has been a cause of celebration by elite citizens for whom homeless people are encroachers and an eyesore to potential investors in the capital. In this case, while commenting on the government's policy of rehabilitating slum dwellers, the Supreme Court remarked that 'the promise of free land at the tax payers [sic] cost, in place of a jhuggi [slum], is a proposal which attracts more land grabbers. Rewarding an encroacher with free alternatives [sic] sites is like giving a reward to a pickpocket.' Over the past years, millions of slum dwellers from the Yamuna Pushta and other *jhuggi* colonies of Delhi have been removed on the orders of the SC and rendered homeless or sent to Bawana, in North west Delhi, without any sanitation, water, electricity, or even drainage (Bhushan 2006; Menon-Sen and Bhan 2008). The courts' allusion to 'development' in their decisions has been seen to represent their commitment to turning Delhi into a world-class city; there has been little appreciation of the anti-poor positions that have deeply informed the ideology behind these judgements.
5. The so-called socialist move to abolish the fundamental right to private property was accompanied by the introduction of the principle of eminent domain, which has allowed the state to acquire land for any public purpose. The havoc that laws like

the Land Acquisition Act, 1894 and the Forest Act, 1927 (until their new versions came into being) have wreaked on the lives of Adivasi (indigenous) communities does not need reiteration here. What is crucial about such a move is that in the name of abolishing private property, the state turned itself into the rightful owner of all landed property, which facilitated its unilateral decision to acquire land whenever there was an industry-induced demand for it.[7]

6. The enactment of the long-overdue Right to Education (RTE) Act, 2009 also works as a spectacle. It guarantees something unprecedented in India's FR history—it translates, for the first time, a directive principle of state policy (DP) not only into an FR but also into legislation. However, with respect to children beyond the age of 14, the state absolves itself of all accountability to guarantee education. Only those with the economic capacity to afford education beyond that age can avail themselves of it; the rest must be satisfied with this tokenistic guarantee. What is interesting is that along with the enactment of the RTE Act, the state is also introducing the Foreign Education Institutions (Regulation of Entry and Operations) Bill, 2010, which will allow a complete takeover of higher education by private universities. Only those who have the private capital to access and afford these universities will benefit—which is a negligible proportion of university aspirants in India (Sadgopal 2010: 17). In other words, the spectacle of the RTE Act is used as a convenient cover for the state to privatize higher education.
7. One way in which the courts avoid the issue of structural exclusion is through the hope that heightened forms of punishment will work as spectacles that will keep the disadvantaged happy about the courts' pronouncements. Take the case of the the Khairlanji judgement in which the ad hoc sessions court in Bhandara district, Maharashtra awarded the death penalty to six upper caste men for the massacre of four Dalits (the 'untouchable' caste) of the Bhotmange family in Khairlanji village on 29 September 2006 (*Central Bureau of Investigation vs Sakru Mahagu Binjewar and Others*, 2008). The verdict, delivered in 2008, was hailed as historic by the Dalit community, despite the

fact that the court reduced the event to just a grave crime and completely ignored the caste character of it. When the case went to appeal to the Nagpur bench of the Bombay High Court 2010, the death penalty was commuted. Dalits were disappointed, but the caste question still did not come up. In the progressive legal imagination, the Khairlanji decision represents speedy justice, and the fact that, culturally, it marked an erasure of a history of deep-seated violence and of caste prejudice did not matter—that was the spectacular potential of the death penalty (Anand 2008; Teltumbde 2010).

8. An illustration of spectacle politics is the government's response to veteran Gandhian Anna Hazare's hunger strike. He demanded the constitution of a joint committee comprising state and civil society members to finalize the Jan Lokpal Bill (a national Ombudsman law for fighting corruption) before its enactment. The fact that the Manmohan Singh government actually accepted all the demands made by Hazare and his team is a spectacular move by the state to posture itself as pro-people, human rights friendly, and committed to rooting out corruption. In contrast, it is necessary to ask why the state has not responded with equal urgency to Irom Sharmila's greater-than-a-decade-long fast demanding the repeal of the draconian Armed Forces Special Powers Act (AFSPA),1958.[8] Does this have anything to do with the strong nationalist narrative that was inherent to Hazare's campaign, with regular refrains of Jai Hind, a huge flexi-banner of Bharat Mata (Mother India) adorning the stage at Delhi's Jantar Mantar where he was fasting, and the patriotic waving of the Tricolour after the government conceded to all demands? Why have the many fasts by Medha Patkar not stopped the SC from allowing the height of the Sardar Sarovar Dam to be raised, even though this decision will result in more areas becoming submerged and more people being displaced? The state's manoeuvre has created a spectacle that has blinded us to the ways in which it selects the fasts that it wants to end (see generally Rehman 2011).
9. For a final example, Manto's prophetic reading of the constitution's spectacle returns as a rude awakening when we remember

1 July 2010, when Cherukuri Rajkumar, also known as Comrade Azad, a spokesperson for a left-wing militant group, was killed extra-judicially by state forces. In January 2011, the SC made a surprisingly sensitive assertion in response to a request for a judicial probe into the killing: 'We cannot allow the republic killing its own children'. The bench added: 'We hope there will be an answer. There will be a good and convincing answer' (Venkatesan 2011). On 19 July 2010, around three weeks after his killing, *Outlook* magazine posthumously published Azad's last work, written in response to an article by veteran journalist B.G. Verghese (Rajkumar 2010). In this piece, Azad rejects Verghese's celebratory belief in India's constitutional democracy. Verghese wrote: 'The Maoists will fade away, democratic India and the Constitution will prevail, despite all the time it takes and the pain involved' (Rajkumar 2010). In response Azad wrote:

> In which part of India is the Constitution prevailing, Mr Verghese? In Dantewada, Bijapur, Kanker, Narayanpur, Rajnandgaon? In Jharkhand, Orissa? In Lalgarh, Jangalmahal? In the Kashmir Valley? Manipur? Where was your Constitution hiding for 25 long years after thousand [sic] of Sikhs were [sic] massacred? When thousands of Muslims were decimated? When lakhs of peasants are compelled to commit suicides? When thousands of people are murdered by state-sponsored Salwa Judum gangs? When adivasi women are gangraped? When people are simply abducted by uniformed goons? Your Constitution is a piece of paper that does not even have the value of toilet paper for the vast majority of the Indian people (Rajkumar 2010).

In just one paragraph, Azad's words captured the essence of the sham that the constitution may be for most of India's poor and disenfranchised people. The cruel reality of his words was reinforced when two weeks before Manto's 100th birthday, the court dismissed the petition seeking a judicial probe into the killing (*The Hindu* 2012). After this order, the SC's bleeding-hearted concern about the death of the 'republic's children' will forever be part of its spectacular history.

Reading Rights Differently

> Rights emblematize the ghostly sovereignty of the unemancipated individual in modernity.
>
> —Wendy Brown, *States of Injury: Power and Freedom in Late Modernity* (1995: 110)

Liberalism's spectacle was best described by the young Karl Marx in his 1844 essay, 'On the Jewish Question', where he complicated the notion of emancipation and offered a critique of liberal rights that we can ignore today at our own peril. Marx questioned why the state should be regarded as the end of all emancipation and suggested that political emancipation by the state is only a masquerade to numb man's consciousness as a species. By distinguishing 'political emancipation' from 'human emancipation', Marx pointed out that the rhetoric of liberal rights ('the rights of man') that the secular state foregrounds is in effect not human emancipation: '[M]an was not liberated from religion; he received religious liberty. He was not liberated from property; he received the liberty to own property. He was not liberated from the egoism of business; he received the liberty to engage in business' (1978: 45).

Wendy Brown, in a trenchant reading of 'On the Jewish Question', writes:

> [T]he ruse of power peculiar to liberal constitutionalism centers upon granting freedom, equality and representation to abstract rather than concrete subjects. The substitution of abstract political subjects for actual ones not only forfeits the project of emancipation but resubjugates us precisely by emancipating substitutes for us – by emancipating our abstracted representatives in the state and naming this process 'freedom.' [...] If [...] the bourgeois constitutional state is premised upon depoliticized inegalitarian social powers, if it depends upon naturalizing [...] abstract representations of equality and community, then *rights* are the modern political form that secure and legitimate these tendencies (1995: 109–111, emphasis in original).

The abstraction of the citizen-subject and the constitutionally guaranteed rights afforded to the intricately manufactured image of the citizen-subject work as a spectacle that blinds us from the violence of constitution-making and the practices through which a *Rechtsstaat* polity is sustained by the state–market collusion in a liberal democracy. While the state creates the rights-bearing, abstract citizen-subject, the market creates the abstract figure of the merit-driven, rational, consuming, and entrepreneurial citizen-subject with individualized desires and privatized ways to satiate those desires. To quote Brown again, 'Liberal equality guarantees that the state will regard us all as equally abstracted from the social powers constituting our existence, equally decontextualized from the unequal conditions of our lives' (1995: 110).

Clearly then, from a Marxist perspective, engaging the state as the only arbiter of emancipation strengthens the state to make the playing field further conducive for capitalism. French historian Fernand Braudel captures this phenomenon sharply when he says, 'Capitalism only triumphs when it is identified with the state, when *it is* the state' (quoted in Hardt & Negri 2000:3, emphasis in original). This especially becomes the case when the responsibility to make and unmake abstract citizen-subjects is shared between the state and the market, and when, on occasion, the market manufactures more idealized forms of citizen-subjects—who are committed to individualized, self-disciplined practices of desire and consumption—than the state.

Human emancipation, thus, can only be achieved when we question the state as strongly as we question the market and when we pay acute attention to the ways in which one feeds off the other. We cannot be blinded by what liberal rights guarantee us, and we need to constantly question the paradigm of liberal rights, which normalizes the rule of the market and makes the rule of law work in sync with it—in effect normalizing inequalities. It is for this reason that we need to read rights differently, to wrest them out of the captivity of rule of law discourses. This task is upon us because of the spectacular potential that the project of liberalism (and neoliberalism, its more advanced avatar) possesses to depoliticize the materiality of the struggles of the rights-less—as has been the case both pre- and post-colonialism. Rather than engaging in an enterprise of abandonment, we must constantly interrogate the law and its promise of emancipation. The tactics through which liberalism's promise seduces us, and the strategic role that law plays in heightening the seduction,[9] must be exposed.

As Nivedita Menon asks, 'What are the implications for the liberatory potential of rights once their meaning is fixed by law?' (Menon 2004: 26). This question bears acute significance especially as most struggles for rights in liberal democracies are about gaining fixed recognition of excluded community identities. This is what John and Jean Comaroff call a 'fetishism of the law', where:

> '[T]he law' [...] is objectified, ascribed a life-force of its own, and attributed the mythic capacity to configure a world of relations in its own image [...] It is a faith owed largely to the fact that the promulgation of a *new Legal Order*, in the upper case, signals a *break with the past*, with its embarrassments, its nightmares, its torments, its traumas (2009: 32–33, emphasis added).

This break with the past is representative of the logic within which legal rights operate, and the New Legal Order (NLO) is the spectacle that sustains this logic—it is the flashpoint (the history-vanishing moment), or the spectacle that announces our journey towards the Promised Land. This promise of the NLO and the imagined break with the past masks the ways in which the NLO continues to unleash violence with impunity. Even if one is able to call the law's bluff, the NLO has amassed enough surplus authority from the faith that people repose in it. This, in turn, allows it to sustain the spectacles of emancipation that continue to make us fetishize the law and its seductive promise of delivering us from all evil.The NLO works akin to the way in which the new economic order works to sustain capitalism's seductive promise of progress despite the acute disadvantage that it makes systemic in the institutions of governance and in the delivery of justice.

The Comaroffs point out the way in which the pervasiveness of neoliberalism across the world, especially in less industrialized countries of the global south, has been accompanied by a pervasiveness of constitutionalism. They note that this enchanted faith in constitutionalism creates a 'culture of legality' that infuses everyday life almost everywhere, 'even when both the spirit and the letter of the law are despoiled, distended, desecrated; even as more regimes suspend it in the name of emergency, expediency, exception; even as they [the state] expropriate its sovereignty unto themselves; even as they franchise it out' (Comaroff and Comaroff 2009: 33).

This is most paradigmatically reflected in the way in which the United Progressive Alliance (UPA) government of India is on the one hand celebrating its pro-*aam aadmi* (common man) commitment by being in a legislative overdrive mode—by passing laws like the National Rural Employment Guarantee Act, 2005, Right to Information Act, 2005, Domestic Violence Act (Protection of Women from Domestic Violence Act, 2005), Right to Education Act (Right of Children to Free and Compulsory Education Act, 2009) Forest Rights Act (The Scheduled Tribes and Other Traditional Forest Dwellers (Recognition of Forest Rights) Act, 2006), and, in the pipeline at the time, the Jan Lokpal Bill. These legislative projects stand in stark contrast to the government's ongoing commitment to the project of divestments, privatization of natural resources, the incarceration of anyone who challenges the state's brutal policies, and the resort to violent military means to achieve the ends of corporate capital's demands on the state. The state's response of 'hyperlegality' (Hussain 2007: 514) is adequately buttressed by the demands of civil society citizenship claims, which lead 'politics to migrate to the court' (Comaroff and Comaroff 2009: 35). Particularly in India, as Julia Eckert observes, 'The "use of the law" now "complements or replaces" other species of counter-politics' (Eckert 2006: 45, cited in Comaroff and Comaroff 2009: 35). This state of hyperlegality is poignantly captured by the Comaroffs when they say:

> [C]lass struggles are giving way to class actions in which people are drawn together by material predicament, culture, race, sexual preference, residence, faith and habits of consumption become legal persons as their common plaints turn them into plaintiffs with common identities. Citizens, subjects, governments, congregations, chiefdoms, communities and corporations litigate against one another in an ever-mutating kaleidoscope [...] often at the intersections of tort law, human rights law, constitutional law and criminal law. Even democracy has been judicialized: few national elections these days go by without some resort to the courts. (2009:35)

This phenomenon of rights-in-the-era-of-hyperlegality is about the emergence of governance mechanisms that promote the withdrawal of the state—'the outsourcing by government of many conventional operations, including those integral to the management of "bare life"'

(Comaroff and Comaroff 2009: 37)—and that simultaneously put in place regulatory governance through legislation. Courts complement this trend by acting as legislators who are continuously meting out rights through a mechanism of classifying population groups demanding legal recognition, much like customized responses to consumer feedback in a shopping mall. What is also characteristic of this trend is the fact that this legalism is promoted equally by the left, a political location that could have ideally allowed a more critical understanding of how hyperlegality is actually capable of entrenching and normalizing disadvantage to the extent of institutionalizing it.

This is an interesting shift in the left's position. It was 'originally' (if one can pinpoint a pristine original moment, that is) concerned more with methods of collective bargaining and other species of counter-politics and viewed the rights question as 'the problem' because of its emphasis on freedom of contract and private property rights (Kennedy 2002: 178). Now, the left is engaging in what Brown and Halley call 'left legalism', in which it 'invoke[s] the liberal state's promise to make justice happen by means of law' (2002: 7–8). While these observations are particular to the situation in the US, they are also applicable to the experiences of present-day India.

The recent set of social justice statutes in India, some of which I mentioned above, is a product of engagement with the law by left-leaning people's movements. But what are the consequences of left legalism in an era of the NLO and GEC? Does the stream of legislations reflect how human rights–friendly the state is, or does it operate as a spectacle that blinds us to the state's corporatized military efforts to forcibly take away Adivasi land?[10] How do those who engage in left legalism gain faith in the rule of law that has historically been the tool for their exclusion and annihilation, both during colonialism and later? What is the left legalist's vision of emancipation? Are these statutes universally emancipatory, or do they mask the violence inherent in their form and operation? Is the state actually committed to emancipation of its marginalized citizens? Or are these statutes a means to make India look like an advanced democracy that has bravely embraced the NLO and adapted well to the needs of GEC by foregrounding its capacity to legislate on issues like '"good governance", "rights" and "development" not so much with a solicitude for the nation-peoples as for the community of foreign investors' (Baxi 2008: 96)? Is constitutionalism in India being 'held hostage by the movement of global capital?' (Baxi 2008: 96).

Brown characterizes this set of paradoxical questions well when she asks, 'When does legal recognition become an instrument of regulation, and political recognition becomes [sic] an instrument of subordination?' (Brown 1995: 99). In her analysis,

> [h]istorically, rights emerged in modernity both as a vehicle of emancipation from political disenfranchisement or institutional servitude and as a means of privileging an emerging bourgeoisie class within a discourse of formal egalitarianism and universal citizenship. Thus, they emerged both as a means of protection against arbitrary use and abuse of sovereign and social power and as a mode of securing and naturalizing dominant social powers – class, gender and so forth. Not only did bourgeoisie rights discourse mask by depoliticizing the social power of institutions such as private property or the family, it organized mass populations for exploitation and regulation [...]. (1995: 99.)

Rights, then, are a hydra-headed organism, and all rights-seeking enterprises—especially those on the left—need to tread cautiously the path of using the law to claim them. While rights emerged as a means to limit sovereign power, once enshrined within a constitutional document, their interpretation, implementation, and desecration remains in the hands of the sovereign only. If we are captive in our articulation of what rights we demand, especially under conditions where our vocabulary is manufactured by the state, then what hope do we have for the future of emancipation for subaltern struggles? Further, what happens when the rights language authored by the state is sponsored by a market-military complex?

A potentially useful starting point for responding to the paradox posed by Brown is to probe how liberalism disciplines our histories and memories of justice. How do we interrogate a political economy that promotes justice as a commodity where its cost is measured in the language in which you ask for it and in the ways in which you publicly and privately 'perform' the rites and rituals of disciplined citizenship? When every governmental articulation of rights can potentially become a spectacle for masking the tactic that is used to construct the ideal rights-bearing subject, which kind of citizen, according to the sovereign, qualifies for emancipation in the spheres of the family, polity, and market? And, to return to Marx, what kind of counter-political engagement is required on the part of people's struggles to create a politics of 'human emancipation' that does not require the scaffolding of the legalistic limits of liberal rights? These are pressing challenges to a justice system that is only made available to those who frame their requests in the language of rights approved by the state and who live as citizens in ways that are approved by the state.

I find instructive the work of postcolonial historian Dipesh Chakrabarty in this regard. In concluding this section, I will make a brief reference to a theoretical schema that Chakrabarty sets up in his book, *Provincializing Europe: Postcolonial Thought and Historical Difference*. He offers a sophisticated analysis of Marx in order to understand the 'life process' of capital through two historical trajectories. In one ('History 1'), capital's universal narrative deals with historical difference by temporizing it and has the ability to subsume all progress under its logic. In the other ('History 2'), the totalizing thrusts of capital constantly interrupt and make room for the politics of human belonging and diversity (Chakrabarty 2000: 47).

Following in the steps of Chakrabarty, this chapter works through two histories of emancipation in contemporary India. One of these, Emancipation 1, follows the liberal teleology of repression to emancipation of the rightsless—a narrative that feeds into and reproduces the magic of modernity. The other, Emancipation 2, is inhabited and performed through bodily habits and unselfconscious collective practices of the everyday and ordinary that are not automatically aligned with the logic of capital. For sake of brevity, the rest of this section will focus more centrally on understanding Emancipation 1, and the chapter will conclude with some provisional glimpses into what Emancipation 2 might look like.

As I have already argued, one powerful tool for the propagation of Emancipation 1 is the legalistic language of human rights, which has become inescapably desirable, despite our critical consciousness about the cruelly liberal genealogy of its idea and practice. For us, human rights remains, to use Gayatri Chakravorty Spivak's expression, 'what one cannot not want' (1993: 46). Wherever one might be placed on the ideological map of the left, even the idea of revolution, inscribed within the political and social practices of liberalism, cannot escape using the vocabulary of rights (Sircar 2010). This consciousness has constituted each of us (and our subterranean others) as 'desiring' nationalist, heterosexual, able bodied, and entrepreneurial subjects to whom liberalism offers means like the market, secularism, merit, multiculturalism, and, of course, human rights law, as remedies for inequality, subordination, and exclusion.

What has also become apparent is that the most legitimate currency of negotiation for social and people's movements today is the language of liberal human rights as a means of 'righting wrongs', rather than contesting oppressive paradigms (Brown 2002: 420). As a result of this, states respond to issues of rights violations through the practice of Emancipation 1, by promulgating a plethora of 'new' human rights—in effect characterizing human rights enunciations as the telos of justice-seeking projects. While this results in more law, it also co-opts claimants into nation-building projects and into a political economy that promotes justice as a consumptive product. It is within the market that the horizon of justice is established today. To ask for justice, re-vindication, or recognition has become, thus, a particular manner of being in the world: which not only confines us to a particular language, but also forces us to perform our claims in a particular way, that is, as the good, nationalist, heterosexual, respectable, able-bodied, and entrepreneurial citizen.

So what would a politics of Emancipation 2 look like? For that, can we engage the law without falling into the trap of liberalism? Can we afford to completely disengage with liberal rights? At what cost do we move beyond the legalese of human rights? Does speaking the liberal language operate as a strategy for people's movements, or is it a co-option of it? What does the left's turn to legalism hold for the future of Emancipation 2? And as Brown enquires, '[H]ow might the paradoxical elements of the struggle for rights in an emancipatory context articulate a field of justice beyond "that which we cannot not want"?' (2002: 432).

Dynamics of Disenchantment

> According to the fable of their constitution, Indians today are all 'citizens'.
>
> —Dipesh Chakrabarty, *Provincializing Europe* (2002: 35)

Chakrabarty's provocation is troubling at this point in history when we are continuing to remain buoyant about the Constitution of India even in the face of growing acts of state violence that are being carried out with impunity. To mark the sixtieth year of the republic, on national television we were comfortably consuming Gulzar's[11] mellifluous rendition of why each citizen needs to defend the Samvidhan (constitution) on one hand, and the prime-time coverage of the state's manufactured constitutional legitimacy for an armed offensive against the 'Maoists' on the other. This despite the fact that the SC has categorically disapproved the arming of the Salwa Judum, a state-sponsored paramilitary group in the state of Chhattisgarh (Venkatesan 2008; Sundar 2016), and has snubbed the government for raising the bogey of 'Naxalism'[12] against human rights activists (Press Trust of India 2010). While India's corporate actors were declaring with pride how the Indian economy braved the recession, they were also condoning the incarceration of Dr. Binayak Sen[13] because his politics would have undermined the credibility of the mining industry's promises of foreign direct investment into India.

The poetics of constitutional magic, the politics of constitutional markets, and the polemics of constitutional coercion make us believe in the fable of citizenship. The power of this fable also disciplines us to almost unquestioningly accept anything that carries the tag of constitutional legitimacy attached to it, such as special security legislations, disinvestment policies, large industrial projects that lead to mass-scale displacement, rights articulated in the language of privacy, and, of course, the 21-month-long Emergency that was declared in India between 1975 and 1977.

The 'dynamics of disenchantment' (Baxi 1985: 107) gets partially allayed by the trust that the rightsless have placed in the constitution because of the creative activist interventions by the SC over the last several years in the form of public interest litigations (PIL) or social action litigations (SAL) to protect and uphold the human rights of a range of disadvantaged communities and individuals. The diamond jubilee of the constitution thus cannot be celebrated without acknowledging the 30 years of 'judicial populism' (Baxi 1985: 107) in India spearheaded by the SC. As Justice Dwivedi observed in *Kesavananda Bharathi vs State of Kerala*:

> The Constitution [of India] is not intended to be the arena of legal quibbling for men with long purses. It is made for the common people. It should generally be so construed as that they can understand and appreciate it. The more they understand it the more they love it and the more they prize it (1973).

If the legitimacy of the constitution has remained intact over 60 years, albeit contestably, this fact is almost singularly owed to the SC's efforts (in response to claims by people's movements and social action groups) through half its life span. As Baxi noted in 1985, 'The Supreme Court *of* India is at long last becoming [...] the Supreme Court *for* Indians' (1985: 107, emphasis in original). Baxi's optimism, however, has waned over time, and he writes in 2002:

> This disenchantment is now more fully voiced when the *still* rightless peoples [...] have to say even to the Supreme Court of India: 'Physician Heal Thyself'. The new zamindari [landlordism] of public interest by courts appears to them no different from its earlier forms and incarcerations, although it provides for many an entrepreneur in the market for human rights activism (2002a: i, emphasis in original).

The impetus for the 'charismatic inaugural moment' (Baxi 2002a: xvi–xvii) of judicial populism was the days of the Emergency during which the SC's role in protecting constitutionally guaranteed FR was itself suspect. In the landmark 1976 case of *Additional District Magistrate, Jabalpur vs S Shukla,* individuals detained without trial challenged the constitutionality of a presidential order suspending the right to challenge detention orders for the duration of the Emergency. They argued that the presidential order and their detentions violated Article 21's guarantee that '[n]o person shall be deprived of his life or liberty except according to procedure established by law.' The SC denied the petitions and upheld the presidential order, opining that 'in times of emergency the executive safeguards the life of the nation' and that during such times its actions cannot be challenged as arbitrary or unlawful. As Desai and Muralidhar note:

> [The *ADM Jabalpur* case] granted virtual immunity to any action of the executive affecting the life and liberty of the citizen [...] The

> judgment brought into question the role of the Supreme Court as the guardian of citizens' liberties. The vigorous growth of PIL was in some measure a reaction to this criticism (2000: 161).

If it was not for the courageously lone dissent by Justice H.R. Khanna in the case, arguing that 'detention without trial is an anathema to all those who love personal liberty', the SC might never have thought of undoing its historic blunder of understanding the 'procedure established by law' laid out in Article 21 to stand the test of fairness, reasonability, and due process (*ADM Jabalpur* 1976: 264). His observation in the *Kesavananda* judgement about why the constitution needs amendments to ensure that the right to life can never be suspended under any circumstance was a brave act of dissent in the spirit of the constitution's revolutionary past:

> No generation has a monopoly of wisdom nor has a right to put fetters on future generations to mould the machinery of governments. If no provisions were made for amendment of the Constitution, the people would have recourse to extra-constitutional methods like revolution to change the Constitution (*Kesavananda* 1974: para 1445).

Today, recourse to extra-constitutional means to change the *Constitution* is active, as evidenced by the militant turn that several peasant movements have taken in the country. The sovereign in India still holds absolute authority to declare a state of emergency (Agamben 2005).

The *New York Times* published an editorial two days after the *ADM Jabalpur* dissent as a tribute to Justice Khanna, stating:

> If India ever finds its way back to the freedom and democracy that were proud hallmarks of its first 18 years as an independent nation, someone will surely erect a monument to Justice H. R. Khanna of the Supreme Court. It was Justice Khanna who spoke out fearlessly and eloquently for freedom this week in dissenting from the court's decision upholding the right of Prime Minister Indira Gandhi's government to imprison political opponents at will and without court hearings [...] the Indian Supreme Court's decision appears close to utter surrender (quoted in Mahapatra 2008).

Although India did find its way back to freedom and democracy—or so we are made to believe—the SC remains subject to the will of the sovereign and extracts public reverence through spectacles. In its post-Emergency decision in *Maneka Gandhi vs Union of India*, the SC affirmed that the doctrine of due process cannot be divorced from the operation of the FR to equality, freedom, and life and liberty, in effect expanding the SC's power to strike down legislation to include the inspection of a statute's commitment to substantive due process (*Maneka Gandhi vs Union of India*; Desai and Muralidhar 2000: 160). Further, pursuant to Justice Khanna's dissent in *Kesavananda*, the 44th amendment to the constitution, which excluded Articles 21 and 22 from suspension during times of Emergency, was passed (The Constitution (44th Amendment) Act, 1978). In 2009, former Chief Justice of India M.N. Venkatachaliah said at a public lecture that the majority decision in *ADM Jabalpur* should be consigned to the 'dustbin of history' (Press Trust of India 2010). So much so that in January 2011, a bench of Justices Aftab Alam and A.K. Ganguly said that the decision was 'erroneous' (*Ramdeo Chauhan at Rajnath Chauhan vs Bani Kant Das & Others*, 2009).

Yet, even after a spectacular history of judicial activism, PIL, and SAL in India, the SC has time and again upheld the constitutionality of draconian special security statutes like the Terrorist Activities and Disruptive Activities (Prevention) Act, 1987, the Prevention of Terrorism Act, 2002, and the AFSPA, 1958, and has found no substantive due process anomaly with these laws.[14] None of the illustrious precedents mentioned above stopped former SC judge Arijit Pasayat from saying at a public event in 2009 that terrorists are animals and thus not deserving of human rights—in effect lending legitimacy to the extrajudicial killings and torture permitted under these laws to ostensibly protect national security (Kumara and Jones 2008). Similarly, the celebratory spectacle of Article 21 and its creative interpretations stopped us from rigorously critiquing Article 22(3), which legitimizes 'preventive detention based on jurisdiction of suspicion [...] as a just order of exception to the precious fundamental rights to life and liberty' (Baxi 2002a: 37).

What, then, has allowed the highest court to maintain its avowed position as the 'Supreme Court *for* Indians' after having compromised on the 'basic structure' element of FR that was ceremoniously asserted as non-derogable through any legislative measure or amendment to the constitution itself in celebrated cases like *Golaknath* (*I.C. Golaknath and Others vs State of Punjab and Others*, 1967), *Kesavananda*, and *Minerva Mills* (*Minerva Mills Limited and Others vs Union of India and Others*, 1980)? In other words, what has sustained our faith in the SC as the ultimate arbiter of fairness and justice when many of its own judgements have grossly compromised basic guarantees of constitutional FR? What role has an activist judiciary played in representing the Samvidhan to the common people to make them 'love it' and 'prize it'?

The sixtieth year of the Constitution of India provides an opportune moment to reflect on what sustains our faith in this document and the institutions that interpret it. The ambitious nature of this reflection demands both time and space that is unavailable for this chapter. However, to make this enquiry worthy of engagement, I will focus, as mentioned earlier, on some critical events in the life and times of the courts and their negotiations with and interpretations and applications of the constitution, paying specific attention to the question of socio-economic rights, primarily between 2000–10. The enquiry is prompted by a need to find out how the Indian economy's liberalization in 1991 impacted the way the courts responded to rights questions. Did they build on the trailblazing history of judicial activism from the 1980s, or did they give in to the corporatized demands of the NLO to keep pace with the march of global capitalism? In other words, how do we understand the trajectory of Emancipation 1 in the history of post-liberalization Indian judicial-constitutionalism?

One trend suggests that in deciding PIL cases where the litigant is seeking redress for socio-economic rights violations, judges have become 'reluctant to penalize the government even when the state fail[s] to fulfill its statutory obligations. Instead, courts adopt [...] *weak remedies* such as setting up committees and [commissions]' (Shankar and Mehta 2008: 147, emphasis added). This emphasis on weak remedies marks a peculiar characteristic of legislative democracies like India, where most socio-economic rights are enumerated in the constitution but are never at par with civil and political rights. This status makes socio-economic rights non-justiciable and only progressively realizable. Given their constitutionally vulnerable status, socio-economic rights are further at a 'systemic risk in legislative democracies because those who benefit from them lack political power' (Shankar and Mehta 2008: 147). In effect, while we might have rights-enhancing judgements from courts that interpret the constitution expansively, these judgements do not transform structures of injustice—rather, they oftentimes normalize them.

A plain reading of the scheme of the constitution, for which one does not require training in law, sets up the spectacular potential of its design. Here I do not refer to the 'expanding horizons of Article 21'[15] that have enabled the SC to use the article to creatively read several rights into the constitution, but rather to the commonsensical distinction between FR and DP. As is evident from the language used, there is a clear hierarchy between these two sets of entitlements. FRs like equality (Article 14) and life (Article 21) are worded in a way that imposes a positive restriction/limitation on state action, namely 'the state shall not deny to any person[…]' or 'no person shall be deprived'. On the other hand, the DPs such as work (Articles 41 to 43), education (Article 45), health (Article 47), and environment (Article 48A) are preceded by aspirational language—'the state shall strive to promote[…]'; 'the state shall take steps to organize[…]'; 'the state shall make provision for[…]'; 'the state shall, within the limits of its economic capacity and development[…]'; or 'the state shall endeavour to secure[…]'. The distinction between the two, then, is a matter of the intention with which they were inserted in the constitution in the first place.

Regarding the DPs, B.R. Ambedkar noted during the Constituent Assembly Debates that it was:

> […] the intention of the Assembly that in future both legislature and the executive should not merely pay lip-service to these principles enacted in this part but that they should be made the basis of all executive and legislative action that may be taken thereafter in the matter of governance of the country (Shankar & Mehta 2008: 148) (quoted in Shankar & Mehta 2008: 148)

Yet, the DPs were, from the beginning, imagined as entitlements that will be progressively realized, contingent upon the economic ability of the state. While the state under the leadership of Jawaharlal Nehru, along with its mutated oppressive avatar during

Indira Gandhi's time, always put rights enshrined in the DPs on the backburner by hiding behind the fig leaf of economic incapacity, it continued to pump money to arm the state—to the extent of investing enough monetary resources to orchestrate the Emergency. 'Progressive realization', it was realized after the scandal of the Emergency, was a myth. As already mentioned, it was with the intention of undoing the damage of decisions like *ADM Jabalpur* that the SC engaged in judicial populism and started interpreting a range of 'new' human rights into the framework of FRs. This liberalization of constitutional interpretation was also accompanied by the relaxation of the rule of *locus standi*, giving rise to the marvel called PIL/SAL. As Baxi notes, this marked the beginning of the moment when the SC started 'taking suffering seriously' (Baxi 1985: 107). Unfortunately, the SC could not sustain the seriousness for very long.

As Radha D'Souza notes, this was the first phase of the PIL/ SAL years (1977–87), during which the SC 'emphasized human rights and facilitated access to justice for marginalized classes and groups' (2005: 488). The second phase (1988–98) is the time when the SC started engaging with PIL primarily on issues of governance (Sathe 2002: 18). And once into the 1990s, specifically 1998 onwards, the third phase began, in which:

> [...] the [SC's] responses to economic legislation in the wake of neoliberal reforms, which include privatization, liberalization, withdrawal of the state from critical areas of decision making, and increased federal intervention in the states among other things [...] raised concerns about the ramifications of PIL in the era of globalization (D'Souza 2005: 488).

Since the beginning of this phase, 'the [SC] has upheld liberalization and privatization but declined to intervene in matters of redistributive justice' (D'Souza 2005: 506). In doing so, the SC fashioned itself as an organ of neoliberal governance, and according to Balakrishnan Rajagopal, started 'sharing the biases of many of the goals and methods of [neo-liberal] governance itself [...] [like] market fundamentalism, state fetishism, and the culture-ideology of consumerism' (Rajagopal 2007: 180).

This turn has been substantiated through an empirical study by Varun Gauri, in which he shows that between 1961 and 2008, the SC's response to socio-economic rights questions increasingly became pro-middle class and anti-poor. One of his data sets represents how the win rates for disadvantaged social classes in selected FR cases before the SC decreased drastically from 71.4 per cent (1961–89) to 47.2 per cent (2000–8). Conversely, the success rates for claimants from advantaged social classes increased consistently, from 57.9 per cent (1961–89) to 73.3 per cent (2000–8) (Gauri 2009:16). As Gauri notes in his conclusion:

> The data here constitute a prima facie validation of the concern that judicial attitudes are less favourably inclined to the claims of the poor than they used to be, either as the exclusive result of new judicial interpretations, or more likely, in conjunction with changes in the political and legislative climate (2009: 13).

Clearly, the 'break with the past' occurred in the period following the flashpoint year of 1991.

In another survey of the SC's docket, Nick Robinson 'finds the court overwhelmed by petitions not from poor or ordinary people but from those with money and resources. In fact, these more privileged litigants very often swamp the court using the very mechanisms that were historically justified to make it more accessible to the less fortunate' (Robinson 2010). In 2007, 40 per cent of the SC's regular hearings were on tax, arbitration, and service issues: 'A disproportionate number of appeals are made up of these cases, which generally involve the more affluent litigants or government lawyers (who do not bear the cost of the appeal themselves)' (Robinson 2010). Robinson's findings show that in the 1970s, around 10 per cent of the cases before the SC were FR writ petitions, of which 5 per cent were admitted, and in 2008, the numbers dropped drastically to 2 per cent, of which none were admitted:

> In 2008, the court received 24, 666 letters, postcards, or petitions asking its intervention in cases that might be considered public interest litigation. Of these, just 226 were even placed before judges on admission days, and only a small fraction of these were heard as regular hearing matters. The rest were rejected (Robinson 2010).

This drop might have had a lot to do with an articulated stand by successive governments and many political parties that have frowned upon judicial activism allegedly usurping turf of the executive (Seetha 2006; TNN 2011). The UPA government (2004–14) had even proposed a national litigation policy to claim damages from those who file frivolous PILs. This move comes at time when it is well known that it is neither poor communities nor the human rights activists who file PIL/SAL on their behalf but rather the state that is the most active litigant (Dey 2009). The troubling concern here is the fact that PIL/SAL has turned into the proverbial Frankenstein that the state is unable to control—which is why it needs to forcibly discredit it. This is bad news for the rightsless, for whom PIL/SAL seemed to be the most powerful means of gaining at least recognition and visibility, if not emancipation and justice.

Through what he calls the 'conditional social rights' approach, Madhav Khosla's reading of the way in which the SC has approached questions of socio-economic rights might help us understand this situation better. As he notes, 'Rather than focusing on the inherent nature of measures undertaken by the state, the conditional social rights approach focuses on their implementation. No judicial review is conducted on the former question, making the right *conditional* upon state action' (Khosla 2011: 5, emphasis in original). He also observes that the conditionality emerges from the fact that many SC judgements have named 'new' rights but haven't elaborated on their content (Khosla 2005: 5). Thus, the articulated right becomes a hollow spectacle: You can celebrate its naming, but you will eventually mourn its non-realization.

This reinforces my earlier point that petitioning the SC to respond to, correct, undo, or remedy violations of FR holds little meaning for the rightsless because the judgement will remain a mere spectacle, and the realization of the right—even when it is upheld by the court—is conditional on political will. Furthermore, the political will to implement a judgement on social rights is contingent upon the state's ostensible economic capacity. The faith in the spectacle of PIL and the resultant fate of resorting to the invocation of constitutional remedies are thus deeply restricted by a double-bound conditionality.

Although compelling, the conditionality argument must also be used cautiously. This approach can absolve the courts of their complicity in crafting a jurisprudence of GEC, which in actuality has been the case where 'the constituency on whose behalf judicial power has been strengthened [through PIL/SAL jurisprudence] began to emerge as the casualty of the exercise of that power' (Ramanathan 2002). In two articles in the *Economic and Political Weekly* written in 2004 and 2009, senior SC lawyer Prashant Bhushan traces a set of SC judgements on issues ranging from national security to development that have gravely undermined the tenets of FR (2004: 1770; 2009: 32). Many of these judgements can be characterized as 'pro-human rights, but anti-poor' (Rajagopal 2007: 157), further enabling the spectacle of Emancipation 1 to thrive. These judgements represent a narrative that endorses the idea that conditions of capitalism will improve human rights guarantees.

As Bhushan angrily notes:

> Since the liberalization of the Indian economy, even the [SC's] rhetoric on socio-economic rights have been weakening. Very often the court has itself ordered the violation of those rights [...] [This] seriously calls into question the commitment of the Indian courts to the rights of the poor and to the constitutional imperative of creating an egalitarian socialist republic [...] Part of the reason for this, undoubtedly, lies in the class structure of the Indian judiciary. The higher judiciary in India almost invariably comes from the elite section of the society and has become a self-appointing and self-perpetuating oligarchy [...] there is no accountability of the higher judiciary [...] Even public criticism of judges has often been held to be contempt of court (2009: 37).

Bhushan's observations are reiterated by Baxi in his readings of the SC's post-liberalization turn. In what he calls the 'structural adjustment of judicial activism', Baxi provides five paradigmatic illustrations of what this turn means (2006).

First, he points to the way in which the SC gave short shrift to a petition that claimed that India's accession to the World Trade Organization violated both FR and the basic structure doctrine. Baxi notes that the SC 'asked the petitioners to return to its powers as and when any such deleterious impact became more manifest!' (Baxi 2006: 23). His second example is the infamous 1989 Bhopal settlement (which may have started the trend Bhushan refers to), in which the SC not only reduced the compensation amount from 3 billion US dollars to 470 million US dollars in the full and final settlement, but also provided Union Carbide Corporation full immunity from criminal proceedings (*Union Carbide Corporation vs Union of India and Others,* 1989). This is an instance of the liberalized turn that may have started off the trend that Bhushan talks about. As Baxi writes, 'The settlement orders mark[ed] the beginnings of a judicially induced/managed Indian transition from the paradigm of the universal human rights of all suffering peoples to that of trade-related, market-friendly human rights paradigm' (2006: 24). Baxi's third illustration refers to the dilution of labour rights by the SC. He points in particular to a 2006 case in which a judge goes so far as to 'suggest that his predecessors labored under the misimpression that ours was a *socialist* constitution!' (Baxi 2006: 23, emphasis in original). Fourth, he comments on the SC's 'meandering jurisprudence' on the Narmada case:

> At one decisional moment, we are told that the height of the dam may not be raised without the utmost solicitous regard for the human rights, and human futures, of the ousted project affected peoples. At another decisional moment stands enacted the mysterious *pari passu* principle under whose auspices, submergence may actually occur with some indeterminate regard for relief, rehabilitation, and resettlement. At a third moment, the affected peoples stand somehow assured of that the court is not powerless to render justice to the adversely affected peoples even as submergence occurs. Who knows what a fourth moment may after all turn out to be? (2006: 25)

The fourth moment Baxi refers to in this passage was, of course, the SC's dismissal of the plaintiffs' petition and its order allowing the height of the dam to be increased. Since then, the door to the SC for the Narmada Bachao Andolan (the plaintiff) has been closed. And this instance also provides a lesson for social movements blinded by the spectacle of PIL/SAL: rather than thinking of the SC as the court of first option in cases of FR violations, it should be considered a last resort. For his fifth illustration, Baxi points to the SC's approval of urban demolition drives that 'that cruelly [impose themselves] on the bloodied bodies of the urban impoverished' (2006: 25). He references, among other cases, the deeply prejudiced *Almitra Patel* judgement discussed to by Bhushan.

Needless to say, both Bhushan's and Baxi's choice and critique of cases are selective. However, they establish those critical events that paradigmatically mark the SC's embracing of the NLO. The trend established by the above judgements illustrate how the SC is constantly pitting the rights of the powerless against the rights of the powerful, ultimately favouring the latter even as it uses the language of rights itself. As Usha Ramanathan comments on the SCs confrontation with conflicting interests:

> The right of over 30% of residents of Delhi to their shelter in the slum settlements was pitted against the need to 'clean up' the city. The right to a relatively unpolluted environment by means of the relocation of industries was pitted against the right of the working classes to their livelihood. The right to life, livelihood and protection from immiseration and exploitation of communities displaced along the Narmada was pitted against the right to water that the dam was expected to reach to the people in parts of Gujarat; it was also pitted against the enormous amounts of money that had already been spent on the dam. Even the right of the victims of the Bhopal gas disaster to receive compensation was pitted against the bureaucratic imperative of winding up the processing of claims (2002).

Outside of the judicial realm, since the 1990s, state policies on social justice have also been designed in such a way that they portray the state as human rights–friendly. However, this image crumbles when the human rights of the powerless come into conflict with the corporatized and militarized agendas of the state. A trend that has also accompanied this process is the individuation of the rights question, whereby the state speaks of rights issues in the individual—and no longer in the collective—sense. If the collective question of entitlement comes up for consideration, it is addressed not as a rights issue that will attract state accountability but rather as an issue of service delivery, which can also be outsourced to non-state actors. Classic examples are the rights to food, education, and health, among others—all of which are being litigated, but only to put in place service-delivery mechanisms and not necessarily to make structural transformations to institutions of subjugation. The dynamics of disenchantment seem more alive than ever before.

Privatizing Emancipation

> Publicity is the very soul of justice [...]
>
> — Jeremy Bentham, *The Works of Jeremy Bentham*, vol IV (1843: 316)

Reading beyond Bhushan's and Baxi's lament, one might refer to the 2009 *Naz Foundation* judgement of the Delhi High Court as an example of the progressive impact liberalization has had on judicial imagination. The decriminalization of same-sex intercourse is clearly an outcome of the gradually increasing cultural acceptance of diverse sexualities that has taken place as a result of liberalization and globalization, as is evident from the court's constant allusions to international human rights law and case law, and precedents primarily from the US. These references made apparent the cultural logic behind the court's judgement: India needs to live up to the progressive developments in other parts of the (Western) world by decriminalizing sodomy. As Anjali Gopalan, founder of petitioner Naz Foundation, said after the judgement was delivered, 'Oh my God, we've finally stepped into the 21st century!' (Flock 2009). This exclamatory declaration seems to be a history-vanishing moment, where the ostensibly progressive present contributes to the making of queer emancipation at the cost of blinding us to a historicized understanding of the cruelly liberal genealogies of present-day India.

While on the face of it this might be a convincing perspective, it must be noted that the *Naz Foundation* judgement builds itself on the foundations of the liberal virtue of 'privacy'. I have argued that the idea of emancipation in the NLO has been privatized and this case is a classic example of that phenomenon. While at first brush the judgement appears progressive, and is indeed historic, it seeks to recognize only the rights of those homosexual men who have the privilege of access to private space. The primacy put on private sex is clearly an elitist qualifier to read down the law because it excludes from its purview a whole range of non-elite and indigenous sexually marginalized people who do not enjoy the privilege of private space (Sircar 2008: 10). The 'privacy' standard is a myth, because those who do have access to private space were already outside of the reach of the law. As Ashley Tellis asks,

'What is the point of allowing consensual sex between private adults of the same sex when most violations are of us in the public realm: in institutions, on the streets, in parks, toilets and wherever else?' (2010). Jason Fernandes has noted that the judgement prioritizes the interests of urban, English-speaking, middle-class leaders of the queer rights movement in India by overshadowing those very sexually marginalized (Hijras, Kothis, Panthis)[16] who they claim to represent (Fernandes 2009). The reading down of the law may thus now ostensibly allow for same-sex acts within private spaces, yet it ironically offers no protection for same-sex practices outside the normative parameters of home and domesticity (Arondekar 2010: 124). My argument is not a dismissal of the judgement or the fact that it might empower the queer community, but rather that the trope of privacy is a contentious one that can, in effect, be more damaging than helpful. Privacy arguments also have the tendency to promote privatized forms of governance among sexually marginalized citizens through practices of individuation.

As Wendy Brown notes in the American context of decriminalization of sodomy on the grounds of privacy:

> Privacy, for example, is for many feminists a site that depoliticizes many of the constituent activities and injuries of women: reproduction, domestic assault, incest, unremunerated household labour, and compulsory emotional and sexual service to men. Yet for those concerned with sexual freedom, with welfare rights for the poor, and with the rights to bodily integrity historically denied racially subjugated peoples, privacy generally appears unambiguously valuable [...] Like rights themselves, depending on the function of privacy in the powers that make the subject, and depending on the marked identity that is at issue, privacy will be seen variously to advance or deter emancipation, to cloak inequality or procure equality (2002: 428).

The lesson, then, is to not treat the liberal virtues of privacy as a universal emancipatory category, but rather as one that has the ability to disenfranchise many sexual-rights agendas that consider, following Bentham, that publicity is at the very heart of justice.

The privatization of emancipation in the NLO has also taken place in the realm of other socio-economic rights such as education. Let me use two examples from the world of advertisements and charity work to explain how this works. As discussed earlier, the right to education, which was originally a DP, has now been made justiciable though legislation and through its migration into Part III of the constitution (as Article 21A). A print advertisement that formed part of the hugely publicized Teach India (TI) campaign (launched in 2008 by the *Times of India*, a private newspaper company and India's largest-circulating English daily) posed the question, 'What is the perfect solution to illiteracy?' In the next line there are two options: 'Govt.' and 'You'. The 'Govt.' option is crossed out, and there is an affirmative tick mark beside 'You'. After this, the advertisement goes on to detail how 'You' can join the TI campaign to 'help change the future of a child forever'. Choosing 'You' over 'Govt.' can imply two things. One is that the government is useless and that it has not been able to ensure education for all children, which is why we should abandon the government and take it upon ourselves to eradicate illiteracy. The other implication could be that providing education to children is not something that the state should do at all and that it is upon private actors—not just individual citizens, but corporate actors and non-governmental entities—to impart education. This call by a corporate entity sends out the message that the protection of children's rights (in this case education) needs to be privatized. This advertising strategy 'engage[s] its audience aesthetically, with promises of pleasure and self-realization' (Mazzarella 2003: 68).

The question of the right to education is completely hollowed out, and education for children turns solely into a matter of individualized compassionate concern. The more you can arouse compassion, the more educated India's children will become; it does not matter whether the right to education is a justiciable right or not, nor whether the state is being held accountable or not. Of course, the *Times of India* cannot be held accountable if it fails to provide universal education. It is their compassionate gesture, outside of their profit-making concerns, that makes them worthy of popular praise and raises their corporate goodwill. This outsourced strategy of privatized and packaged emancipation, which is appealed for through publicized calls, fuels a thriving compassion industry and creates a culture of impunity that allows the state, as well as those who claim to replace the state, to get away with accountability.

Private capital's campaign to end discrimination has taken another interesting turn and has given Emancipation 1 a new dimension altogether. An advertisement on the matrimonial pages of the *Times of India* appealed to those who pay to advertise in their pages to 'drop social pre-conditions like caste, religion or dowry requirements', and in return they would give the advertiser 15 per cent off on advertising rates.[17] Ostensibly, this is a progressive move, but it is a move that asks the potential advertiser to privatize the practices of what Amartya Sen calls 'identity disregard' (Sen 2006: 20), the implication being that in the consumptive markets of neoliberalism, identities don't matter—which, Sen notes, is a myth. What gets passed off as progressive in the present instance is actually a move towards privatizing the practice of non-discrimination as a public issue. For instance, some progressive-thinking liberal person might believe strongly in the message that the advertisement is conveying and accordingly drop identity-based marriage preconditions. But will the same person support affirmative action as a state policy in private organizations in India? Practice of identity disregard, then, is a privatized issue of self-governance that necessarily has no connection to ending structural prejudice—be it cultural, social, economic, or sexual. Emancipation 1 seduces people to end discrimination through the economic incentive of discounts. This is another dimension of the operation of Emancipation 1, and it is at the heart of how the NLO functions.

The Curious Case of *Taking the State to Court*

> Judicial process and institution cannot be permitted to be scandalized or subjected to contumacious violation in such a blatant manner [...] Vicious stultification and vulgar debunking cannot be permitted to pollute the stream of justice.
>
> — Justice A. S. Anand, *Narmada Bachao Andolan v Union of India* of(1994: 3)

In this penultimate section, I share an anecdote about what happens when the spectacle of judicial/legal emancipation is resisted and punctured. There could be many ways of doing this—perhaps, for example, by taking inspiration from Ambedkar's burning of the *Manu Smriti* at the Mahad Satyagraha in Maharashtra in 1927 and publicly burning copies of anti-poor judgements. I, however, will examine a very benign form of resistance.

In 2001, German sociologist Hans Dembowski's book, *Taking the State to Court: Public Interest Litigation and the Public Sphere in Metropolitan India*, was published by Oxford University Press (OUP) in India. Soon after its launch at the 2001 Kolkata Book Fair, the Calcutta High Court started contempt-of-court proceedings against Dembowski, the publisher, and others, and OUP discontinued distribution of the book. To this day, neither have the contempt proceedings been heard nor has the book been reintroduced into the market. The book is, however, freely downloadable on the Internet.[18]

The SC's position on works criticizing the judiciary can be gleaned from its order reprimanding Arundhati Roy for insulting the SC in her essay, 'The Greater Common Good' (Roy 1999). Justice Anand made it amply clear that the court will not tolerate anyone polluting the 'stream of justice' (Bhushan 2001). The exception, however, is the court itself, as was evident from the cases referred to above in the previous section. So what was in Dembowski's book that the court saw as having the potential to pollute? *Taking the State to Court* is a dense sociological and ethnographic reading of environmental cases in the Calcutta High Court. While a detailed discussion of the contents of the book is beyond the scope of this chapter, suffice to say that apart from the book's research being based in Kolkata and Howrah, its theoretical insights were aimed at examining the relationships between civil society and the judiciary in fashioning a public sphere. The book also provided a very useful sociological discussion of the history of judicial activism in India. Until chapter 6, the book discusses various facets of the cases that it studies. It is in chapter 7 that Dembowski offers a more personalized ethnographic reading of judicial and court culture in Kolkata. And this, it seems, was the central 'pollutant' for the court.

As Dembowski mentions in a paper that he presented at a conference at Jawaharlal Nehru University, Delhi, in 2008:

> So why were some judges obviously unhappy with the book? The answer probably lies in chapter 7, which moves on from 'hard' case-study facts derived from court orders, government plans and other written documents. Chapter 7 examines day-to-day life in the High

> Court and civil society, including rumours of corruption. The image that emerges of the High Court is one of an institution that does not enjoy undivided popular trust. While this image may not be favourable, I would still insist that it was true at the time and that my description would hardly seem unfair to critical readers without personal stakes in the matter (2008: 4).

He concludes the book by stating, 'Public Interest Litigation has, several times, made a difference in people's immediate surroundings. While it does not provide an easy road to official accountability and democratic deliberation, it does raise hope for change' (2001: 211).

My reading of Chapter 7 does not provide me with any poisonously pollutant material that can do any harm to the court's stream of justice or injustice. In my view, what Dembowski has written does not even qualify as contempt under the Contempt of Courts Act, 1971. Rather, it falls squarely within the exceptions of 'fair and accurate report[ing]' (section 4) and 'fair criticism' (section 5). Yet the court's censorious response to a book that did not in any militant way call the judiciary's spectacular bluff is a brutal affront to academic and creative freedom in this country. Is the spectacular façade of the judiciary so fragile that the only way it can stop people from scratching its surface is by criminalizing them? The curious case of Hans Dembowski brings home the fact the high court and the SC in India use the spectre of contempt to muzzle any resistance to the spectacles of emancipation that judicial imagination manufactures for us.

It is apt to close this section by quoting at length that part from Roy's 'The Greater Common Good' that made her culpable of contempt, leading to a day's incarceration:

> I stood on a hill and laughed out loud
>
> [...]
>
> Why did I laugh?
>
> Because I suddenly remembered the tender concern with which the Supreme Court judges in Delhi (before vacating the legal stay on further construction of the Sardar Sarovar Dam) had enquired whether tribal children in the resettlement colonies would have children's parks to play in. The lawyers representing the Government had hastened to assure them that indeed they would, and, what's more, that

> there were seesaws and slides and swings in every park. I looked up at the endless sky and down at the river rushing past and for a brief, brief moment the absurdity of it all reversed my rage and I laughed. I meant no disrespect (Roy 1999).

Letting Hope Elope with Justice? A Closing Refraction

> Your courtroom turns into an ominous circus.
> Two shows everyday, entry free. As the
> High Priestess you let hope elope with justice…
>
> And to make sure that you never turn blind,
> Or bored, or fall asleep, each plaintiff applies
> A paste of bloodred chillies on your open eyes
>
> —Meena Kandasamy (*Ms. Militan*cy 2010: 28–9.)

I will end this chapter with a concluding refraction (not a conclusion)—a poetic detour of sorts—that will provide hopeful glimpses of what Emancipation 2, as I imagine it, might look like. I think detours are necessary, as they allow us to traverse uncharted paths to arrive at our favoured destinations. Sometimes detours make us re-imagine our destinations and lead us to places that we did not plan to go to. Detours are inevitable in any ethical voyage because our journeys are concerned not just with the destination but also with every bit of the journey itself, which is why I think it would be apt to begin the concluding section of this chapter by sharing Naxal ideologue and poet Srijan Sen's poem, 'Das Kapital':

> Karl Marx wrote 'Das Kapital'.
> His readers swelled their own capital.
> The lessons that they drew from his pages […]
> Was invested in building palaces.
> Then they made the profound assertion:
> 'Das Kapital' needs full 'revision'! (2009: 72)

Through a cruel hilarity, Sen points at a paradox that is embedded in ideas and texts that promise emancipation. As a committed Marxist, I am deeply appreciative of Sen's provocation because it forces me to think of detours—not to abandon Marxism, but to rethink the paths that have lead to the profound assertion that *Das Kapital* needs full revision.

This poem for me is not one that denounces Marxism; rather, it calls for a more rigorous engagement with it. It cautions us about unquestioningly believing in the political emancipation promised by the liberal incantations of constitutionalism. The poem urges us to interrogate rights as constitutive of oppressive systems of power rather than as a body of knowledge or a tactic of management that is outside of it.

Judicial pronouncements are also texts of emancipation, and they hold the cruel capacity to unleash brutal violence. As Robert Cover states:

> Legal interpretation takes place in a field of pain and death. A judge articulates her understanding of a text, and as a result, somebody loses his freedom, his property, his children, even his life. Interpretations in law also constitute justifications for violence which has already occurred or which is about to occur. When interpreters have finished their work, they frequently leave behind victims whose lives have been torn apart by these organized, social practices of violence. Neither legal interpretation nor the violence it occasions may be properly understood apart from one another (1986: 601).

What is required, then, is a re-imagining of emancipation by searching for and archiving material practices of being that embody insurrectionary knowledge: knowledge that brings an understanding of rights as embodied practices of resistance that disturb the linear trajectories of its constitutional narratives and emancipation, which reproduces the magic of modernity and normalizes inequality. What comes to mind from the recent history of contemporary India is the July 2004 protest outside the headquarters of the Assam Rifles in Imphal, the capital of the north eastern state of Manipur, where groups of middle-aged women stripped naked, shouted slogans, and carried banners that read, 'Indian Army Rape Us!' The protest was a spontaneous response to the arbitrary abduction, rape, and murder of Manorama Devi by the armed forces on mere suspicion of being an insurgent (Rehman 2008; Human Rights Watch 2008). What does the corporeality of this protest do to our constitutional morality in a location where the law has been central to the normalization of state violence? The violent letter of the law (the AFSPA, 1956), which allows the army to kill on suspicion, and the fragility of our spectacular hope in constitutional protection was powerfully shattered by the protest that questioned not only the perverse masculinity of the state but also the very structure of the law that perpetuates the state's monopoly over violence through constitutional sanction.[19]

Do we abandon Emancipation 1? Where do we look for Emancipation 2? How can we stop hope from eloping with justice? Nivedita Menon provides an inspirational direction:

> I understand emancipation as a process without closure, it is not a goal that we can reach. Each victory becomes the site of a fresh cooptation, but conversely too, each defeat releases new potential to resist oppression. To move away from legal and state-centered conceptions of political practice is to recognize political practice as the perpetual *attempt* to eliminate oppression rather than the *achievement* of this elimination. Nevertheless 'emancipation' remains a horizon that should drive our political practice (2004: 20, emphasis in original).

Emancipation 2, thus lies in the contested cultures of the quotidian, the cacophonous politics of the street, and the mundane negotiations of the everyday and the ordinary, what Asef Bayat calls 'nonmovements': 'the collective endeavors of millions of non collective actors, carried out in the main squares, back streets, court houses, or communities' (2010: ix). Emancipation 2 is about the unrelenting journeys that are full of detours for finding new meanings for our human condition beyond greed and civilizational domination.

I will end, finally, with another poem. This one is called 'Right' and is written by Naxal poet Cherabandaraju:

> I will not stop cutting down trees
> Though there's life in them.
> I will not stop plucking out leaves,
> Though they make nature beautiful.
> I will not stop hacking off branches
> Though they are the hands of a tree.
> Because –
> I need a hut (2009: 56).

Our constitutional rights vocabulary is woefully inadequate in responding to this deeply unsettling paradox. I, for one, would unflinchingly support the extension of Cherabandaraju's poem to a hypothetical but altogether conceivable claim by a mining company that we must keep hacking down trees '[...] because – we need a factory'. I can imagine the company going on to wax eloquent about how that factory will help people build concrete houses, hospitals, and schools. Huts—they are primitive! Their prototypes can adorn exotic resorts that are built by cutting down trees in forests, destroying beaches, defacing hills, and displacing people, but 'real' huts, and the real people who inhabit them, should become extinct.

In the second half of 2011, while the state was caught in one of modern India's most complicated governance crises—that of corruption—the SC restored some hope. A most unexpected spectacular moment came on 5 July 2011, when the SC, hearing a petition on human rights violations carried out by a civilian group called Salwa Judum also referred to as special police officers (SPOs)—tribal youth trained to fight Maoist insurgents—armed and aided by the state of Chhattisgarh, ordered that the vigilante civilian group be disbanded and declared that it was unconstitutional on the part of the state to carry out, in the name of fighting Maoism, armed operations that resulted in grave violations of human rights of poor tribals (*Nandini Sundar & Others vs State of Chhattisgarh*, 2007). In a rare acknowledgement of the devastating consequences of neoliberal economic policies of the state and, in particular, the mining industries, the SC noted in unambiguous terms:

> The culture of unrestrained selfishness and greed spawned by modern neoliberal economic ideology, and the false promises of ever increasing spirals of consumption leading to economic growth that will lift everyone, under-grid this socially, politically and economically unsustainable set of circumstances in vast tracts of India [...] Predatory forms of capitalism, supported and promoted by the State in direct contravention of constitutional norms and values, often take deep roots around the extractive industries (*Nandini Sundar & Others v State of Chattisgargh*, 2007: 9).

Most of us on the left end of the ideological spectrum hailed the judgement, and we celebrated the achievement of those who fought the legal battle and of those who have bravely resisted the state's violence in Chhattisgarh and other places in India where mining industries have devastated the lives and livelihoods of poor indigenous populations. This was a classic instance of left legalism's triumph.

This seemed like a repeat of the act of historical rectification that the SC carried out in the wake of the Emergency. Our faith in the law, like Ustad Mangu's, was seemingly restored. But the celebration was temporary. On 18 November 2011, in response to a challenge to the SC order by the state, it was clarified that the ban on SPOs and the fact that the Salwa Judum was declared unconstitutional will be confined to the state of Chhattisgarh (Venkatesan 2011). There was hardly any questioning of this shift in the SC's stand that can now, in effect, allow the state to replicate the formation of vigilante groups in other parts of India ostensibly facing the Maoist threat. The spectacle of the SC's strong indictment against neoliberalism-induced state violence was ultimately truncated.

In November 2011, the Chhattisgarh government declared that it had complied with the SC judgement and has disbanded all SPOs. On 26 January 2012, India's Republic Day was celebrated, to mark the anniversary of the adoption of the Constitution of India in 1950. On the same day, the president honoured Ankit Garg, a police officer from Chhattisgarh, with a gallantry medal for his relentless fight against left-wing extremism in the state. Garg has been accused of torturing and sexually abusing in custody Soni Sori, a tribal school teacher from Dantewada, for allegedly having Maoist links. Sori had alleged that Garg watched as junior police personnel stripped her naked, administered electric shocks, and assaulted her: 'According to her lawyers, a medical examination found two stones in Ms. Soni's genital tract and another in her rectum' (Sethi 2012).

New constitution, new constitution… What am I talking about? It is the same old constitution.

Notes

1. A definition of neoliberalism that I wish to work with is by Harvey, D. *A Brief History of Neoliberalism*. New York: Oxford University Press (2007: 2) ('Neoliberalism is in the first instance a theory of political economic practices that proposes that human well-being can best be

advanced by liberating individual entrepreneurial freedoms and skills within an institutional framework characterized by strong private property rights, free markets and free trade. The role of the state is to create and preserve an institutional framework appropriate to such practices. The state has to guarantee, for example, the quality and integrity of money. It must also set up those military, defence, police, and legal structures and functions required to secure private property rights and to guarantee, by force if need be, the proper functioning of markets. Furthermore, if markets do not exist (in areas such as land, water, education, health care, social security or environmental pollution) then they must be created, by state action if necessary. But beyond these tasks the state should not venture.'; for a detailed account of the consequences of the adoption of neo-liberalism globally see, Klein 2007.

2. For discussions around these themes, see Bhargava (ed.) 2008; Hasan, Sridharan and Sudarshan (eds.) 2004; Chatterjee (ed.) 1997; Samaddar 2007; Samaddar 2007a.
3. On modernity, the violence of modern constitulionalism and its connection to colonialism/imperialism, see Baxi 2000: 1184–85. ('Much of the business of "modern" constitutionalism was transacted during the halcyon days of colonialism/ imperialism. That historical timespace marks a combined and uneven development of the world in the processes of early modernity[...] Constutionalism inherits the propensity for violent social exclusion from the "modern".')
4. Section 377 is the anti-sodomy provision in the Indian Penal Code of 1860, which was 'read-down' by the Delhi High Court on July 2, 2009. Post this judgement, the provision stands decriminalized as far as adult, consensual sex between adults in private.
5. The argument that the very existence of Section 377 on the law books for over 150 years in India has normalized non-legal forms of homophobia and discriminations against homosexuals and other sexually marginalized persons draws on the work of Ryan Goodman on South Africa in which it was shown that despite the South African constitution's recognition of the right against discrimination on the basis of sexual orientation, homophobia continues in ways that the law cannot detect or prosecute. See Goodman 2001: 651–53.
6. The arrests and charges against those who have been released on bail were done on mere suspicion based on either their work with indigenous people's movements and against indiscriminate corporate mining, or their religion. For testimonies by those who have been arrested and tortured under anti-terror laws in India, see Preeti Verma, *The terror of*

POTA and other security legislation in India (Delhi: Human Rights Law Network, 2004).

7. For a sharp analysis of the first amendment which introduced, among other significant changes, the state's right to acquire land, see Menon 2008: 189; Bhargava 2008: 189–210.
8. Irom Sharmila Chanu is a human rights defender from India's northeastern state of Manipur where she has been on hunger strike for the past 12 years in protest against the AFSPA which gives the army extraordinary powers. She has been in captivity of the Indian state, locked up in a hospital, and is being force-fed through her nose. For more on Irom Sharmila's protest, see Mehrotra 2009.
9. While capitalism as an ideology puts into operation a political formation of governance like liberalism, neoliberalism is the condition where practices of state liberalism get naturalized and internalized by individuals who inhabit a liberal state formation. This understanding of neoliberalism marks a departure from the more popular economistic explanations of the term that is marked by the hyper-efficiency logics of the Chicago Boys team led by Milton Friedman, who advocated for a complete hollowing out of the state from areas of economic transactions—particularly in times of crisis—to allow the market to take over and determine the course of the future, in turn militarizing countries across the world in the name of bringing prosperity. The market, unfortunately, is no holy cow and acts the way it is made to by the powers that be. Economic neoliberalism contributed centrally to the present crisis of global recession. While many consider the crash of the global markets as capitalism's foot-in-the-mouth moment, it in no way marks the death of neoliberalism as a cultural phenomenon. Because culturally, it has very smoothly done three things to ensure its robust and brutal longevity: first, it has enabled the mutation of the state into a firm; second, it has given birth to the responsibilized and self-governing citizen; and third, it has constantly projected experiences of human precarity (or risk, in more Foucaultian terms) as entrepreneurial opportunity. These three ramifications of neoliberalism on human sentiments have had devastating consequences on the idea and practice of human rights. As the state mutated into the firm, people were told not to claim rights and accountability, but to treat it as a service provider. If the service provider fails to deliver, you can always outsource the service to a private agency—don't blame the state, just replace it when it fails. The new mantra of citizenship was for people to become self-disciplined, where you will not depend on the state for essential entitlements like health and education, but earn it for yourself through competition.

People were told to ignore that society had inherent inequalities that deeply impaired some people's ability to compete on an equal playing field. If you are failing, it's your responsibility. The vulnerability of human lives was turned into economic opportunities for corporations—thus the birth of private insurance, and the near death of free primary healthcare.

10. For the Indian state, corporate, and military nexus, particularly in the context of Adivasi land acquisition for mining, see Roy 2011.
11. Gulzar is an award-winning Urdu poet and a songwriter for several critically acclaimed Hindi films.
12. Naxalism is a militant ideology that emerged out of the 1967 peasant uprising for land redistribution from the Naxalbari district in the state of West Bengal, India. Naxal movements are still active where struggles against land acquisition by the Indian state exist. Naxalites are interchangeably also called Maoists because they organize under the Communist Party of India (Maoist). For a historical account, see Banerjee 1984.
13. Binayak Sen is a medical doctor, human rights activist, and member of the People's Union for Civil Liberties. He has been involved with public health work in remote areas in the state of Chhattisgarh for several years, and has been critical of the government's policies on land acquisition and eviction of poor peasants. In May 2007, he was allegedly falsely arrested by the police on charges of sedition and for being an alleged Naxalite. After several failed attempts, the Supreme Court of India finally granted him bail in March 2011. See generally Vaid 2011.
14. These three laws have been declared constitutional by the SC—despite widely recorded evidence of how they have unleashed and legitimized police and army brutality particularly against 'suspect' populations—in the following three cases respectively: *Kartar Singh vs State of Punjab*, 1994; *People's Union for Civil Liberties vs Union of India*, 2004; *Naga People's Human Rights Movement vs Union of India*, 1997.
15. For a discussion on the 'expanding horizons of Article 21', see Singh 2001: 175.
16. These are identity categories that non-elite, sexually marginalized persons in India use instead of the category of gay. Culturally, the performance of these identities is also very different from being gay or only homosexual.
17. Advertisement on file with author.
18. For the full text of the book, see Hans Dembowski, *Taking the State to Court: Public Interest Litigation and the Public Sphere in Metropolitan*

India. Accessible at https://www.asienhaus.de/public/archiv/taking_the_state_to_court.pdf

19. Despite the Protection of Human Rights Act, 1993 that established the National Human Rights Commission (NHRC), Section 19 of the act denies the NHRC any authority to investigate human rights violations by the armed forces. The NHRC, on receipt of any complaint, can only seek a report on the alleged violation from the central government.

2

Beyond Compassion

Children of Sex Workers and the Politics of Suffering*

(with Debolina Dutta)

> ... the essence of 'compassion' is nothing other than the narcissistic desires of an exploitative bourgeoisie to feel good about itself.
>
> — Natan Sznaider, *The Compassionate Temperament* (2001: 11)

> ...the aesthetics of compassion [...] opens a hornet's nest of problems about what responses should be desired and when private responses are not only insufficient but a part of the practice of injustice.
>
> — Lauren Berlant, 'Compassion (and Withholding)' (2004: 9)

The Incitement

On the evening of 3 March 2009—the International Sex Worker Rights Day—over 3,000 children of sex workers (aged between 6 to

* Researched and written through 2008–10 in Kolkata and New Delhi, as a response to the Oscar-winning documentary film, *Born into Brothels* (2004). This essay is dedicated to Durbar Mahila Samanwaya Committee for what we continue to learn about the ethics of scholarlship from their activism.

25 years) from Sonagachi[1] and surrounding red-light districts from Kolkata marched through College Street holding up placards and shouting slogans demanding the guarantee of their mothers' right to livelihood as sex workers and their rights as children against stigma and discrimination. One of the most popular slogans being shouted was against the then women and child development minister of India: '*Renuka Chaudhary'r Kalo Hath Guriye Dao, Guriye Dao*' ('Smash Renuka Chaudhary's Black Hand'). This reprise of provocation came at a time when most of urban India was hailing Chaudhary's tough stand against the assault by a Hindu right-wing group on women at a pub in Mangalore, a city in south India.[2]

Using this slogan, the children in the march were alluding to the amendment that the women and child development ministry had been pushing for in the Immoral Traffic (Prevention) Act, 1956—to criminalize clients of sex workers—a move that would render their mothers unemployed (Faleiro 2006). In addition, they were also protesting against a provision in the same law that allowed the state to forcibly take away children who were said to be living off the earnings of their mothers as well as living with them when they crossed 18 years of age.

This is one of the many incidents in the exercise of political agency by children of sex workers that inspires this essay.[2] We attempt to foreground the experiences of these children from Sonagachi to challenge the singularity of focus on suffering that their ostensible plight has attracted. To challenge this singularity does not mean to dismiss it, but to bring to light the multiple and overlapping realities of coercion, celebration, negotiation and determination that mark their lives. It is also an attempt at exposing how a singular focus on suffering works to erase the multiplicity of their lived experiences—in turn, denying these children an opportunity to be recognized as citizens who have the agency to give meaning to how their histories and stories are represented.

The roots of this singularity of focus lie in the terms 'children' and 'innocence', although semantically distinct, having attained a state of synonymy because of the poetics of compassion. Imageries of suffering carry with them notions of idealized victim subjects who attract the most amount of compassion. Children—especially from non-Western geographies—are such a group, for whom vicarious appeals by activists, philanthropists, and the state alike contribute towards a discourse of compassion that is globally throbbing with funds, protective laws, and images. It is accepted common sense that children are the worst victims of scourges like trafficking, sexual abuse, exploitation, homelessness, hunger, and armed conflict. Given the kind of connection that this discourse of compassion has established between 'children' and 'innocence', the objective of compassionate interventions, many a times well-meaning and significant, becomes to protect and preserve the innocence of which children are at the risk of being robbed, rather than protecting their rights against stigma, discrimination, and equal access to education, housing, and healthcare.

In the context of sex-trafficking and 'prostitution' the focus on children's plight has attained a special place in the global attempts at protecting child rights. The phenomenal popularity of the Oscar-winning documentary, *Born into Brothels* (*BiB*) (Briski and Kauffman 2004) triggered a response in huge Western human rights organizations like Amnesty International to look anew, with enhanced vigour and compassion, at the pitiful lives of children of sex workers.[3] Representations like *BiB* churn out highly aesthetized images of acute vulnerability and suffering—ones that propose a straightjacket response to save these children: raid, rescue, rehabilitate—because their cultures, communities, or mothers cannot/will not do so.

While the 'truth' about the plight and vulnerability of these children cannot be denied, it is only one aspect of their lives. While these children are at the receiving end of disadvantage—because of the locations where they live, the profession of their mothers, as well as being burdened by the hierarchy of age—they are also active agents in resisting disadvantage and formulating daily negotiation strategies which are an exemplary show of resilience. Although age is a factor that results in violation of the rights of these children, age also becomes the reason because of which compassionate interventions do not consider them as citizens whose say matter.

This essay offers a critique of such images of children of sex workers through the documentation of the work of a group called *Amra Padatik* (AP), which has been formed and run by the children of sex workers of Kolkata's Sonagachi red-light district. We foreground the experiences of members of AP to replace the traditional three Rs (raid, rescue, rehabilitation) response to child trafficking with three counter Rs: resilience, reworking, and resistance (Katz 2004).

It was during our documentation of the changing contours of the agential practice of the Durbar Mahila Samanyaya Committee (DMSC) (Dutta and Sircar 2008: 3)—a sex workers' collective with over 65, 000 women and trans sex-worker members in Sonagachi—that we had first watched *BiB*. There were strong protests by DMSC regarding the way in which the film completely ignored their collective struggles and how sex-worker mothers were represented as incompetent and uncaring guardians of their children (Gayen 2005). It was at the same time that AP was taking shape, and it was a unique political practice that came to our notice. It seemed to us that just the way in which *BiB* portrays, most interventions to protect the rights of sex workers' children seldom recognize the potential of the attempts made by these children to collectivize and engage in advocacy for their own cause. Like colonial interventions to 'save the brown woman', or to train indigenous children into 'whiteness', these initiatives look at children of sex workers as those who cannot even be considered to have a voice of their own. Such initiatives consider their mothers to be inept parents. As recourse, they strongly believe in the logic of 'rescue through removal'. This was evident in many such covert operations carried out in other parts of India, notably in Sangli, Maharashtra (Gupte et al. 2007).

The ethical basis of our arguments is inspired by postcolonial feminist insights that have powerfully critiqued compassion-driven interventions to save Third World women and pull them out of the clutches of poverty, deprivation, gender-based violence, and indigenous patriarchy (Mohanty 2003; Narayan 1997; Kapur 2005). Popular representations have naturalized the fact that these children live in 'hell holes' and the only way to protect them from all 'evil' is to take them out of it. Civil society interventions seldom create enabling conditions for these children to enjoy the child rights guaranteed to them, nor do they let them positively respect their mothers' livelihood choices.

This chapter emerged out of a three-year-long project with the members of AP, which concluded in 2009 with *We Are Foot Soldiers,* a documentary film (Dutta and Sircar 2011). This chapter draws on interviews in the film to listen to three founding members and two office-bearers of AP, in order to understand how these children practise resilience through tacit negotiations between transgression and conformity. We foreground these negotiations to demystify the culture of fear that is associated with the lives of the children of sex workers—not to underplay the acute experience of disadvantage in their lives, but to foreground the fact that they can also be politically astute citizens and decision-makers in policies that concern their lives.

As researchers from 'outside', we are acutely aware of our locations of privilege due to class and age. We would like to emphasize here that our engagement with the members of AP—through interviews and interactions—were designed to ensure that we do not reduce the children to mere sources of information retrieval. Our attempt is to convey their own vision of themselves, not find a definition that will make them easily understood to mainstream society. In the process of foregrounding their stories of resilience and resistance, we will recognize loss, instead of fixating victimhood as an identity. As researchers, our attempt is to be ethical witnesses to the emotional and political lives of these children rather than remain purely objective spectators (Cubilie 2005).

Suffering Children and the Discontents of Compassion

In a print advertisement appealing for sponsorship for the education of the girl-child the copy reads: 'This is 4-year-old Shreya. Her parents abandoned her and vanished. If you turn the page, you'll do the same'. This advertisement for the corporate-supported charity *Nanhi Kali* (NK) uses the classic tool of pity to seduce compassion out of the viewer. The copy is accompanied by the photograph of a little girl whose innocent gaze stares right into viewers' eyes. The copy further goes on to appeal: 'With no one left in the world, Shreya doesn't have the slightest hope of facing the future, unless she gets an education'. In another NK brochure, Shreya's close-up has an accompanying dialogue bubble where she's saying: 'My parents can't send me to school, can you?'[4]

Little Shreya is clearly this corporate-charity initiative's poster girl. She is at once abandoned and *with* her parents. These two representations of Shreya paint contradictory pictures of who she really is. She is not just a sweet and sorry face; she has a name too. But sometimes she has her parents *with* her (albeit they cannot afford to send her to school), and sometimes she is an orphan 'with no one left in the world', her parents having done the vanishing act. On the first occasion, she is being spoken about, and in the next, she utters a line about her plight, which becomes the cue for the rest of the copy to continue speaking *about* her. The advertisement predicts what the future holds for Shreya: 'She will end up house-bound, exploited as a maid or a child prostitute, be married off early and could even die during childbirth!' The predictions make viewers of the ad imagine the gamut of disadvantageous situations that Shreya will be forced into if they do not contribute monetarily towards her education. The advertisement packs in all the punches, by even predicting that she might die at childbirth—when she's alive at four years of age!

Our objective here is not to discredit the intentions of this charity initiative, but to understand the kind of imagery and language that is getting used to arouse compassion in the liberal consumer of '*infotainment*' (Kleinman and Kleinman 1997: 1, emphasis in original). But is such a reading against the grain of any significance? For compassionate liberals who choose to contribute to NK, these conflicting representations of Shreya's plight are not of any consequence. What is important is that the representation seduces them to practise philanthropy, irrespective of concerns regarding what such a contribution does to the real question of children's fundamental right to education guaranteed by the constitution that the state is supposed to protect and fulfil. What also does not get questioned is why education is privileged over all other children's needs. In such projections of children's vulnerability, language and photography are used together to both produce and fixate meanings. Evidently, education for NK is the panacea for all the disadvantages that poor and orphaned girl children face, and universal education to the girl child can be ensured only if the compassionate philanthropist in each of us can be aroused through the unified working of image and text. Be it the orphaned Shreya or the Shreya as the daughter of poor parents—irrespective of the face remaining the same, and the life story changing—it attracts compassionate attention. This call to compassion uses the already established popular imaginary of the many Shreyas in India to send out the message that the protection of children's rights (in this case education) needs to be privatized.

What is also interesting about the NK advertisement is that the child is not depicted with a sad, droopy face, but with a bright smile, or a spark of excitement in her eyes, calling out endearingly for our compassion, giving us an exclusive opportunity to redeem our failure to respond to their plight for so long. Pictures like these imply that even after being denied their right to education, these children are still smiling—and it is now up to us to ensure that the smiles remain on their faces by providing them with education. They are not complaining or protesting, all they want is our compassion—Rs1,800 in case of NK. Feelings, then, are captive within the binaries of happiness and sadness for underprivileged children—you have to either look so sad and depressed that people pity your situation, or sweetly smile so that people find you cute enough to change your life. This advertising strategy 'engage[s] its audience aesthetically, with promises of pleasure and self-realization' (Mazzarella 2003: 68)—the pleasure of providing education to a hapless child that builds our self-worth for being the ones to do it.

Evidently, compassion is aroused not only at the level of benign philanthropy, but gets culturally appropriated into a more active and privatized 'let's-change-the-future-of-the-nation' attitude. The question of the right to education gets completely hollowed out, and education for children turns into only a matter of individualized compassionate concern. The more you can arouse compassion, the more educated will India's children become—it doesn't matter whether the right to education is a justiciable right or not. Of course, Mahindra & Mahindra Ltd. (which is NK's key philanthropic supporter) cannot be held accountable if they fail to provide universal education. It is their compassionate gesture, outside of their profit-making concerns, that makes them worthy of popular praise and raises their corporate goodwill.

Writing about the commercial appropriation of images of suffering Arthur and Joan Kleinman have remarked:

> Images of suffering are appropriated to appeal emotionally and morally [...]. [I]mages of victims are commercialized; they are taken up into processes of global marketing and business competition. The

> existential appeal of human experiences, their potential to mobilize popular sentiment and collective action, and even their capability to witness or offer testimony are now available for gaining market share (1997: 1).

Consequently, it is expected that 'good citizens' will respond with compassionate and rational commitment (Höijer 2004: 513). As Höijer points out, this compassion gets heightened when the image represents an 'ideal victim': 'as a cultural-cognitive construction, the discourse of global compassion designates some victims as "better" victims than others' (2004: 516). Women, children, and the elderly share top positions, but children on most occasions outshine the others.

It is useful to quote Höijer again:

> A child is [...] the most ideal victim in the perspective of compassion. When a child shows his/ her feelings by crying or looking sad, we may feel pity both through our own memory of being open and vulnerable to the treachery of adulthood, and in terms of our adult identity – our *desire to protect* the child. When the child stares into the photographer's camera she or he may be perceived as looking directly at you as an audience, reminding you of her or his vulnerability and innocence (2004: 522, emphasis ours).

The 1972 image of Phan Thị Kim Phúc (clicked by Associated Press photographer Nick Út)—the naked Vietnamese girl fleeing after a napalm bomb was dropped on her village, Trang Bang—has attained iconic status as a testimony of how damaging and traumatic the impact of armed aggression can be, brilliantly captured in the 1974 Oscar-winning documentary by Peter Davis called *Hearts and Minds*. What makes the compassion quotient of the image even more powerful is that the frame is shared by visibly terrified and crying children (along with Phúc) in the foreground, without any adult family/community member with them, and armed soldiers in the background. Út went on to win the Pulitzer Prize and the World Press Photo of the Year for this photograph. Phúc migrated to Canada, was named UNESCO Goodwill Ambassador in 1997, and had songs and books written on her. She is well-known for her work to aid child victims of war around the world. However, when you see a recording of this scene in *Hearts and Minds*, the same moment in history captured on a video camera widens the frame and shows you that there are other adults from their community running along with them—who were excluded from Út's photographic frame.

The compassion aroused by this photograph might work in ways that challenge our sceptical submissions above. Compassion can result in extremely powerful and useful responses. We are raising questions about how representations of suffering, especially of children, essentialize, naturalize, or sentimentalize suffering:

> There is no single way to suffer; there is no timeless or spaceless universal shape to suffering [...]. Individuals do not suffer in the same way, any more than they live, talk about what is at stake, or respond to serious problems in the same way. Pain is perceived and expressed differently, even in the same community (Kleinman and Kleinman 1997: 2).

What the Kleinmans are concerned about in their influential essay are the uses to which representations of the experiences of suffering are put (1997: 3). Following a similar argument, our essay is concerned with enquiring into whether representations of suffering children result in securing their rights. Is there a causal connection between the existence of compassion and guarantees to human rights of children? When the suffering of children acquires fixated meaning, do our compassionate responses also become fixated on only certain kinds of remedies—and certain kinds of children? What are the consequences of advocating for such remedies? What role do the suffering children and the communities that they are a part of play in charting the direction of our compassion, beyond being the pitiful, horrifying, endearing, sad, captive faces and bodies?

Consider the photo depicting a vulture perched near a little emaciated girl in Sudan who has collapsed from hunger trying to crawl her way to a nearby UN food camp. The photographer Kevin Carter of the *New York Times* (*NYT*) won the 1993 Pulitzer Prize for capturing this devastating image of starvation that has been used by several development and human rights organizations working in Sudan and generally on hunger. The photo evokes memories of the devastating images of the children of Biafra with distended stomachs from the late 1960s, during the Biafra liberation war in Nigeria.

A year after being awarded the Pulitzer, Carter killed himself. In a suicide note he admitted to not having been able to deal with the trauma of his experiences in Sudan. The Kleinmans offer an incisive discussion on how the event of Carter's death created a more complex reality about the effects of the appropriation of the image of suffering that he had captured when alive. Further in the essay they raise some critical questions regarding this particular photo that bear significance with regard to our argument in this chapter. While not disputing the enormous achievements of the photograph in attracting humanitarian and donor agencies to compassionately invest in developing Sudan, the Kleinmans examine the moral and political assumptions that accompany this photo:

> There is [...] the unstated idea that this group of unnamed Africans [...] cannot protect their own [children]. They must be protected, as well as represented, by others. The image of the subaltern conjures up an almost neocolonial ideology of failure, inadequacy, passivity, fatalism, and inevitability. Something must be done, and it must be done soon, but *from outside* the local setting. The authorization of action through an appeal for foreign aid, even foreign intervention, begins with an evocation of indigenous absence and erasure of local voices and acts (1997: 7, emphasis in original).

Our essay asks critical questions about *all* efforts that use images of suffering to evoke compassion from outside as the means to help suffering subjects. Do such interventions effect an erasure of local experiences of coping, negotiation, and resistance? Does the affective nature of such representations allow the status quo of disadvantage and exclusion to continue, while do-gooding goes on, because suffering at distant lands perpetuates a universal teleology of what modernity, progress, development mean for children's lives and rights? What are the cultural invectives that accompany such representations to justify a repeat of the colonial project of civilizing the native, or saving the native child's innocence from the barbarity of backward cultures?

These questions are not only directed at Western outsiders who capitalize on experiences of suffering in the global south, but also at people like us from Southern countries who make a living out of either creating spectacles of suffering, or keep building on those spectacles.

However, despite the sincerity of compassionate responses, as a sceptic like Guy Debord would say, all that remains at the end is a 'graveyard of good intentions' (1983: 84). Representations of suffering have attained a form of 'commodity fetishism', which culturally homogenizes what constitutes suffering, and the kinds of representations of suffering that are saleable enough to arouse compassion. Experiences of suffering can now only be identified through representations: 'Everything that was directly lived has moved away into a representation' (Debord 1983: 1). Thus, only representations can create spectacles, not everyday experiences of negotiations. In effect, when we make compassionate interventions, we do so as responses to spectacles, especially where we invest in the creation and circulation of those very spectacles of suffering.

Practising Compassion, Aesthetising Suffering, Customizing Children

It might seem, given our arguments in the previous section, that we are not in favour of initiatives that arouse compassion through the depiction of acute suffering. Our own engagements with issues of human rights, and specifically our work with children of sex workers in Kolkata, does emerge from a sense of compassion that we feel for the disadvantageous lives of these children. Compassion, thus, can mean different things to different people. What we are concerned with is not so much the idea of compassion itself, but the representational practices of arousing and responding to it that emanate from such an idea. We had used the terms compassion and pity interchangeably in the last section to establish how pity is actually a vicissitude of compassion. Pity operates on an understanding of distantiation, which evokes compassionate responses from afar, seldom making a difference to the structural causes behind the suffering in question (Johnson 2011: 621–43). Distantiation works to establish a feeling of secured insulation: Thank God, we will never face anything like that; we can never let our children suffer that way.

As the Kleinmans observe:

> One message that comes across from viewing suffering from a distance is that for all the havoc in Western society, we are somehow

> better than [the native society]. We gain in moral status and some of our organizations gain financially and politically, while those whom we represent, or appropriate, remain where they are, moribund [...]. This 'consumption' of suffering in an era of so-called 'disordered capitalism' is not so very different from the late nineteenth-century view that the savage barbarism in pagan lands justified the value of our own civilization at a higher level of development – a view that authorized colonial exploitation (1997: 8).

Compassion that is mediated through images engage the viewer voyeuristically by aesthetizing suffering and turning it into a spectacle. Especially when compassion is understood as the only link to justice without attention to structures of injustice, it can become, a form of 'sentimental liberalism' that is an end in itself, 'affording the viewer the pleasures of vicarious suffering and virtuous feelings of compassion, but returning us to a private [civilized and insulated] world far removed from the public sphere [the location of suffering]' (Woodward 2004: 71). An emotion of this kind is 'deliciously consumable, cruelly ineffective and morally bankrupt' (Woodward 2004: 71).

In the context of children, there has been an unproblematic acceptance of the liberal values of 'play' and 'training' as the two primary attributes of modern childhood, which have become the *leitmotif* of children's human rights: 'a life free of labour and exploitation' (Uberoi 2006: 88). Compassionate interventions thus respond best to representations of suffering children who are shown to be denied opportunities to play (in parks or with toys) and learn (through formal systems of education and care, as is offered in school or children's homes). The response is always to restore and rescue the innocence of these suffering children by creating opportunities for playing and learning, through a fixed set of aestheticized tools: building colourfully decorated safe homes, segregating underprivileged children (including disabled children) in the name of special care, teaching them painting, photography, poetry, and most importantly, providing them ostensibly with secular education, to overcome their conditions of grief, and even to physically lift them out of surroundings that do not encourage play and training. Understandably, *BiB* and the other initiatives to save children of sex workers from their plight (that we discuss below), follow this very trajectory of intervention: lift them out, give them things to play with (like a camera or a paintbrush), replace their incompetent parents with foster parents, and train them to become more cultured and civilized than their mothers, parents, or communities.

This is what Patricia Uberoi aptly calls the condition of manufacturing the 'customized child' (2006: 95): a subjectivity that emerges out of a confluence of representational, cognitive, and corporeal practices of liberalism that inform the operation of compassion.

Representing Ugliness, Beautifully

The representations that we discuss below have attained popularity and fame, not simply because of their high compassion-arresting quotient, but also because of their sophisticated aesthetics on display. Irrespective of whether one agrees or disagrees with the content and perspectives of these representations, all of them represent what is perceived to be ugly, beautifully—where ugliness becomes the 'other' of beauty.

The moral universalism of compassion is what leads us to create idealized notions and practices of childhood with which suffering children must be endowed. In the process of manufacturing the customized child through compassion that is driven by aesthetic representations, universal guarantees to the human rights of children remain grossly unattended, several times even hindering their protection and fulfilment.

We want to discuss a photo that the Kleinmans make a reference to, which is not reproduced in their essay alongside the one by Kevin Carter. It is the photo of a bare-chested, coyly smiling small girl at the Kandupatti brothel in Dhaka, Bangladesh that appeared in *NYT* on 9 April 1993, accompanying an article titled, 'The Sex Market: Scourge on the World's Children'.[5]

The Kleinmans' offer a critique of the photograph by arguing that the representation of the girl would have been considered child pornography had it not appeared along with this article. They refer to the photo as an illustration of the aesthetization of child sexual abuse:

> The purpose of the picture and the accompanying story is to expose the degradation of child prostitution, a phenomenon greatly increasing in

> the era of AIDS. But the picture simultaneously appeals, probably not entirely without intention, to a prurient sensibility. It is clearly not enough to picture a child's body for sale; the picture needs to recreate the atmosphere of sexual desire. Thus, the media, by the success of its artistry, gets caught up in the very processes it seeks to criticize (1997: 11).

Having cited the Kleinmans heavily in this paper, we are both happy and alarmed by their reading of this photograph. The argument about how aesthetization of suffering attracts compassion, where the consumer and producer of news/information work in complicity, is critical to understand the politics of representation. What alarms us are the problematic assumptions that even the Kleinmans make when they are consuming images of aesthetized suffering.

Based on the *NYT* article the Kleinmans assume, without verification, that the girl in the photograph is a child prostitute, dressed up with 'tousled adult hairstyle, many bangles on her arms, earrings and a necklace' (Kleinman and Kleinman 1996: 11) being exhibited on the streets for soliciting clients. The photograph is originally part of a collection of photos of the red-light districts in Bangladesh called 'Daughters of Darkness', which was put together by photographers from a Bangladeshi media collective called Drik.[6] The blurb accompanying the photograph in the Drik collection reads: 'A minor girl child, daughter of a prostitute, amongst the clients in the background and a passer-by prostitute in the foreground. Growing up in a brothel environment doesn't leave children here with much option and usually turns them into young prostitutes.'[7] While there is no denying that the threat of the girl children of sex workers being forced into their mothers' profession is indeed a cause for concern and adequate steps need to be taken to stop that from happening, compassion makes the Kleinmans conflate issues to arrive at *a priori* assumptions that the presence of a girl child in a brothel means that she is a child prostitute or that girl children of sex workers will inevitably become prostitutes.

The location of the photograph also has a history that never got researched either by *NYT* or the Kleinmans. The sex workers of Kandupatti have resisted eviction threats for a long time, taking care of their children and other family members, but were finally forcibly evicted by the government in 1999, with no shelter for them or their children. Ulka, Bangladesh's first sex-workers' collective, had been resisting these threats through the 1990s and valiantly struggled against the evictions by forming alliances with other women's rights groups (Institute of Development Studies (IDS) 2005: 37). The Kleinmans were caught up so much with the artistry and geography of the photo that their aesthetic judgement had to elicit compassion, in effect, fixating the subjectivity of the child.

It is this conflation that the acclaimed documentary films *Selling of Innocents* (Gupta 1997) and *BiB* deepen with more aesthetic finesse. These films go a step further to illustrate how compassion should be practised with the objective of customizing the childhoods of suffering children in red-light districts in India, be they trafficked children or children of sex workers.

Selling of Innocents (*SoI*), a 1997 Emmy-award-winning documentary, claims to do an exposé on the horrors of child trafficking from Nepal to India, the abject conditions in which prostitutes and their children live in the dingy brothels of Kamathipura in Mumbai, and lauds the heroic efforts of people who have supported law-enforcement agencies in raiding, rescuing, and rehabilitating trafficked victims from Mumbai's brothels.

From a pro-sex-work feminist perspective, there are strong arguments to critique the image of the helpless sex worker as a victim that the film represents, as also the continuous conflation between trafficking and sex work that the film perpetuates (Kempadoo 2005; Doezema 2010). Discussing those arguments are beyond the scope of this essay. But what is of relevance are the slippages in the narrative of the film that repeat the compassion-driven assumptions that the Kleinmans made while discussing the Kandupatti photograph.

The visuals of Kamathipura illustrate how the brothel spaces are occupied by women and children—the men keep moving in and out of the frames. In an opening scene of the film, the voiceover says: 'These girls have been cheated, kidnapped, beaten, and sold into bondage. They are modern-day sex slaves.' The accompanying visual shows the camera moving through a brothel. The vagueness with which the voiceover identifies the women and children makes it unclear whether the small girls and even smaller children seen in the film are child prostitutes, children of sex workers, or minors who have been trafficked into Kamathipura. All of them are bundled together and labeled with an identical subjectivity that remains constant throughout the film.

The film uses under-lit, grainy, slow-moving images, and haunting background scores to complement the stories of horror that the trafficked underage girls share: they have no one to turn to, nowhere to go—unless people watching the film respond. The camera travels between Mumbai and some villages in Nepal from where, the film claims, underage girls are being duped and trafficked into brothels in Mumbai for two reasons: poverty and deep-seated patriarchy. The camera travels with a social activist named Vinod Gupta who, along with the police, conducts sudden raids on brothels to 'rescue' trafficked children and young girls; and visits a shelter home for trafficked children run by Anuradha Koirala in rural Nepal. The film advocates spreading education among women and children to combat the cruelty of 'sisters and daughters [being] sold every day'. The film concludes with the visual of a huddled group of little children sleeping together in a room with the voiceover saying: 'These are the children of the prostitutes. They sleep while their mothers work. *Who will help them avoid their mother's fate?* What songs do they hear? If nothing is done to stop sex trafficking, this is the next generation of Kamathipura girls' (emphasis ours).

Rather than focusing on the problems with the way in which it represents trafficking and sex work, we will critique the film on three other counts, given the thesis of this essay. First, that the kind of compassionate response that a film like this is expected to attract would have contributed towards a positive transformation in the suffering lives of the sex workers and their children in Kamathipura. But as Svati P. Shah notes in her reading of *SoI* and similar spectacles of suffering on Kamathipura:

> Visual and textual representations of Kamathipura, however, rarely function to mobilize actions or interventions directed among or toward people living and working in the district. If disseminating these kinds of images did inspire their viewers to action, one might imagine the scene in Kamathipura to be somehow productively changed following the release of a film or media story which depicts

sex workers in the district as impoverished and abused. Rather, any pre-existing negative conditions in the red light area seem to be maintained or intensified as a result of these representations. In other words, the effect of these representations is to maintain Kamathipura as an exceptional space as compared to the normative social spaces at which images and stories about prostitution in Mumbai are targeted. As Kellner writes, 'the spectacle is a tool of pacification and depoliticization' (2006: 280).

Thus, our second critique is that spectacles of suffering of the *SoI* kind, in attempting to highlight their own work, invisibilize the already existent collectives and negotiation strategies that the sex-worker mothers use to ensure that their children are not trafficked. In that act of erasure both the consumer of the film and the filmmakers are complicit. By invisibilizing the everyday practices of struggle and negotiation, the filmmaker assumes the position of the compassionate outsider who is the messiah of all the change that will now happen in the lives of these women and their hapless children. In an interview to the website *Adventure Divas*, Ruchira Gupta, the producer of the film, was referred to as a 'Muckraker'—the compassionate liberal who goes so far as to wade through filth to save victims of trafficking. She said this about her interventions at Kamathipura:

> Six years ago, when I came into this brothel, they [the prostitutes] were so timid and they were so scared, they were not willing to even talk to each other. They did not let outsiders in, and today, six years later, you can see the laughter and the joy that they have.[8]

Gupta's indication suggests how these women today have a voice only because of the organization called Apne Aap Women Worldwide that she has set up after being deeply moved by the experience of making the film—as if to say that the women could have done nothing if she did not arrive.

Our third critique is regarding the unqualified assumption that the film makes: that sex workers' girl children will always become sex workers. It is an assumption based on the understanding that the mothers do not have any control over themselves, let alone their children. Being born in a brothel inevitably means that you have been trafficked into sex work anyway—your mother was forced into prostitution, you were conceived because of forced sex, you were born into a cruel and ugly world without any choice—it is all in the continuum of a generational trafficking trail. As a child of a sex worker you have only two possibilities of hope: that sex work is abolished and you are rescued and rehabilitated along with your mother; or, because that will take time, some compassionate soul should come and lift you out of the cruel and inhuman brothel space, sent away to a 'safe' home, away from your mother, and taught the finer cultures of life.

Zana Briski and Ross Kauffman's Oscar-winning *BiB* begins where *SoI* ends. Now that *SoI* has established how existentially trafficked the lives of children of sex workers are, 'Zana Aunty'—with an advanced degree in theology from Cambridge University—comes from New York to save the children of sex workers in Kolkata 'from "dead end" lives, where the boys have limited prospects and the girls are merely being groomed to "go into the line" as prostitutes' (Kapur 2007: 224). The synopsis of the film reads:

> *The most stigmatized people in Calcutta's red light district, are not the prostitutes, but their children.* In the face of abject poverty, abuse, and despair, these kids have little possibility of escaping their mothers' fate or for creating another type of life [...]. Trying to evade a doomed future, they embark on a transformational journey with New York based photographer Zana Briski, who teaches them photography. This humorous and heartfelt story portrays the power of art and the courage of those willing to change their own lives (emphasis ours).[9]

The film, a first-person journey, begins with Kochi (who is one of the eight children), a 10-year-old girl at the time of filming, saying: 'The men who enter our building are not so good...they are drunk, they come inside and shout and swear. The women ask me, "When are you going to join the line?" [...] They say it won't be long'. Quite clearly, this establishes the justification for Briski's project: she will use the 'restorative power of art' to help these children overcome their fears, and get them out of the brothels. This film marks a departure from *SoI* as far as it foregrounds the children of sex workers as active subjects in the film, who are not only present, but also speak.

Despite the grim brothel atmosphere in Kolkata as well, the children are shown forgetting their miseries in the company of Briski, their 'saviour', who introduces them to cameras and photography as a means to capture moments from their lives, and the way they want to look at life. Needless to say, the creative inclinations of the children and Briski's lessons result in the children taking excellent photographs. But while the children go on capturing life on the streets of Kolkata, Briski and Kaufmann represent a highly skewed picture of their lives. They capture day-to-day moments from these children's lives like fetching water, watching TV, and most prominently, their interaction with adults—either other sex workers who live in the same building as theirs, or their mothers. At every such interaction the adults are shown verbally abusing them and even physically beating them, abusing each other, or drugged. Sex workers are thus fixated as uncaring, irresponsible, and incompetent parents who cannot ensure a 'customized' childhood for their children. Don't the children share any happy and intimate moments with their mothers, or parents? Has there been a complete breakdown of interpersonal support from other sex workers in the Sonagachi community towards these children? Are Briski and Kauffman the only people who they can trust to make their lives better, and make their aspirations and dreams come true?

After *BiB* won the Oscar in 2005, DMSC, the sex-workers' collective operating in Sonagachi, sent a strong protest letter in which they argued, inter alia, that the film's portrayal of how uncaring sex workers are towards their children completely disregards the decade-long efforts of the collective to work for the rights and dignity of sex workers and their children. In response, Briski decided not to screen the film in India on the flimsy ground of protecting the identity of the children, though by that time the children, their mothers and their families had 'become a part of global public consumption' (Kapur 2007: 224).

The film anaesthetizes suffering to mask its politics. The method of practising compassion that the film advocates is that of rescue through removal and relocation; repeating in a far more sophisticated and creative way the same strategy that *SoI* advocated. Briski's mission of ensuring an idealized childhood can only be attained, as she says in the film, by getting these children out of the brothels—because they are from 'bad backgrounds'—and admitting them in a boarding school where they can learn and play. She insists on a boarding school to ensure that the children do not get the opportunity to return to the red-light area where their families live. She laments the fact that for children to be able to get admission in schools, the parents cannot be criminals, but 'the problem is that their parents are all criminals—prostitutes, selling alcohol…' Speaking about the brightest of the children, Avijit, Briski fears that 'he will turn out to be a pretty bad kid if he doesn't get any help […] he wants to be good, but he has no guidance'—apart from her of course.

Briski is shown to be going through harrowing times dealing with the bureaucracy in Kolkata—to get the children admitted to schools and get a passport issued for Avijit so that he can attend an international photo exhibition in Amsterdam. The segment in the film which documents Avijit's visit to Amsterdam shows how ebulliently he inhabits the foreign space—as if he belongs there. When his photos are exhibited, they are not described just as photos but as photos by the child of a sex worker, which seems necessary to appreciate them as aesthetically appealing.

The film concludes by showing who from among the eight children joined the school where Briski wanted to admit them, and the ones who were pulled out by their parents or family. After demonizing sex workers as bad mothers, and brothels as evil spaces in the closing, the film states that it has been made 'in honour of the women and children of the red-light district'. In the name of compassionate intervention, the film reifies the brothel as a space where children remain existentially trafficked, unless they are removed from there. To translate their compassionate vision into reality, *Kids with Camera*—the organization that Briski and Kauffman founded, tried setting up Hope House, a 'safe' home for the children of sex workers in Kolkata, where they can be kept safely away from, as their website says, the 'squalid rooms and chaotic conditions of the congested red light district'.[10]

While Ruchira Gupta's *SoI* does not show any children of sex workers as speaking subjects—they are mutely suffering the fate of being 'born into brothels'—her organization Apne Aap Women Worldwide carried out an innovative book-writing project in 2005 with a group of children of sex workers from Kolkata's Kalighat and Sonagachi red-light districts. The back cover of the beautifully designed book, titled *The Place Where We Live is Called a Red- Light Area,* reads:

> The red-light areas of Kolkata are ghettoized localities, disregarded by modern progress. Crime and corruption exist without fear of law. Violence is a way of life and death and disappearance forgotten easily… Apne Aap decided to bring together some children from these areas to tell a story, make a drawing and describe their dreams, hopes and aspirations. It was a book-writing project, a narrative therapy project and an advocacy project, all rolled into one. It was also a breaking of the silence surrounding the lives of children in red-light areas. What emerged was a stunning body of work on life and living in red-light areas, of violence and death, of naked human trafficking and soul destroying prostitution, of disease and HIV/ AIDS and almost impossibly and inspirationally, of dreams and aspirations…[11]

A visual presentation of the book, available on YouTube, begins with:

> You are about to begin a visual journey into the minds and souls of children from a marginalized world. Violence is part of their daily lives, rape and trafficking frightening realities. The images that follow break their silence.[12]

Evidently, there is no dearth of images in the public domain of suffering children, especially in connection with sex work and trafficking. So on that count, this book does not break any silence. What might be of relevant concern is whether our compassion for these children, being aroused by these images, is doing anything to secure their human rights? Where this book does mark a departure from existing images of suffering children is that here the children are themselves engaging in a project where they are talking about their lives—like *BiB*—without simply remaining objects of compassionate representation. The important thing to note is that rather than being bare testimonies, their voices have been aesthetized through drawing and painting, representing the ugliness of their lives beautifully. But here too, a moral universalism takes over the representations. The book hardly has any positive drawings or quotes from children where they talk about play, or enjoying their lives, unless they are talking about what they aspire their future to be like—a deferral of sorts. The drawings illustrate either scenes of soliciting, beating, sex or crying women and children.[13] In a quote by 14-year-old Aradhana, she says:

> The red-light area is bad because it causes AIDS. The disease spreads through the women who do bad work here. I would like to close it down to stop AIDS and the bad work; the people living in our locality have very bad manners. They are quarrelsome and use bad language. They never behave properly with any person...[14]

There are striking similarities between the images depicted in the book and the visuals captured on film in *BiB*. There are two very important inferences that we draw from this. First, in spite of *SoI* and Apne Aap's book being activist interventions and *BiB* being a creative intervention, the politics that inform them are the same. There is a collapse that takes place between the poetic and political here, which is where the liberal appeal of *BiB* lies. Although Briski says in as many words in the film that she is not a social worker, or an activist, her intervention is as politically motivated to rescue as that of law-enforcement agencies in *SoI*, or the way in which the Immoral Traffic Prevention Act (IPTA), 1956 operates in India. So our second inference is that interventions in the name of protecting the rights of children of sex workers—irrespective of whether the pursuits are governmental, activist, philanthropist, or creative—work in the same way to disenfranchise the children, if they are not considered as agents whose voices are primary in determining the policies that can protect their rights best.

The ITPA follows the same logic of rescue through removal that Briski talks about in *BiB*. Section 4 of the law criminalizes any person above the age of 18 who lives off the earnings of a sex worker. Despite the fact that this section applies only to adults, it is meant to prosecute pimps or brothel owners, and is a protection against children being arbitrarily removed from brothels, even though the police rampantly carry out 'rescue' operations and pick up children from brothels on the pretext that they have been trafficked. The very location of the children within brothel spaces becomes the reason for their forced removal. As per Section 16, a magistrate—even based on unverified information from the police—can order a minor to be 'rescued' from brothel premises and produced before the court without informing the child's mother or family. The child is also not informed or her opinion sought during such acts of 'rescue'. Law-enforcement agencies thus find a compassionate justification for carrying out these acts of arbitrary detention.

In a display of outright missionary zeal, far more in-your-face than Briski's, and even more arbitrary than police raids, was an incident that took place in Sangli, Maharashtra, in May 2005. Members from an evangelical organization called Restore International (RI), who were foreigners, came to conduct a survey in the brothels of Sangli. Later, they informed the district superintendent of police that the survey had revealed that there are minor girls in the brothels. In response, around 200 police personnel, mostly plainclothes male officers, conducted a raid accompanied by Greg Malstead from RI. The raid was conducted with complete disregard for the work that Sangram, a sex workers' collective, has been doing in Sangli to secure the rights of women in prostitution, and to stop trafficking in minors.

The raid yielded a total of allegedly 35 'minor' girls, of which two were schoolgoing girls who had come home for vacations. The girls were sent to a remand home in Sangli. The first medical report stated that there were only four minors out of the 35. The police went for a re-examination and the resulting medical report stated that an additional 13, which raised the total number to 17, were minors ranging from 16 to 19 years of age. The 18 majors were released to their parents and the 17 sent to the Child Welfare Committee (CWC) at the insistence of a lawyer from Prerna, an NGO in Mumbai.

The CWC then appointed a probation officer (PO) to investigate and submit a report regarding the parents of the 17 girls. Sangram pleaded on behalf of the two schoolgoing girls who submitted their school credentials to the CWC. By the time they were released they had been in a remand home for 15 days. Restore International did not come to their rescue, much less make any effort to counsel them about this gross violation of their rights. Parents of the remaining 15 then appealed to the CWC that they should be given custody of their children and were also willing to give an undertaking that they will ensure that their children will not return to live in the brothels. They had school-leaving certificates for 12 of the girls stating that they were 18 and above. The CWC then released 9 girls to their parents on the basis of the PO's report. Restore International went against this order of the CWC by filing a case in the Sangli Sessions Court. Later, the rest the girls were released—some of them had produced proof of age to establish that they were major, and a couple who were actually minors were released on humanitarian grounds because they were pregnant.

A statement released by Sangram during this fiasco said:

> What is the best solution for a 'girl child in need of care and protection'? A simplistic solution - such as raid and rescue - only offers patchwork relief, and takes away the rights of the girl child by inflicting untold violence on her in the process. The 'raid, rescue and rehabilitation' model blames the community, pushing it to a corner of no return. Such strategies that have violated the rights of the women in prostitution have not yielded good results for generations. We need solutions that are long term and those that can be implemented effectively. We need strategies that will strengthen women to resist being pushed into those corners and build the will to reject the unacceptable and illegal violation and sexual abuse of the girl child. The collectivization of women in prostitution, which is a rights based approach, is one such strategy. It creates a space for women in prostitution to collectively look for solutions to their problems. It helps them to access information and education about rights and to take informed decisions.[15]

Sangram's attempt to confront this evangelist 'raid, rescue, rehabilitation' brigade led to murkier events later in the year when they were accused of thwarting the raids, forcing the CWC to release the minors (despite them producing majority certificates), and engaging in child trafficking.[16]

In another incident in May 2007, members of a group called Freedom Firm (closely associated with RI) arbitrarily raided a brothel in Miraj, a small town close to Sangli. A member from that group entered a brothel as a decoy customer to find out whether there are trafficked minors or child prostitutes. In a desperate attempt to expose that there indeed were child prostitutes, the decoy customer allegedly molested the 13-year-old daughter of a former sex worker. The police and the media colluded in the operation, with local newspapers flashing the girl's photograph saying that she was a child prostitute. An independent fact-finding report on this incident, titled 'In the Name of Rescue', revealed the extent to which missionary compassionate zeal can go to rampantly violate the rights of children of sex workers, or other children who live and work (not sex work) within sex-worker communities.

The *SoI* and *BiB* narratives on film and the more material practices of compassion in the Sangli and Miraj cases clearly establish the trouble with the monochromatic nature of these representations and the unidirectional responses they attract. The problem with such representations is that they singularly invoke compassion and continuously propagate half-truths about the lives of these children and their families. These images have nearly clogged every mode through which knowledge about their lives gets circulated today, effecting either an erasure or deferral of the daily practices of resilience and resistance in their lives.

In the 'Political Society' of Sex Workers' Children

De-centring hegemony is easier said than done, especially when the ones undertaking that task contribute to the longevity of an oppressive order. In this section, we as human rights activists and researchers question the ethics of our politics. A politics that thrives on what Mark Seltzer calls 'wound culture': a culture's collective fetish for spectacles of suffering (Seltzer 1997: 3–26). Our task is not to effect a second act of erasure of experiences from the lives of the children of sex workers by overlooking the stigma and disadvantage of which they are at the receiving end.

What provides a basis to our critique of the discourse of compassion is our engagement and interactions with Amra Padatik (AP), the collective of children of sex workers in Sonagachi mentioned earlier. Founded in 2005, AP is run by children of sex workers and functions under the aegis of the organization run by their mothers, called Durbar Mahila Samanwaya Committee (DMSC). Even though AP might often come across as reiterating DMSC's politics, what is novel about it is that the children who started this initiative have very powerful individual life stories to tell—stories that challenge, critique, and confront the meta-narrative of the innocent-victim-child so successfully created through the kinds of images and texts we have discussed in the essay.

While we do not claim that AP and the experiences of its young members are paradigmatic of the lives of all children of sex workers in Kolkata, we do believe that witnessing their practices of negotiating with life offers valuable lessons for compassionate interventions that intend to save them from their misery. Listening to their stories of struggle and triumph also give researchers, activists, and philanthropists alike an opportunity to be critically self-reflexive and attentive to their own modes of working for, on, or with these children.

To recognize children of sex workers as transformative agents requires a shift in the terminology and frame of observation through which their lives have been represented so far. Clearly, all the interventions discussed above are 'civil-society' engagements—where people whose rights and citizenship privileges are not under threat because of their location, identity, or politics are negotiating with the state for the rights of others. It is on the strength of their privileges that they can choose to direct compassion at the less privileged. This understanding of civil society—primarily comprised of law-abiding non-state actors like NGOs, charities, corporate houses, funding agencies, the mainstream media—are characterized by the liberal virtues of free association, constitutional guarantees to equality and freedom, deliberative processes of decision-making, contractual transactions, capital accumulation, private property, and the like. These are the virtues that 'civil society' wants to endow the disadvantaged and suffering with—akin to the colonial attempts of 'civilizing the native', though maintaining incommensurability of status, deferral of opportunities and exceptionality of their locational identity. For Partha Chatterjee, civil society is bourgeoisie society (2004).

'Political society' on the other hand is inhabited by those who have been subjects of bourgeoisie (historically colonial) exclusion, experiments, and pity, but never agents who have had the opportunity to question, interpret, and shape their own histories. While 'civil society' comprises citizens, 'political society' is the realm of illegality, inhabited by 'populations'—homogenized masses of non/illegal citizens whose lives need to be managed by 'civil society' actors, including the state. Inhabitants of 'political society' are constantly negotiating through everyday practices and processes to confront the violence of exclusion and compassion that 'civil society' directs at them, but not necessarily in the language of liberal rights. Chatterjee distinguishes the two thus:

> Civil society is typically about a kind of free associative, modern bourgeois life. It is quintessentially *bourgeois* politics. The challenge [...] in most of the non-Western world is that most people are *not* bourgeois. What sense does it make to use the forms of modern law and modern administrative procedures on populations that cannot *survive* if you simply insist on protection of private property, equality of law, freedom of contract and these kinds of things? Most of these people would simply *die* or they would rise in revolt and break down the whole structure (quoted in Sheikh 2007: 89, emphasis in original).

Chatterjee recognizes that because of electoral compulsions, on several occasions, civil society and the state overlook the political practices of survival within political society that violate the rules of civil-society behaviour. In other words, civil society sometimes offers benign toleration which can take the forms of indifference, or compassion (for example, the ways in which squatters, prostitutes, illegal migrants are tolerated for the sake of ensuring a definite vote bank). Chatterjee's focus on electoral compulsions of the state automatically excludes children from the purview of 'political society' because of age. However, we find his conceptualization useful to locate the experiences of resilience and resistance of AP within 'political society'.

By foregrounding the voices of these children, our objective is to challenge the traditional three-Rs model (raid, rescue, rehabilitation) of securing their rights with three counter Rs: resilience, reworking, resistance. This counter lens, developed by Cindi Katz, allows us to foreground agency in place of victimhood to examine the 'creative reworkings' (2004: 240) and the diverse and inventive ways in which these children cope with the intrusions of different forms of stigma and sympathy into their everyday lives. Katz refers to these strategies as a 'revolutionary imagination' in political consciousness bound with everyday acts and the remaking of social life. These are also the 'spaces of hope' that are found in the ordinary exchanges between the children and communities as they act out their dreams and futures. Katz hopes that 'a politics intent on locating practices [of resilience, reworking, and resistance] that scratched at, and under certain conditions might completely break down, hegemony' (Katz 2004: xi).

Resisting Compassion

> In recognizing[…] the oppression of children[…] a radical approach would also recognize *children as resistors to that oppression*. This means *refusing* to collaborate in the censorship of children's contemporary and historical struggle against injustice…
>
> — Jenny Kitzinger (1990: 176, quoted in S. Grover (2005: 536), emphasis in original)

Our conversations with children of sex workers from Sonagachi are an attempt to read resistance into their everyday and ordinary experiences of negotiating stigma and discrimination. These conversations powerfully militate against the aesthetized representations of suffering that have attracted compassionate responses from the likes of Briski and Kauffman.

It is simplistic to talk about the rights of children of sex workers by only laying threadbare the entangled realities of their lives. Their lived experiences are so layered that no representation can ever justifiably capture the complexities. What rights do you prioritize and protect, when the very mechanisms of protection disenfranchise them and mute their voices? Which is why we must listen to them.[17]

AP's mission statement reads:

> Our goal is to establish the rights and dignity of all marginalized people and their children through social and political changes. With our involvement in this global movement, we are determined to improve the quality of life and social status of the sex workers and their children (AP Mission Statement 2005).[18]

What is unique about this declaration is the clarity with which children have been able to respond to their lived realities, and that is what allows them to think of building bridges of solidarity with other marginalized groups. Since being set up in 2005, AP has mobilized close to 1,500 members, who are children of sex workers from Kolkata and its suburbs. The organization believes that a primary means to secure and guarantee the rights of sex workers' children is for them to also join the struggles of their mothers, because they feel that the question of their rights as children is undeniably connected to the criminalization of sex work and the societal indignity that their mothers face. These children have seen how their mothers have collectivized to fight for their rights through DMSC, and their coming together draws inspiration from that.

As Chaitali, AP's first president (then a 17-year-old girl) says: 'It all began when Gobinda, Mithu, and I—all children of sex workers—were discussing how our mothers say that the work they do is not bad and that they should have their rights. We wondered what we thought as their children. That is when we realized that we should have more discussions like this. So we started talking to more children like us and felt that we had some specific problems and need to come together and form a collective to be able to address them.' A question that they kept confronting was why aren't they as children able to respect their mothers' profession, when it is her money that runs the house and takes care of their education?

The first impetus was an incident where Gobinda (AP's founding secretary, then 18 years old) was refused an admission form after his board exams because of a TV interview where he had mentioned that he was a sex worker's child; the other children supported him, rallied outside the school, and made sure that he got the form. Similarly, when another child was harassed by the landlord after his mother died, the children went and made sure that he was not evicted.

Mithu (a founder member of AP, and 28 years old at that time) feels that one of the major reasons why it was necessary for children of sex workers to collectivize was because their stigma was intrinsically connected to that of their mothers, irrespective of whether, as a child, you liked what your mother did or not. As Mithu says, 'According to the law [ITPA], children of sex workers cannot live on their mother's earnings after the age of 18 years. But where will the children go after that? You cannot do anything these days with being a graduate, which means at least 21 or 22 years. They don't want us to earn or do anything in life? Is the child of a doctor or lawyer penalized because he or she is living off the earnings of their parents at 18 years of age? I had to discontinue my school because of this. My mother wanted to get me married before that. And I was married off at 14.' Mithu, a mother now, is certain that she will not marry off her children before they reach the age of majority and have completed their education.

It was through the sharing of experiences like these that Gobinda, Chaitali, and Mithu started reaching out to other children of sex workers beyond Sonagachi, in Rambagan, Boubajar, and some districts in and around Kolkata urging them to attend meetings, to share their own experiences of being children of sex workers, and the kinds of problems that they face because of their identity. What was being built was a children's movement where they were not merely passive recipients of welfare measures as victims, but active agents who were participating in demanding their rights. They were advocates in their own right.

This is representative of the first of the three counter Rs: resilience, reflective of their ability to confront the stigma that mars their lives. As Mithu asserts, 'We must publicly declare that we are children of sex workers. If that is the label that stigmatizes us, we should make people hear it even more.' Closely connected with this practice of resilience is reworking, the second of the three counter Rs. Reworking builds on acts of resilience to 'make and remake social facts and collective identities' (Katz 2004: 247).

Through the meetings and discussions that these children were organizing emerged a collective understanding that they needed to find an identity for themselves to be able to advocate for their rights better. Since the formation of AP, these children have always introduced themselves as *jouno kormir shantan* (child of a sex worker)—in stark contrast with representations like *BiB* where erasing this identity is their only way to escape stigma. One might argue that for AP, this assertion is reflective of the internalization of their hapless fate, fixating their identity. Our interactions with other members suggest a far more complex reason behind this. It will be incorrect to say that there is no internalization; however, assertively taking on the identity is a political and strategic act to reclaim the dignity of sex workers and their children; to reclaim the dignity of that very identity which ascribes indignity to every aspect of their lives. As one of the children (who did not want to be named) we interviewed said, 'We are denied rights and dignity because we are *jouno kormir shantan* [...] we'll use the strength of calling us by that very name to reclaim rights for our mothers and us.'

Taking on the identity of *jouno kormir shantan* led to another critical consciousness among the children. Claiming their rights was not necessarily an attempt at gaining 'mainstream' acceptance. They were aware that their situation required special rights, so they referred to children who are not *jouno kormir shantan* as *shadharon shantan* (ordinary child). The use of the word *shadharon* instead of its vicissitude *shubhubik* (normal)—points at how the discourse of normalcy (that makes deviants and victims out of them) is not part of their political vocabulary.

This distinction that they make between their own self-asserted identity of *jouno kormir shantan* and *shadharon shantan*, however, does not in any way signify that they consider all their rights and needs as special. There are aspirations that they have of an ideal childhood and future—but the process of achieving that does not have a customized model which is divorced from their present realities, or comes at the cost of moving out of the red-light area. It was only because of the continued effort of AP, especially Gobinda, that they were able to convince the Indira Gandhi National Open University (IGNOU) to open a study centre at Sonagachi in March 2008. Children of sex workers who are school dropouts, but have crossed the age of majority can enroll for free at the study centre to complete a bridge course called the bachelor's preparatory programme. Even sex-worker mothers are joining this course (*The Telegraph* 2008).

The AP members, however, do not stop to critique their own achievements, which is reflective of their self-reflexivity as activists. As Ratan Dolui (19 years old and the then secretary of AP) says:

> The IGNOU centre was a very important achievement, but we now realize that it is not useful for us because after passing out from IGNOU you cannot get into any other university, you have to only continue with IGNOU. These IGNOU classes were only publicity stunts. To publicize their work for children of sex workers IGNOU agreed to set up a centre at DMSC. Their books are in English, teachers don't come. Most of us cannot follow English so language becomes a barrier for us to access what they offer.

Ratan is doing his master's in social work from Rabindra Bharati University. Pinky Das (16 years old and the present president of AP) concurs with Ratan.

During our interactions with these children, we always wondered whether the experiences of children of sex workers are gendered, and they perceive being *jouno kormir shantan* differently. While girls and boys do get socialized differently, the disparity in gender roles that we see in case of *shadharon shantans* is much less ingrained when it comes to children of sex workers. For the girls, seeing their mothers work as breadwinners for their families instills in them a different idea about what their socialized roles should be. Also, their exposure to their mothers' work, and being informed at an early age about issues of sexuality, make them far more knowledgeable than other children. For instance, Ratan, having been part of a peer-education programme run by an organization called Cini-Asha since his childhood, is now the repository of knowledge on safe sex and sexuality and is always sought out by young boys in his locality for information on sex.

The descriptions of the relationship that these children share with their mothers offer a far more complex experience than of the kind popular representations circulate. Gobinda, for example, shares a very good relationship with his mother and he proudly told us that she takes very good care of him. During the interview he said that he could not stay and have lunch with us because his mother had made lunch for him and she would feel bad if he did not eat that food.

For Mithu, her childhood experiences are little different. She remembers being angry with her mother because she could never tell her friends where she lived. She felt bad when she saw other children 'proudly' go to school and tuitions and play. 'I have told my children that you tell everyone where you live and if they still maintain their relationship with you then it's fine, otherwise forget them,' she says. Mithu remembers that her mother married her off when she was 14 years old because she was scared about Mithu being forced into prostitution. While her mother lives with her now, she also shares a very nice relationship with her mother's *babu* (permanent client), who she calls her father. 'My father has married again and doesn't live with us anymore, but he loves me a lot. I always listen to what he says,' adds Mithu.

Chaitali laments that she could not stay with her mother when she was a child. 'I have not been able to enjoy my childhood. I was kept away from home and my mother. I couldn't spend time with my friends. They never came home. I couldn't have a normal life,' she says. What is interesting about both Mithu's and Chaitali's experiences is that while stigma is a burning reality in their life, for them the ideal childhood is about staying with their mothers and not shunning the location of the red-light area that they inhabit, unlike the logic of interventions from outside that can only imagine them having better lives when they are physically lifted out of the brothel space away from their mothers. Many of the children we interviewed emphatically said that the very act of forcibly taking them away from the mothers in the name of 'rescue' is no different from trafficking.

Ratan's mother is dead. He remembers how she used to be tortured by her *babu*. When she passed away he was evicted by the *malkin* (brothel keeper) because he was not the tenant. But he has negotiated and settled the matter. This is a predicament that many of these children face if they are living with their mothers when they die. Is 'rescue' the most effective intervention in such a grave situation? Ratan continued to stay in the red-light area, in the same house that his mother did, and is now a postgraduate student. Similarly, Gobinda works as a clinic attendant at a health clinic in Chetla and is applying for a position of a school teacher through the West Bengal School Service Commission this year. Their achievements bust the myth that children living in red-light areas are doomed.

Pinky now lives in her mother's house in Narendrapur. A man, who she refers to as *kaku* (uncle), also lives in the same house but separately. Her mother has moved out with another client and Pinky does not know anything about her mother anymore. She thinks that her mother is dead. 'I hate my mother, but I know *jouno kormi* mothers do care about their children,' she said. Her mother had sent her to a shelter home at a very early age so that Pinky could study and her life wouldn't be adversely affected. Pinky's experience, then, follows the 'rescue through removal' logic that her mother had used, and not an outsider. Yet, Pinky's experience of being at shelter homes tells us why she is now back in the community working for the rights of children like her.

> Shelter homes are a good thing. They can be really helpful for children who are orphans or whose sex worker mothers are unable to take care of them, but they should be *nijer barir moton* (like your own home). They shouldn't be like jails where children have no freedom, don't get to eat properly, study properly. From my experience, I can say that shelter homes can be a very unsafe place. A friend of mine got so badly beaten up by the matron that she broke her spinal cord. A male teacher at the home where I used to live had tried to molest me.

> Moreover, as children of sex workers—because we carry our stigma everywhere with us—we are even more ill-treated in these homes compared to the other children.

She goes on to point out a cruel reality about shelter homes in West Bengal: 'There is a strange rule in government homes that girls have to leave the shelter homes and be on their own after they are 15 years of age. Most have no source of earning at 15 and have no place to go'. Pinky now shares her house with Pratima and Priyanka who have had to leave their shelter homes after turning 15. Pratima accompanies Pinky to all AP meetings to learn how the organization works before she formally joins. Pratima said that they have lot of fun staying together at Pinky's and she would like to call their present residence a 'happy home'.

The idea of home is also troubled by their experiences. While all those we spoke to believe that they should not be forcibly taken away from their mothers and feel the need for living at a place that they can call home, they remain sceptical about whether marriage is the most secure way of ensuring that they are closest to the imagination of an idealized home. Since most girls are married off while they are minors in the hope that they will live away from the red-light area and their future will be secure, all of them are very critical about child marriage. As Chaitali says:

> I am a victim. I know what it is to be married off when you are a child. I remember how much I had to suffer. I don't want that to happen to anyone else. It is also necessary for us to understand that child marriage is no different from trafficking. But look at the hypocrisy in our society—while child marriage receives societal approval, sex work is shunned. When I didn't know what marriage was I had to get married. But now when I love someone I cannot marry because I know he will never respect me and be able to accept who I am, because I have chosen to become a sex worker.

Acutely aware of the perils of child trafficking and the processes through which it happens, young members of AP in some districts in West Bengal are continuously working towards preventing it. In an incident that took place in the Kalna district in July 2006, the district head of AP, Chandni Ghosh, a student of standard 4, along with other members, received information about a girl locked inside one of the houses in the red-light area. They immediately located her, contacted the local office of DMSC, and rescued the girl with the help of the police.[19]

The experience of police raids in brothels from a very early age has made the children very sceptical about the role of protection that the law enforcers play. Mithu described an incident where, during her pregnancy, she had come to visit her mother and the police suddenly raided their house. 'I was eating lunch. But we were all so scared that my mother made me run. In that pregnant state I ran for my life. I fainted after that and was really sick. Since then, I have developed a phobia about the police. Even now when I go for some work to meet the police I cannot talk. Simply put, I hate the police. They only abuse power. I am still very scared of them and cannot erase that memory out of my mind.' Pinky, who along with her work with AP has also been involved in the national campaign against child labour, says: 'I feel very angry at policemen. I have seen so many incidents where the police are beating up children on platforms and pavements mercilessly. But I cannot do anything because even my position is vulnerable. But some day I want to be able to give it back to them. Hit them back!'

As an advocacy group run by the children themselves, AP's concerns reach far beyond their condition as children of sex workers only within the red-light district. One of its first publicly released posters was a statement by the children against the US-supported Israeli bombings in Lebanon (2006), in which they strongly decried war. The concluding sentence of the poster said: 'We are kids; we have to be alive in the future. So let's stop all wars'.[20]

This endeavour is reflective of what politics of solidarity can do in place of politics of pity. The organization responded to the suffering people in Lebanon not through a statement that evoked any feeling of helplessness, but one which powerfully asserted a position of unanimously resisting any kind of aggression against the weak. In 2009, AP also brought out a rally to protest the racist attacks on Indians in Australia. That's the final of the three counter Rs—resistance, where they will confront being slotted as victims, who can only be concerned about their own suffering.

The troubles with victim-rhetoric that films like *BiB* perpetuate have not escaped AP members' scrutiny. As Gobinda says:

> The lives of sex workers and their children have become consumable products in the market. The mysteries surrounding the places where they live, the criminality of their livelihood, the helplessness in their lives have become very saleable topics for making films. *Born into Brothels* which won the Oscar capitalizes on this very image of helplessness in the lives of sex workers and their children. The film represents us as children whose lives are perpetually in peril. That we will all grow up to be bad people if we stay in the red-light areas and the only way out is to rescue us out of the brothels. This entire perspective is so disrespectful towards our mothers.

Pinky is more ruthless in her criticism:

> I have watched *BiB*—will anyone dare to make a film so unethically on anybody else's child? What did she do with all the Oscar money? I would have understood if she had secured the future of the children featured in the film with that money but she only made a good name for herself. How can anyone invade anyone's privacy like this? Why were the children asked to take pictures secretly? That is a ploy. Did she take permission before using the pictures of the women inside brothel spaces and sometimes even when they were with their clients? They show one woman changing her clothes. Will that not badly affect her child when his/her friends see that picture? Do you think they will not tease her and it will not be shameful for the child? If she really cared for the child she would never have done that. The directors only show the sex workers talking in foul language. Do you think other people living in good houses don't abuse? But can anyone dare to secretly shoot that and make a film on that? I know respectable people who live in good houses and ill-treat their children. Will you ask them to send their children to shelter homes? I feel very angry with the filmmaker for insulting us like this. Even our collectivization and struggles find no mention in the film.

The narration of these experiences—although fragmented—disturb the neatness with which the images of the 'suffering' lives of children of sex workers consume us. Clearly, they have had very difficult lives—but their entangled realities don't paint a picture of helplessness, but one where, in the face of acute stigma, they are powerfully resilient, reworking through the odds and resisting discrimination with equal gusto. Needless to say, AP's existence as a group owes a great deal of the strength to DMSC as an organization. Yet, it is an initiative that has sustained over five years, and had its first general election in 2009. Clearly, lending children of sex workers with the opportunity to voice their opinion makes them politically assertive and socially conscious citizens.

The starkly contrasting picture of the lives of children of sex workers who are part of AP is not an attempt to romanticize their 'political society'. Several of the images in *SoI*, *BiB*, or Apne Aap's book are something that many AP members will also identify with. Yet, in the face of adversity their response is not only despair, fear, and suffering. We will end this section by sharing two lengthy testimonies by Gobinda and Chaitali to illustrate how despair is being confronted with grit by these children. We offer no analysis of these testimonies to ensure that they remain unmediated by us as outsiders, being aware of the perils of having translated them from Bangla already. We remain accountable to all the children we interviewed for representing them. These two narratives are from the first interviews that we did in 2007 and they remain the most powerful.

Gobinda

My mother is a sex worker from Sonagachi. She used to pay someone to take care of me, in a 'family house', from the time I was six months old. That's where I grew up. When I was two years old, I would visit my mother and stay with her sometimes. I remember, when clients visited her, she would ask me to sit outside. Later, at the age of five, my mother took me to Ranaghat, where I was admitted to a home for sex workers' children. That's where I started studying and completed standard 4. From there I moved to another school to study further. That same year, during Durga Puja, my mother had to take me out of school because my classmates had found out that I lived in a home for sex workers' children and they made fun of me because of that. I started staying with my mother and took admission in another school by hiding my identity. Even there my friends found out that I stayed in Sonagachi and started misbehaving with me. I had to leave that school as well, and went to stay at my maternal uncle's house. Once again I took admission in another school by hiding my identity. At that point, my mother's earnings were very low.

She couldn't pay my uncle for my expenses. It was here that I studied till standard 10 […]

I was once interviewed on a Bengali TV channel as a sex worker's child who had passed the standard 10 board exams. This led to further harassment and I wasn't given admission forms in many schools. Finally, I got admitted in standard 11, in yet another school closer to Sonagachi. Alas, there too friends found out that I was a sex worker's child. One day, in class, when the teacher was telling us about HIV/AIDS, he mentioned that it spreads through sex workers. I couldn't help but interrupt him and tell him that it wasn't true—in fact, sex workers were doing a lot of work at Sonagachi to control the spread of the disease. This, of course, didn't go down very well with him and I was reprimanded […]

Sometimes I used to feel, why does Ma need to do this work when it brings so much misery and pain to my life […]. *I wanted to open a factory where only sex workers would work, including my mother* […].

But later when I met other sex workers' children through DMSC and discussed this, we all realized that society was to be blamed for the way we were being treated, and not our mothers. They were only trying to earn a living to support their families and children— and there was no reason why people should think of them as 'fallen' women.

Through Amra Padatik we are trying to reach out to as many children of sex workers as possible—talk to them about our experiences and unite them to fight against the stigma and disrespect that is meted out to us and our mothers because they are sex workers. We have already got some financial support and are working hard to develop a plan of action for the next few years.

We believe that, as children, it is our responsibility to be part of our mothers' struggles. We are our mothers' foot soldiers who will lead their struggle from the front […].

Chaitali

As a child I used to stay with my mother—but my house felt like a jail. My mother kept me in a separate room and told me that she used to do 'bad' work. I would go to school and come back home. I didn't go out with friends because my mother always wanted me to get back home fast so that I was safe. I used to see men come and go but never understood what they came for. My mother also worked in a hotel and I hardly spent time with her. The landlord and his wife were good people and loved me a lot. I spent a lot of time with them. Once when I was around 10 years old, there was some property dispute in the family, and I heard my grandmother mention that I was 'jarok santan' (bastard child) and so I had nothing to do with the family property. I also heard her say bad things about my mother. That's when I started wondering, what is it that my mother does? And I started to hate it [...] *but now that I understand everything I don't hate it anymore* [...].

At the age of 13, I was married off to a sex worker's son. They lived in a 'family house' outside Sonagachi. This is where I came to know about sex work, drinking, and all such things. It's funny that I had no idea about all this when I used to stay with my mother. I had a very unhappy marriage and was made to do all the housework. They would always speak badly about my mother. I gave birth to a child soon after marriage and had to take care of him too. People keep talking about child trafficking into sex work, but I can tell from my personal experience that child marriage is a form of child trafficking. If only my mother's work was not stigmatized, she wouldn't have to worry so much about my safety and think of marriage at such an early age as the only means to my security. When the marriage became unbearable, I left my in-laws and came back to stay with my mother.

I tried taking up some job. But at every place people made sexual advances. I couldn't continue anywhere. It was then that I got involved with DMSC [...].

In 2005 we formed Amra Padatik [...]. *Whenever sex workers' children are in some trouble we go and help them. When Gobinda was refused an admission form after his board exam because of a TV interview where he had mentioned that he was a sex worker's child, we supported him and made sure that he got the form* [...]. *Another child was harassed by the landlord after his mother died; we went and made sure that he wasn't evicted* [...].

Over the next few years we are planning to start tutorials and install computers at all DMSC health clinics where children from those areas can come and meet each other [...] *and build support groups for each other so that they don't have to face the hardships that I, Gobinda, and a lot of us have faced* [...].

Beyond Captivity

The vision with which Gobinda, Chaitali, and Mithu founded AP has progressed—not necessarily in the way structured projects progress, but in directions that have continued to foreground the voices of children of sex workers as active citizens with politically astute perspectives on their lives as well as the conditions of rightslessness around them.

Captivity in brothels can be one of the many experiences that mark the lives of the children of sex workers. However, for those of us who deduce that through looking at them from afar, it is simply a perceived experience. Even if we work to establish its reality, it would still never qualify to be the only one. It is this recognition of a layered existence, of multiple childhoods, and a challenge to any morally universalist notion of customized childhoods which will allow us to resurrect a more agential politics for claiming children's human rights based on solidarity.

There's an urgent need for developing and emulating practices of research, representation, and intervention that foreground the issue of child rights—not from a-saviour-from-outside point of view, but one that shifts our observational frames to put the voices of the children of sex workers at the centre of human rights concerns. They must be regarded as powerful advocates of their own rights. It is important to acknowledge that they know best what will ensure them a more dignified life free of compassionate attempts to 'rescue' them and aesthetized methods of training and play that attempt to customize their lives according to the visions of kindhearted outsiders. Such attempts are, at best temporary, and at worst, come at the cost of abrogating their rights.

Unlearnings

When we watched *BiB*, we had already been associated with DMSC as feminist allies for many years. We supported their struggles for the right to sex work, and the rights of sex workers. We had been part of their rallies and written about their activism. As human rights lawyers, we had done legal-awareness workshops with their members. In the course of our interactions with sex-worker activists, we learned a key lesson in feminist politics that was conveyed to us through a well-known slogan of the global sex workers' rights movement: 'Nothing about us, without us'. We learned that the communities of people that a feminist engages and works with, must be regarded as active subjects capable of knowing, evaluating, and deciding on what is best for their lives; that the feminist-self who claims to be an ally in the struggles of marginalized people must not also claim superiority of knowledge and being.

Over the years, during our visits to DMSC's offices in north Kolkata, we'd meet many of the children of the sex workers milling about and participating in the collective's work. We'd join them to raise slogans at protests. Yet, until we had watched *BiB*, it did not occur to us with as much clarity that children of sex workers are a group that is used as the bait by abolitionist feminists to trump arguments in favour of the right to sex work. *Born into Brothels* was, in many ways, an extension of such a feminist position, and reinforced a similar image of the agency-less Third World sex worker.

Strangely enough, as pro-sex-work feminists, we had seldom thought of the children of sex workers from DMSC as fully agential subjects. Our focus was almost solely on the rights of sex workers. This included their right to the custody of their children, but not necessarily the children's right against forced removal from their mothers. However, the fact that the children had stakes in their mothers' struggles, that they too were political actors who were an integral part of the sex workers' rights movement, didn't dawn on us until we attended the protest rally that was led by AP that we narrate at the opening of this essay.

It was at this rally that we conceived the idea of a project on the collectivization of children of sex workers, and their activism as political actors.[21] We felt that it was necessary for the global human rights world, of which we were a part by virtue of our profession, to hear this story that we were learning from.[22]

As feminists whose politics was strongly informed by a postcolonial sensibility, we assumed that our idea already carried an ethical heft. As part of our participatory methodology, we decided to organize a meeting with a group of members from AP to share the idea with them and to get their feedback. While the group, comprising AP's office holders Pinky, Gobinda, Ratan, Mithu, and Chaitali, was happy about a project of this nature, they raised doubts about its transformative capacity. They were concerned that as researchers we will end up publishing the outcome in English, that too in some academic journal, which in effect, will not be of any use to them. It would only benefit us. We had embarked on the project from a pro-sex-work feminist position to counter abolitionist feminism's disregard for the voices of sex workers and their children. In our minds, we were their feminist friends, and the abolitionists were the foes. The meeting made clear that our feminist good intentions were not good enough. The suggestion came from one of them that we make a film that can both offer a counter-story to that of *BiB*, and one that AP can use as a part of their own advocacy work. Both Pinky and Gobinda had watched *BiB* and they were troubled by how a film that demeans them and their mothers could find such widespread appeal, not only globally, but also in India.

In 2011, we completed making the documentary film *We Are Foot Soldiers*,[23] which featured the five members of AP mentioned above as the protagonists. Alongside, we published an article that accompanied the film (Sircar and Dutta 2011: 333–49). While writing the article was a rehearsal of activist-academic conventions in feminism and jurisprudence, making the film was a provocation to unlearn a lot of these very conventions. It was not our inexperience in the technique of filmmaking that was the cause for this provocation. That challenge, although pertinent, we had overcome by bringing on board kindred friends who had the technical knowledge.[24] Rather, it was the challenge of thinking about a form of storytelling that was able to bring our pro-sex-work feminism into conversation with the politics of AP without letting it become the explanatory framework for our narrative. How do we tell a story which is both ours and theirs? How do we tell a story in which the aesthetics will not overwhelm the politics and vice versa?

The film was a collaborative exercise and yet not. The story couldn't be told without the children of sex workers being featured in it. Not only were their voices and images paramount, they were also involved in the planning of the film. In fact, on one occasion during the shoot, sex workers who have come to consider the camera as an extremely invasive tool, and justifiably so, objected to our filming. It was Gobinda who negotiated with them on our behalf. He convinced them that this project was telling their story and was important for their activism. It appeared to us that the children were, through such active participation, already assuming ownership of the film that was seeking to tell their stories.

As directors we exercised creative control and authority. At the time of filming, we decided to never enter the frame of the camera during interviews. We intended the audience to see what we saw, to become a part of our point of view. That space on the screen, within the frame, was exclusively for our five protagonists. At the time of editing, we followed AP's earlier suggestion about organizing the narrative in a way that can be used later as an advocacy tool and to that end, we divided the film into a set of themes—breaking stereotypes, resisting stigma, and so on—that were strongly articulated by them. We translated the spoken Bangla into English subtitles. Even as we tried to maintain fidelity to language, we exercised some latitude with trying to convey ideas and not just be literal. From over 12 hours of footage, the decisions to retain what would be a part of the 26-minute-long final cut was ours.[25]

Of course, these are standard dilemmas regarding the ethics of documentary filmmaking, especially when there is a clear differential in power between the filmmakers and the human subjects of the film. But for us, negotiating these dilemmas were more than a practice of professional ethics. These negotiations enabled us to witness a material encounter between our feminisms and a politics of their childhoods. Within pro-sex-work feminist discourses, the children of sex workers often appear either as an apology or a justification for their mothers' choice of occupation. Through conversations with our protagonists, we realized that such discourses overridden with sex work must be kept at bay if the children had to occupy centre stage in a narrative about their lives. This necessitated that we, as well as the sex workers, had to remain out of the frames; and thus, we decided to not interview any sex-working mothers.

The encounter between feminisms and childhoods that we saw was not one of rivalry, but unfolded as a dialogue in which we had to confront that feminism, even the most good-intentioned and self-reflexive versions, must recognize its limitations. For us, this recognition hasn't been a paralyzing force. The encounter has shown us the merits of unlearning to make way for learning anew.[26]

Notes

1. Sonagachi has been a zoned red-light district in Kolkata since the days of colonial occupation. Its proximity to the Calcutta Port enabled easy access to sailors and officers of the East India Company to the 'prostitutes'. In those days, the red-light district was marked out for the purposes of quarantine and surveillance by the Contagious Diseases Act to protect English soldiers. For a detailed historical insight into Sonagachi, see Banerjee S. 2000.
2. Our use of the term children does not denote minors; it refers to those born to sex workers, or those whose mothers sell sexual services for a living.
3. Amnesty International USA published a Companion Curriculum for *Born into Brothels* to be used by teachers in schools. The curriculum is available at http://www.amnestyusa.org/education/pdf/bornintobroth-elscurriculum.pdf; last accessed on 15 September 2010.
4. Advertisement copy on file with authors.
5. Simons, M. 1993. 'The Sex Market: Scourge on the World's Children', *New York Times*, April 9. Accessible on http://www.nytimes.com/1993/04/09/world/the-sex-market-scourge-on-the-world-s-children.html; last accessed 15 September 2010.
6. The photo can be viewed at http://www.collectivelens.com/photo/daughters-darkness-0
7. http:// http://www.collectivelens.com/photo/daughters-darkness-0
8. http://www.adventuredivas.com/docs/india/holy-cow/
9. http://www.indianvibes.de/newgenerations/?portfolio=born-into-brothels
10. http://dev.kidswithdestiny.org/projects/hope-house
11. http://apneaap.org/wp-content/uploads/2012/10/6-The-Place-Where-We-Live.pdf
12. https://www.youtube.com/watch?v=9xSMbMT69Vo
13. In a striking contrast of sorts, the Sampada Gramin Mahila Sanstha (*SANGRAM*), a sex-workers' collective in Sangli, Mahatashtra in western India came out with a book of testimonies of sex workers' children, titled *Brothel Born and Bred: Children of Sex Workers Speak* (December 2008). Each testimony in the book powerfully captures the hope and determination in the voices of the children of sex workers who have been featured, who respect their mothers' profession and dream of a future that includes not just education for themselves but better lives for their mothers within the brothel space. To read, visit https://www.sangram.org/upload/resources/brothel_born_and_bred.pdf

14. http://apneaap.org/wp-content/uploads/2012/10/6-The-Place-Where-We-Live.pdf
15. On file with authors.
16. This backlash against Sangram has connections with a larger politics of international funding for HIV/AIDS and anti-trafficking work.
17. All conversations with AP members quoted in this essay were conducted in Bangla. Extracts have been translated into English by us.
18. On file with authors.
19. *Kalna Theke Bolchhi, Nishiddho Palli Theke Kishori Uddhar*, 31 July 2006 (on file with authors).
20. On file with authors.
21. The initial funding for this project came from the National Child Rights Fellowship that we had received from Child Rights and You (CRY) in 2009 to write a research paper on Amra Padatik's activism.
22. We want to note that the lives of the children of sex workers aren't homogenous. There are many different forms of sex work—brothel-based, home-based, street-based etc. —which means that the lives of the children take varied forms along with the forms in which sex work is practised. While the children of sex workers living in brothels become easily identifiable, and therefore more vulnerable on certain counts, it also means that they are likely to have a community of people, including other sex workers' children, around them that is not available to children of home-based or street-based sex workers. Such specificities make their life experiences significantly varied and this deserves to be kept in mind.
23. *We are Foot Soldiers* [documentary film]. 2011. Directed by Debolina Dutta and Oishik Sircar. India: Public Service Broadcasting Trust.
24. Our team comprised Anindya Shankar Das, Prachi Tulshan, Anirban Ghosh, and Sakyadeb Chowdhury. We would like to acknowledge the inspiration drawn from Shohini Ghosh's important documentary film on DMSC. See *Tales of the Night Fairies.* 2002. Directed by Shohini Ghosh. India: Mediastorm Collective.
25. The decision to keep the film to exactly 26 minutes wasn't entirely ours. All Public Service Broadcasting Trust (PSBT)-funded films are broadcast on national television, and thus must meet a particular time slot.
26. 'We Are Foot Soldiers' is regularly used by both AP and DMSC as an advocacy tool.

3

Bollywood's Law

Cinema, Justice, and Collective Memory*

Law tells stories, just as stories are told about law.

—Peter Goodrich, 'Law by Other Means' (1998: 114)

[...] to see what law is go to the cinema; to see what cinema is go to the courts.

—Ranabir Samaddar, 'Beyond the Frame of Practical Reason' (2015: 71)

The Work of Reconstructive Imagination

In 2013, a Bollywood film[1] called *Kai Po Che* (Kapoor 2013a)[2] received both popular and critical attention from audiences and commentators alike. The retelling of the 2002 anti-Muslim pogrom in Gujarat—a sophisticatedly planned ethnocide that targetted Muslims, unlike its popular characterization as a riot, which is spontaneously provoked mob violence[3]—is part of the film's fictional plot and cathartic closure, and was one of the major reasons for this

* Written through 2014–15 in Melbourne, Cambridge, and Dublin; in the wake of Narendra Modi being elected as prime minister of India.

attention. While on the one hand, it was praised for taking a sensitive look at the pogrom and spoke of friendship, hope, and forgiveness in the midst of mindless religious hatred (Patel 2013), on the other hand, there was a lot of criticism about the cunning ways in which the film avoided questions of accountability, downplayed the enormity of the event, even as it acknowledged the trauma (Janmohamed 2013). When I first watched it on a pirated DVD in Melbourne, I felt that the film, in its narrative and aesthetic reconstructions of the pogrom, revealed—more than concealed—the workings of a nationalist, secularist, and developmentalist rationality in postcolonial India that has come to texture the mnemohistories of collective memory of the pogrom. As I read it, not only did the film not depict the violence in all its nuances (which was the standard critique), it also glorified love for the New India—a neoliberal and Hindu nation (a key element of Hindu right-wing discourse which provided the ideological justification for the violence) as the panacea for everyone who was affected by it. To put it simply, I, too, felt that the film lacked in its retelling of the events of 2002.

A few months after the film's release, a PIL was filed in the Gujarat High Court in Ahmedabad, demanding that its clearance by the Central Board of Film Certification (CBFC) in India be cancelled.[4] The CBFC had rated the film 'U', making it universally eligible for viewing without any age restriction. A news headline reporting the incident read: 'PIL against *Kai Po Che* for "biased" portrayal of Gujarat riots' (*The Times of India*, 3 May 2013). The petitioners, a lawyer named Bhautik Bhatt and another applicant, took issue with the representation of the 2002 violence in the film for its anti-Hindu bias. As the judgement noted, the two reasons for which the petitioners approached the court were: first, 'the film defames group of a certain community, in the guise that the members of the minority community were victimized'; and second, 'the film does not approach the topic evenhandedly and projects one community being more responsible than the other' (*Bhautik Vijaykumar Bhatt vs Central Board of Film Certification*, 23 September 2014: 1).

I was a little taken aback.[5] *The 3 Mistakes of My Life*, author Chetan Bhagat's novel on which the film was based, the film's publicity and trailers, and even the theatrical release did not attract any attention from the Hindu Right—including the ruling BJP in Gujarat at that time. It was primarily secular-leftists like me who found the film problematic for its bias in favour of Hindus, for not depicting the atrocity in all its nuances, and for explaining the causes of the violence through *realpolitik* framings that displaced its deep ideological foundations (Sircar 2013a; Mukherjee 2013; Ghufran 2013). And here, the petitioners felt that even in the film's soft pedalling of the violence carried out by Hindus, it depicted the majority community in a bad light. I did not think the petition stood any chance in court. The film could not have been challenged on its reconstruction of facts, because it did not make any claims regarding historical accuracy. It was, after all, a work of fiction, adapted from a novel. The filmmakers did not feel the need to offer a standard disclaimer regarding the story's relation to the pogrom. The court in its 2014 judgement rejected the petition by stating why the freedom of speech and expression of the filmmakers cannot be curtailed, especially because it was 'made on an imaginatory [sic] topic'. It might have been possible to restrain exhibition if the film had provoked sectarian violence because of the reasons that the petitioners had stated. However, as the judges noted: 'Nothing untoward has happened or [been] reported. The viewers across the country, with due maturity, have absorbed the theme' (*Bhautik Vijaykumar Bhatt vs Central Board of Film Certification*, 23 September 2014: 3).

Yet, the same sequence of fictive events—or 'imaginatory', as the court called them—in the film are considered a watered-down version of the *real* violence by some like me, and by those like Bhatt as being biased against Hindus. This encounter between law and film opens up a contestation about the truth claims that constitute collective memory in the realm of filmic reconstructions of mass atrocity. *Kai Po Che* (KPC) participates in the 'ideoscapes'[6] and 'lawscapes'[7] of collective memories which I consider to be mnemonic in nature, doing, what Jan Assman would describe as 'the ongoing work of reconstructive imagination': 'the past cannot be stored but always has to be "processed" and mediated' (1997: 14).

This reconstructive imagination also points at the complicated intimacies between law and the aesthetic, and the ways in which their encounter processes and mediates collective memory. The aesthetic provides the fictive grounding for the film, while the legal provides the traction for making, or appealing to, truth claims. The critics of *KPC*—both groups that point at the film's pro- and anti-Hindu bias—are engaged in contestations about the ways in which the stories of the pogrom are actively reconstructed and remembered. In recognition of this law–aesthetic conversation, this essay attempts to chart a response to the question: Do our legal investments in establishing the truth about the violence of Gujarat 2002 keep alive a faith in the aesthetic (in this case the cinematic) as an active archive of collective memory, and consequently, as a credible jurisprudential source that engenders imaginations of justice?

Law and image/imagination have played an important role in the making of collective memories of Gujarat 2002. This is the case especially for those like me who experienced it from a safe distance, consuming the unfolding of the horror on television screens or in newspapers, and continue to do so, given that the Gujarat pogrom has come to be one of the most mediatized events of mass violence in contemporary India (Ohm 2010: 123–44). The event's contested narratives are shaped through a set of iconic photographs—like Qutubuddin Ansari begging for mercy with folded hands or Ashok Mochi's war cry against Muslims with outstretched arms (Sahni 2012; Hazra 2012)—and landmark criminal trials of highly localized massacres—like the Best Bakery and Gulberg Society cases (Dhavan 2003; Katakam 2012)—that have not only produced a surfeit of reportage but have also offered templates for popular culture and aesthetic reconstructions in film, literature, and art. Despite their perceived incommensurability, law and image/imagination are porous archives seeping into each other constantly, and they share a tendentious intimacy in making, managing, and ordering collective memory.

Law and image, notes Cornelia Vissman, share 'a troubled relationship' (2008: 1). She identifies jurists as those who are most uncomfortable with images: 'Jurists fear images foremost and by vocation. After all, they are expected to establish order, a mission they see frequently challenged by the ambiguity of images' (Vissman 2008: 1). As Peter Goodrich critically observes: 'law [...] is a text that negates its images and denies the figurations of fluidity in its texts' (Goodrich 1995: x). Commenting on the 'aesthetic question' in law, Costas Douzinas and Lynda Nead write: 'Modern law is born in its separation from aesthetic considerations and the aspirations of literature and art, and a wall is built between the two sides [...] Art is assigned to imagination, creativity and playfulness, law to control discipline and sobriety' (Douzinas and Nead 1999: 3).

However, despite this historical opposition between law and aesthetics, one is deeply implicated in the other; they share a relationship that is troubled because of their collaborative contestations and not because of their antithetical orientations. There is an 'enriching asymmetry of their encounter' that connects 'justice [or injustice] and beauty [or the ugly]' (Ben-Dor 2011: 1). Clifford Geertz's observation that law, 'here, there, everywhere, is a distinct manner of imagining the real' (1983: 184) is a reminder of 'the imaginative life of the law and the way law lives in our imagination' (Sarat 2011: 2). In conceptually understanding law's imaginative habitations, particularly as they appeal to the visual, Richard Sherwin writes:

> If law is to be treated as part of contemporary visual culture, and of that need there be no doubt, it is not enough to consider the way in which law partakes in various aesthetic, cognitive and cultural codes that different visual media deploy. Law also shares in the various normative aspirations and afflictions that are bound up in the culture at large. For this reason, we must also be attentive to cultural conditions (2011: 3).

Collective memory is one such cultural condition which is paradigmatic of the contested collaborations between law and aesthetics. Collective memory—a term originally coined by sociologist Émile Durkheim, and subsequently developed by his student Maurice Halbwachs—is a mode of active remembering—unlike the hegemony of history—that is only possible to produce in groups, and not individually. As Halbwachs notes in his classic work, *On Collective Memory*: 'It is in society that people normally acquire their memories. It is also in society that they recall, recognize, and localize their memories' (1992: 38). Within group formations, collective memory is not generated only through commemorative interactions between group members, but also draw on 'publicly available commemorative symbols, rituals, and technologies' (Olick, Vinitzky-Seroussi, and Levy 2011: 21): 'collective memory is the *active past* that forms our identities' (Olick 2007: 20, emphasis mine).

In the context of the Gujarat pogrom, both law and cinema are 'publicly available commemorative symbols, rituals, and representations' that are in continuous engagement with an 'active past', one whose meanings and truths are being revealed and regenerated through continuous collaborative contestations—the ongoing investigations, trials, political rhetoric, and aesthetic memorializations. Legal and filmic reconstructions of the pogrom are archives that both lend to and derive meaning from their collective public reception and response.

A Small Retelling

Gujarat 2002 has been one of the most litigated, mediatized, and politically polarizing events of mass atrocity in contemporary India. The version of the events of the pogrom and the narrative that I hold on to through this chapter is aimed at foregrounding the 'small voices', to borrow historian Ranajit Guha's expression (1996: 1–12), that struggle to keep alive a certain memory of the pogrom in an India where they are constantly being 'drowned in the noise of statist [and increasingly corporatist] commands' (1996: 3), that propagate a dominant memory.

It has been over a decade since the western Indian state of Gujarat experienced one of independent India's most violent mass atrocities against its Muslim minority population.[8] Postcolonial India has experienced many incidents of anti-minority mass religious violence since the Partition in 1947: notably, the ongoing persecution of Muslims by the occupying Indian army in Kashmir, the 1983 massacre of Bengali Muslim immigrants from Bangladesh in Nellie, Assam, the anti-Sikh violence of 1984 in Delhi, the anti-Muslim violence of 1992 in Bombay (now Mumbai), and the anti-Christian violence in Kandhamal, Odisha in 2008. All of these events have been part of a larger script that animates the violence of postcolonial state-making. However, during Gujarat 2002, the sophisticated organization of the violence, the macabre forms of brutality, and the extent of state involvement, particularly police inaction and complicity, was unprecedented (Chopra and Jha 2014). Although official estimates state that the violence lasted for three days, many Gujaratis say that it lasted for as long as three months (Ghassem-Fachandi 2012: 1).

The killings, rapes, arson, and destruction continued unabated, yet despite a complete breakdown of law and order and grave instances of police inaction, a constitutional state of emergency was not declared by the president of India. It can be argued that such a decision reveals how the federal government—which at that time was the Hindu nationalist BJP-led NDA coalition—condoned the event.[9] This failure to impose president's rule rendered the violence as not deserving of federal attention in political and public consciousness, even though it could be considered to be a situation where there was a complete breakdown of the constitutional machinery.[10]

Starting on 28 February 2002, Hindu militant mobs—with active support from Hindu right-wing political factions like the Rashtriya Swayamsevak Sangh (RSS), the Vishwa Hindu Parishad (VHP) or the World Hindu Council, and the Bajrang Dal—singularly targeted Muslim across urban and rural Gujarat: killing close to 2,000 people (which included some Hindu, Christian, and Parsi lives as well), 'disappearing' an estimated 2,500 people, and driving tens of thousands homeless (Human Rights Watch 2002). Sexual violence was rampantly used to murder Muslim women, including those who were pregnant, which in turn was meant as a humiliation of the entire Muslim community (International Initiative for Justice in Gujarat 2003). Homes and property owned by Muslims were pillaged and burnt. Several mosques were desecrated and razed to the ground and roads paved over them. The violence targeted Muslims across the board, irrespective of their class status and residential locations (Engineer 2003).

That Muslims could be attacked in such a systematic manner without much resistance from the community was not only because of the state administration's complicity and police inaction. The sophisticated organization was also made possible because an attack on Muslims had been planned well in advance. This planning included the advance accumulation of arms by Hindu militant groups (Setalvad 2017: 213) and legislative planning of the city of Ahmedabad over many years, which resulted in the creation of Muslim ghettos whose captive populations were easy to attack (Rajagopal 2011; Jaffrelot and Thomas 2012: 43–81). The violence, thus, was not akin to a 'riot'—a spontaneous conflagration—but a result of long-term and systematic planning aided through state support that characterizes a 'pogrom' (Setalvad 2013: 10).

Even over a decade after 2002, many Muslims are still displaced, and many victim-survivors await compensation for damages (Amnesty International 2012; Choksi 2014). The criminal justice processes trying some of the perpetrators have been under threat of being compromised by political interference (Jaffrelot 2012: 77), the intimidation of witnesses and judges (Misra 2015; Johri 2015; Human Rights Watch 2004), and faulty investigations by the police and special investigation agencies (Mitta 2014; Ayyub 2016; Farasat and Jha 2016). By the Gujarat government's own admission made to the Supreme Court of India, of a total of 4,252 cases that victim-survivors registered with the police, nearly half were summarily closed by the police and thus never progressed to the trial stage (Chopra and Jha 2014: 174). For the few cases that did get to trial, some in the first instance resulted in full acquittal of all accused due to lack of evidence, reflecting the police's tardy investigation.

State impunity in India, especially for mass anti-minority violence, is strengthened by the active cooperation of the criminal justice system, and local political and patronage networks (Hoenig and Singh 2015; Nainar and Uma 2013). If lower conviction rates in the post-pogrom trials are one way to measure state impunity, then Gujarat has been particularly notable. As of 2012, in comparison to the national conviction rate of 18.5 per cent for cases related to riots, the conviction rate in cases related to the pogrom in Gujarat was 1.2 per cent (International Human Rights and Conflict Resolution Clinic 2014: ii). Despite the failures in investigation and prosecution related to criminal trials arising out of the pogrom, the judiciary has projected itself as an able and willing neutral arbiter of justice that is not complicit with the deep structures of Hindutva's anti-Muslim prejudice. This has been called the 'impunity effect': 'how a majoritarian regime conducts farcical legal proceedings that allow it to acknowledge, yet benefit from, state-backed violence against minorities' (Chatterjee 2017: 118).

Since the 2002 pogrom, Gujarat, under the chief ministership of Narendra Modi (since 2014, the prime minister of India) of the BJP, has been celebrated as one of India's most developed states with unparalleled urban and industrial infrastructure, and has become a preferred destination for corporate investments by multinationals. Due to the projections of rapid growth rates and ease of doing business, the Gujarat Model has been showcased by political parties and industrialists as a template for development in the New India. These projections have been questioned by scholars who have argued that Gujarat's growth is built on the structural marginalization of populations like Muslims, Dalits, and Adivasis. The Gujarat Model has been analysed as playing a role in consolidating the state's Hindu majoritarianism, and has also been deployed to whitewash the memories of 2002 (Sood 2012; Sud 2012; Chandoke 2012: 10–11; Jaffrelot 2015: 820; Hirway, Shah, and Shah 2014).

Modi's critics, particularly the secular-left, allege that he—along with other politicians in the Gujarat BJP—oversaw the planning and execution of the 2002 violence. It has been argued that the pogrom was meant to be a definitive step towards furthering the Hindu Right's vision of establishing India as a Hindu *rashtra* (Shani 2007; Balagopal 2002: 2117). Hindutva's neo-fascist vision, inspired by Zionism, wants to establish India as the holy land of Hindus only (Gregor 2006: 197–227; Noorani 2017; Sen 2015: 690). Muslims and Christians who are in the territory of India are outsiders because their holy lands are elsewhere. According to Hindutva ideology, those who follow Islam and Christianity must assimilate if they wish to stay in India, or their forced removal or killing will stand justified.[11] In the making of such an ideology against Abrahamic monotheism, Hindutva, ironically, advances an idea of Hindu religion tied to a single all-powerful god in the mythological figure of Ram.[12]

Gujarat has been considered by many as the Hindutva Laboratory that experimented with the pogrom in furtherance of its neo-fascist mission by teaching Muslims in India a lesson (Spodek 2010: 349–99). Modi and many of his ministers in Gujarat have been named in independent fact-finding reports (Concerned Citizens Tribunal 2002), survivor testimonies (Citizen's Initiative 2002), revelations by public servants (*The Hindu*, 20 August 2009; *The Times of India*, 1 October 2012), media investigations (*Tehelka*, 2 November 2007), and statements by the Supreme Court (*Zahira Habibulla H. Sheikh vs State of Gujarat*, 12 April 2004) for having ordered the police to step back and let the mobs rein free, for having instigated the mobs with their inflammatory anti-Muslim speeches,[13] and for justifying the pogrom by citing the Godhra train-burning incident of 27 February

2002 that killed 58 *kar sevaks* (Hindu pilgrims) as the legitimate cause for this *pratikriya* (retributive action) by angry Hindus.

The incident of the burning of compartment S-6 of the Sabarmati Express, carrying kar sevaks returning from Ayodhya,[14] allegedly by Muslim mobs at Godhra station in Gujarat, has come to stand as the temporal and ideological justification for the pogrom, or as the 'precipitating event' (Nussbaum 2004: 2). In line with the Newtonian explanation that Narendra Modi provided to rationalize the violence—'every "action" has an equal and opposite "reaction"'[15]—almost all references to the Gujarat pogrom till today continue to replay this cause-and-effect logic of equivalence: the Muslims burnt the Hindus in the train, so now the Hindus are taking their revenge on the Muslims.[16] Collective memory of the pogrom has thus been mobilized through the marking of Godhra as a singular history-vanishing 'flashpoint'[17] that turns Hindus into victims, and blinds us to the deep and dispersed structures of prejudice which informed how the pogrom was meticulously planned much before the train caught fire. It also masks the historical and economic antecedents of Hindutva in Gujarat that did not erupt only as a spontaneous and reactionary response to Godhra (Yagnik and Sheth 2005).

The foregrounding of this small retelling gains special significance at this particular point in contemporary Indian history, because Narendra Modi, the current prime minister of India, representing the Hindu nationalist BJP, was the chief minister (CM) and the home minister of Gujarat in 2002. The pogrom was orchestrated under his watch, and it has been argued on the grounds of empirical evidence that it is the pogrom that consolidated the Hindu vote in Modi's favour, and led to him winning four consecutive state elections in Gujarat as CM since 2002 (Kumar 2002: 270–5; Iyer and Shrivastava 2018: 104; Kenny 2017). In 2014, a sophisticated, media-managed mixture of soft Hindu nationalism and robust neoliberal developmentalism was the resounding campaign call that got Modi elected as prime minister in an election that saw a clear majority emerge for a single party for the first time since 1984 (Bobbio 2013: 123–34; Chacko and Mayer 2014: 518–28; Simpson 2006: 331–48).

During the run-up to his prime ministerial campaign, Modi was exonerated in 2012—given a 'clean chit'—by a Supreme Court of India–appointed special investigation team (SIT), which was tasked with specifically looking into three major massacres committed during the pogrom. The SIT's ostensible independent functioning has been questioned for procedural, investigative, and ethical lapses, especially in the way it has been complicit in protecting Modi from being criminally prosecuted (Mitta 2014; Setalvad 2013: 10–13; John 2017). A protest petition by Zakia Jafri, a victim-survivor, against the SIT's exoneration of Modi was also dismissed by a court in Ahmedabad in 2013, upholding the 'clean chit' (*Hindustan Times*, 26 December 2013). In response to this judicial exoneration of his accountability as head of state, Modi tweeted 'Satyameva Jayate', or 'truth alone triumphs' (*Hindustan Times* 2013), a Sanskrit expression from an ancient Hindu religious text (the *Mundaka Upanishad*) that has been secularized to accompany independent India's national emblem, and that serves as a foundational idea of Indian constitutionalism (Debroy 2012).

In fact, if postcolonial India's ostensibly secular legal system, with particular regard to the apex court, had to write its autobiography, it would repeat and echo Modi's tweet with equal exuberance when it comes to the judiciary's performance in delivering justice in cases of mass anti-minority violence, including Gujarat 2002 (Grover 2002: 355–88). Despite the failures in investigation and prosecution, judicial rationality—even in its condemnation of Modi as a 'modern day Nero' (*Zahira Habibulla H. Sheikh vs State of Gujarat*, 12 April 2004)—has projected itself as an almost transcendental arbiter, uncontaminated by any complicities with the deep structures of anti-Muslim prejudice of Hindutva that formed the foundations of the pogrom. In fact, in 1994, it was the SC that granted judicial imprimatur to the idea of Hindutva, recognizing it as a way of life rather than neo-Fascist ideology, providing much fillip to the institutionalization of Hindutva, which has only been strengthened over time (Cossman and Kapur 2001; Sen 2010).

Modi's version of the truth about Gujarat 2002 can be gleaned from his response in an interview to Reuters, where he likened his feelings for the victims as the sadness that a person in a car would feel if the driver runs over a puppy (Colvin and Gottipati 2013). Regarding continuing to fund relief camps for the Muslims displaced by the pogrom, Modi has expressed eugenicist panic about how they can turn into 'child producing centres' that will breed more Muslims (*Outlook*, 30 September 2002). The possibility of him expressing even an iota of remorse for the pogrom had turned so absurd that a news outlet had to speak of it in the form of an April Fool's day joke (*Firstpost*, 1 April 2013). His standard refrain whenever asked about the 2002 violence has been to say: 'Why even talk about 2002? [...] It's the past. What does it matter?' (quoted in Dalrymple 2014).

Beyond an Amorphous Politics

It is this 'let's move on' rhetoric that has animated a lot of the dominant legal and aesthetic discourses about how to remember the Gujarat pogrom. This point of view, however, is not reflective of a practice of denial, but one which, even while acknowledging the horror of the pogrom, either traces everything about it back to what it believes to be its originary cause, Godhra, or it relegates 'all violence to an amorphous "politics"' (Ghassem-Fachandi 2012: 2). Such relegation works to guard against 'summoning a past that still vividly lurks in the present', (Ghassem-Fachandi 2012: 2–3) and as Ghassem-Fachandi further notes:

> Such interpretations elide the more disturbing realization that not only do political parties manipulate constituencies for electoral gain, but people themselves become complicit in this by inhabiting representations, participating in acts and thoughts that have effects beyond the mere political calculations of those who organize violence. The political machinations of the pogrom reveal only half the story (2012: 3).

It is an attention to the mnemohistories of collective memory that can open up space for ways of remembering the pogrom that do not necessarily use the scaffolding of an amorphous politics to make the pogrom intelligible for public consumption and memorialization. The work of reconstructive imagination, in the way I use it in this chapter, is thus not about testing the mimetic accuracy of *a posteriori* narratives of the pogrom—in this case law and cinema—but to lend solidarity to the 'right to story-telling that the vulnerable in Gujarat are asked to, [and sometimes have been forced to] abandon' (Visvanathan and Setalvad 2014: 122).

This essay is interested in understanding the discursive intimacies and encounters of law and cinema in doing the work of reconstructive imagination that engender collective memories of the Gujarat pogrom. In these times of information overload—particularly in the way Gujarat 2002 has been spectacularized in media publics (Jain 2010: 163–79)—I argue that what should concern the critical jurisprudent is not a contest between memory and forgetting, as most on the secular-left in India continue to claim and fear with regard to the neoliberal whitewashing of the memories of the Gujarat pogrom, but rather the *ways* of remembering that are brought into being by the collective workings of law and cinema.[18]

In the last 13 years since the 2002 pogrom, a significant archive of memorialization in Bollywood films has come to exist. The most notable of these films are *Dev* (Govind Nihalani 2004), *Parzania* (Rahul Dholakia 2005), *Firaaq* (Nandita Das 2008) and the previously mentioned *Kai Po Che*—all which use the Gujarat pogrom as part of their narrative plots to reconstruct the events of the pogrom, and also to offer political and cultural commentary on the event.[19] Rather than *KPC*, which I referred to in the beginning, in this chapter, I will focus on *Dev*—the first Bollywood film memorializing the pogrom that was released in 2004.

Dev is a part of popular Hindi cinema of Mumbai, which in recent times, as Ashish Rajadhyaksha notes, has 'Bollywoodized' Indian cinema,[20] having turned it into a 'culture industry', that is constantly 'being created and marketed' as an aesthetic genre, industrial product, and economic practice (Rajadhyaksha 2008: 20). In its culture-industry avatar, cinema occupies an extremely significant place in India's cultural, political, and public life and in the wake of Bollywoodization, in its transnational economic lives (Mishra 2002; Ganti 2013). M. Madhava Prasad has called Indian cinema 'a site of ideological production [...] as the (re)production of the state form' (Prasad 1998: 9). Bollywoodization has entrenched this further, with the emergence of 'techno-nationalism' as '*the* Bollywood thematic' (Rajadhyaksha 2008: 29, emphasis in original). This thematic proffers 'a discourse of love and a discourse of law—the two fundamental registers of universality' (Prasad 2008: 46) that has made Bollywood cinema 'indispensable to the State' (Rajadhyaksha 2008: 34). It has made the film industry win 'for itself, a distinct, even unique, space for spectatorial address and spectatorial attention that even today is not shared by any of its other ancillary industries [like] [...] television [...]' (Rajadhyaksha 2008: 35). Bollywoodization's spectatorial affects, both inside and outside the theatrical space, and across geographical locations, are sutured through the cinema's address that produces a distinct public of cinematic citizens (Liang 2005: 366–85) where the 'ticket-buying [or DVD buying] spectator assumes certain rights like that of 'the right to enter a movie theater, to act as its privileged addressee' (Rajadhyaksha 2008: 33). As a community of cinematic citizens, 'spectators were, and continue to be, symbolically and narratively, aware of these rights, aware of their political underpinnings, and do various things [...] that constitute the famous "active" and vocal Indian film spectator' (Rajadhyaksha 2008: 33). By virtue of this status, the cinematic citizen carries the authority to pass judgement on a film's form, content, and context.

These observations are significant because it is in the realm of the state/nation/affect analytic that cinema's relationship to law and memory is both forged and fraught. Bollywood cinema, thus, provides a valuable archive for an analysis of how collective memories of the Gujarat pogrom and its relation with law, are actively engendered and ordered. While photographic or documentary images of 2002 have focused on phantasmagoric violence, films have woven fictive representations of the violence with narratives of the everyday and the ordinary that Bollywood's many publics can connect with at the level of the quotidian and not the exceptional. The use of music and songs, typical of this genre, add texture to the fictive narrative that enhance their affective appeal, especially how it has been used in the conjuring of a national imaginary in the New India (Dutta 2013: 231–45).

Bollywood cinema's reconstructive imagination of the pogrom not only commemorates the event, but also develops a vision of cinematic justice that calls on imaginations of law to play a specific role in the memorialization of the pogrom. I will demonstrate how *Dev*, even while recognizing the horror of the pogrom, offers a vision of justice that valorizes the violent techniques of postcolonial state-making, which actually formed the foundations for the pogrom. In its memorialization of the Gujarat pogrom, *Dev*'s filmic archive of collective memory works as a 'narrative compact' (Basu 2012: 12) between law and cinema to engender a particular way of remembering: one that aligns itself with the state-making practices of the new postcolonial India, even as it acknowledges the horror of the event. This way of remembering works through what I provisionally call a 'developmental juridical rationality', practised through the triad of secularism,[21] legalism,[22] and developmentalism.[23] This rationality, even as it condemns the visible violence of religious sectarianism, keeps the deep-seated structural and ideological violence of the putative secular postcolonial Indian nation against its Muslim minorities intact.

Cinema as Minor Jurisprudence

In its examination of the Gujarat pogrom, legal analysis has remained mostly concerned with the institutional discourse of trials, investigations, judgements, and legislations, focusing on criminal-law issues related to impunity, constitutional issues related to the rule of law and secularism, and human-rights and international-law issues related to the freedom of religion, citizenship, and transitional justice. However, the aesthetic dimensions of law have not been attended to in this body of legal work on Gujarat 2002, despite the fact that law occupies a significant place in all aesthetic reconstructions, particularly films.[24] As I understand, this is because, on the one hand, law in jurisprudential analysis of the pogrom has seldom been imagined as an aesthetic category and on the other, it is constantly burdened by the demands of being a problem-solving practice, meant only to deliver justice as quantifiable result: convictions, compensation, reparations, and legislations.

I understand cinema as a credible source of jurisprudence that we encounter as the subterranean other of the hegemonic jurisprudence of state legalism. The state, in practising its sovereign craft to mete out justice for the victim-survivors of the pogrom, had turned *parens patriae.* This doctrine has been used as a 'spectacle of emancipation' and parental care by the state to absolve itself of accountability in cases of mass harm in India (Sircar 2012: 527–73), is aptly captured by the Ciceronian maxim, *salus publica suprema lex* (the safety of the state is the supreme law). The working of state law towards justice for victim-survivors is a means for the very state that enabled the pogrom, to secure its symbolic and its sovereign power, to keep intact the 'weighty mythology' of what Sudipta Kaviraj has called 'the imaginary institution of India', born out of a 'narrative contract' between history-making and the nation, which makes the idea of the Indian nation an 'ideological construct' (2010: 167).

Aesthetics, and in this case cinema, thus, enters collective memory of the Gujarat pogrom not as an end to state law, but as an encounter with what Peter Goodrich calls a 'minor jurisprudence' that repeatedly challenges 'the dominance of any singular system of legal norms', and 'neither aspires nor pretends to be the only law or universal jurisprudence' (Goodrich 1996: 2). I do not think of minor jurisprudence as equivalent to legal pluralism. I use the expression to not talk about a diversity of legal imaginations, but how law needs to be understood as an assemblage, or what Deleuze and Guattari have termed 'the machine of justice' (1986: 81). A recognition of law as an assemblage of minor jurisprudences is an assertion that there is nothing like a major jurisprudence—because the machine of justice is a constantly mutating assemblage based on the jurisdiction of minor jurisprudence that it is located in.

I also do not valorize minor jurisprudence in the aesthetic archive merely as a romanticized category of resistance to hegemonic state law. Creating a hierarchy between law and aesthetics defeats the very aim of thinking about their conjoined habitus—narrative compact—in the making of collective memory, and their consequent ordering through juridical developmental rationality. Rather, my account of minor jurisprudence in reading *Dev* is a story of complicities—between law and aesthetics, their inflections and contaminations, their leakages and seepages. Understanding minor jurisprudence as such becomes necessary given why I have chosen to characterize Gujarat 2002 as a *pogrom*, and not as riot or genocide, as it has generally been understood in most of the existing literature on Gujarat 2002.[25]

I draw on the work of Parvis Ghassem-Fachandi, who understands a pogrom as 'an event driven by [the narrative compact of] words and images, as much by the associations and invocations that precede it as by those that accompany it. The enactment of the Gujarat pogrom followed a script collectively shared on the streets and in the media representations' (Ghassem-Fachandi 2012: 1): 'the pogrom was an acting out of [this] imaginary script' (Ghassem-Fachandi 2012: 64–5). The narrative compact of law and cinema—in the ways in which it has contributed to the making of a 'disgusting' Muslim subject—has been 'the symbolic repository to imagine violence' (Ghassem-Fachandi 2012: 65) that was already being performed in Gujarat much before the actual violence began on 28 February 2002. And by extension, has also contributed to imaginations of post-violence justice. As Ghassem-Fachandi writes:

> As informed by this script, the pogrom violence was motivated not merely by an 'initial' violent attack—the burning of Hindu pilgrims in Godhra—but by a mimetic desire that preceded the Godhra incident and provided a rationale for the enactment of violence (2012: 65).

This script of violence emerges out of the entanglements and intimacies between law and aesthetics, both as method and meaning, that frames and orders collective memories of the pogrom. Taking minor jurisprudence of the cinematic archive seriously can show what Shoshana Felman calls the 'juridical unconscious' (Felman 2002) in this script, which is the affective life of the law as lived in the cinematic publics of Bollywood.

A Jurisprudential–Aesthetic Reading of Bollywood's Law

Given law's symbolic and spectral presence in the way the filmic reconstructions of Gujarat 2002 frame collective memory, it is imperative that law is understood as a discursive category that is not restricted only to the texts of legislations and judgements in its making of collective memory, but also informs aesthetic imaginations of justice. I use a jurisprudential–aesthetic lens as a method of reading *Dev* to understand the work of law *as* and *in* aesthetics, in fashioning particular ways of remembering the pogrom. By *law as aesthetics*, I mean its aesthetic incantations beyond its scriptural organization and articulation, and by *law in aesthetics*, I mean the form and place of law in aesthetic imaginations of justice. Such a reading renders visible the workings of the law–cinema narrative compact in the making of collective memories of the pogrom, and managing the aftermath of atrocity.

Building on such an understanding, the jurisprudential–aesthetic lens as a method of reading cinema seeks to avoid the two standard approaches in law and film scholarship. The first is to not 'reduce film to a resource for specific legal issues, points or questions', and the second, to not let 'each medium [law and film that is] retreat [...] to its own corner relatively unscathed and looking pretty much as it had before the encounter' (Seymour 2004: 107). This method will read law's representations, not in the corrective or mimetic, but the 'affective register', that is, to read *Dev* not only for the story of the pogrom that it tells, but also the intensity it generates through its visual and auditory dimensions in engendering particular ways of remembering the pogrom (Buchanan and Johnson 2009: 39).

The minor jurisprudence of cinema will thus be considered as a 'system of memory' (Goodrich 1996: 1). The significance of unravelling minor jurisprudences in the aesthetic archive of cinema lies in the fact that the 'moving image provides a domain in which legal power operates independently of law's formal institutions' (Sarat, Douglas, and Umphrey 2005: 1). In lending meaning to social relations, law and film share a relationship, in which they use their distinctive and discursive narrative styles to make powerful symbolic gestures towards witnessing and truth telling. As Jessica Silbey writes:

> The affinity of law and film lies in their mutual manufacture of truth through strategies of representation and storytelling and also in the power of these truth claims to structure and regulate social relations. Film, no less than law, changes our perceptions of reality; it shapes our understanding of the world. The power of both film and law derives at first from the intensity of the personal faith in believing what we see [and hear] (*bearing witness and judging based on the act of witnessing*) (2014: 26, emphasis added).

Imaginations of cinematic justice, thus, emerge from this relationship that law and film share in their ability to open up the space of affective reception such that the act of embodied witnessing and the responsibility of judging coalesce in the spectator. By cinematic justice I do not only mean the representation of law and justice in film, but more importantly, as Alison Young puts it, 'how cinema is jurisprudence', in how it generates judgement outside of the scriptural confines of law books, and the architectural confines of the courtroom (Young 1997: 31). A double-play between law and the aesthetic language of cinema, one which undermines and reinforces imaginaries of justice simultaneously, is what the interpretive work of the jurisprudential–aesthetic lens aims to demonstrate in *Dev* as an instance of Bollywood cinema's mnemonic reconstructions of collective memories of the Gujarat pogrom. Such a reading shows us the way Bollywood's visions of cinematic justice do not make its spectators forget the pogrom, but at the same time, orders the *ways* in which it is remembered.

Since 1991, when the Indian economy was liberalized—that temporal marker of the birth of the New India—mainstream Hindi cinema's form, content, reach, and consumption started appealing to an audience that cut across class, caste, religion, gender, and national barriers. What was once, in the words of Ashis Nandy, 'a slum's eye view of politics' has today also become a '*haute bourgeoisie*', view of politics as well (1999: 1, emphasis in original). There does not, any longer, remain an older binary opposition between a '"low", popular, resistant Hindi cinema and a hegemonic "high" literary culture in India' (Virdi 2003: xi). What makes Bollywood cinema attract such wide-ranging appeal is what Ranjani Mazumdar refers to as its 'techno-folk form'—like Rajadhyaksha's 'techno-nationalism' discussed before—which is achieved '[by] combin[ing] folk traditions with new cinematic technology [that offers an] unabashedly hybrid cultural form that narrates the complicated intersection between tradition and modernity in contemporary India' (Mazumdar 2007: xvii). This hybridity is sustained by invoking symbols of developmentalist desire on one hand—democracy, rule of law, wealth, the market, glitz, fashion, technology, urbanity, exotic foreign locales, the good life—and on the other, by appealing to mythopoetic tropes of secular relationality in the family, community, and most importantly, the nation.

The complicated intersection between developmentalist desires and tropes of relationality does not always happen through neat categorizations of the former as markers of modernity and the latter as tradition, particularly at a time in the new postcolonial India where the lines between the state and the market are increasingly getting blurred. Bollywood primarily produces privately funded cinema, so while the films can be said to have deep investments in a proto-neoliberal ethos, they cannot be said to have a direct connection with promoting state propaganda. Yet, as filmmaker Saeed Mirza has sharply noted: '[a] certain kind of cinema exists only because a certain kind of state exists',[26] as is evident in the recent instances of growing intimacy between Bollywood and the BJP government (Sharma 2019). M. Madhava Prasad, in his book, *Ideology of the Hindi Film: A Historical Construction,* studies 'cinema as an institution that is part of the continuing struggles within India over the form of the state' (Prasad 1998: 9). Although written in 1998, within a few years of India liberalizing its economy, Prasad's observations still carry trenchant currency:

> Cultural production too registers this reality through the recurring allegorical dimension of the dominant textual form in the popular cinema. [...] What the allegorical dimension of texts represents is the continuing necessity to conceive the state form which will serve as the ground for cultural signification. Through the allegorical scaffolding, texts register the instability of their ground of practice and signification, as well as the continuing possibility of struggles *over* the state, of struggles to reconstitute the state (1998: 9, emphasis in original).

The most potent site for contests over the allegories of the state form is cinema in general and Bollywood cinema in particular. In the mythology of the New India—marked by the narrative contract between Hindutva and neoliberalism—the state and the nation seamlessly merge as a dominant allegorical trope in this kind of cinema, which, historically, as many have claimed, has been 'an exemplar of secularism', with 'Islamicate roots' (Chadha & Kavoori 2008: 131). As Jyotika Virdi writes in her analysis of representations of the 'nation' in mainstream cinema:

> Popular films touch a major nerve in the nation's body politic, address common anxieties, and social tensions, and articulate vexed problems that are ultimately resolved by presenting mythical solutions to restore an [sic] utopian world. The situation, complication, action and resolution in all popular film narratives both creates and is created by a collective social imagination [...] The concept of nation subtends that imagination in Hindi films, and centres its moral universe. All ethical dilemmas revolve around the nation; good and bad, heroes and villains are divided by their patriotism and anti-patriotism (2003: 9).

Law, in all its discursive forms, is the scaffolding that plays the role of framing the allegories of the nation-state form. The Indian cinema does not have a distinct law-film genre, although, as Prasad has pointed out, in the wake of Bollywoodization, a 'post-national aesthetic' has developed 'where the old dramatic courtroom confrontations seem to have lost their place', replacing law as one of the fundamental registers of cinematic universality with a rise in an Anglicized register of love (Prasad 2008: 47). This replacement, however, as I understand, is that of law's identifiable statist symbols, like the courthouse and the courtroom. But even in this new discourse of love, the meta-trope of the nation, and the sub-tropes of community and family, draw on dharmic thinking (traditions of Hindu Law founded on the 'Dharmaśāstra')[27] in moments of 'acute crisis' (Virdi's ethical dilemmas), 'to close the gap between the fallible world of human law and a divine ontology of justice' (Basu 2010: 3). As Anustup Basu, writing about imaginations of justice in the Bollywood aesthetic, explains, 'Law, it must be remembered, is for judgment, not justice. The former is an earthly discursive phenomenon, prone to error and adjustment; the latter is a divine ideal toward which historical procedures of judgment aspire but never quite reach' (2010: 3).

This ancient-mythical rendering of justice in Bollywoodized cinema, seems to coincide with what has been referred to as the 'dream life of law', or the 'mythic discourse', in the law-film genre in the West, where '[i]nasmuch as legal legitimacy is derived from society's perceptions of historical and cultural truths, generating myth is crucial to building legitimacy' (Sarat, Douglas, and Umphrey 2005: 11). To quote Sherwin: 'The battle to control the constitutive norms of myth by taking over the means of cultural production is crucial to many aspects of law and politics' (2005: 106). The trope of the myth, as Silbey notes, plays a role in connecting law, film, and memory: 'film, like memory can be mythic […]. This mythic memory is law's popular consciousness' (2014: 31). The mythic in the cinematic allegories of law and justice draws on dharmic thinking, which affectively marks the Hinduness of the nation-state's imagination in Bollywood cinema. Keeping this myth alive, even when fractures and fragments on the nation's filmic canvas contest it, is the ideological script for Bollywood cinema. This mode of dharmic address is directed at the spectatorial publics of a community of cinematic citizens for whom the secular nationalism of Hindu thought is held up, as Tejaswini Niranjana notes, as 'a marker of the readiness to enter the "modern" age, and the modern person produced as "Indian" was the free, agentive, romantic subject of liberal humanism' (quoted in Liang 2005: 372). This modern cinematic citizen is also a mythic construction, 'while allegedly a neutral category, is invariably marked invisibly as middle class, upper caste, Hindu and male' (Liang 2005: 373).

Keeping this specificity of the Bollywood aesthetic in mind, my reading of *Dev* attends to the mythic in the cinematic allegories of law and justice. The work that dharmic thinking does in Bollywood's legal imaginary, as I will show, affectively marks the Hinduness of the nation-state and its secular constitution.

Dev: A Hindu Constitution?

Made by critically acclaimed filmmaker Govind Nihalani, with superstar Amitabh Bachchan in the lead, *Dev*'s narrative centres on the violence of Gujarat 2002, though it is not represented as a pogrom, but as a riot. Released in 2004, *Dev* was the first Bollywood film made on the Gujarat pogrom. Its theatrical release took place a few months ahead of India's general elections in 2004 (in which the Hindu right-wing BJP was voted out at the centre, though it continued to win elections in Gujarat), and soon after the controversial Best Bakery case (which was one of the major criminal trials arising from the killing of 14 people at a bakery in the city of Vadodara during the pogrom), was shifted out of Gujarat to Mumbai based on an order by the SC (to ensure a fair trial and guard against the intimidation of witnesses).[28]

Dev opens with a standard disclaimer: 'All characters and incidents in this film are fictitious and bear no resemblance to any person living or dead or to any incident whatsoever. Any similarity so perceived is purely coincidental'. Despite the fact that *Dev*'s story is located in Mumbai, and makes no mention of the Gujarat pogrom, the *pure coincidence* is that the key moments in its plot and narrative borrow from events that happened in 2002 in Gujarat. The violence against Muslims in the film is preceded by a precipitating event like that of the Godhra train-burning incident. *Dev*, interestingly, even in its non-naming and non-identification with the Gujarat pogrom, frames its narrative in the same chronology as the 2002 pogrom, the death of Hindus in the train compartment is replaced by a bomb blast at a Hindu temple that becomes the trigger for the killing of Muslims. In fact, it was because of these striking similarities with actual events from 2002 that legal action was initiated against *Dev* by private petitioners—much like *KPC*—who demanded a ban claiming that the film could instigate sectarian tensions because audiences would identify the connection between the plot and the pogrom (Pandya 2004).

As journalist Ayesha Khan reports, when *Dev* released in Vadodara, theatre owners put out advertisements in local dailies calling on both Hindus and Muslims to come and watch the film, to get as much business as possible, fearing that it might be banned by a court order. The fact that *Dev*'s story was similar to events related to the pogrom, was apparent from the text of an advertisement, which read: 'Watch Vadodara's Zaheera Sheikh-inspired Kareena Kapoor's role. Naked portrayal of riots, inactive police force and non-performance at the behest of the chief minister'. In fact, as Khan noted, the audiences would shout out 'Zaheera Sheikh' when actress Kareena Kapoor appeared on the screen (Ayesha Khan 2004). In another reported incident, during the screening of the film in Jamnagar, a city in Gujarat, Hindu and Muslim audiences engaged in a heated argument on the film. In consequence, the theatre authorities had to stop the screening and also refund the price of the tickets to the audience (Pandya 2004). *Dev*, it is possible to argue, brought into being, through its surrogate address about sectarian violence, cinematic publics that identified the film with the Gujarat pogrom, despite its disclaimer of being fictitious.[29] This identification also was not mere familiarity with the event. As Martha Nussbaum wrote, commenting on her experience of watching the film in an Ahmedabad theatre: 'the mood of the audience was staunchly anti-Muslim' (Nussbaum 2007: 10).

Like any other Indian film approved for public exhibition, *Dev* inaugurates the legal–aesthetic narrative compact of cinematic citizenship by displaying a certificate from the CBFC which declares its images and sounds as legitimate speech, an archive of state-sanctioned memory, and its audience are made the contractually rightful recipients of its memorial narrative. The film was classified for viewing as

'Adults Only', constituting an imagined mature cinematic public, as was referred to in the *KPC* judgement discussed at the beginning of the chapter, who might be able to absorb the film without being provoked to resort to violence, unlike the murderous mobs during the pogrom. The CBFC certificate can be read as what Goodrich has called 'obiter depicta' (Goodrich 2014)—an iconic legal emblem that any film-watching Indian would be extremely familiar with. The certificate, carrying the secular insignia of the Indian state, lends life and form to the relations between law, cinema, memory, the nation-state, and the citizen. It activates a state-making and state-preserving rationality in the New India that attests to Bollywood's 'cinematic apparatus and its pedagogic role as the disseminator of modernity' (Prasad 2008: 46).

The English and Hindi titles of *Dev*, digitally stylized to emerge out of flames, suggesting a trial by fire, is accompanied by an intense background score in which a chorus of deep male voices recites a Sanskrit *shloka* (chant) from Chapter 2, Verse 27 of the *Bhagavad Gita*: 'Karmanye Vadhikaraste Ma Phaleshu Kadachana, Ma Karmaphalaheturbhurma Te Sangostvakarmani'. Its English translation means: 'You have a right to perform your prescribed duty, but you are not entitled to the fruits of action. Never consider yourself the cause of the results of your activities, and never be attached to not doing your duty' (Prabhupada 1983: 69). It is this message from the *Gita*—'of action without consequence' (Kapila and Devji 2010: 271)—that frames the ethico-juridical universe that the film conjures.

The invocation of the Hindu holy book and the use of language in the title sequence offer a telling instance of how Hindutva ideology subliminally informs *Dev*'s affects of initiation and spectatorial address. The use of English and Hindi in the titling suggests the practice of what Prasad has called the 'structural bilingualism of the Indian nation-state': 'a state of affairs where the multitude of Indian languages (here counted as one) function under the direction of a meta-language in which alone the national ideology can be properly articulated' (Prasad 2008: 45). It is through Bollywood cinema that the meta-languages of English and Hindi have thus emerged as 'defining the linguistic order of new India' (Prasad 2008: 45), in which English works as the language of secular neoliberal aspiration, and Hindi as that of secular nationalist unity: a classic instance of techno-nationalism or folk-nationalism at work. What this has done is to wipe out the Islamicate presence of Urdu—much in line with what the proponents of Hindutva would ideally want—as a language that would always appear on film posters (Mazumdar 2003), and opening title sequences of Bollywood cinema 'as a matter of routine' (Prasad 2008: 46).

The seamless blending of the Sanskrit shlokas from the *Bhagavad Gita*, and the English–Hindi titling of *Dev*, initiates the pedagogical project of Bollywood cinema in naturalizing Hindutva's secular narrative that reduces anti-Muslim violence to tragedy and politics, and celebrates the mythical Hindu foundations of modernity in India that the constitution is popularly believed to enshrine.[30]

Dev's story is set at a time in India—taking its cue from the Gujarat pogrom—that is rife with sectarian tensions. The main character in the film is Dev Pratap Singh (played by Amitabh Bachchan), a joint commissioner of police in Mumbai. The film's subtitle—'He chose to walk the razor's edge…'—is a comment on Dev's personality: a police officer who does not fear to stand by his convictions, and takes his responsibility as a policeman of upholding the rule-of-law and protecting the nation-state from 'terrorists' so seriously, that he is known for carrying out and defending extrajudicial killings. The film portrays Dev's belief in the supremacy of law as a virtue, especially in the way he repeatedly declares in the film that he does not discriminate between terrorists based on their religion. The intensity of the virtue is established when the film opens with Dev defending his act of shooting a protesting college student for rebuking the authority of the police. Such a portrayal is, by extension, a comment on the rule-of-law as a value-neutral idea that is purely committed to maintaining national security by killing anyone, irrespective of identity, who poses a threat to the nation-state.

The other important character in the film is Dev's very good friend and colleague, Tejinder Khosla (played by Om Puri), whose ideology turns him into Dev's antagonist. Tejinder identifies Muslims as the Outsiders who are the reason for India's ills. His mission, in the fight against terrorism, is to root out all Muslims, to annihilate them. The Outsider metaphor has been repeatedly used in Bollywood cinema in its representations of Muslim characters; and despite continuing to narrativize the Muslim as exoticized, marginalized or, and more increasingly, demonized (Chadha and Kavoori 2008: 131), *Dev*, in Bollywood's 'techno-nationalist' tradition, rehabilitates the fractured nation through the tropes of familiality, diversity, nationalism, and a belief in the rule-of-law.

A parallel narrative in the film portrays the lives of a young Muslim man called Farhaan Ali (played by Fardeen Khan), who has just returned to Mumbai after completing his law degree from Vadodara, and his girlfriend Aaliya (played by Kareena Kapoor), a college student in Mumbai. They live in a densely populated Muslim community housing complex called Noor Manzil, located in a working-class area. Farhaan's father, Ali Khan, is a respected local Muslim leader, who has a lot of faith in Indian democracy and pluralism and believes in the ideologies of non-violence and pacifism of anti-colonial leaders like Mohandas Karamchand Gandhi and Khan Abdul Gaffar Khan. The trope that Ali's character follows is that of a *good* Muslim, who believes in the constitutional vision of 'unity in diversity' (Singh and Deva 2005: 649–86) and is an exception to the rule of the *bad* Muslim as terrorist (Mamdani 2004). Farhaan, however, feels that the lofty ideals of constitutional equality have turned into a sham, and that innocent Muslims are being persecuted by the Indian state and its police in the name of fighting terrorism. It is here that an invocation of law sets up the crisis in the film, which unfolds as an ideological conflict, on the one hand, between Farhaan, as a Muslim and a law graduate, whose lived experience considers the constitution to be a document worthy of suspicion, and on the other, Dev, as a police officer, whose lived experience suggests that even extra-constitutional violence by the police is justified to uphold the constitution.

Soon after Farhaan's return to Mumbai after graduation, at a peaceful protest demonstration against police brutality against Muslims, Farhaan's father is killed by the police, when Dev orders his cadres to open fire after the crowd turns violent. Farhaan vows to take revenge on Dev. Taking advantage of Farhaan's rage, a fundamentalist Muslim politician offers to train him as a jihadi. The politician's character, of course, is created using the tropes of the *bad* Muslim, in contrast to that of Ali Khan.

Farhaan fails an assassination attempt against Dev, but is then surreptitiously, without his knowledge, made to plant a bomb outside a

Hindu temple. The bomb blast—akin to the Godhra incident but in this case, made clear as to have been carried out at the behest of the Muslim politician—kills several Hindus, provoking retaliation against Muslims. This *pratikriya*, of the kind that followed the Godhra train burning—is openly led by a right-wing Hindu politician, pointing at the connivance of political leaders in fomenting the Gujarat pogrom. The violence is represented as a reactionary and spontaneous outrage, like a riot, and not a sophisticatedly pre-planned pogrom. Farhaan survives the blast, and realizes that he was being used as a foot soldier by the Muslim politician to serve his sectarian agenda. Aaliya also survives the retaliatory violence, though she witnesses the killing of all her family members. In the middle of the violence, Dev helps Farhaan take Aaliya to the hospital, and this effects a change of heart in Farhaan and his hatred for Dev subsides.

While the Hindu mobs were on the rampage killing Muslims, Dev, as part of the anti-terrorism team led by his friend and colleague Tejinder, was ordered not to take action to stop the mobs. This order came from the Hindu CM, who, much like Narendra Modi, asked Tejinder to ensure that Hindus get to freely vent their anger against Muslims for this blast. Dev arrives at the scene to find that Tejinder is waiting with the police squad, allowing the Hindu mobs a free rein in killing Muslims. Dev ignores Tejinder's orders and goes ahead with his team of policemen to stop the killings, but his efforts are in vain and several people die.

Dev is deeply distraught about not being able to uphold the rule-of-law to save the victims, in spite of having the opportunity and authority to do so. He realizes the extent of the ideological differences between him and Tejinder. Despite political pressure, Dev organizes a public meeting at the site of Noor Manzil, where he urges people to come forward to lodge their first information reports (FIR), and also identify any policemen or politicians who were involved in carrying out the violence. Despite threats to her life Aaliya comes forward to testify and inspires other women to do the same.

The mise-en-scène comprises a large makeshift tent, which has been erected right outside Noor Manzil. Inside the tent there is a table with the necessary legal documents in which FIRs will be filed. There are local leaders sitting on chairs behind the table. Dev speaks through a microphone that carries his voice to the residents of Noor Manzil who have gathered on their verandahs to hear him speak and be spectators of what is on offer, lending a theatrical feel to the space. This space of the public meeting can be read as an allegory for what Dorsett and McVeigh have called a 'jurisdiction of conscience' (Dorsett and McVeigh 2012: 112), in which it is not the victims who have to go to the law—that is, go to police stations to file their FIRs to put the law in motion—but it is the law that has ceremonially travelled to them. The camera is placed behind the group of women who have gathered on the balcony to listen to Dev speak. In Dev's authoritative and amplified address as the sole judge in the situation, the spectator in the film watcher is also interpellated as a recipient of that judgement. The point of view accorded to the spectatorial public, thus, allows them legitimate entry into this jurisdiction of conscience. The jurisdictional boundaries between the private space of Noor Manzil and the public space of the police station merge, and Dev embodies state law and carries it to Aaliya and other victim-survivors. The theatrical arrangement of the space also lends to it the form of a public court handing out popular justice outside of the architectural confines of a courtroom. However, here Dev presides as the judge and jury. This is especially the case when, on Aaliya's identification of the erring policemen, Dev suspends them without a hearing, and orders that a charge sheet be filed against them.

Meanwhile, Farhaan and Aaliya take refuge at Dev's home, where it is decided that Dev will present his eyewitness account of police and political inaction and collusion in carrying out the violence. He submits his report to the CM, but also decides to depose in the court, since Dev is aware of his anti-Muslim ideology. Farhaan expresses his fear that Dev's life will be under threat if he goes ahead with his decision to expose police and political complicity. Dev invokes the morality of the Sanskrit shloka from the *Bhagavad Gita* with which the film opened to emphasize that life or death does not matter as long as he continues to fight for the truth to uphold the rule-of-law until his last breath. Tejinder tries to dissuade Dev, but Dev stands by his convictions. In the climactic scene, set right outside a symbolically imposing court building, Dev is shot dead by Tejinder. In a show of secular solidarity Farhaan, a Muslim, lights fire to the Hindu Dev's funeral pyre, a duty that in Hinduism is supposed to be the privilege of the son. Later, unable to deal with the trauma of having murdered his friend, Tejinder kills himself.

The film ends with Dev's wife handing over a file—a record with all the necessary evidence that Dev had collected and a document memorializing Dev himself—to Farhaan, who finally dons the lawyer's attire and walks up the stairs of the courthouse, following Dev's instructions that he must keep faith in the law and begin litigation for the rights of the dead and the violated.

Dev, in an all-black attire, seated against a black background, in his transcendental post-death avatar fades in, repeating with singular intensity, in Amitabh Bachchan's 'inimitable throaty baritone' (Kabeer 2002: 42), the *Bhagavad Gita*'s juridico-ethical morality of relentlessly fighting for truth irrespective of consequences. The scene invokes *darsana*—a technique particular to Indian cinema's aesthetic that demonstrates 'the power exercised by the authoritative image in Hindu religious culture' (Vasudevan 2012: 233). The imagistic and acoustic intensity in this ostensibly secular scene accords Dev the power of divine authority. In death, he is deified. Farhaan looks up at the courthouse in hope, but it is Dev's spectral presence that guides him. The symbolic message with which the film ends is that the Muslim Farhaan, having given up on the path of violence to seek justice, will now follow the path of the law to seek justice for the violence against his community, and as a tribute to the Hindu Dev's courage and sacrifice.

Dev offers a memorial reconstruction of Gujarat 2002 that reduces religious strife in India to an amorphous politics of equivalence and linearity. In such a way of remembering, first, the violence is judged to be an outcome of a cause-and-effect logic that begins with one community casting 'the first stone' (Setalvad 2017: 78), and the other justifying it through retaliation; second, a precipitating event is identified and made foundational to the narrative of violence; and, third, the violence is seen as a consequence of the sectarian agendas of individual fundamentalist politicians who spread hate to gain political mileage. This way of remembering conceals the ideological and structural foundations that lend legitimacy to anti-Muslim hatred in the New India. The film's assessment of religious violence is that ordinary Hindus and Muslims are the victims, first as pawns in the hands of politicians who brainwash them to propagate their violent agendas, and second as the innocents who get killed because of this violence. The idea that both Hindus and Muslims bear the brunt of this equally lends a democratic logic to religious violence, and equalizes its consequences for majority and minority communities. The film emphasizes that both sides suffer, that sectarian violence does not choose its victims based on religion, much like Dev's secularism tells him not to kill terrorists based on their faith, but extrajudicially execute them nevertheless. The chronology of events in both the factual record of collective memory, and cinema's fictitious record, follows a linear narrative where the cycle of violence is always initiated by the unruly and anti-national Muslims, which is the reason why the tolerant Hindus are forced to retaliate. As Sunera Thobani writes:

> In the cinematic Gujarat—and India—[…] [t]he deeply institutionalized inequities and imbalance of power between Hindus and Muslims is rarely allowed to enter the frame, and if it is, the good intentions of the secular Hindu hero/heroine becomes a mitigating factor—his/her ideals and values, his/her personal acceptance of Muslims will set everything right. The Muslims who do not abide by these ideals and values are hopelessly naïve, and the proof of Muslim loyalty is, without exception, subservience to the values and embrace of enlightened Hindu characters, most of whom are secularists (2014: 493).

This ordering of collective memory has been a standard refrain of the Hindu Right to justify violence against Muslims, citing, inter alia, the 'invasion' of India by the Mughals and the Partition in 1947 as the original reasons (Josh 2018: 175). In an opening scene, Farhaan is questioned by a police officer on a train. When he learns that Farhaan is Muslim, he conspiratorially asks whether he has relatives in Pakistan. Later, expressing anguish, Farhaan tells his father: 'How does it feel to be a Muslim in India? To be repeatedly reminded that you belong to Pakistan?' *Dev*'s narrative acknowledges this prejudice against Muslims in India, and simultaneously normalizes it by valorizing the way in which Dev repeatedly and unquestioningly connects 'terrorism' to the work of infiltrators and brainwashed Muslim youth who have become anti-nationals.

The role of law is two-fold—both metaphoric and material. Its appearances are metaphorically embodied in the character of the film's protagonist Dev. He embodies the characteristics of the ideal nationalist: a benevolent patriarch, Hindu, secular, liberal, and an unshakeable believer in the rule-of-law—he is the good secular Hindu hero. Dev's beliefs are so powerful that they can, on the one hand, justify extrajudicial killings, and on the other, inspire a young Muslim gone astray to repose faith in the law in his quest for justice. In the traditions of the classic psychoanalytic reading of the law of the father, the good secular Hindu in Dev, and his unwavering belief in the rule-of-law, turns him into a father figure for the fatherless Farhaan, and in the film's affective address to the cinematic publics. In the 'world of danger' that the film conjures, Dev and his *Gita*-inspired juridico-moral universe offers succor for 'certainty and security' and embodies the role of the 'father substitute' (Sarat 2000: 13). '[T]he father is the infallible Judge', writes Jerome Frank, 'the Maker of definite rules of conduct. He knows precisely what is wrong and [...] sits in judgment and punishes misdeeds. The Law... inevitably becomes a partial substitute for the Father-as-Infallible-Judge' (quoted in Sarat 2000: 14).

In material form, secular law steps in to resolve the 'acute crisis' or 'ethical dilemmas' that *Dev*'s protagonists confront. For Dev, the primary dilemma was, on the one hand, to uphold the rule-of-law to end terrorism and sectarian violence, and on the other, to stay loyal in his friendship with Tejinder. Dev's decision to stand firm on his conviction in the rule-of-law comes from a certain belief in constitutionalism, which becomes apparent in a very didactic scene in the film where Dev and Tejinder are discussing over a drink what the foundations of their conscience are. This discussion takes place in Dev's elite living room over a drink.

> *Dev:* One thing is clear, Mr Tejinder Khosla, your and my *Gitas* are different. My *Gita* is the Constitution of India, and the rule-of-law. What is your *Gita*?
>
> *Tejinder:* It is like this dear Dev. If there is a nation, only then will there be a Constitution. Without the nation the Constitution and rule of law have no basis. My *Gita* is Power. The power to completely annihilate the enemies of this nation.
>
> *Dev:* Oh dear Tejinder! Power, you see, is not in the police, the army, or weapons. A nation's power lies in its political organization, its economy, in its justice system, in social equality, and religious harmony. And all of this is given to us by our Constitution.[31]

Also present in the living room is Dev's wife, Bharti, who has been listening in silence. The conversation briefly turns to her when Tejinder apologizes for not including her in the conversation, and requests her to share what her *Gita* is.

> *Bharti:* I have no *Gita*, only a dream. An ordinary person's dream: who wants a nation that doesn't just provide food, clothing and shelter, but also respect and justice; the freedom to think and choose. What happened? Have I asked for too much?
>
> *Tejinder:* You have asked for the whole of Ramrajya, Bharti!
>
> *Bharti:* And Ramrajya isn't possible in Kaliyug, right?[32]

The *Bhagavad Gita*, it is apparent, is a metaphor with a shared meaning for all the three characters in this scene. It is being invoked as a reference to a foundation of their conscience and imagination as citizens of the Indian nation. The conversation is set up primarily to demonstrate the ideological differences between two friends, and inaugurates the 'ethical dilemma' that will serve as the 'acute crisis' that demands resolution in the film's climax. Tejinder's *Gita* is power, which, in line with John Austin, considers postcolonial state sovereignty to be illimitable by a document like the constitution (Abbas and Kumar 2012: 154–5). For Tejinder, the power to protect the sovereignty of India from its enemies (who for him are Muslims) must override constitutional restrictions on the use of force. This has historically been the case with special security legislations in India that have always been upheld by the SC despite their provisions being draconian and in contravention of guaranteed rights in the Constitution of India.[33]

Dev's rival *Gita*, the guiding source of his conscience, is the 'material' Constitution of India, which can be 'grasped only by properly grappling with the deeper societal context in which formal constitutional development is embedded' (Goldoni and Wilkinson 2018: 569). This societal context is the story of the New India and of religious violence that the film tells. However, the depth of Dev's living room constitutionalism is much like Hans Kelsen's 'basic norm' (Raz 1974: 94). He 'presupposes' the constitution as the normative basis of sovereignty and human flourishing for India's postcolonial social context,[34] which for him is founded on the secular religious ideas of Hinduism enshrined in the *Gita*. Dev's assertions about the constitution point to his passionate investments in the triad of secularism (religious harmony), legalism (the justice system), and developmentalism (the economy). It is this belief in the constitution that convinces Dev to depose in court against the misdeeds of the police and politicians who supported the pogrom, the court for him being the highest institutional authority that upholds the constitution.

Bharti's intervention in this conversation offers yet another rival imagination. While on the one hand she does not consider the *Gita* to be the foundation of her conscience, on the other, she dreams of a future India of prosperity and rights for all, only possible in Ramrajya, the kingdom of the mythological Hindu god Ram. That imagination for her has become an impossibility in Kaliyug—'the dark age' (Madan 2003: 298), 'the era of greatest spiritual decline in Hindu cosmic time' (Lothspeich 2007: 159; Ahmad 2017: 57). Hindutva politics in modern India continues to be mobilized most powerfully around the figure of Ram, and in the campaign to build a temple in Ayodhya at the exact location where he was born. It was at this location that the Babri Masjid was demolished in 1992 by cadres of Hindutva activists to make way for the building of the temple. The vision of achieving Ramrajya, or what has been called 'pure Hindu rule' (Malik 2005: 99), has also been an articulated promise of Hindutva political parties to rescue India from its Kaliyug (Udayakumar 1997: 11).

Thus, all the three characters offer rival visions of their attachment to and imagination of the Indian nation-state. While each of these visions is presented as secular, the foundational ethos remains Hindu. In particular, to strengthen the integrity of Dev as the film's hero, this narrative equates the Constitution of India to the *Bhagavad Gita*. Dev's conscience—captured in the affective force of the Sanskrit shlokas that opened the film—considers the idea and imagination of the constitution to be sacred, as is borne out by Dev's own invocation of the *Gita*. By doing this, Dev Hinduizes not only his own conscience, but also the conscience and legal foundations of the nation, in keeping with an Indian Supreme Court judgement from 1994 that did not find any reason for Hindutva ideology to be considered antithetical to secularism (Cossman and Kapur 2001).

The location of this conversation is also pertinent to my jurisprudential–aesthetic reading. The art direction of the living room makes the space look agnostic to the religion of the Hindu characters present. Their clothing also provides no indication of their religion or religiosity. These particularities are of significance for two reasons. First, they produce a sense of seamless cohabitation of the secular and the religious when it comes to Hinduism. Second, they provide a contrast, in art and costume direction, to the representations of the domestic spaces inside Noor Manzil, where specific kinds of clothing—the skullcap, the veil and the *lungi* (Indian sarong)—and identifiable Islamic symbols, greetings, rituals, and gestures make the space and its inhabitants look overtly Muslim. The affect of secularity that the living room scene and its screenplay generate, despite the exchange between the characters being imbued with Hindu metaphors, in effect secularizes Hinduism and Hinduizes secularism as 'cultural common sense' (Nanda 2007: 39).

Dev is the hero of the film—he is characterized as progressive, secular, and liberal (the unmarked Hindu in secular police uniform). He does not hate Muslims, but at the same time, likens the secular constitution to the Hindu holy book. The film, though, draws a distinction between Dev's good Hinduism and Tejinder's bad version. The good version rationalizes, modernizes, and secularizes the imagined Hindu foundations of postcolonial India by using the constitution as an alibi, whereas the bad version offers extra-constitutional justifications for the annihilation of Muslims. Both these versions ultimately celebrate two versions of Hindutva ideology. Dev's version speaks more to Hindutva's neoliberal avatar that speaks of developmentalism and legalism as a means of assimilating the Muslim as 'reluctant citizen' into the Hindu nation's fold (Visvanathan and Setalvad 2014: 125). If Muslims resist this tactic, it will be 'read in jurisprudential terms as a self-imposed injury of an ethnic group caught in a time-warp and reluctant to embrace citizenship and development' (Visvanathan and Setalvad 2014: 125). Farhaan's lawyerly transformation into the good Muslim citizen, as a seeker of justice using constitutional means, rehabilitates him as a Muslim and champions the promise of Dev's *Bhagavad Gita* as constitution.

This script has also been the secular rhetoric on the basis of which Narendra Modi had appealed for votes during his prime ministerial campaigns. Time and again Modi has referred to the constitution as the 'holy book' that should drive his 'India First' mission (*Business Standard*, 12 January 2014). Similarly, since Modi's win in 2014, there have been attempts to include the *Gita* as a secular pedagogical text in school curriculums in BJP-ruled states in India (Mohan 2015). This secular rhetoric of constitutionalism has been a part of Indian juridical governance techniques since 1976 when the word 'secular' was inserted into the text of the constitution for the first time through The Constitution (42nd Amendment) Act.[35] Dev's valorization of the constitution as his holy book is a narrative that even the secular-left in India would subscribe to. The secular rhetoric, thus, works as a mask to cover the Hindu foundations of the constitution. Pointing out the 'Hindu bias' in the Indian constitution, Pritam Singh writes: 'The progressive and genuinely secular forces in India need to recognize a bitter truth, namely that uncritically claiming a secular heritage from [...] the Constitution of India is to play a potentially losing game from the very beginning against their *Hindutva* opponents' (2005: 911, emphasis in original). The appeal to the constitution, like in *Dev*, as the panacea for all injustices against Muslims, and the contradictory projection of it as a sacred text that is secular, is, in fact, institutionalized within India's juridical imagination.

In the Best Bakery case (*Zahira Habibulla H. Sheikh vs State of Gujarat*, 12 April 2004), where the SC, after ordering that the case be shifted out of Gujarat for fear for political manipulation by the state and to uphold constitutional standards of a fair trial, tried Zahira Sheikh—the key witness who turned hostile due to political threats against her family and her—held her guilty for contempt of court. In sentencing Zahira, the same court that expressed anguish over how the justice process in Gujarat was weighed against its Muslim-minority population, and how that was an affront to our constitutional principles of secularism, began the judgement by quoting from the *Manusmriti*—a classical Hindu religious scripture that also forms the basis of Hindu law—on the duties of a witness.[36] In upholding the secular constitution, the court, much like Dev, Hinduized it. As Kalpana Kannabiran notes:

> [...] by drawing justification from the Manusmriti to negate the liberty of a Muslim survivor of Hindu fundamentalist assault—the

> Supreme Court demonstrated by its own example the way in which discrimination interlocks with the loss of liberty in the case of persons belonging to religious minority communities, especially the women of these communities. [...] [T]he normativization by constitutional courts of conservative Hindu legal traditions embodied in the Manusmriti, and the situated reading of the constitution within the ideological frameworks of orthodox Hinduism, sharpens the crisis of constitutional disarticulation on the critical issue of non-discrimination. (2012: 298).

For Farhaan, the dilemma was between subscribing to his father's belief in the non-violence and pacifism of freedom fighters like Gandhi and Khan, as the way to respond to the discrimination faced by Muslims in India, or to take the path of violence. After his brush with violence, and seeing Dev firmly standing his ground to side with his constitutional beliefs, Farhaan also reposes faith in the justice system—the courts—by taking up litigation to fight for Dev's cause and for the Muslims of India, and in turn, to resolve his own dilemma. Aaliya too—in resolving her dilemma of whether to speak up as an eyewitness in front of the same police force that aided and abetted the violence—believed in Dev's promise at the public hearing, ensuring that if people lodge FIRs the police will ensure justice by arresting and charging the individual wrongdoers—a gesture towards individual criminalization as a way of ending impunity.

In the *law in aesthetics* register, the legal process, particularly criminal law, is represented as a trustworthy venue for justice seeking. Like the protagonists of the film, the audience is called on to repose faith in the law. This is the performance of a particular kind of state-making and state-preserving rationality that displaces structural concerns about state accountability. Legal culpability is individualized, and is singularly focused on specific politicians or a prejudiced police officer like Tejinder. Responding to the Gujarat pogrom where all investments are directed at individual criminalization of perpetrators, does very little to challenge the historical, structural, and ideological foundations that resulted in the pogrom occurring in the first place. Convictions can, in fact, create an illusion of the restoration of rule-of-law and the state's commitment to liberal rights, which demands that we repose faith in New India's state-making practices.

As Ratna Kapur has argued in her assessment of the justice-seeking mechanisms post the Gujarat violence:

> The story of the Gujarat riots and subsequent efforts to address the harms and injuries through prosecution and apology does not pay attention to the institutional discursive mechanisms within a democratic polity that can produce moments of extreme violence, moments that cannot be written off as aberrational and deviant [...]. 2002 cannot be addressed exclusively within a prosecutorial, or reparations framework that seeks to prosecute individual wrongdoers who carried out such atrocities and provide compensation to those who suffered [...]. [T]he riots were a logical product or outcome of a discursive strategy partly in and through liberal rights discourse and not in opposition to such rights (2006: 889).

By extension, the film addresses its cinematic publics, especially Muslims, to repose faith and trust in the constitution and the courts. The idea of the constitution and the institution of the court are represented as incorruptible foundations of the nation–state which can weather all crises, and can, in consequence, unshakably guard the nation. The courthouse outside which Dev is murdered, and the steps of which Farhaan climbs in his advocate's attire, the sun shining on him, is an imposing building, painted white, and its environs look sanitized. The only traces of memory of the violence are in the fading stain of Dev's blood on the steps leading to the court (right beside Farhaan), and the file in Farhaan's hand that contains all the evidence that Dev had gathered.

These material locations of law, and the location of the elite drawing room where Dev and Tejinder pontificated on constitutionalism, are set up, in my reading, in contradistinction to the squalid and lawless Muslim ghetto of Noor Manzil—which, when introduced early on in the film, was shown to be a hideout for a Muslim militant. For those like Farhaan and Aaliya, who are the victim-survivors of the pogrom, they had to exit that lawless location, find refuge in Dev's secular home, and then enter the ostensibly secular space of the court in search of justice. The jurisdictional organization of the city and that of law and legalism are, thus, clearly identified in its aesthetic representations.

The *way* of remembering that *Dev*'s reconstruction of the pogrom engenders, is that religious strife is a doing of individual evil politicians, that violence begets violence (and Muslims generally tend to start it), so trust the constitution and courts; they are secular, they will ultimately deliver justice. More importantly, it is the trust in the constitution and the conviction to stand by the rule-of-law that also resolves the enmity between the Muslim Farhaan and Hindu Dev. The intensity of the constitutional resolution is so powerful that Farhaan is able to overlook the fact that it was because of Dev's extra-judicial orders that his father and many other Muslims were killed in the police firing. Despite developing an endearing feeling towards Farhaan, Dev, in fact, never expresses any remorse about his orders that killed Farhaan's father—he is placed above the audience's moral judgement because that was in the realm of his *Gita*-inspired dharma (juridico-ethical duty) to protect the nation. Farhaan, similarly, never demands justice for Dev's act of ordering the killing of his father and many other Muslims at the protest rally.

Dev's reconstructive imagination records a memory of the pogrom where, while the phantasmagoric violence is recognized, the structural othering of Muslims in India is rationalized. It is the appeal to such a rationalization that produces and mobilizes judgement by calling on the film's spectatorial publics. It is the possibility of such judgement that frames the mnemohistory of the pogrom in the film, where secular Hindus like Dev, despite their belief in the Hindu foundations of the nation and its constitution, are rehabilitated in the eyes of the Muslim citizen as being fair to Muslims as long as they stand by the constitution and the rule-of-law. The Muslim victim-survivors of the violence in the film ultimately repose faith in Dev's Hindu constitution, and in the secular courts as the ultimate arbiters of justice. It is the rationalities of legalism and secularism that elide the Hindu foundations of the Indian nation-state, its constitution, and courts, which order and lend meaning to law's institutions and imaginaries of justice. The memorialization of the pogrom in *Dev*, thus, happens through the projection of the performance of state legalism, which is designed to restore faith in the capacity of secular law to deliver justice in response to an event of religious violence. *Dev* ends outside the courtroom and the audience does not yet know whether the promise of secular law that the film has celebrated will be fulfilled.

A Provisional Closure

My reading of *Dev* through the jurisprudential–aesthetic lens has demonstrated the aesthetic forms that law takes in the making of imaginaries of cinematic justice, and in rationally ordering a way in which collective memory of the pogrom is actively reconstructed in Bollywood cinema. Despite not being a law film, this way of remembering that *Dev* engenders is framed by a Bollywoodized imagination/imagery of law and legalism. *Dev* recognizes the scale of the violence (chronology and facts aside), and also reposes enormous faith in the constitution and rule-of-law as unquestionable paths to justice. While *Dev* condemns the violence, and mourns the dead, at the same time it also reifies constitutional secularism and legalism as part of New India's state-making arsenal, the embrace of which will provide the most effective closure to the trauma of the pogrom. The foundational Hinduness of the nation-state and its buttressing by secularism and legalism is never questioned by the memorial reconstructions of the pogrom in the film. The landscape of cinematic justice that is painted rationalizes the pogrom as aberrant—one that does not fit the way the Indian nation-state conducts its governance—and offers visions of reconciliation and resolution that are deeply invested in the very structures that enabled the pogrom in the first place.

It is this particular form of ordering of collective memory that I have called 'developmental juridical rationality': the ordering of collective memory through the combined working of the triad of secularism, legalism, and developmentalism. My reading of *Dev* was aimed at demonstrating the working of the first two techniques in the triad, and offers some brief sense of how the third works.

Drawing on Michel Foucault's analytic of 'governmental rationality', and later critiques and interventions by postcolonial and other critical scholars, I provisionally develop this conceptual category that explains how the New India conducts its state-making and state-preserving practices. Foucault notes that the purpose of government is to secure the 'welfare of the population, the improvement of its condition, the increase of its wealth, longevity, health et cetera' (Foucault

1991: 100). To do this, writes David Scott, government 'arrange[es] things so that people, following only their self-interest, *will do as they ought*' (Scott 1995: 202–3, emphasis in original).

Secularism, legalism, and developmentalism are projected by the New Indian nation-state as governmental practices for the welfare of its population, which is legitimated by the filmic reconstructions. The cinematic public is addressed to identify with these practices as virtues of governance, and hence, conduct themselves *as they ought*. According to Hindutva ideology—its two different hues embodied by Dev and Tejinder—such conduct involves the pursuance of self-interest for welfare, health, wealth, and longevity, which is attainable only through the revival of Hindu India. The existence of Muslims who behave as reluctant citizens, thus, is a hindrance to the achievement of the welfare of (Hindu) populations.

In Foucault's formulation, the conduct of government in modernity is arrived through a periodization from control over the individual body (punishment), to panoptic control (discipline), to inducing violence-free self-discipline *en masse* (biopolitics). Achille Mbembe argues that in postcolonial locations the operation of governmental rationality works in ways where control over minds is coexistent with brutal violence over bodies (2003: 3). Thus, by developmental juridical rationality, I mean a particular way in which a state's governance tactics order the conduct of politics in a neoliberal 'postcolony'.[37] Such a tactic valorizes accelerated legalism and developmentalism as primary markers of secular constitutionalism and modernity, and is simultaneously accompanied by a conjuncture of violence and violation—thanatopolitics: 'killing rather than simply as allowing to die or exposing to death' (Gupta 2012: 17)—against minority groups, that remain implicitly tied to the Indian state's rational performances and enactments of legalism, not exceptionalism.

In this chapter, my attempt was to bring into conversation law and aesthetics and Indian film studies to take the minor jurisprudence of Bollywood cinema seriously as a memorial archive through which we can read the Gujarat pogrom both as a concentrated instance of the making of collective memory and the managing of its aftermath through cinematic imaginations of justice. In reading *Dev* through the jurisprudential–aesthetic lens, I demonstrated how aesthetic reconstructions of the Gujarat pogrom call on the law to generate a way of remembering that is ordered by the workings of a juridical developmental rationality that recognizes the violence of the pogrom, but at the same time, valorizes the state-making practices of the New India that laid the foundations of the pogrom.

The many cinematic publics of Bollywood reconstructions of the pogrom—including the other films that have memorialized the pogrom—can be said to have elicited three kinds of responses from urban, Hindu middle classes who voted Modi to power: they were either happy about what happened to Muslims (because they deserved it), or they were repulsed by them (too much gore is not good for our happy lives), or it generated, as Anuja Jain says, 'a "politics of pity", which had the polarizing implications of creating a binary of the "fortunate us" and "unfortunate them"' (2010: 163). Given how Modi has been deified in India, and the two repeated landslide victories of the BJP in 2014 and 2019, pity, in my reading, is the closest sentiment of attachment that the elite and middle classes, as well as the secular-left, have come to express for the victim-survivors of the Gujarat pogrom. This sentiment, even while expressing feelings of injustice done to Muslims, have exacerbated anti-Muslim prejudice manifold and entrenched a deeper belief in the need for Muslim assimilation into Hindu ways of living and behaving; else their annihilation can be successfully rationalized and memorialized for national posterity—in law, in cinema, in our storytelling of small lives in the New India.

Notes

1. Though it is commonsensically understood to be so, especially outside of India, Bollywood is not synonymous with Indian cinema. It is one kind of Indian cinema. Bollywood can be loosely understood as Hindi mainstream cinema produced in Mumbai. In this chapter I use it in this way, remaining attentive both to the uniqueness of the genre and to its universalizing weight that flattens the idea of Indian cinema.
2. The film's second title in English was *Brothers... for Life.*
3. Later in the chapter I provide a brief retelling of what this event was, and also an explanation for why I use 'pogrom' to characterize the violence.
4. The Central Board of Film Certification (CBFC) in India, also known as the Census Board, a statutory body established by the Indian

Cinematograph Act of 1952, makes it mandatory for films to apply for a censor certificate before they can be publicly exhibited. The CBFC also classifies films based on their content for universal or restricted viewing. The board's decisions to censor films considered sexually explicit or communally sensitive tend to reflect the moral and political views of the government in power. The CBFC's decisions have met with resistance from both free-speech advocates and right-wing conservatives. On the history and politics of film censorship in India, see Bhowmik 2009; Mazzarella 2013.

5. *The 3 Mistakes of My Life*, the novel on which the film was based (Chetan Bhagat 2008), the film's publicity and trailers, and even the theatrical release did not attract any attention from Hindu right-wing parties—including the ruling Hindu nationalist BJP in Gujarat at that time—as has been the case in the past with most other feature and documentary films on the pogrom (P. Menon 2004; Bandukwala 2007).
6. Arjun Appadurai understands 'ideoscapes' as composed of elements of the Enlightenment world-view, which consists of a concatenation of ideas, terms and images, including 'freedom', 'welfare', 'rights', 'sovereignty', 'representation', and the master term 'democracy' (Appadurai 1996: 299).
7. Drawing on the work of Andreas Philippopoulos-Mihalopoulos, I understand the 'lawscape' as imaginations of justice that are 'so thick with law that, just like air, the law is not perceived. It becomes "invisible", white noise, thin air. It becomes an *atmosphere*—there but not there, imperceptible yet all-determining' (Philippopoulos- 2013: 2, emphasis in original).
8. The account that follows is based on a select set of fact-finding reports, investigative, and academic works that can be broadly and loosely classified as left-secular, human-rights affirming. I am sympathetic to these tellings, and draw on them, because of my own ideological and political alliance to the left-secular and human-rights groups and individuals that have authored these, and also because these have been considered credible accounts by victim-survivors of the pogrom. I spent time in Ahmedabad, the capital city of Gujarat in 2002, right after the pogrom, as part of a fact-finding team constituted by the South Asia Human Rights Documentation Centre, New Delhi. I revisited Ahmedabad and Vadodara in 2014 for my doctoral research. On both these occasions, in my conversations with victim-survivors, some of the reports that they have expressed faith in are the ones that I draw on in my brief retelling of the pogrom in this essay. All these sources have also been consistently referenced in the literature on the pogrom that I have read.

9. This was evident in the way the then BJP prime minister, Atal Bihari Vajpayee, at a speech delivered in Goa in April 2002, justified the pogrom, by citing Muslim separatism as its foundational cause, and rationalizing such alleged Muslim behaviour as an affront to Indian secularism. He is recorded to have said: 'Wherever Muslims live, they don't like to live in coexistence with others, they don't like to mingle with others; and instead of propagating their ideas in a peaceful manner, they want to spread their faith by resorting to terror and threats' (quoted in Varadarajan 2002: 450–1).
10. The imposition of Emergency, or President's Rule, has been a practice of considerable debate in Indian constitutional jurisprudence, especially given the history of the widespread abuse of power and the violent throttling of dissent under the Emergency rule experienced from 1975–7 during Prime Minister Indira Gandhi's leadership. I draw attention to the non-imposition of an Emergency during Gujarat 2002 as an attempt by the state to treat the event as an ordinary occurrence, not recognizing the complete breakdown of law and order deserving special interventions from the central government to stop the violence.
11. Many scholarly works have traced the origins of Hindutva ideology to that of European fascism. See Ahmad 2002: 129; Basu, Datta, Sarkar, Sarkar, and Sen 1993; S. Sarkar 1993: 163; Casolari 2000: 2018; Casolari 2011; Banaji 2016.
12. See generally Figueira 2002; Ahmed 2017; Udayakumar 1997: 11; Wariavwalla 2000: 593; Jaffrelot 2008; Bal 2018.
13. Rakesh Sharma's 2002 documentary film *Final Solution* carries footage of several such hate speeches by Narendra Modi and many others. To watch the film, visit https://vimeo.com/ondemand/32491/110332012; last accessed on 20 May 2015.
14. In Ayodhya, on 6 December 1992, militant Hindu mobs led by key leaders of the BJP demolished the Babri Masjid (built in 1527 by Babur, the first Mughal emperor of India) because they claimed that the mythological Hindu god Ram was born exactly where the mosque stood. The demolition led to widespread anti-Muslim violence, and erupted in the Bombay riots of 1992. Both the demolition and the Bombay riots catapulted the BJP as a party of national significance, leading to them winning the general elections in 1998 and installing Atal Behari Vajpayee as India's first BJP prime minister.
15. Quoted in Mitta 2014: 237.
16. Atal Bihari Vajpayee, the BJP prime minister in 2002, buttressed this logic to justify the pogrom when he said at the Goa speech: 'What happened in Gujarat? If a conspiracy had not been hatched to burn alive

the innocent passengers of the Sabarmati Express, then the subsequent tragedy in Gujarat could have been averted. But this did not happen. People were torched alive. Who were those culprits? […] The subsequent developments were no doubt condemnable, but who lit the fire? How did the fire spread?' (quoted in Varadarajan 2002: 450–1).

17. Jasbir K. Puar, citing David Kazanjian, understands a 'flashpoint' as 'a centripetal turbulence of illumination so powerful that it may blind the past even as it spotlights the present and lights up the future' (2007: xviii).
18. I have repeatedly used the expression secular-left in this essay to identify a certain political position that I ally with. In making the instant claim, my aim is to in fact argue against that very position. This particular political juncture in the New India is indeed a moment of reckoning for the secular-left for having failed to offer any meaningful resistance to the collective rise of the combined forces of Hindutva and neoliberalism, a brand of politics of which Modi is the torchbearer. Despite its best intentions, the secular-left's failure in its attempts to keep alive the small memories of Gujarat 2002 can be blamed on its logic of positing secularism and Hindutva in untouchable opposition. Such a clear opposition overlooks how Hindutva politics speaks and gains recognition through the very language of secularism and liberal rights. The secular-left's Manichean logic of thinking of Hindutva as evil and secularism as sacred forecloses readings of the practices of postcolonial secularism that are foundational to the advancement of Hindutva politics and neoliberalism, and even works as a cover for the secular-left's own complicities with developmentalism, legalism, and indeed Hindutva.
19. As far as I am aware, there are four other Bollywood films in which the pogrom features either centrally or marginally as part of the fictive plots. These are: *Chand Bujh Gaya* (2005), *Road to Sangam* (2009), *Mausam* (2011), and *Rajdhani Express* (2013). Of these, *Chand Bujh Gaya* was involved in litigation to fight cuts demanded by the CBFC because the character of a minister in the film allegedly resembled Narendra Modi, and *Rajdhani Express* was taken to court by Qutubuddin Ansari, a pogrom victim-survivor, who alleged that the film used his photograph, which had turned him into the iconic face of the pogrom, without consent.
20. Bollywood does not carry a stable meaning. As M. Madhava Prasad writes: 'It is precisely the act of naming that is the most interesting aspect of Bollywood. It is a strange name, a hybrid, that seems to at once mock the thing it names and celebrate its difference […]. Today, the term "Bollywood" has become naturalized not only in the

English-language media, which is probably the term's original habitat, but also the Indian-language press, not only among journalists but also film scholars' (Prasad 2008: 41).

21. 'The modern concept of secularism in India [...] is borrowed from western history and has been, during the last one hundred years or so, a symbol of the efforts to interject history and redesign contemporary Indian life according to the demands of that history. This concept has a clear normative component: religion and ethnicity should be banished from the public sphere and an area should be marked out in politics where rationality, contractual social relationships, and *realpolitik* would reign' (Nandy 1995: 41, emphasis in original).
22. 'Legalism' is understood as a governmental obsession with 'rule following', and an overreliance on law reform as forms of governance practice. See Shklar 1964; Brown and Halley 2002.
23. 'By developmentalism—to be distinguished from development—I mean an ideological orientation characterized by the fetishization of development, or the attribution to development of the power of a natural (or even, divine) force which humans can resist or question only at the risk of being condemned to stagnation and poverty' (Dirlik 2014: 30–1).
24. Two notable exceptions are Nussbaum 2007 and Kapur 2006: 885–927.
25. For a discussion on conceptual distinctions and similarities between these terms see Brass 1996 and Brass 2006.
26. Quoted in Prasad 1998: 1.
27. As Donald R. Davis, Jr. writes: 'Dharmaśāstra' are 'a specific genre of text in the Sanskrit language', that 'contain Hindu jurisprudence, a way of thinking about law from a distinctively Hindu perspective' (Davis 2010: 12–13). Hindutva ideology has historically drawn its inspiration from 'Dharmaśāstra', among other classical Hindu legal texts (Sharma 2002: 1–36).
28. See Dhavan 2003: 1.
29. This particular spectatorial identification also carried strong juridical-aesthetic traction, given that Zahira Sheikh in the Best Bakery judgements was repeatedly referred to as the 'star witness'—like that of a movie star—and was accorded fallen celebrity status by the media, not so much for the violence she witnessed and experienced, but for being the unreliable Muslim who flip-flopped on her testimony, ultimately being convicted for perjury by the Supreme Court of India.
30. While the use of English has powerfully aided the processes and practices of Bollywood in its transnational developmentalist avatar, the way in which Hindi has come to displace Urdu can be read as the fulfilling

of a juridical mandate enshrined in Articles 343 and 351 of the Indian constitution that make Hindi the official language of India, and directs the state to be duty-bound to promote and spread it 'relying *primarily* on Sanskrit' (P. Singh 2005: 921, emphasis in original).

31. My translation from Hindi to English.
32. My translation from Hindi to English.
33. See Singh 2007.
34. See generally Kumar 1999: 500.
35. Accessible on http://indiacode.nic.in/coiweb/amend/amend42.htm; last accessed 20 June 2015.
36. The *Manusmriti* form a part of the 'Dharmaśāstra' texts and serves as an important source of what constitutes Hindu law. Several parts of the *Manusmriti* are outrightly discriminatory towards women, and Dalits (see Doniger and Smith 1991). As has been argued, it is in fact the anti-Dalit foundations of Hindu scriptures that form the basis of the birth of Hindutva ideology in India. See D. Menon 2006. For the historical connections between caste, Hindutva, and violence in Gujarat, see Shani 2007.
37. I deploy postcolony as a cartographic and ideological category, and not simply a geographical one. To quote Mbembe at length:

> The notion 'postcolony' identifies specifically a given historical trajectory—that of societies recently emerging from the experience of colonisation and the violence which the colonial relationship, par excellence, involves. To be sure, the postcolony is chaotically pluralistic, yet it has nonetheless an internal coherence. It is a specific system of signs, a particular way of fabricating simulacra or re-forming stereotypes. It is not, however, just an economy of signs in which power is mirrored and imagined self-reflectively. The postcolony is characterised by a distinctive style of political improvisation, by a tendency to excess and a lack of proportion as well as by distinctive ways in which identities are multiplied, transformed and put into circulation. But the postcolony is also made up of a series of corporate institutions and a political machinery which, once they are in place, constitute a distinctive regime of violence. In this sense, the postcolony is a particularly revealing (and rather dramatic) stage on which are played out the wider problems of subjection and its corollary, discipline (1992: 3).

4

New Queer Politics

Notes on Failure and Stuckness in a Negative Moment*

A Dangerous Commonsense

What happens when queers become democracy's 'favourite minority' championed by the capitalists, the liberals, the conservatives, and the leftists, all singing in the language of rights? It marks the inauguration (or culmination?) of a moment that is not *bad* but *dangerous*. 'If everything is dangerous', Michel Foucault writes, 'then we always have something to do. So my position leads not to apathy, but to a hyper- and pessimistic activism' (Foucault et al. 1983: 231–32). The commonsense opposite of bad is good—and the good in this situation, of all of these apparently oppositional political positions becoming strange bedfellows to turn queers into rights-bearing subjects, as I will argue, is what makes this a dangerous commonsense.

* Written through 2015–16 in Melbourne and Sonipat; in the wake of the *Koushal* judgement of the SC reinstating Section 377 of the IPC. I dedicate this piece to the memory of Sharmila Rege (1964–2013), teacher extraordinaire, who taught me to appreciate both the possibilities and perils of intersectional politics.

This chapter is interested in understanding the emerging intimacies between queer politics, the Hindu Right, and neoliberalism in what I am calling the New India (and its global mutations) as a concentrated instance of the way 'queer'—both as identity and discourse—is being depoliticized, individualized, and responsibilized. My allusion to the newness of an India, and of queer politics, is not a discovery, but the acknowledgement of a continuum. This chapter is a demonstration of my hyper- and pessimistic activism that eventually leads to an acknowledgement of failure. I did not set out with this intention, but that is what it has come to—as you will see.

The chapter is organized as follows: first, it describes the mise-en-scène of the time and place of queer politics that I have characterized as the New India. In doing this, I foreground some key places and characters. The attention to place is important because I am not offering a theoretical exegesis which is portable. What I offer might find resonances elsewhere (and I indicate these through this chapter); but the political framing cannot be extrapolated unproblematically. However, I am not provincially located—both in terms of my training in common law across continents and the transnational traditions of *queerfeministmarxistpostcolonial* thought and practice that have inspired me.[1] This is especially apparent in the ease with which I deploy 'queer' as politics and theory to speak of non-Western locations, even as the term carries complicated, and even violent, legacies in its journeys through the Global South (Tellis and Bala 2015). Second, I zoom in to closely see how the field of queer politics in India is textured by law's flashpoints framed by the language of rights, particularly as these are sequestered by the demand surrounding the decriminalization of the colonial anti-sodomy law. I read, see, and listen to a set of visual and legal texts to show how these demands reify the intimacies between queer politics, Hindu right-wing nationalism, and neoliberalism. I use these reified instances to zoom out and connect with other locations where queer politics has or is taking a similar turn. I establish this connection to suggest how those troubled by these dangerous instances are related through experiences of failure rather than triumph, and that to acknowledge failure responsibly might offer a way of building 'affective communities' (Gandhi 2006) of queer kinship. I end on a note of hopelessness (not apathy) because resistance and solidarity are romantically overrated, and much of the cause for the dangerous commonsense we have built for ourselves.

When Was the New?

Of the many photographs of posters and banners at the 2014 Delhi Queer Pride march that flooded social media, there was one that caught my attention because of how appropriately it queered the times we were in. The 2014 Pride march was being held in the aftermath of two events that held special significance for queer politics in India. The first was the SC's December 2013 *Koushal* judgement[2] that re-criminalized adult, consensual, and private sex by overturning the landmark 2009 Delhi High Court *Naz Foundation* judgement[3] that had ruled Section 377 of the IPC, 1860 (which criminalizes 'carnal intercourse against the order of nature') to be unconstitutional (Bhaskaran 2002).

The second event was the election of Narendra Modi of the Hindu nationalist BJP as the prime minister in May 2014. Although the BJP has been driven by a neo-fascist ideology of establishing a Hindu *rashtra*[4]—even through mass violence against Muslims and Christians—for his electoral campaign, Modi produced a sophisticated narrative of soft fascism and hard neoliberalism that led to the BJP's historic win in the 2014 national elections.[5] The party's coming to power is not good news for queer rights in India, since the party has consistently maintained its opposition to homosexuality—characterizing it as a Western decadent import that is against their understanding of 'Indian' culture—and had strongly supported the *Koushal* decision.

So now, about the poster at the 2014 Delhi Pride march: this one depicted Modi's face painted with rainbow colours, carrying the line: 'I love Amit Shah' (Bhattacharya 2014). Shah is Modi's closest aide in the BJP—formerly the president of the party and now India's Home Minister. Their relationship goes back to the orchestration of the 2002 Gujarat pogrom under their watch (discussed in Chapter 3),[6] followed by the extra-judicial killings, or fake police encounters, of Muslim youths who were alleged to have plotted Modi's assassination (Agarwal 2013). Shah delivered a speech at an election rally in Muzaffarnagar in Uttar Pradesh in 2014, in which he instigated

Hindus to take revenge against Muslims (Press Trust of India 2014b). A queering of the Modi–Shah fascist camaraderie, as a quirky comment on the BJP's anti-homosexuality position, and the charge of the Modi–Shah homosocial intimacy, were what I guess the poster was invoking. Of course, it was also an expression of irreverence, puncturing Modi's hyper-masculinized and deified image in public culture, by playing on the relationship between the prime minister and his closest aide.

Around the same time as the Delhi Pride march—which was held in late November—I was in Mumbai, travelling in a taxi to the Santa Cruz airport to catch a flight back to Kolkata, my hometown. The traffic was extremely sluggish, as it always is in Mumbai. As I approached the airport, two things caught my attention. The first was a huge procession of the Bajrang Dal—the militant youth wing of the Sangh Parivar (Collective Family of Hindu Right-Wing outfits) (Jaffrelot 2005a) of which the BJP is also a part. A resounding slogan in Hindi being shouted on loudspeakers by those in the procession was: '*Katwa Pachtayega Ram Ram Chillaye Ga*', which translates as, 'The circumcised Muslim will repent; he will have to cry out Lord Ram's name'.[7] The fascist insinuation was unambiguous.

Closer to the airport, I saw posters of the Shiv Sena—another militant Hindu fascist political party that carried out the anti-Muslim violence in Mumbai in 1992[8]—pasted on street walls. They carried the photos of Bal Thackeray,[9] the late Shiv Sena supremo,[10] alongside B.R. Ambedkar, the chairperson of the Indian constitution's drafting committee and an inspiring leader of the anti-caste movement.[11] Ambedkar has been the beacon of the Dalit movement in India, and for his entire life, was a very strong critic of the Hindu religion, which, he has argued, was the basis of caste oppression in India (Ambedkar 2014). Although ideologically oppositional, to see Ambedkar and Thackeray together was not altogether surprising, because this was clearly the Shiv Sena's way of appealing for votes from the Dalit constituency in Maharashtra, and thereby mobilizing and consolidating an anti-Muslim electorate (Narayan 2009). However, this projection of Hindu–Dalit solidarity was not only a marker of the Hindu Right's attempts at forging new identitarian intimacies, but also a means to achieve its old desire of establishing Hindu Raj (rule) by eliminating the Muslim.[12]

In his tract *Pakistan or the Partition of India*, published in 1940, Ambedkar had cautioned against what I understand as a constitutive foundation of the New India. Ambedkar predicted: 'If Hindu Raj does become a fact, it will, no doubt, be the greatest calamity for this country. No matter what the Hindus say, Hinduism is a menace to liberty, equality and fraternity. On that account it is incompatible with democracy. Hindu Raj must be prevented at any cost' (Ambedkar 1940).[13]

Narendra Modi's election as prime minister in 2014 was a chest-thumping[14] return of Hindu Raj (in its repackaged neoliberal avatar)[15] to majority power after a decade.[16] And if one takes even a cursory look at the attacks on dissent and diversity that the new BJP government (or those part of its patronage networks within the Sangh Parivar) has carried out or legitimated in its two years in office, that is enough evidence to recognize that Indian democracy is in for a raw deal as far as the treatment of its religious minorities are concerned (Dayal 2015).

Some of these incidents of hate and bigotry have included the banning of beef eating in BJP-ruled states, because the cow is considered as holy for Hindus by the current political dispensation (despite the fact that it is a staple source of protein for the poor across religious denominations, is part of Islamic and indigenous culinary cultures in India, and historically Hindus have been beef-eaters (Jha 2009); to the attack on churches, to the lynching of a Muslim man in Uttar Pradesh by a mob of Hindus for allegedly storing beef in his fridge, to the intimidation and murders of activists and intellectuals for speaking and writing against the Hindu Right's fascist politics; to the slapping of the draconian sedition law to incriminate students and academics as 'anti-national' at the Jawaharlal Nehru University in Delhi for questioning India's armed occupation of Kashmir; to a vigilante Hindu cow-protection group's public flogging of Dalit youth for allegedly skinning a dead cow in Gujarat; to legally establishing India as the land of the Hindus by bringing an amendment to the Citizenship Act, 1955 which will grant asylum only to persecuted Hindus from other countries in South Asia; to name just a few.

In response to some of these events in 2015, many prominent writers, artists and filmmakers protested by returning the awards that they had received from the Indian state previously (and not necessarily from the BJP government) in recognition of their work. Author and activist Arundhati Roy, on returning her national award, wrote:

> I want to make it clear that I am not returning this award because I am 'shocked' by what is being called the 'growing intolerance' being fostered by the present government. First of all, 'intolerance' is the wrong word to use for the lynching, shooting, burning and mass murder of fellow human beings. Second, we had plenty of advance notice of what lay in store for us — so I cannot claim to be shocked by what has happened after this government was enthusiastically voted into office with an overwhelming majority. Third, these horrific murders are only a symptom of a deeper malaise. Life is hell for the living too. Whole populations — millions of Dalits, Adivasis, Muslims and Christians — are being forced to live in terror, unsure of when and from where the assault will come (2015).

Roy's comment bears testimony to the fact that other political forces, particularly the parliamentary Left in India, have failed miserably to prevent the advent of Hindutva politics.[17] This recognition requires that questions be asked about the Left's own insidious complicities with the ideologies and practices of both Hindutva and its vicissitudes in neoliberalism.

A few months into 2015, from within the grim shadows of Modi's rule in India, emerged two instances of queer visibility and assertion in full rainbow radiance. The first was what has been called India's first gay matrimonial advertisement that the daily *Mid-Day*, published (after being rejected by several other newspapers) (Inani 2015). It was inserted by Padma Iyer, mother of Harish. Harish is a prominent gay rights activist and media personality. Through the advertisement, Padma was seeking a groom for her son. Media outlets from around the world covered it as an event of radical significance in conservative India, and social media started celebrating it as a landmark for gay rights in a post-*Koushal* and Modi-fied India. The ad read: 'Seeking Well-Placed, Animal-Loving, Vegetarian, GROOM for my SON (36, 5' 11") who works with an NGO, Caste no Bar (Though IYER Preferred)' (Borges 2015).

What makes the advertisement worthy as a marker of its time in the New India, is not only that a gay matrimonial appears in mainstream

English media in a country where non-procreative sex stands criminalized, but also that this gay marriage solicitation carries a Brahmanical qualification in parenthesis which reinforces the very hierarchies of caste and endogamy legitimated by Hindu religion that Ambedkar had fought against. Iyers are Tamil Brahmins, mostly middle classes, but the topmost in the graded hierarchy of Hindu castes (Fuller and Narasimhan 2014).

These hierarchies that have for many years been propagated with celebratory zeal by the huge market for heterosexual matrimonials,[18] was now being wholeheartedly embraced by queers. On social media, the celebrations surrounding the advertisement were also accompanied by—though not in as many numbers—criticisms of its embedded casteism (Bhattacharya 2015). In response, Harish Iyer tweeted: 'that was not discriminatory tho [sic]. :) that's more like knowing someone from a familiar territory' (Iyer 2015). Of course, since when did listing personal preferences for soliciting a prospective spouse become discriminatory? Yet, Iyer's claim to 'familiar territory' in this case seemed to have been deployed as an alibi for reifying the insidious violence of sexual, caste, and class normativities, in the name of achieving marriage equality—much like the way in which race violence in Charleston was displaced by the celebrations surrounding the US Supreme Court decision in *Obergefell vs Hodges* legalizing same-sex marriage in June 2015.[19]

The second was an instance of another first. This time, it was a video called *The Visit* for the ethnic-wear brand Anouk, touted as 'India's first lesbian ad' (Johri 2016a). It shows a young urban couple, relaxed and confident in their skins and wearing Anouk apparel, in their very tastefully decorated house (with a poster of *A Clockwork Orange*, fluttering curtains and the soft glow of the setting sun streaming in), waiting to welcome the parents of one of them. The couple speak in English with each other—because they don't speak the same language, thus implying their cross-cultural relationship—and in the vernacular to the parents (on the phone), thus suggesting the ease with which they traverse between tradition and modernity (something that Anouk as a brand wants to stand for).

The video builds up a calm anticipation of a coming-out encounter, where the couple are going to tell the parents about their romantic relationship. One of them asks: 'Are you sure about this?' The one whose parents are on their way replies: 'I am sure about us, and I don't want to hide it anymore.' The video ends with the words 'Bold is Beautiful' on the screen, and the couple holding hands walk out of the frame to meet the parents, who we don't see.

While both the advertisements locate the normalization of queer liberation in domestic monogamous conjugality—which is a dream for many, and might in fact be a powerful public assertion to challenge the compulsorily heteronormative idea of the family—access to the domestic space and the relationship of conjugality is mediated through caste and endogamous marriage in the first, and in the second, through class as the marker of queer consumerism. Interestingly then, even while queering the discursive pitch, as it were, both the advertisements reinforce some of the very foundations that form the base of the idea of the New India, particularly that of privatization of liberation, and in effect marks a smooth spread of the 'epistemic violence' (Spivak 1998: 271) of the caste–class–sexuality complex from heteronormativity to 'homonormativity' (Duggan 2002: 175).[20]

How does one make sense of this moment in India's present, especially in the context of how it might impact queer politics, and the renewed legal struggles to decriminalize gay sex? Commenting on the simultaneous rise in the decriminalization of sodomy and legalization of gay marriage across several Western countries on the one hand and that of the spread of queer imperialism on the other, Nikita Dhawan wrote in a 2013 essay: 'For queer politics, it is the best of times, and it is the worst of times' (2013: 191). Her remark is apposite for the New India—where the ostensible conservatism of Hindu right-wing nationalism and its declared homophobia is coexistent with the narratives of queer liberation championed by neoliberalism. What, however, makes this moment of immense significance for queer politics in India is not so much the polarization between the best and the worst of times, but the growing intimacies between them—even as they might seem to be in opposition. Attending to these intimacies becomes imperative to make better sense of why it was under the BJP government's rule that the SC finally decriminalized Section 377 in 2018.

My thoughts on queer politics in New India are a response to a persistent discomfort with the emerging intimacies between claims for queer rights on the one hand and the conjoined narrative of *acche din* or good days that right-wing Hindu nationalism and neoliberalism currently espouse.[21] It is this ongoing phase of the simultaneous workings of Hindutva and neoliberalism—that I characterize as New India—inaugurated, if one has to identify a temporal marker, in the early 1990s—with the liberalization of the Indian economy in 1991, which also coincided with the chronological end of the Cold War and the beginning of the World Bank–initiated structural adjustment programmes in India, the escalation of militarization of Kashmir by the occupying Indian army, and the demolition of the Babri Masjid in Ayodhya by huge Hindu militant mobs a year later in 1992, led by key BJP politicians. The state supported 2002 anti-Muslim pogrom in Gujarat under Modi's leadership as chief minister and home minister; the Congress government's armed offensive against Adivasis to forcefully clear them off mineral-rich lands for acquisition by mining companies during its rule from 2004–14; and Modi's win in 2014, are all part of this New India's curated continuum.

Queer politics have not been immune to these key events in contemporary Indian history. Which is why the articulation of queer-rights claims cannot be understood through the unproblematized opposition that is generally drawn between the conservatism of non-Western primitive cultures and religions and non-heteronormative sexualities on the one hand, and the happy marriage between queer rights and the modern, neoliberal, militarized, and corporatized Indian nation-state on the other. Needless to say, the story is more complicated than that.

Although there have not been many attempts to write a historiography of the contemporary queer movement in India,[22] it is necessary to emphasize that the movement is not of recent origin, and has had very diverse and vibrant political roots. Having sustained its struggles despite not finding allies in both communists and feminists in India through many of its initial years—both these groups 'decrying lesbianism as an elitist deviation from real political issues' (N. Menon 2007: 23; Rege 1996: 1,359)—the movement continues to negotiate with such fraught encounters. I feel this historiographical 'lack'—to borrow from Dipesh Chakrabarty—could be read 'otherwise' (2000: 34), as a productive impossibility perhaps that is a testimony to the coexistence of many queer movements in India (not necessarily even called by this name), which resist the imposition of a homogenous historical narrative for the sake of academic intelligibility or curatorial desire.

While it is true that the queer movement is not homogenous in character,[23] there is certainly an urban, anglicized, and elite dominant voice within it—particularly those that have led the legal struggles against the anti-sodomy law—that gains most visibility and stands in for what has come to be identified globally as *the* Indian queer movement. This is the movement that I have been a part of—as an activist, academic, and intervener as a group of law professors in the SC in support of the *Naz Foundation* judgement[24]—and my reflections in this chapter emerge from these engagements. My aim is to do an 'otherwise' reading of queer politics in India, but not with the aim of romanticizing the idea of the 'lack', or by resisting it. While I remained committed to the movement against Section 377 at the time of writing this chapter, I was and am troubled by the fault lines that are emerging with the increasing visibility of a homogenous looking and sounding queer movement in India—mobilized around the legal challenge—in these times of Hindutva and neoliberalism. In carrying out this task I disclaim any objectivity in my views, as might have already become clear by now.

Law's Flashpoints

The law's flashpoints have been treated as harbingers of the history of queer politics in New India. As a result, they have turned into history-vanishing moments: 'a centripetal turbulence of illumination so powerful that it may blind the past even as it spotlights the present and lights up the future' (quoting David Kazanjian in Puar 2007: xviii). And when a history of struggle is reduced to flashpoints like landmark judgements, it is a truncated, blinkered history that results in a sanitized politics. 'A politics', as I have written with Dipika Jain elsewhere, 'that fossilises the past, valorises the present, and simply paints a clean picture: no contradictions, no contestations, no mess. A picture that irons out the unruly creases of historical inexplicability and is ready to adorn the manicured walls of an aesthetically curated memory museum' (Sircar and Jain 2017: xi–xii).

As is the case in many other parts of the world, the primary visibility for the queer rights movement in India has come from its almost singular engagement with the law, aimed at challenging Section 377 of the IPC, 1860, an antiquated Victorian provision that used to criminalize 'unnatural' sex, which basically includes all forms non-peno-vaginal, penetrative, non-procreative sex.[25] There has been a lot of documentation on how this federal law (along with a gamut of local laws), have been used, especially by the police, as a tool to persecute the sexually marginalized—especially in public places—whose vulnerabilities are further exacerbated due to their class-, caste-, gender-, and religion-based marginalities (People's Union for Civil Liberties, Karnataka 2001). After a very long and sustained legal battle, the Delhi High Court in its July 2009 *Naz Foundation* decision read down Section 377 by decriminalizing all forms of adult, consensual, and private sex, from the ambit of this law.[26] To advance a creative reading of equality and non-discrimination, the judgement was inspired by B.R. Ambedkar's notion of 'constitutional morality' which trumped conservative 'public morality' as a test to determine the law's unconstitutionality (Kannabiran 2012: 433–43).

The judgement was hailed, as Anjali Gopalan, founder of the petitioner organization Naz Foundation, exclaimed, 'Oh my God, we've finally stepped into the 21st century!' (Flock 2009). This symbolic civilizational uplift for India propelled by the judgement, announcing its membership into the moral universe of neoliberal modernity, valorized privacy as the qualifier for queer liberation. The primacy put on private sex—similar to the kind represented in the two advertisements discussed earlier—was the qualifier that enabled the reading down of the law, and effectively excluded from its purview a whole range of non-elite and indigenous sexually marginalized people who do not enjoy the privileges of private space.[27] The 'privacy' standard is a 'spectacle of emancipation' (Sircar 2012: 527), because those who do have access to private space were already outside of the reach of the law (Sircar 2008: 10–17). As Ashley Tellis has rightly questioned: 'What is the point of allowing consensual sex between private adults of the same sex when most violations are of us in the public realm: in institutions, on the streets, in parks, toilets?' (Tellis 2010). Similarly, Jason K. Fernandes has argued that 'the judgment responds to the interests of urban, English-speaking, middle-class leaders of the queer rights movement in India, by overshadowing those very sexually marginalised (Hijras, Kothis, Panthis) who they claim to represent' (2009). Anjali Arondekar has raised concerns about how 'the reading down of the law may thus now ostensibly allow for same-sex acts within private spaces, yet it ironically offers no protection for same-sex practices outside the normative parameters of home and domesticity' (2010: 113, 124). Transgender activists Raina Roy and Indira have pointed out that 'the link between IPC 377 and gay/lesbian criminalisation or liberation is more symbolic than material', because in practice the police 'rarely [...] use legal excuses to harass, abuse or rape socio-economically marginalised transgender and gay people. And when they do, they often evoke other laws concerning public order, decency, sex work or obscenity' (quoted in Boyce and Dutta 2013).

It is necessary to note that despite the Hindutva hatred of Muslims and other religious minorities in India, when it came to opposing the *Naz Foundation* judgement in the SC, a look at the list of appellants curiously revealed how right-wing Hindu, Muslim, and Christian groups had all suddenly become strange bedfellows united in their firm belief that decriminalizing Section 377 would shake up the foundations of all religions, and result in the definite degeneration of 'Indian culture'. Religious groups across denominations came together in solidarity against the judgement as part of the appeal that was filed by Suresh Kumar Koushal. A Hindu astrologer from Delhi, Koushal expressed his thoughts with bigoted creativity on why he challenged the judgement in the SC. In an interview with *The Hindu*, he had said: 'You can't allow anal intercourse. The back portion of a body is for throwing out the waste of the body. It is like an exhaust fan. If you allow it, then it is like reversing the motion of the earth, like reversing the blood flow' (Pisharoty 2013). Clearly, all the religious groups that joined Koushal in his appeal collectively shared a commitment to such bigotry.

New Emergences

The euphoria of the *Naz Foundation* judgement, however, was short-lived, because in December 2013, the SC in its anti-minority rights *Koushal* decision dismissed it. One of the primary grounds for dismissal was, as the court defying an empirical impossibility stated:

'lesbians, gays, bisexuals or transgenders' are a 'miniscule fraction of the country's population' hence Section 377 cannot be said to be adequately discriminatory against them as they do not constitute a reasonably classifiable group of people under the equality clause (Article 14) of the Constitution of India (read with the right against discrimination in Article 15, and the right to life in Article 21), to warrant the law being declared unconstitutional.[28]

The SC also adopted a hands-off stance in *Koushal*—in strange contradistinction to its own activist histories of protecting fundamental rights (Baxi 1985b: 107–32; Sathe 2002)—by saying that changes to the law should be brought through legislative action by the parliament, and that it falls outside of the court's purview to do so. In response to this 'jurispathic' (Cover 1983: 4–68,) judgement, Pratiksha Baxi powerfully wrote—albeit in a romantic display of 'left legalism' (Brown and Halley 2002a)—that it 'directs law's violence on the body of the Constitution of India. Proclaiming colonial law as constitutional, the Supreme Court negates its role in the making of postcolonial constitutionalism' (Baxi 2013).

The responses to the *Koushal* judgement, particularly on social media and activist circles, generated a discourse that characterized it as backward and the *Naz* judgement as forward. This linear progressive logic was expressed through the hashtag #nogoingback, and an image of 377 captive within a prohibition sign, which went instantly viral leading to mobilizations for protests on 15 December 2013, that came to be called the 'Global Day of Rage' across many locations in India and around the world (Nashrulla 2013a). Indira Jaisingh, women's rights activist and former additional solicitor general of India, called out the court's 'medieval mindset' (Special Correspondent 2013), while HIV/ AIDS and gay rights activist Ashok Row Kavi said that the court has 'put the clock back' (Pawar 2013). Author and poet Vikram Seth noted that the judgement 'takes us back to a position of barbarism' (Times News Network 2013). While it is true that all of these responses that deemed the judgement retrograde and resisted a return to an undesirable past, were speaking up against Section 377's colonial inheritance by courts and communities in independent India—it is also true that all of these comments seemed to express anguish about how the judgement is antithetical to their idea of New India—modern, global, progressive. As Paul Boyce and Aniruddha Dutta attentively commented in the din of a raging cacophony of protests:

> For lots of activists, the decision has significant symbolic implications in terms of India's image in the international arena. India had previously [post *Naz*] looked relatively progressive on the world stage in terms of minority sexual rights. This was part of a package of other attributes, such as growing socio-economic liberalism and urbanising modernity in the sub-continent, often associated with sexual progress despite their problematic impacts in terms of poverty and the wealth gap. Now, a more regressive image suddenly seems to have taken centre stage. The Supreme Court decision is especially important not only because it stirs up a new set of concerns for same-sex desiring and practising people in India, but because it appears to upset an equivalence between legislative progress on sexual rights and the image of India as a modern, secular and progressive nation (2013).[29]

It is necessary to understand how this logic came to prevail over the framing of contestations over queer rights in India. This backward/ forward logic is located on contentious foundations that open up articulations of queer rights claims to troubling appropriations by Hindutva and neoliberal narratives. In fact, what emerges is that the lines between progressive and regressive have increasingly blurred when queer victories and defeats are characterized as forward/ backward.[30]

The *Koushal* decision came a few months before India's national elections in 2014. In the din of statements by political parties on the judgement, the then ruling party, the Indian National Congress, declared that they will support a legislation in parliament to repeal Section 377. The Congress party even went on to include this commitment in their election manifesto (Shukla 2014). Such a commitment by a major political party has been unprecedented, and only goes to show the impact that the anti-377 movements have had on the public and political consciousness in India. Of course, this also points at how urban and elite queers (and their corporate allies) were being considered as a constituency worthy of being a sizeable vote bank in the pre-election moment. While the Congress' move was celebrated by many, I would argue that it was used as a convenient ploy for the then ruling government to portray itself as progressive (in contrast to the right-wing and Hindu majoritarian BJP, its biggest opposition), and taking attention away from the fact that it is the same government which has unleashed brutal armed violence against India's Adivasi populations, at the behest of huge mining corporations (Roy 2009). This was a classic instance of the perverse use of the promise of law reform to the sexually marginalized on the one hand, and to carry on legalized violence on peasants and ethnic minorities on the other.[31]

The BJP on the other hand was the only major political party, poised to win the elections, which made public statements saying that they will never support the decriminalization of Section 377 (*Firstpost* 2013a). They set up 'homosexuality' against the idea of their Hinduized definition of 'Indian culture', merrily sidestepping the fact that this 'anti-sodomy' law that they so strongly wished to support was in fact a colonial legacy.

So, as I said in the beginning, the BJP's coming to power is certainly not good news for queer people, and for those who are committed to the queer and sexuality rights movements in India.[32] Of course one didn't have to wait for the BJP's win to understand this. Other members of the Sangh Parivar that the BJP is a part of have a checkered history of carrying out vandalism against all kinds of expressions of non-heteronormative sex and affirmative representations of female sexuality. Instances include, the violent censoring of Deepa Mehta's 1996 film *Fire* (Kapur 2000: 53–64), the hounding of painter M.F. Husain out the country for painting the Hindu goddess Saraswati in the nude in 2006 (Tripathi 1997: 90), or forcing the pulping of historian Wendy Doniger's book *Hindus: An Alternative History* in 2014 (Taylor 2014: 717), and forcing the Tamil writer Perumal Murugan to declare his literary death by the public burnings of his book *Madhorubhagan* in 2015 (Kannabiran 2015: 76)—just to name a few instances.[33]

An annual fixture of several Hindu right-wing political outfits for many years has been to vandalize gift shops and beat and intimidate (heterosexual) couples who celebrate Valentine's Day in public (Varughese 2014: 93). In 2009, women were attacked and publicly beaten by members of a Hindu group called Sri Ram Sene for going to have a drink at a pub in Mangalore (Sengupta 2009). In recent years the Hindu Right has used the bogey of what it calls 'Love Jihad' to vilify Muslim men in love with Hindu women, on the pretext that they are trying to convert Hindu women to Islam by luring them into marrying them (Gupta 2009: 13).

Another judgement that came after *Koushal* deserves a brief mention here. In April 2014, while the general elections that Modi went on to win were on in full swing, in *National Legal Services Authority (NALSA) vs Union of India*,[34] the SC recognized transgender persons as the 'third gender', ordered that their FRs in Part III of the Indian constitution be protected, and upheld their 'right to decide their self-identified gender'. The judgement also directed central and state governments to treat transgender persons 'as socially and educationally backward classes of citizens and extend all kinds of reservation in cases of admission in educational institutions and for public appointments [to them]'. One might say that *NALSA* overcame the concerns about elitism which I had earlier raised to critique the *Naz Foundation* judgement for its primacy on privacy. But, only contingently.

The decision was hailed by the media and by activists alike for its progressivism, and was unanimously welcomed by political parties across the spectrum. By comparing it to the regressive decision in *Koushal*, many queried how the same SC, in a matter of months, could deliver such a rights-affirming judgement in favour of India's sexually marginalized. One primary distinction between *Naz*/*Koushal* and *NALSA* is the issues that were adjudicated upon—the legitimacy of non-procreative sex (primarily between gay men) in the former, and the right of a culturally identifiable sexually marginalized group to a life of dignity in the latter.

Of course, these are related issues—and all three cases were concerned about the violence faced by non-heterosexual persons because of the existence of a law, and due to societal prejudices—but sex as *behaviour* was attached with a certain kind of repugnance in *Koushal* that was not attached to sex as *identity* in *NALSA*. The latter remained sanitized of offering an opinion on Section 377 (and deferred it to *Koushal*), and, by extension, on the legitimacy of non-procreative sex. The judgement speaks in the liberal language of human rights (much like *Naz*), that, while on the one hand, serves as the foundation of its celebrated progressivism, but on the other (unlike *Naz*), depoliticizes sex (as act) by treating transgender persons as subjects of welfare and uplift, thus ordering that they be treated akin to a constitutionally designated group called other backward classes, who are considered to be socially and educationally disadvantaged.

In doing this balancing act between being rights-affirmative and sex-agnostic, *NALSA* avoids provoking moral panic, or the ire of the sex-phobic Hindu Right. Much like the two advertisements discussed earlier, *NALSA* offers a seamless fusion between tradition (its references to Hindu mythology for tracing the history of transgender persons in India) and modernity (drawing on international human rights law on gender identity and sexual orientation for affirming their rights). The *NALSA* judgement's recognition of the rights of transgender persons frames their identities and lives as lacking—'absence of procreative capability' and 'backward'—and thus 'constitutes them as biopolitical subjects for care and management by the state' (Dutta 2015: 225). Even as it grants citizenship status, albeit a graded one, such a framing keeps transgender persons at a safe—thus, uncontaminateable—distance from the heteronormative institutions of marriage, family, and property devolution/ownership that form the foundations of New India, and from which the idea of the Hindu nation draws its cultural, political, and economic capital.[35]

In May 2014—a month after the *NALSA* judgement—television music network Channel V produced a video called 'The Seatbelt Crew' made by the advertising firm Ogilvy and Mather, featuring a particular cultural group of transgender women (hijras) promoting road safety in India (Seervai 2014). The video shows a group of hijras, all dressed in identical blue saris and purple blouses, like that of airhostesses, carrying out a safety drill at a traffic signal to educate car drivers about the importance of wearing the seatbelt (V with U 2014). A traffic signal is that liminal location that is used by many hijras to earn money by begging. In return they offer blessings. In the video, the members of the hijras crew say they will exchange their blessings with those abiding by the rule of wearing the seatbelt while driving.

Hijras begging (or sex working) at traffic signals, and other public places, like on trains, are oftentimes ridiculed, and even beaten and harassed in this conduct of a precarious livelihood practice. They are regularly at the receiving end of egregious forms of harassment and violence from the police, whose acts are legitimated by various public decency laws.[36] Hijras' mere public presence is considered a nuisance, despite the fact that they are accorded a perverted sacredness to give away blessings on occasions like birth and marriage. They are called to bless the newborn or the newly married so that they absorb any possibility of reproductive incapacity that they are thought to have already been cursed with (Jaffrey 1996; Reddy 2005).

The video, it seems, takes a cue from *NALSA* to represent hijras through a liberal rights frame that is meant to make them look and do something more respectable than begging or soliciting sex at traffic signals. It aims at transforming them into responsibilized subjects: pleasantly feminine creatures, neatly dressed with understated make-up, stripped of the radical performance of sexuality that their public presence as beggars or sex workers otherwise embody. The class–caste–sexuality compact of both heteronormativity and homonormativity in this video narrates a story of amelioration that offers a sense of respectability and responsibilization by turning hijras into educators as a rehabilitative gesture, but they remain captive in their liminal public location at traffic signals. This compact actively works to prohibit their presence in any imaginary of the domestic private space of productive/procreative conjugality as celebrated in the two previous advertisements. While monogamous gay and lesbian emancipation is tied to practices of privatized conjugality, hijra emancipation seems contingent upon public performances of respectability and responsibilization, and individualized compassion towards their lack and backwardness.[37]

Hinduizing the Neoliberal Queer

In the new emergences discussed above, we will be missing something crucial in these mobilizations around sexual politics in general and queer politics in particular in India if we continue to read them through the forward/backward logic that posits peoples, parties, and publics based on their political ideology neatly on either side of the progressive/regressive divide.

In response to the BJP's coming to power, the popular argument that most on the secular-left (including me) tend to make is that the onslaught on sexual rights will increase manifold. This, I believe, is a different kind of moral panic that, just like the Hindu Right, reinforces a false opposition between religion and queer sexuality. I call this false, because not only is there brilliant historical evidence of queer sexuality in abundance in religious/spiritual art and literature from India (Vanita and Kidwai 2000), but also that such an argument presumes that a queer person cannot be a Hindu right-winger.

The rise of the Hindu Right in India has, in fact, seen a simultaneous rise of the neoliberal and Hindu queer subject, who performs, 'homonationalist' (Puar 2007) and 'homocapitalist' (Rao 2015: 38) practices with aplomb in their ostensibly chic queer lifestyles. These subjects might in fact celebrate Modi's win, because many upper-class, upper-caste Hindu queer people believe that Hindu India was always open to non-normative sexualities, but it was only when the Muslim 'invaders' plundered India that India's tolerance with sexual diversity took a plunge.[38] This is a narrative that is perfectly compatible with that of the Hindu Right. Such an argument, versions of which have been propagated by many right-wing queers, allows the Hindu Right to Brahmanize India's erotic pasts through the creation of the imagined evil Muslim homophobic outsider.

When Modi came to power, I had argued that we'll be mistaken to write off the BJP as a party that will never support queer rights, despite its public stand against Section 377 (Sircar 2014). If neoliberalism has wholeheartedly been embraced by the Hindu Right, it wouldn't be surprising if, in its developmentalist avatar, the BJP starts supporting queer rights, albeit one which promotes an essentialist version of Indian history that is Hindu, and thus tolerant of sexual diversity. If this serves their sectarian interests better, and enables them to find another way to Hinduize Indian history, then BJP will do this, as is evident from the Rashtriya Swayamsevak Sangh (RSS, which is the ideological fountainhead of the Sangh Parivar) spokesperson Ram Madhav's indication of the possibility of a softened stand on Section 377 (Kumar 2014); or Harsh Vardhan, the former BJP health minister, publicly saying that irrespective of Section 377 the government should protect the human rights of gays (Press Trust of India 2014a). The BJP's second law minister in Modi's cabinet, Sadananda Gowda, was reported in national media to have said the following about decriminalizing Section 377: 'The mood appears to be in favour of it.' He later retracted his statement, saying that he was misquoted. Subhramanian Swamy, a member of the BJP's national executive, tweeted a corrective: 'I think the law minister was misquoted, our party position has been that homosexuality is a genetic disorder' (*FirstPost* (FP) Politics 2015). Although the BJP's party position continued to offer bigoted explanations for its stand against Section 377, the fact that some of its ministers made public statements that are open to the idea of a rethink on the law indicates that once they are able to work out the immense possibilities in Hinduizing the neoliberal queer as a means to forward their agenda of establishing a Hindu rashtra, they might just go ahead and do it. And so it happened in 2018. Days following the *Navtej Johar* judgement, social media was filled with celebratory messages and memes. India, these declared, has finally rid itself of a colonial taint. The judiciary was congratulated for enabling a decolonization of sorts. From Uber to Farhan Akhtar, all joined in the rainbow-unfurling party.[39] The trending hashtags were #loveislove and #lovewins and in one such meme, the first hashtag features as the text written inside the map of India—marked by its political boundaries and filled with rainbow colours. If you paid attention it wouldn't be hard to notice that the cartographic imagination that love and the rainbow covered included Kashmir as an integral part of the Indian nation (Krishna 1994: 507). The win for love in India seemed to have reinforced an idea of the Indian nation that does not violently occupy Kashmir through its army. Queer emancipation from a colonial law seemed to happily coexist with India's colonial control over Kashmir. Both were being celebrated with equal aplomb. I don't see this as conspiratorial, but the condition of queer politics in the New India.

Outside of the speculations concerning the political parties discussed above, I have written elsewhere about how the attachment of nationalist pride to public queer rights articulations has been evident at many pride parades in India.[40] For example, at the Delhi Queer Pride march I attended in 2010, there were passionate cries of 'Jai Hind' (Victory to the Nation); and as an activist friend from Mumbai mentioned, that at the Mumbai Queer Pride march that same year, participants held hands at the end to sing the Indian national anthem—despite resistance from some. What imaginations of queer belonging does the singing of the national anthem signify, especially for the Muslim/Adivasi/Dalit queer? How would she reconcile her experience of alienation as a citizen by the Hindutvavadi Indian state, with the feeling of queer solidarity that she seeks at a pride march?

The national anthem also made an appearance on a talk show on the English news channel CNN-IBN during a discussion about whether independent India is open to homosexuality. This programme was being aired during the Independence Day week in 2009, just a few weeks after the delivery of the *Naz* judgement on 2 July. The experts invited to speak were responding to a CNN-IBN–*Hindustan Times* survey in which almost 70 per cent of the respondents felt that homosexuality should be illegal in India (Sharma 2009). There were a range of speakers represented by activists, filmmakers, politicians, academicians, and a Hindu conservative.

The discussion sparked many a fire, but was hackneyed—the same arguments and the same defences that are not worth repeating here. Yet, the unprecedented openness with which the audience was engaging with the issue of homosexuality on primetime television was an encouraging sign. The findings of the survey (even if statistics are graver than damned lies) did throw light on the societal prejudice that queers face in India, despite progressive judgements like *Naz*.

The sharp divide in beliefs and perspectives among the panellists on issues of sexual morality finally reached a climax through a moment of nationalism-induced catharsis. Sagarika Ghose, the anchor, abruptly ended the show by asking everyone to stand up to the national anthem. And as per her instructions everyone did—the conservatives, the liberals, the fence-sitters, the homosexuals, the heterosexuals, the non-heterosexuals—everyone stood upright soaking in the buoyant verses of 'Jana Gana Mana' and it seemed a perfect end to the crisis of India's morals, culture, sexuality, and religion where nationalist pride erased all differences and made us realize that, after all, we are all 'Indians' first.[41]

These instances of the 'nationalist resolution of the homosexual question'—to queer Partha Chatterjee's phrase (Chatterjee 1999: 233)—take on more significance in a BJP-ruled India, if one considers the slickly designed and en masse produced placards at the 2014 Delhi Pride carrying the Hindi words '*Ek Bharat*' (One India) in Devanagari script, printed over pastel shades of rainbow colours. The choice of the nomenclature Bharat (as the Indic equivalent of India) interestingly carries both Hindu and constitutional precedents. Article 1 of the putatively secular Constitution of India opens with the words: 'India that is Bharat […]', and there is ample evidence of the Hindu influences in the records of the Constituent Assembly Debates that lead to the insertion of this article (P. Singh 2005: 909). Upendra Baxi has questioned the exclusionary basis of this constitutional equivalence:

> Does it contain codes of memory and identity of some vision of pre-British, even millenarian, Hindu empire and civilization? What would the word 'Bharat' mean, for example, to a Konyak Naga, a Bhil, a Santhal, and a Bodo person/ woman? What would this mean to India's Islamic peoples, among them the Bohras, Meos, Khojas, the Ahmadiyas, the Shias and the Sunnis? And what may this notion convey to Indian Christians, the Parsees and the microscopic Jewish communities? And how may [we] relate the idea of Bharat to the diasporic Tibetan, Pakistani, and East Bengal (Bangladeshi) migrants to India after the independence? How may be one an *Indian* without at the same time being a *Bharati*? What mix of human rights and rightlessness does this all signify? (2003: 11, emphasis in original).

I read the queer articulation of Ek Bharat at a pride march as signifying the very troubling, inseparable vision of sexual unity conditional on secular (read: Hindu) assimilation; which is equally troubling when read the other way: as secular unity predicated on sexual (read: homonormative/homonationalist) assimilation.

For the 2015 Mumbai Pride march, an image that was circulated as a social media announcement, replicated the poster of the 2001 HBO TV series *Band of Brothers*, which was on American sacrifice in World War II (Katyal 2015). The Mumbai Queer Pride march announcement carried the identical landscape of silhouetted army men, with the text replaced as: 'Queer Cadets and Allies / Pride is Coming'. By identifying the trope of war that connects the two images, Akhil Katyal offered a trenchant reading of the Mumbai Queer Pride march announcement that celebrates an emergent queer subject that he calls 'The Homo Pathetic'. It is useful to quote Katyal at length:

> What strange twist of fate in our times brings on this convergence of war brouhaha and modern queer politics, of war flags and rainbows? Is it that strange after all? In these times of the Homo Pathetic (THP), I suggest it is not. [...] On his way to the Holy Grail of gay rights [the

> Pride March], he is the victim better than any other. He is the most tortured being on earth. No one's suffering; no one's pathos equals his. All women, Dalits, black folks, the poor, the droned-out war-refugees, and half those LBT's all add up and produce a quantity of pain that is not even enough to sugar the morning tea of the Homo Pathetic. He out-victims them all. And in order to do something about his pain, he will use any war-justifying, bloodshed-glorifying, trench-beautifying god-damn image of American exceptionalism, if that is what it will take to bring him two inches closer to his goal of gay rights (2015).

Also, take the example of the media and activist response to India's vote at the UN against granting benefits for partners of same-sex employees in 2014 (*Express News Service* 2015). There is no doubt that the Indian state needs to be questioned for its practices of institutionalized homophobia, as well for finding a cover for its homophobia by justifying its decision on grounds of procedural anomalies (Haider 2015).

Yet, it is necessary to take note of the fact that the ostensibly secular-liberal response in India was an expression of shock regarding the company of states (who also voted against the resolution) that India was in. Like one media headline said: 'India stood with Iran, Saudi and Pakistan in failed attempt to block benefits for gay UN staffers' (*Scroll* 2015). Another read: 'Despots, Religious Extremists: Company India Keeps on Gay Rights' (*IndiaSpend* 2015). These 'despotic' states clearly included a lot of Islamic countries (though it was Russia that led the failed initiative to defeat the secretary general's decision). What surprised me was why shock was being expressed at the company India keeps. Isn't the present Indian government a religious extremist one? Wasn't it the highest court of the country that reinstated a law that was discriminatory towards the sexually marginalized? So isn't India, in fact, in the right company? Or, as Madhavi Menon rightly asked: was there an underlining Islamophobia, wrapped in secular homophilia that provoked these media and activist responses? (2015).

A similar logic also worked through the legal activism prior to the *Naz* judgement, where an advocacy document featuring an open letter arguing for the repeal of Section 377 (signed by eminent Indians including Nobel laureate Amartya Sen, novelist and poet Vikram

Seth, and essayist and Booker Prize winner Arundhati Roy, among others), carried a map of the world, with countries—from the Third World (the Middle East, Africa, the Caribbean, and South and South East Asia)—that criminalize sodomy marked out in orange, asking the question: 'To which world must India belong?'[42] 'The question relies', writes Rahul Rao in his analysis,

> for its persuasiveness on what it knows to be the predisposition of an elite Indian audience, desperate to break away from the Third World to take its rightful place at the table of the powerful. The irony of deploying both tropes in combination – blaming the colonial West for its imposition of the sodomy law and urging its repeal through an imitation of the postcolonial post-Wolfenden West – is either lost or slyly concealed in an attempt to appeal simultaneously to what are thought to be the divergent preferences of cultural nationalists and neoliberal modernizers (2014: 199).

To return to the immediate aftermath of the post-*Koushal* moment in December 2013: the social media outrage surrounding the dismissal of the *Naz* judgement by the SC was acknowledged by several lifestyle brands that came out with advertisements celebrating queerness, clearly indicating the neoliberal market's recognition of elite queers as consumers (Nashrulla 2013). While corporate India's response can be read as progressive, yet at the same time, its appeal was specifically aimed at a particular class of queer consumers (or those aspiring to join that class)—'experts in the art of self-conduct' (Cossman 2007: 2–3)—who can afford these products and invest in fashioning an elite queer lifestyle. The advertisements were reflective of an atmosphere where only a select few could rejoice in the queer-friendliness of corporate benevolence at a time of mourning. Mind you, there were no freebies. These were advertisements to raise sales, smartly packaged in a rainbow wrapper.

Two months later, in February 2014, while the election campaigns in India were going on at a feverish pitch and media psephologists were almost unanimously speculating a certain win for the BJP, the World Bank released a report titled *The Economic Cost of Homophobia and the Exclusion of LGBT People: A Case Study of India* (Badgett 2014). The report's findings suggested that discrimination against LGBT people made the Indian economy lose between 0.1 per cent and 1.7 per cent of its GDP in 2012. In 2012 it was the Congress government in power, and Section 377's decriminalized status accorded by the *Naz* judgement was still valid. It seems to me that the timing of this report's release in 2014 was meant as a message to the neoliberalism-loving BJP, slated to come to power, to pay heed and better its performance in comparison to the Congress's.[43] It might also be indicative of the World Bank's greater trust in Modi's neoliberal vision, which made it release the report specifically at that time. This report forms part of the proliferation of International Financial Institutions' support for LGBT rights. Rao identifies this as the workings of what he calls 'global homocapitalism' (Rao 2015: 38). As he writes in his analysis of the report and the connection that it draws between economic growth and the end of homophobia in India:

> Queer visions of the good life become mortgaged to limitless growth, which is itself further insulated from environmental, equity, and other critiques. Beholden to capitalism, the prospects for a queer Green or a queer indigenous politics become increasingly remote. In the political context of the [World] Bank's work in India, the Bank's overtures to queers should invite us to interrogate the queer movement's relations with other social movements – those of farmers, fishworkers and adivasis (forest dwellers) to name only a few – that have struggled against the effects of Bank-led policies for decades. [...] [I]t is sobering to imagine what queer adivasis might make of a Bank project that hailed their participation (as queers) in the very processes that are destroying their lifeworlds (as queer adivasis). That the intersectionality of queer and Adivasi is virtually unthinkable in the imaginary of the Bank and possibly the mainstream of the queer movement in India begs important questions [...] (2015: 41).

This global, neoliberal market as queer ally inaugurates new narratives of progress that are more comfortably aligned with Hindutva than one might expect. A Bollywood-style music video, called *The Welcome*, produced by Free & Equal, the UN campaign for lesbian, gay, bisexual, and transgender equality, also released in the aftermath of *Koushal*, is an instance of the phenomena I am describing (UN Human Rights 2014). The video features Bollywood actor Celina Jaitley (who has also been a vocal supporter of gay rights), and shows a very affluent family—given the set-up of the location, the dresses, the upholstery, and so on—getting ready to welcome a male member of the family and his significant other, who the family doesn't know is also a man. When they arrive, and it is revealed that the partner is male, there is a still stare on everyone's face. But in a few seconds the eldest member of the family, the grandmother, smiles. The couple touch her feet (a Hindu custom), and then they all dance together to the song. The UN web page offers a subtitle to the video, which reads: 'Love is a family value'.[44] Along with Hindutva and neoliberalism, we see the narrative of human rights, and in the case of this particular video, that of marriage equality, entering the scene of New India's new queer politics.[45]

While I'd happily celebrate the successful Bollywoodization of the UN, and am aware of the power of popular culture as a tool for social change, it's necessary to ask: Whose rights is the UN talking about in this video? What class is depicted? What kinds of clothes and accessories are they wearing? What cars are being driven? What kind of houses do they live in? What's the religion of the family? The video clearly marks the spectacular arrival of the uber-cool queer subject, and the progressive Hindu family in India; and for the global audience, it is also adequately orientalized with all the grandeur of colours and dances that Bollywood's reductionist and fantastic vision of India has come to signify (Joshi 2015).

This video, in many ways, seems like a precursor to the two advertisements that I discussed in the beginning of this article that locate articulations of queer emancipation in the homonormative family and in monogamous conjugality, and yet, the aesthetic tropes that are used to fashion this narrative of emancipation, privatizes the world of queer liberation and struggle to reinforce class, caste, and religious hierarchies and prejudices. One can argue that the video neatly invisibilizes the indigenous queers of India, who are at the receiving end of a combination of oppression based on class, caste, sexuality, gender, religion, and language. Not to say that representing them would've made the video a better advocacy tool—because the chances of exoticizing indigenous sexualities for the hegemonic consumption of a global (overwhelmingly white) saviour publics of queer compassion would have made it into a perfect tool for marketing Third World queer suffering.

Civilizational Scripts

My rather meandering account of new queer politics in the New India is closely tied to ongoing and emergent dimensions in global queer politics—of which I have provided some indications. This story will remain incomplete if I do not speak to some of these connections. I'd like to recollect two incidents that I was part of that offer some insights into how a certain civilizational script has come to frame the narrative of global queer politics today.

In June 2010, I was in Berlin to speak at a conference (where one of the first versions of this chapter was presented), and my visit coincided with the city's huge corporate-funded pride event called the Christopher Street Day (CSD) parade, which I attended. At the culmination of the parade a large and colourful crowd had gathered in front of a stage on which American queer theorist Judith Butler was to be awarded the Zivilcourage (Civil Courage) Prize. Butler was introduced as a 'determined critic' by one of the organizers and was called on stage to accept the award. She took the award in her hand, went up to the microphone, and said:

> When I considered what it means today to accept such an award, I believe that I would actually lose my courage, if I would simply accept the prize under the present political conditions. [...] I must distance myself from this complicity with racism, including anti-Muslim racism. We have recognized that lesbian, gay, trans, queer people, can be used by warmongers.[46]

By making her refusal clear, Butler went on to say that queers are being co-opted into the politics of racist hatred that justify the war on terror, and they have been used to advocate in favour of anti-immigrant policies and media campaigns in the name of protecting the 'modern' and 'progressive' culture of Germany from contamination by the 'backward' and 'homophobic' outsider, who is almost always cast as Muslim.

Butler offered the prize to anti-racist queer groups in Berlin, who she acknowledged are more deserving of it because of their consistent resistance against practices of racism and Islamophobia among queer organizing in Berlin. There was resounding applause from the crowd. While some of the organizers tried to say things to defend themselves, all was drowned out in the cacophonous uproar. Queer politics in Germany, and especially those associated with the organization of the CSD parade, have for years been complicit in perpetuating racism that characterized Muslim immigrants as homophobes and thus inassimilable into German 'culture'.

One instance of this is the support that many queer groups in Germany had shown for what has been called the 'Muslim Test', which has now been revoked. The test was exclusively meant for people who sought immigration into Germany from a so-called 'Muslim' country. It required that those seeking immigration respond to questions like: 'what would you do if your son comes out to you as gay?' (Corbet 2006). Jin Haritaworn with Tamsila Tauqir and Esra Erdem, writing about queer support for anti-immigrant policies in western Europe, have called this a practice of 'gay imperialism' (Haritaworn et al. 2009: 71), which is a formation that speaks of queer rights in the language of exclusionary nationalism. A nationalism that instrumentalizes a discourse of queer rights to achieve the ends of a virulent racism that makes legitimate the bogus explanations for the war on terror—that it will bring democracy, peace, rule of law, and freedom for the 'gay Muslim victim' in the 'primitive' Islamic countries that are militarily invaded by the West. Commenting on how the 'Muslim Test' aimed to elevate 'gender and sexuality to mainstream political status' in Germany, Haritaworn, Tauqir, and Erdem observe: '[W]e find it vital to note that its main basis is not a progress in gender and sexual politics but a regression in racial politics' (2009: 79).

There was, the last I heard, a similar test for immigrants to the Netherlands. In this test immigrants from a specific set of non-western countries were made to watch a video showing two gay men kissing in a park, and a topless woman bathing. Being able to watch these videos unflinchingly was understood as a marker of whether prospective immigrants can embrace 'modernity', and thus be worthy of being allowed legal entry. Citizens of the USA, Australia, New Zealand, Canada, Japan, and Switzerland applying for immigration to Holland were exempted from taking this test (Associated Press 2006).

An influential and growing body of critical scholarship, primarily by queer of colour academic-activists have powerfully critiqued practices of gay imperialism, which have come to be identified as critiques of 'homonationalism' (Puar 2007). A necessary function of homonationalism—a condition that Jasbir Puar identifies as having emerged in the aftermath of the 11 September 2001 attacks on the World Trade Centre in the US[47]—has been to mobilize dominant queer publics contingent upon their performance of an overt patriotism and jingoistic nationalism. Haritaworn, Puar, and veteran activist Scott Long, all of who have consistently challenged the racism embedded in such a narrative of queer emancipation in the West through their writings, have also been at the receiving end of attempts to censor their views, and have even been threatened with criminal defamation cases for calling out the racist and Islamophobic agenda of prominent Australian-British activist Peter Tatchell.[48] As Butler's refusal speech highlighted, such mobilizations—in favour of gay imperialism and against those who critique it—have recruited queer voices to lend support to anti-immigrant state policies and provided a means to mask the racism of Western queer organizing in the name of protecting queer rights globally.

Homonationalism has been very effectively put to work in projecting militaristic Western nations as queer friendly. This is operationalized through the practice of what has come to be called 'pinkwashing' (Mikdashi 2011), applied particularly to identify Israel's queer rights propaganda as a means to justify its apartheid against Palestinians. Pinkwashing has been used by the Israeli state quite effectively in advertising campaigns in Western Europe and North America to build a brand of queer-friendly nationalism that takes attention away from its violent occupation of Palestine. As Puar writes:

> Israeli pinkwashing is a potent method through which the terms of Israeli occupation of Palestine are reiterated – Israel is civilised, Palestinians are barbaric, homophobic, uncivilized, suicide-bombing fanatics. It produces Israel as the only gay-friendly country in an otherwise hostile region. This has manifold effects: it denies Israeli homophobic oppression of its own gays and lesbians, of which there is plenty, and it recruits, often unwittingly, gays and lesbians of other countries into collusion with Israeli violence towards Palestine (2010).

Anti-occupation queer groups outside of Israel, like Toronto's Queers Against Israeli Apartheid (QuAIA), have challenged the attempts at pinkwashing the Toronto Pride. But such resistance has met with QuAIA being denied inclusion in the city's pride march. The group was part of the parade for the several years, but the organizers imposed a ban in 2010. Apparently, the reason for the ban had to do with the accusation by the pro-Israel and Jewish lobbies (which included Zionist queers) about how the term 'Israeli Apartheid' was anti-Semitic (Grant 2012).

Interestingly, QuAIA's challenge to their exclusion was on the grounds of their freedom of speech and expression (a liberal rights claim that Canadian democracy prides itself for) and that in a recursive way, as Michael Connors Jackman and Nishant Upadhyay point out, has contributed to a discourse of 'whitewashing' the settler-colonial inheritances of anti-pinkwashing queer activism in Canada. As Jackman and Upadhyay write:

> [W]e question how (settler) queer politics is produced and maintained by settler colonialism. Queer settlers are complicit in reimagining and reproducing the same nation-building narratives that it produces and maintains. Whiteness and queerness within the settler state create ambivalent and racial state hierarchies, naturalizing the settler state as non-colonial and 'normal' (2014: 200–1).

This critique would very well apply to my location in Australia. I mentioned in the acknowledgment section of this book that the land of the University of Melbourne on which this essay was written belongs to the Wurundjeri People of the Kulin Nation. I provide this acknowledgement to foreground how I am—even as a non-white skilled temporary migrant from a postcolonial country to Australia—a beneficiary of the ongoing loots of settler colonialism.

If one end of homonationalism has been to use the civilizational logic of human rights to construct the bogey of the Muslim homophobic outsider, thus justifying anti-immigrant policies to keep the most vulnerable of refugees out, the other has been to use that same logic to construct the queer Muslim victim, and let her in. This show of benevolence—again in the name of protecting the human rights of queer people fleeing persecution from non-Western lands—plays out a script of civilizational hierarchy in a settler-colonial context like Australia.

This brings me to my second incident. In January 2014, I was on a panel at the Melbourne Law School to reflect on the consequences of the *Koushal* decision. During the discussion, a man raised his hand to ask a question. He introduced himself and an accompanying colleague as representatives of the Australian government's Refugee Review Tribunal—an independent statutory body that hears reviews of 'protection visa' refusals to asylum seekers by the department of immigration and citizenship. He asked whether, in the light of the *Koushal* judgement dismissing *Naz*, persecution based on sexual orientation in India will increase resulting in more asylum claims to Australia.

The question caught me completely off guard. First, I wasn't even aware that there were a sizeable number of applicants from India to Australia who were seeking asylum for persecution based on sexual orientation. So I couldn't have provided him with an empirically sound answer. Second, I was in a dilemma about whether what I say might play any role in prejudicing asylum applications from Indians fleeing persecution for their sexual orientation to seek refugee status in Australia. And third, I wondered why he was interested in the numbers going up—was that an expression of compassion, or paranoia? I don't remember clearly, but I must have mumbled something that was quite incoherent to him, and he clearly didn't look satisfied.

While on the one hand I thought that it was quite considerate of the Refugee Review Tribunal to send in their personnel to know more about whether *Koushal* would increase incidents of persecution, given how widely the judgement was criticized globally, with a Global Day of Rage protest being held in Sydney. On the other hand, I wondered what this interest meant in the context of Australia's continuing egregious treatment of 'bad asylum seekers' (because they arrive by boats and are accused of jumping the queue—in other words, not being well behaved) (Kapur 2005: 128). Australia's horrific policy on indefinite detentions (Saul 2012: 685), and a history of white-settler supremacy demonstrated with chilling effect in cases like the Tampa affair (McMaster 2002: 3), the Children Overboard controversy (Slattery 2003: 93), the detention of children in mainland and offshore centres like Nauru (Triggs 2014), and the lip sewing protests by detainees on Christmas Island (Pugliese 2002), all of which seem to keep alive the spirit of the White Australia Policy, putatively abolished in the late 1970s.

It is indeed true—as I later found out—that there are queer people from India who do seek asylum here,[49] and they must have the right to flee persecution and seek refuge in a country like Australia where same-sex sexualities are not criminalized—though homophobic and transphobic violence, including against indigenous queer people, has been historically widespread (Robinson 2008). However, we need to be attentive to the civilizational script that this 'worse the better' (Bhaba 2002: 155, 162) narrative of international asylum law might both draw on and contribute to. It indeed can be a narrative that uses queer rights and the projection of Australia's benevolence towards persecuted queers from a non-Western location as the marker for its civilizational hierarchy.[50]

Sample this piece published a few days before the Indian general elections in 2014 on the LGBT lifestyle website in Australia called *SameSame* titled: 'Escaping India's Anti-Gay Laws: "Coming to Australia is the Runaway Plan"' (Rognstrand 2014). The author, soon after mentioning how there has been a space for articulations of queer sexuality within ancient Hindu culture, quotes a member of the All India Muslim Personal Law Board (AIMPLB)—a conservative Sunni non-governmental all-male body that was a co-appellant in *Koushal*—stating how homosexuality is a sin in Islam. It is the homophobic and conservative Muslim who is quoted as the only non-queer person in the piece as an example of India's conservatism, in contradistinction to references of Hindu traditions of openness to queer pasts. In fact, the AIMPLB—which leading Islamic law scholars in India feel should be abolished (Ashraf 2015)—is used in the article as a representative of all Muslim attitudes to homosexuality in India. There is, of course, no mention of the Hindu Right's position, and scant recognition of the very visible and vibrant struggles of the queer rights movements.

Where on the one hand Australia continues to mete out barbaric treatment to poor asylum seekers fleeing persecution through its inhuman mandatory detention policies, it seems to welcome relatively well-off queer asylum seekers from India (because they don't arrive by boats) to mark itself as more progressive than the countries (almost always non-Western) that criminalize sodomy. However, for queer people from the Africa or the Middle East who arrive here in boats in extremely precarious conditions, the experience is quite different (Seuffert 2015: 39–83).

Interestingly, even in the case of regular immigration (those not fleeing persecution) especially in the post 11 September 2001 years, while there was a 'cut back with the introduction of new border "protection" policies' for Asians; '[s]amesex [...] migration flourished with gay and lesbian Asian migrants making up the largest successful group in [...] the [interdependency] visa class (Yue 2014: 114). As Audrey Yue writes:

> [S]ame-sex migration policy organizes sexuality around the hetero-normative institutions of intimacy and the family, incorporating the queer migrant as a good citizen through self-cultivation and disciplinary regulation. The queer migrant provides a critical platform to question how the state uses the language of intimacy in its progressive same-sex migration policy to silence the struggles of subordinate groups and to assimilate select gays and lesbians into a global and national discourse of identity and capital, thereby sustaining the core values of the Eurocentric nation (2008: 239).

In doing this—both in case of queer asylum seekers and same-sex migrants—it can be argued that Australia cultivates its international image as a state that is queer friendly, while at the same time continues to devastate the lives of its aboriginal citizens, and keeps out the bad unassimilable refugee. Could this be Australia's home-grown pinkwashing strategy that doubles up to also whitewash its settler-colonial presents?

Performing Stuckness in a Negative Moment

The word 'complicated' is poor academic gloss for the description and critique that I have narrated of queer rights struggles in many parts of the world that are up against the combined forces of nationalism and neoliberalism, both succumbing to and resisting their seductions. In this chapter I have rehearsed and revisited concerns drawing on, inspired by, and in conversation with a community of activists and academics who are a part of queer, feminist, sex worker, Dalit, secular, indigenous, anti-colonial, and anti-capitalist struggles in India and elsewhere. My aim in sharing these ideas is not to paternalistically say that the queer movement(s) ought to do better, or that it needs to work harder towards achieving a purer version of its politics.

I also do not mean to draw unhelpful identitarian and ideological distinctions between good and bad queers. Rather, this is an exercise of participating in collaboratively building a community where we can speak about our failures fearlessly. As I have learnt from Judith/Jack Halberstam:

> Failure suggests a historiographical method within which we must write queer history not simply as a record of heroes, martyrs, forebears, but also as a record of complicity, cowardice, exclusion and violence – in other words, any history, LGBT history included, contains episodes that are shameful, racist, complicit with state power, orientalist, colonial and so on. To leave that history out is to commit to normative models of self, time and the past/future (2012).

On the one hand, I continue to feel politically compelled to repeat these arguments given the re-invigorated onslaught of Hindutva and neoliberalism and its devastating impact on precarious lives in India. However, on the other, my own investments and complicities in the very structures I critique (particularly my locations within a heterosexual upper-caste marriage and the neoliberal academy) have resulted in my arguments taking the posture, I believe, of what Lauren Berlant has brilliantly termed the 'performance of stuckness':

> It is a record of where we got stuck on a question for long enough to do some research and write out the whole knot until the original passion and curiosity that made us want to try to say something about something got so detailed, buried, encrypted, and diluted that the energetic and risk-taking impulse became sealed and delivered in the form of a defense against thinking any more about it. Along the way, something might have happened to the scene the question stood for: or not (2014).

While both Halberstam and Berlant are writing from a location with its own queer histories and politics, I locate my stuckness in the New India, by borrowing from what Achille Mbembe has referred to, in his reflections on the Rhodes Must Fall movement at the University of Cape Town, as a 'negative moment'. He describes it as follows:

> A negative moment is a moment when new antagonisms emerge while old ones remain unresolved. It is a moment when contradictory

> forces – inchoate, fractured, fragmented – are at work but what might come out of their interaction is anything but certain. It is also a moment when multiple old and recent unresolved crises seem to be on the path towards a collision. Such a collision might happen – or maybe not. It might take the form of outbursts that end up petering out. Whether the collision actually happens or not, the age of innocence and complacency is over. (Mbembe 2015)

I feel a combined sense of both fear and pleasure at getting stuck in this negative moment in New India. I wonder where I—and indeed the communities I am learning from and thinking with—might take our complicities and contaminations to. Those like me who inhabit this 'double-bind' (Spivak 2012: 97–118) of being complicit and contaminated at the same time, have with difficulty moved from performing a politics of confrontation to a politics of self-reflexivity, and now are stuck with and at the limits of both these practices of politics (Sircar 2015: 44). This stuckness, I believe, must provoke the inauguration of thinking about the conduct of politics (and critique) as an ethic of responsibility,[51] as a counter to the politics of responsibilization and civility that the New Indian nation-state and neoliberal queer mobilizations globally espouse. To be stuck in this negative moment might, in fact, demand that we slow down to spend more time to create spaces and languages of speaking about failure, or even sometimes practising silence with responsibility (Marle 2003: 239; Fitzpatrick 2012: 193–210).

So at the end, almost always, there remains that same burning question that we have inherited from Lenin: 'What is to be done?' (1999). Where is hope then (Duggan and Muñoz 2009: 275–83)? Hope, I believe, has been too overrated by the radical-thought, liberal-conduct types (like me). Hope lies in the unremarkable quotidian—no amount of research or writing by the likes of us will ever be able to account for it, leave alone even bring a semblance of intelligibility.[52] That is where hope lies I think—our inability to recognize it, interpret it, theorize it, articulate it. Hope is the nemesis, the point of breakdown, of the hubris of our interpretive projects.[53]

It should constantly remind us of our inadequacy. And it is that inadequacy, that failure that our political work—on the streets, in classrooms, courtrooms, and bedrooms—should honestly speak of.

Let some things remain outside our reach. We've perversely saturated our lives with it. Let our writings not have the ability to colonize the hope of others whose miseries we write about and make careers out of (Smith 2012). As old-fashioned as it may sound, even our genuine expressions of solidarity are in need of constant decolonizing at a time when transnational radical politics seem to be reliant almost entirely on virtual affects circulated and consumed through neoliberal networks of knowledge (Land 2015). It is apt to close by recollecting some very powerful words by the late human rights lawyer and activist from India, K. Balagopal: 'To condemn oppression is to condemn a little bit of oneself' (2000: 1,075). Maybe this is how we can record a queer history of our failures and stuckness at this negative moment in the dangerous commonsense that is the New India. If at all.

Notes

1. I do this to guard against my account being read as what Leela Gandhi would call 'postcolonial revenge'. This gesture indicates my deep suspicion towards both relativism and universalism. I remain unsure about whether I place myself between these locational indices or beyond (Gandhi 1998: x). See generally Chakrabarty 2002.
2. *Koushal vs Naz Foundation*, 2014, 1 SCC 1 (India). *Accessible on* http://indiankanoon.org/doc/58730926/; last accessed 5 July 2019.
3. *Naz Foundation vs Government of Delhi*, 2009 111 DRJ 1 (DB).
4. See Casolari 2000: 218 (connecting Hindu nationalism and Fascism); see also Casolari 2011; Banaji 2016.
5. See generally Periscope 2015 (critical analysis of a range of aspects related to Modi's 2014 win).
6. See Ghassem-Fachandi 2012 (rich ethnographic study of the pogrom).
7. The Hindu god Ram was the mythological figure who was deployed by the BJP in 1992 to mobilize militant groups of *kar sevaks* (pilgrims) in the city of Ayodhya to raze to the ground the Babri Masjid, built in 1527, on the pretext that the mosque was built exactly where Ram was born. The demolition of the mosque was followed by widespread rioting in many parts of India, and particularly in Mumbai where the Shiv Sena—a Hindu fascist political party—carried out a well-planned attack on the city's Muslim population.
8. See M. Menon 2011 (detailed study of the 1992 anti-Muslim riots in Mumbai).

9. '[…] in an interview in the *Time* magazine in the immediate aftermath of the riots of 1993, Thackeray did not mince words on his agenda for the Muslim minority in India. When questioned on the role of the Shiv Sena in the riots, Thackeray replied: 'I want to teach Muslims a lesson.' When questioned on the fact that Muslims were fleeing Mumbai in droves, Thackeray replied, 'If they are going, let them go. If they are not going, *kick them out.'* In an exchange that reflects his long-standing admiration of the Hindu Right for Nazi Germany, he responded to the charge that 'Indian Muslims are beginning to feel like Jews in Nazi Germany', by saying, 'Have they behaved like the Jews in Nazi Germany? If so, there is nothing wrong if they are treated as Jews were in Germany.' (Kapur and Cossman 1999: 8–9, emphasis in original).
10. See Anandan 2014 (close journalistic account of Bal Thackeray and the Shiv Sena).
11. See Jaffrelot 2005b (historical account of Ambedkar's political life).
12. Since having come to power the BJP has been trying very hard to appropriate Ambedkar's legacy to forward its fascist agenda, even as Hindu Right groups have been unleashing egregious forms of violence against Dalits. See Teltumbde 2016.
13. It is necessary to note here that at the time that Ambedkar wrote this, he considered the Indian National Congress to be as much a vehicle for establishing Hindu Raj as the BJP is today.
14. Modi has been quoted as saying: 'Only a man like me with a chest of 56 inches could achieve what I did in 2002 in Gujarat'. As Harsh Mander writes: 'The macho metaphor of the 56-inch chest (*chappan chaati*) returned frequently in Modi's election speeches when he sought re-election in the winter of 2007'. See Mander 2009: 48.
15. See Nanda 2009 (astute analysis of the combined rise of Hindu nationalism and neoliberalism in India).
16. Since the BJP's coming to power, several smaller Hindu Right groups have publicly supported Donald Trump's politics of hatred against Muslims. One of these groups, notably the Hindu Sena, has even celebrated Trump's birthday by cutting a cake, and also bursting crackers when Trump won the US elections. Much like the bigoted machismo of Modi that is hailed by the Hindu Right, the Hindu Sena has called Trump a 'fighter and savior of humanity' (Agence France-Presse 2016).
17. See Anand 2011: 1 ('[H]indutva ("Hindu-ness", shorthand for Hindu nationalism) in India is a chauvinist and majoritarian nationalism that conjures up the image of a Hindu Self vis-à-vis the threatening minority Other.').
18. See generally Banerjee et al. 2009: 33–72.

19. The Iyer advert and the Obergefell decision are not equivalent events. I compare them because of the identical responses that they have generated: of how queer celebrations have come to mask caste/race violence and prejudice. Commenting on the Obergefell judgement on her Facebook page, Kimberlé Crenshaw wrote:

    Nine dead people – killed while worshipping – are now afterthoughts, to be squeezed into the celebration of American Democracy. So now […] Black people can marry whomever they please, but we can't vote, worship, represent our people, swim, shop, or walk the streets without fear of being discriminated against or even killed. So on this day of sorrow and celebration, this is what democracy looks like. (2015)

20. As Lisa Duggan writes: 'Homonormativity: a politics that does not contest dominant heteronormative assumptions and institutions—such as marriage, and its call for monogamy and reproduction—but upholds and sustains them while promising the possibility of a demobilized gay constituency and a privatized, depoliticized gay culture anchored in domesticity and consumption' (2002: 175).
21. '*Acche din aane waale hain*' (Good days are coming) was the campaign slogan for the BJP in its run up to the 2014 elections.
22. See Arondekar 2009; Dave 2012; Puri 2016 (some notable recent projects that attempt to do this).
23. My identification of something by the name of the queer movement might in fact be the imposition of a homogeneity that I have cautioned against. Both in terms of identity and politics, the word queer has had a troubled journey in India, especially in the way in which it subsumes within itself a whole range of non-elite and indigenous sexualities that resist neat identification. My use of the word is meant to both indicate my own class position that enables me to use it with such ease, as well as the class dynamics of what is now called the queer movement in India. On this point, see Tellis 2012: 142–56.
24. The text of the intervention application is accessible at http://orinam.net/377/wp-content/uploads/2014/01/377_ReviewPetition_RatnaKapur.pdf.; last accessed 5 July 2013.
25. See Bhaskaran 2002: 15–29 (analysing the law's colonial legacy.).
26. Sheikh 2013: 104–32 (giving a detailed narrative of the social life of the *Naz* case and its aftermath, and a trenchant reading of the judgement.).
27. See Mandal 2009: 525–40 (analysing the limitations of using the right to privacy argument to decriminalize sodomy).
28. The SC used this logic to also state that because 'in [sic] last more than 150 years less than 200 persons have been prosecuted (as per the reported orders) for committing offence under Section 377 IPC […]

this cannot be made sound basis for declaring that section ultra vires the provisions of Articles 14, 15 and 21 of the Constitution' (*Koushal vs Naz Foundation*, 2014).

29. Boyce and Dutta also point out that the 'media reaction' and 'extensive liberal outrage' against the judgement might lead to Section 377 'acquiring more dangerous connotations than it ever did before; over the years, many more people – including the police – have come to know that it might be used as a stick with which to beat LGBT people'.
30. See generally Cossman 2000: 49–59 (for an exploration of the limitations accompanying legal victories).
31. In making this argument I don't mean to suggest that queerness is urban and ethnicity/race is rural. My intension is to emphasize on how democratic statecraft works through a certain kind of biopolitical logic, in which management of marginalized populations are carried out by articulating progressivism in favour of one to mask violence against the other. Even as I say this, I am aware that both queerness and ethnicity are intersectional and co-constitutive categories. I thank Rahul Rao for helping me articulate this.
32. Emphasizing on this relationship of antagonism between the Hindu Right and the queer movement in India was a poster at the 2016 Delhi Queer Pride march which carried the message 'Homos Hate B.J.P.'. For a photo of the poster, see Speed News Desk 2016.
33. Artistic or creative representations of sexuality have been at the receiving end of threats and intimidation by right-wing Muslim outfits as well, though the instances have been lesser in comparison. There are two notable instances in this regard. First has been the continued threats and violence that exiled Bangladeshi author Taslima Nasrin has faced for her writings criticizing Islamic fundamentalism in both Bangladesh and India. Interestingly, the Hindu Right has cunningly used this as an opportunity to project itself as secular by championing Nasrin's right to free speech against her censorship by right-wing Muslim groups. The second is Salman Rushdie's book *The Satanic Verses* (1989), which was banned by the Congress government even before a fatwa against him was issued by Ayatollah Khomeini. The book continues to remain banned in India, and Rushdie even had to pull out of the Jaipur Literary Festival in 2012 following threats from local Muslim clerics. See Dhavan 2008.
34. *National Legal Services Authority vs Union of India*. Accessible at http://indiankanoon.org/doc/193543132/; last accessed 5 July 2013..
35. For a discussion on the connections between the construction of the Hindu nation and queerness, see Bacchetta 1999: 141–66.

36. Siddharth Narrain 2013. Policing Hijras, *Infochange Agenda*. Accessible on http://infochangeindia.org/agenda/access-to-justice/policing-hijras.html; last accessed 5 July 2013.
37. Four key legal developments had taken place since during the writing of this article that are not analysed here. (i) In August 2016, pursuant to the *NALSA* judgment, the Transgender Persons (Protection of Rights) Bill 2016 was introduced in the Lok Sabha (the lower house of the Indian Parliament). The Bill has been strongly criticized by many activists. Those interested can read the text of the Bill at: http://www.prsindia.org/uploads/media/Transgender/Transgender%20Persons%20Bill,%202016.pdf; last accessed 5 July 2013. See, Datta 2016 (for a sharp analysis of the politics surrounding the Bill). (ii) In response to a set of curative petitions filed against the *Koushal* judgment, which was joined by a new petition filed by three gay celebrities, the a two-judge bench of the Supreme Court referred the matter to the Chief Justice of India (CJI) in June 2016. The CJI is yet to hear it. See, Vishwanath & Ratnam 2016. (iii) Shashi Tharoor, a Member of Parliament from the Congress party introduced a private member's bill in the Lok Sabha to decriminalize Sec. 377. The bill was defeated in December 2015. See Press Trust of India 2015. (iv) In December 2016, the HIV/ AIDS (Prevention and Control) Bill, 2014 was tabled in the parliament in a form that dilutes the rights to accessible treatment and drugs. Despite years of work put in by activists, in the Bill the state has privileged prevention efforts as part of its responsibility and deprioritized its responsibility to provide free access to medicine and treatment. The current Bill says that the state will provide treatment 'only as far as possible'. If passed, such a provision will have a devastating impact on people living with HIV/ AIDS, which includes the sexually marginalized as an especially vulnerable and stigmatized group. This development is especially alarming given the crisis of India's AIDS programme is due to government apathy. See, Krishnan 2016; Gahlot 2015.
38. For an instance of this, see Johri 2016b.
39. https://newsd.in/uber-india-celebrates-first-valentines-post-decriminalization-of-377/; https://twitter.com/faroutakhtar/status/1037593200402153472
40. Sircar 2012. Homonationalism: Queer Tales of Queer Prides, Infochange. Accessible on http://infochangeindia.org/human-rights/rights-and-resistance/homonationalism-queer-tales-of-queer-prides.html; last accessed 5 July 2013.
41. In a show of judicial overreach which reeks of overzealous nationalism, the SC has recently ordered that the national anthem be played in every

movie theatre before a film is shown with an image of the Indian flag on the screen. The order has also mandated that it is a constitutional duty to stand up when the anthem is played. This order has reversed a prior judgement in which the same court had said that not standing up for the national anthem does not amount to disrespect for the nation. Irrespective of this new judgement, over the years, there have been many cases of viewers being beaten and harassed inside cinemas for not standing up when the national anthem plays. This has been the case in states like Maharashtra where this practice was already being followed on executive orders. Interestingly, Rabindranath Tagore, the poet who wrote the song 'Jana Gana Mana' that later became the national anthem of India, was a strong critic of nationalism. See Liang 2016.

42. Open Letters, *New York Times*. Accessible on http://www.nytimes.com/packages/pdf/international/open_letter.pdf; last accessed 5 July 2013.
43. It is, thus, of little surprise that in November 2015, P. Chidambaram, India's former finance minister under the Congress government, and Arun Jaitley, the current BJP finance minister, made public statements on consecutive days in support of the decriminalization of sodomy. One wonders, had they read the World Bank report together? See Johari 2015.
44. UN Human Rights Office. Free and Equal. Accessible on https://www.unfe.org/en/actions/the-welcome; last accessed 5 July 2013.
45. For a powerful critique of derivative imaginations of marriage equality in India, see Manayath 2013 ('So we seem to want same-sex marriages to protect the legal rights of urban middle-class gay or lesbian identified men and women who might want to contract a legal marriage to ensure that they are able to access corporate and state benefits that accrue to couples. This urban minority, and its desire for a global LGBT identity, is increasingly the focus of much of LGBT legal rights work, even as it claims to speak for all people expressing transgressive erotic desires. This subsuming of the hijra into the global language of LGBT rights is reflective of the many ways in which legal LGBT activism in the country directs itself.')
46. For the full version of Butler's speech translated into English from German, see http://www.egs.edu/faculty/judith-butler/articles/i-must-distance-myself/ and the YouTube video of Butler's refusal is accessible on http://www.youtube.com/watch?v=BV9dd6r361k; last accessed 5 July 2019.
47. My identification of this event as '11 September 2001' rather than '9/11' is purposeful. The spectacular common sense that the expression

'9/11' has been endowed with has turned it into a history-vanishing event which forces an erasure from collective and cultural memory the many September 11s—both real and metaphorical—that have preceded it. See Aguilera et al. 2006.

48. Publishers Raw Nerve Books and Routledge pulled out writings by Haritaworn, Tauqir, and Erdem (Haritaworn et al. 2009: 146), and Long (2009: 119) respectively after they were threatened with defamation suits by Tatchell; See Puar 2011: 113 for an account of how a talk by her in Berlin on homonationalism and Palestine/Israel was almost cancelled.
49. I thank Sara Dehm for sending across a list of cases adjudicated by the Refugee Review Tribunal of Australia concerning Indians who were seeking asylum for persecution based on sexual orientation. These cases can be found on the Australian Legal Information Institute website, in the Refugee Review Tribunal of Australia database, by doing a search using the strings 'India' + 'sexuality' + '377'.
50. Interestingly, a reversal of this position was articulated by Senator Eric Abetz and Federal Agriculture Minister Barnaby Joyce who were reported to have said that if Australia achieves marriage equality its Asian neighbours would view it as decadent. This sentiment—which is ridden with ignorance more than anything else—effects an erasure of the diverse and rich histories of non-normative Asian sexualities and ongoing politics of rights claims, and consequently presents Asia as always already homophobic. It sounded like saying Australia's sexual mores are so much more progressive than Asian countries, and because we are open to diversity, we will be sensitive to Asian conservativism to same sex marriage. See Chakraborty 2015: 'The pronouncements of Abetz and Joyce effect a curious reversal of the business-as-usual moral hierarchy between the West and the Rest that measures democracy and progress in terms of a hegemonic conception of sexual freedom (among other things)'.
51. For a gesture in this direction, see Dave 2012. See also Dorsett and McVeigh 2012: 470–93; McVeigh 2014: 471–92 (for discussions on the question of responsibility in the writing of jurisprudence).
52. See Dhawan 2012: 47–60. Dhawan accounts for 'the challenge of representation and the problematic role of the (postcolonial) feminist who attempts to recover and represent the perspectives of those who are illegible and unintelligible within hegemonic frameworks and thereby rendered ethically, politically and rhetorically illegitimate'.
53. Here I have in mind the argument by Gayatri Chakravorty Spivak on the politics of translation and the limits of interpretation in the foreword to her translation of Mahasveta Devi's short story 'Draupadi'. See Devi 1981: 381– 402.

PART II

… IS PERSONAL …

5

The Silence of Gulberg

Refracted Memories, Inadequate Images*

The Tragedy of Repetition

The 2002 Gujarat pogrom was an essential marker of the ideology of the Indian nation as Hindu supremacist (celebratory for some, devastating for others), and now it serves additionally as a marker of the governmentality of the Indian state as neoliberal triumphalist (celebratory for the same lot, and devastating for several more). The spectre of the pogrom inhabits public consciousness in India in a way where memory and forgetting are not racing against each other, but are constantly on a collision path. Like magnets, when they reach the point of collision, they repel each other. Their paths are located on a Mobius strip: so if you start with memory, you encounter forgetting charging at you with teeth-gritting glory, and if you start with

* Written through 2015 and 2017 in Melbourne and Sonipat; trying to make sense of what it means for me to remember the Gujarat pogrom. I thank the Lalakiya family in Ahmedabad for hosting me with such care during my visit in 2014. I acknowledge the support of Ravi Nair for inviting me to join the South Asia Documentation Centre's fact-finding team that visited Ahmedabad in 2002. Sincere gratitude to Farooq and Imtiaz for their generosity with time and for trusting me with their stories.

forgetting, the phantom of memory will always be surreptitiously lurking at you. The consequence is an uneasy coexistence where the primary concern is not whether Gujarat should be remembered or forgotten, but *how* do we remember *what* happened in 2002. While forgetting here is not about denying what happened, memory is about selecting which story to tell. And every story claims to be 'the truth', in which forensic truth is competing against experiential truth is competing against neoliberal truth is competing against electoral truth is competing against artistic truth.

With the competing narratives of 'truth' that have been in circulation since the Sabarmati Express's coach number S6 catching fire in Godhra on 27 February 2002, to the election of Narendra Modi as the prime minister of India in 2014 and again in 2019, to the judgement in the Gulberg Society massacre case in 2016, among others, there are stories after stories—official, legal, colloquial, fabricated, imagined, hopeful, utopic, devastating, disgusting. Events that have transpired between then and now have only proliferated spirals of impunity, the celebratory hand-in-hand march of Hindutva and neoliberalism, the spectacular rise and rise of the idea of Narendra Modi, the co-option of the Muslim vote bank by the BJP, the sophisticated marketing and distribution of fear, the sanitization of the public sphere in Gujarat, and the unending trials— legal and personal.

I was a law student in Pune when news of the Godhra train burning and the later events of a violent Hindu 'revenge' against Muslims started coming in. Most of the English-language media was critical of the Modi government (Desai 2004: 228–34), but their characterization of what was happening in Gujarat followed the standard cause-and-effect explanation. This is what what Teesta Setalvad has called the 'who cast the first stone' thesis (Setalvad 2017: 78): 'every act of violence of the majority Hindu is an act of retaliation of the perennially and permanently barbaric Mussalmaan' (ibid.). The Newtonian physics of Modi's immediate response was to say 'every "action" has an equal and opposite "reaction"'.[1] And Godhra was marked (for posterity) as a singular 'flashpoint'[2] moment that performs a 'moral inversion'(Mander 2017) where India's majority Hindus become victims of its minority Muslims. The art of mobilizing public opinion through the marking of a singular event as 'history vanishing' (Puar 2007: xviii) was mastered by the US government when 11 September happened, and it has been used to justify all the military aggressions and invasions that the US has carried out in the name of self-defence and democracy since then. Godhra has been made to occupy our memories in an identical manner: it is the flash that blinds us to the history of how the pogrom was founded on the deep and dispersed structures of Hindutva which enabled its planning well before the train caught fire (Setalvad 2013). It also masks the historical and economic antecedents of Hindutva in Gujarat that did not erupt only as a spontaneous and reactionary response to Godhra (Yagnik and Seth 2005, Spodek 2011).

The ability to apply nuance, to see through the spectacle of this blinding flashpoint at my first experience of surrogate consumption of real-time mass violence, was pretty low. A mix of bewilderment, anger, and numbness was what I felt. The only previous occasion in my lifetime when I had heard about 'communal' violence was a decade ago in 1992 when the Babri Masjid in Ayodhya was demolished by militant Hindu mobs followed by an anti-Muslim killing spree (Noorani 2017). At that time, as a school student, all I looked forward to in the distant city of Calcutta were the curfews, because that would mean not having to go to school. During the long periods of curfew, I enjoyed watching cricket matches on TV without my mother constantly asking me to go study (because exams were indefinitely postponed), and playing cricket on the street with friends during the two-hour curfew breaks that were allowed once a week. The brutality of the violence was conveniently censored by my parents and its antecedents had already been mythologized on state television (Rajagopal 2001, Farmer 1996: 98–118). While some information did reach me, the lack of discussion in our 'secular Hindu' family about the demolition and the ensuing killings did not make it so obvious. Some unrest was happening somewhere else in India, and the curfew was just a way to keep us safe, was the standard refrain. I did not complain.

Ten years later, in 2002, when I was looking at the grotesque images of heaps of dead bodies, maimed and charred, and deserted streets and burnt houses, and desecrated mosques, on live 24/7 television (privatized news channels were enjoying their fledgling liberated status covering the violence without regulation after several years of state control) (Jain 2010: 163–79), the language that was put into circulation to characterize what was happening followed the cause/effect logic. The violence was almost universally being referred to as the 'post-Godhra riots'. Everything that was happening was being traced back to Godhra. We were surreptitiously being told that our memory scales must have a limit: do not look beyond Godhra; Godhra should be the only source for your explanations; treat Godhra as exceptional, so that what has followed it, despite the unprecedented levels of brutality, becomes routine. It took some time to understand that the violence was far from a riot. It was a genocidal massacre, or more aptly, a pogrom.

When you type 'Gujarat 2002' into Google even today, the first link that comes up is the Wikipedia entry, and it starts with the following words: 'The 2002 Gujarat violence was a series of incidents starting with the Godhra train burning and the subsequent communal violence between Hindus and Muslims…'[3] A Google image search throws up photos, the first of which are images of the burning train compartment.[4] The significantly detailed April 2002 Human Rights Watch report on the carnage titled 'We Have No Orders To Save You: State Participation and Complicity in Communal Violence in Gujarat', opens with the sentence: 'The ongoing violence in Gujarat was triggered by a Muslim mob's torching of two train cars carrying Hindu activists on February 27, 2002.'[5] In several critical and closely documented publications on the violence—academic, activist, journalistic—Godhra has been marked as what feminist philosopher Martha Nussbaum has called 'the precipitating event' (Nussbaum 2007: 2). The 'post-Godhra riots' adage continues to be a part of the conscious and unconscious vocabulary for most Indians, and despite the activism, civil society outcry, several detailed fact-finding reports, enquiry commissions, sustained and selective media coverage, and some convictions, Godhra remains that flashpoint moment that blinds us to the long-term organized and meticulously planned continuum of anti-Muslim hatred that resulted in the Gujarat pogrom.[6]

In this chapter, I intend to weave the experiential, literary, and analytical to offer a memorial account that will try to treat the Gujarat pogrom and its aftermath not as an exceptional, but an ordinary event. Rendering Gujarat 2002 as exceptional tends to serve the purpose of allowing secularlists like me to disavow their own complicities in the ideological makings of the event and the memories of it that are kept alive. My narrative—organized as a bricolage—aims to bring together my own experience of being in Ahmedabad in the wake of the pogrom, a later visit that took me there over a decade after the event, and combine it with critical refractions (not reflections). Reflection has the possibility of being a self contained engagement; on the other hand, refraction carries the potential to destabilize and bend our disciplined contours of thought. Refraction does not necessarily suggest a 'moving away' from issues at stake, but a critical engagement that confronts not one, but competing truths (Sircar 2011: 182-228, Jay 2003: 2). Thus, I do not claim to reveal the neutral truth about the pogrom.[7] My account critiques what I disagree with, but without rejection, recognizes the partiality of my own view, and prioritizes the question of suffering, without fetishizing it (Kennedy 1982: 600, Davies 2008: 199).[8] I do this to let neither my subjectivity nor factual objectivity get the better of each other in the making of my memory of Gujarat 2002.

Storytelling Atrocity

On our way to Chamanpura, a working-class locality in Ahmedabad, Farooq bhai suggested that we pick up Imtiaz. It was well past lunch time, but he insisted that we visit Gulberg Society before heading to Teen Darwaja to eat kabab and halwa. Farooq had been driving me around the city since morning. I had got to know him a few days back when I arrived in Ahmedabad—having hired his auto rickshaw at the railway station. On the way to the place where I was staying, I had told him why I was in the city—to look for public remnants of the 2002 anti-Muslim pogrom for a research project on collective memories of mass violence. I felt embarrassingly voyeuristic to say this even as I wanted to befriend Farooq, but his relaxed disposition had offered an invitation that allowed me to rest the inhibitions of a first meeting. He very forthcomingly agreed to show me around a few days later.

It was winter—sometime around late November in 2014—but the Ahmedabad sun was scorching hot. I was distraught—hungry, sweaty, and deeply shaken by the visits to some of the key locations in the city which experienced massacres of Muslims by mobs mobilized by neo-fascist Hindu militant groups[9] (with active state support) during the Gujarat pogrom. These locations were pointed out to me by Farooq because 12 years later, they carried no visible scars on the city's gaudy body decorated by huge hoardings publicizing the

2015 Vibrant Gujarat Summit, where Ban Ki-moon, the then UN secretary general, had accepted the invitation to be the chief guest (PTI 2014).

The summit has been an annual fixture for the state to project it as India's most investment-friendly destination for transnational corporations. Gujarat's developmentalist refashioning of itself by Modi—under whose watch (and alleged active connivance) as chief minister and home minister, the 2002 pogrom was carried out—catapulted him to national politics, and ultimately got him elected as India's prime minister in mid-2014 (Jaffrelot 2015: 820–38). The summit has also been the location where, year after year, world leaders and India's richest industrialists line up to offer heaps of praise for Modi's neoliberal economic vision (Bobbio 2013: 123–34). It is a meticulously planned attempt by the government to thwart efforts that try to keep alive the memories of the pogrom. Sample this quote by industrialist Anil Ambani: 'Narendra bhai has been described in different ways. My personal favourite comes from what his name literally means in Sanskrit – a conjunction of Nara and Indra. Nara means man and Indra means king or leader. Narendra bhai is the lord of men and a king among kings.'[10] The deification of a man who is alleged to have personally overseen the design of the pogrom, who has never expressed any remorse about the murder of thousands of Muslims as the accountable political authority in that state, and who has carried on spewing hate speech with impunity, says a lot about the intimacies between neoliberalism and Hindu fascism in the New India.

Away from the mask of the hoardings, many of the locations that Farooq took me to were mosques and Sufi dargahs of great historical significance that were completely razed to the ground and paved over. Fancy cars drove over these well-tarred 'smooth roads' now—a metaphor that has come to symbolize Gujarat's projection of itself as India's most economically advanced state. The warts—of what remained of those Muslims who survived the pogrom—were preserved as cruel reminders on the cartographic and cerebral margins of the city. These were the squalid ghettoes into which Muslims displaced by violence were forced to live (Mahadevia 2007: 341–89). One of these ghettoes—ironically called Citizen Nagar—was built as a location for rehabilitating the survivors (Gupta 2011). The whole area did not have roads, sanitation, or hospitals. It was located right beside the place where the sewage and garbage of the entire city was dumped. Muslims who lived there were thus reminded—through this perverse rehabilitative gesture of the state—of their status being equivalent to the refuse of the city. This was a milder reincarnation of the message, though a more persistent one, that the Hindu Right conveyed to Muslims through the mass killings of 2002.

For a more unambiguous message consider the several incendiary flyers, leaflets, and pamphlets that were circulated by the militant mobs as they ran rampage through the killing streets of Ahmedabad. One of these, signed by a leader of the VHP, a close ideological ally of the BJP, carried the following verse:

> The volcano which was inactive has erupted
>
> It has burnt the arse of miyas [Muslim men] and made them dance nude
>
> We have untied the penises that were tied till now
>
> We have widened the tight vaginas of the bibis [Muslim women][11]

I have used the term pogrom to characterize the 2002 Gujarat violence. Many others have used genocide. Both of these terms carry derivative valence, and enable making Gujarat 2002 intelligible to a primarily international audience for whom the Holocaust is the most identifiable point of historical reference. Riot—'a euphemism for communal murder' as M.G. Vassanji puts it (2007: 264)—has remained the preferred term in India, given that it is the only way collective violence is defined in the criminal law. In Gujarat, I seldom heard these English terms being used to speak of 2002. Some of the vernacular terms used were *dhamaal*, *hullad*, *aandhi*, *toofan*, and *qayamat*. I point to this politics of naming not only because it provides a sense of the difficulty in drawing equivalences between the English and vernacular expressions through translation, but also because there is always a tendency in written, photographic, and cinematic accounts to spectacularize the event, to render it exceptional, to use the universal force of a term of capture the phantasmagoria. In doing so—despite all good intentions—we risk taking attention away from the quotidian practices of Hindu nationalism—within families to state institutions—that morally legitimized the killings of Muslims in 2002, and continues to feed a scary culture of state impunity. The danger is that such representations of the violence can potentially either set in a sense of fatigue even amongst the most compassionate, or as Bhrigupati Singh notes: 'Potential consumers of such images will then increasingly require ever more detail in words and images of hurt and suffering to authenticate reality' (2002).

A Charred Roseleaf

In 2002, Zakia Jafri used to live in Gulberg Society, a lower- to middle-class Muslim residential complex in Chamanpura. A visit to its abandoned ruins was the last destination on my human rights tourism agenda for the day. Imtiaz Khan, who Farooq picked up on the way, was also a resident of Gulberg. He had escaped death, but had seen his family members and many residents being burnt alive, hacked to death, or raped on 28 February 2002, when armed mobs numbering in thousands, attacked the Muslim-majority residential colony. Imtiaz has been a key witness for the prosecution in the resulting criminal trials related to the massacre, which, at that time, were due to resume in December 2014.

I felt a sense of discomfort about Imtiaz accompanying us to Gulberg. Of course, there couldn't be a better guide for me, as Farooq had suggested. However, it felt parasitic to take him away from work on a weekday and to make him recollect memories of trauma for a complete stranger. I expressed my concern to Farooq. He assured me that I had nothing to worry about, and that Imtiaz was always willing to spare time for those who wanted to know about what really happened at Gulberg. I was not a journalist, I told him when we met, and clarified that I was not out to uncover any hidden truths. In response, Imtiaz offered a knowing smile.

Much like Farooq, Imtiaz was comforting and friendly. He looked my age, mid-30s—though I never asked. He was married, with two children, and lived in a different part of the city. He was the first victim-survivor of the pogrom I was meeting on this trip. The last time I was in Ahmedabad in April 2002, I spent many weeks at the Shah-Alam Dargah (a mosque which was converted into a makeshift camp for the displaced) collecting testimonies as part of a fact-finding team of lawyers from Delhi. I knew about the massacre at Gulberg Society then, but never managed to find the time, or the courage, to see any more of the devastation in Ahmedabad.

Gulberg—meaning roseleaf—was built in the 1960s. As Amrita Shah, a recent chronicler of the city has written in *Ahmedabad: A City in the World* (2005): '[it was][...] a genteel complex of bungalows generously spaced out with spreading trees and a high surrounding wall giving it a measure of privacy and exclusion rare in the shabby neighbourhood' (2015: 18). One of its well-known residents was Ehsan Jafri—Zakia's husband—a former Congress parliamentarian, a socialist, trade unionist, and poet. While the society was under siege on 28 February, many Muslims had sought refuge in Jafri's home, hopeful that given his stature they would be safe.

As has been recorded in many independent fact-finding reports, Jafri made several calls to high officials in the government to send police protection. The police commissioner is reported to have come in the morning, and promised that he would send his forces. But they did not intervene when the armed mobs broke through the walls. The April 2002 Human Rights Watch report, '"We have No Orders to Save You": State Participation and Complicity in Communal Violence in Gujarat', details the active role that the police played in enabling the mobs to carry out the violence. Jafri's calls to Modi also yielded no response. A total of 69 people were killed in the massacre, the second largest of all the killings in the pogrom. The mob used weapons ranging from stones and bricks to swords and iron rods. Gas cylinders were used to set the houses inside Gulberg on fire. The attacks on Muslim women took especially macabre forms—many were gang-raped, their breasts and vaginas mutilated, pregnant women's wombs split open, and then thrown into fire (Kumar 2017). Jafri was murdered. As the report, 'Crimes Against Humanity', by the Concerned Citizens Tribunal notes: 'He was stripped, paraded naked [...] His fingers were chopped off and he was paraded around in the locality, badly injured. Next his hands and feet were severed. He was then dragged, a fork-like instrument clutching his neck, down the road, before being thrown into fire.'[12]

Zakia Jafri, Ehsan's 77-year-old widow, has carried on a valiant legal battle since 2002—with support from activist and human rights defender Teesta Setalvad—to hold Modi criminally and administratively culpable, as the head of the state, on the grounds of chain-of-command responsibility. The Gujarat judiciary has time and again come under great criticism for being politically biased against the Muslim victims, and for colluding with the state administration to safeguard leaders of the Hindu Right who led and instigated the murderous mobs. Two key trials were ordered by the SC to be held in Mumbai, to avoid subversion of justice by the Gujarat government. The biased operation of the Gujarat judiciary was further reflected when Zakia's protest petition against the SC-appointed special investigation team (SIT) for exonerating Modi was rejected by the Ahmedabad Metropolitan Court in December 2013. The Gujarat High Court heard an appeal against this decision in September 2015 (Nair 2015). In the run-up to the appeal, the Modi government began intimidating and harassing Teesta Setalvad and Citizens for Justice and Peace, the organization that she had co-founded with her husband Javed Anand in 2002 to provide legal aid to the victims of the Gujarat pogrom. Setalvad and Anand 'faced court proceedings on fabricated charges of embezzlement, misuse of funds and 'anti-national propaganda' (Front Line 2016: 14). They averted an arrest when the Bombay High Court granted anticipatory bail in August 2015. A decision on the appeal is yet to be delivered.

A separate criminal trial for the Gulberg Society massacre—in which Imtiaz was among the 338 witnesses who testified—began in 2009, and ended in September 2015. The verdict by a special court was delivered in June 2016 in which 24 of the accused were convicted, and 36 acquitted. Zakia Jafri had expressed her disappointment with the judgement and said that she will continue to pursue other legal options to indict Modi.[13] Her son Tanvir wondered how the court thought only 24 people could have killed 69 people and burnt down an entire housing complex. In reconstructing its account of the events from 28 February, the judgement said that the mob that attacked Gulberg turned violent because Ehsan Jafri provoked it by opening fire. None of the independent fact-finding reports found evidence to such effect. The judgement dismissed a contention of the prosecution which argued that the Gulberg Society massacre be considered a crime of conspiracy, thus, planned and premeditated (Sen 2016).

Violating the Solitude

Gulberg Society was located on a very noisy and crowded road. Given that the criminal trials related to the massacre were still proceeding, I expected that the site would be guarded by the police. There were none. Embedded in the wall to the left of the entrance, camouflaged in the yellow paint of an advertisement, was a notice from the Gujarat government which declared that this was police *sampatty* (property). The notice carried the official insignia of the Indian state (Figures 5.1 and 5.2).

The two photographs below were not taken when I first entered Gulberg Society. I was hesitant to pull out my camera. It was only after we had spent a while walking through the desolate houses within the compound that I asked for permission to take photographs. I was perspiring profusely—and held the camera in one hand, as I wiped my brow with a handkerchief in the other. My fingers were greasy with sweat, and I ended up touching the lens repeatedly. The

Figure 5.1 The entrance to Gulberg Society
Source: Oishik Sircar.

Figure 5.2 Police *sampatty* (property)
Source: Oishik Sircar.

photos were originally taken in colour. However, even in the black-and-white versions reproduced here, readers might notice a smudge on the right-hand corner of some of the photos. While the smudge speaks of the inadequacy of the quality of the photos, I feel it also speaks of the inadequacy of a photographer to record visual testimonies of trauma. All recordings of testimony—in text, image, or sound—are always already contaminated by the technology of the medium, and the perspective of the medium user.

In the time that we spent inside the compound, I never took out my diary to take notes; it felt disrespectful to not look at Imtiaz when he spoke to me about what had happened. His descriptions were monotonous and chillingly matter-of-fact. I did not see him flinch as he offered a clinical narration of the events. These were much more detailed than those recorded in the fact-finding reports that I had read. For every killing that he narrated, he pointed out the exact location of its occurrence. I clicked photographs during the silences in-between, as we walked from one *a posteriori* scene of violence to another (Figures 5.3 and 5.4).

I did not have any presuppositions about what I wanted to capture in my photographs. My shots were not organized for a photo essay. It was something I thought I should do as a researcher. The photos were meant to be a visual record for my memory's sake. When I looked at them much later, I realized that there was one compelling strain running through all of them—that of a haunting emptiness. Gulberg had no human inhabitants any longer. It required the stories of someone like Imtiaz to frame the human emptiness and fill it with meaning. Without the stories, the photos remain ordinary images of abandoned houses where stray dogs now lived, barking disappointment at our presence. But even without the stories, the affect of abandonment inside Gulberg generated an intensity that only my body bears testimony to. Words or images are inadequate records.

Figure 5.3 *A posteriori* scenes of violence 1
Source: Oishik Sircar.

Figure 5.4 *A posteriori* scenes of violence 2
Source: Oishik Sircar.

After he finished, Imtiaz and Farooq sat on the steps to the entrance of what used to be his home. They asked me to take my time and look around. The quietness that descended—with the dogs also retreating to their dens—as I walked through the empty buildings felt like what John Berger has evocatively called 'the accumulated absence of sound' (1976: 9). The silence defeated the sense of growing sadness and anger that I was keeping captive inside me. The anger was disciplined to submission when it confronted silence, while the sadness sublimated.

Gulberg Society was covered in unruly foliage. Ehsan Jafri's home had a huge creeper that had covered an entire side of the building. The pink flowers on the creeper's green expanse offered comforting relief from the burnt surfaces of the buildings. The silence and the foliage had turned Gulberg into a sanctuary for its dead (Figure 5.5). If there was one place the dead might be able to rest, it was possibly here. Not in the courts, not in the solidarity marches and candlelight vigils, and certainly not in the PhD thesis I was writing at that time.

Figure 5.5 Silence and foliage
Source: Oishik Sircar.

To mark 10 years of the pogrom in 2012, Citizens for Justice and Peace brought together many civil society groups to organize a memorial meeting at Gulberg Society. On our way out Imtiaz pointed at a worn-out, dust-covered poster that was put up during that meeting. On the map of Gujarat, it depicted the locations where mosques and dargahs were desecrated between 2002 and 2007, and the numbers of Muslims who had gone missing since the pogrom. It was a strange map—it had no numbers, and thus carried no evidentiary testament (Figure 5.6). Perhaps, it did not wish to reduce violence to statistics. There has been a talk of turning Gulberg into a Museum of Resistance to honour the lives of the dead, and to document the struggles of those living for justice. Imtiaz disagreed with the idea. He said that he did not want to remember the dead by museumizing them. 'Building a museum would mean that we will never be able to come here to spend time with our dead in silence,' he said. I wondered, whether through my photographs I was contributing to an archive of museumization of Gulberg's silent traumascape; that I

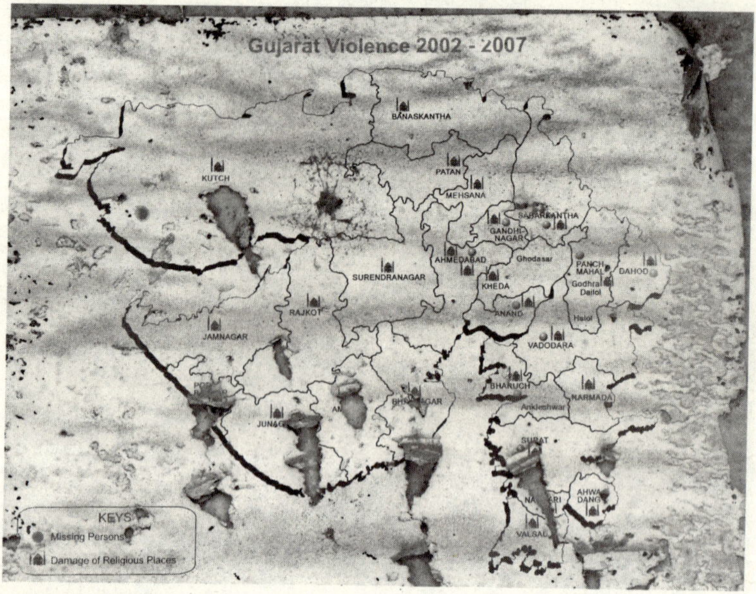

Figure 5.6 A map with no numbers
Source: Oishik Sircar.

was, to borrow from Milan Kundera's comment on Kafka's writings, violating the solitude (2005: 111).

I could not resist taking a last photograph much against Susan Sontag's belief that 'there is no final photograph' (2007: 127) (Figure 5.7). As we were about to exit, I saw a cart of a local music band with four loudspeakers fitted on top parked in front of Gulberg's tallest building. The juxtaposition of the loudspeakers and the silent monument was a strange frame of contradictions. The dead must be allowed to rest in peace, but even the loudest of screams from victim-survivors and activists have not been able to disturb the growing cultures of impunity for mass crimes, and violence against the marginalized, that the Indian state continues to enjoy.

As we left the compound in Farooq's auto rickshaw, I looked back and spotted the Gujarat government's notice stating that Gulberg was police property. The state had already laid claim to Gulberg's silence.

Figure 5.7 'There is no final photograph'
Source: Oishik Sircar

Remembering, Mourning

I have seldom thought about silence with much seriousness, until the point at which I stepped into Gulberg Society. Much after the visit, I was reminded of this quote from Amitav Ghosh's novel, *The Shadow Lines*:

> The enemy of silence is speech, but there can be no speech without words, and there can be no words without meanings – so it follows, inexorably, in the manner of syllogisms, that when we try to speak of events of which we do not know the meaning, we must lose ourselves in the silence that lies in the gap between words and the world. This is a silence that is proof against any conceivable act of scorn or courage; it lies beyond defiance – for what means have we to defy the mere absence of meaning? Where there is no meaning, there is banality, and this is what this silence consists in, that is why it cannot be defeated – because it is the silence of an absolute, impenetrable banality (2008: 240).

'Breaking the silence' of impunity is understood as a standard objective of any human rights or justice-seeking enterprise. The work of a human rights defender, campaigner, activist, or advocate is considered to be one that verbalizes and visualizes the unheard and unseen voices and experiences of the violated. The recording of testimony in fact-finding reports, the oral presentation of witness accounts in tribunals, public hearings, or courts, the photographic or video documentation of atrocity on social and news media carry a moral charge that is meant to challenge public apathy, appeal to the global publics of compassion, as well as demand state accountability. The material that constitutes written and imagistic records of human rights violations are accorded the status of evidence, and thus by extension, truth. There is a sense of normative good attached to such material, and those producing that material—the organizations, or the persons—carry a moral heft.

The act of breaking silence is an interpretive practice in which we—activists, researchers, journalists, artists—who take on the persona of the human rights worker treat silence as an empty vessel and fill it with our words, images, or sounds. Whatever be its form —legal, literary, visual—interpretation, as we know, is an activity fraught with the possibility of exacerbating the very violence that we claim to seek justice for. When confronted with silence, the practice of interpretation faces an ethical crisis.

In a sequence of frames in Art Speigleman's graphic work of non-fiction *Maus*, the narrator Art meets with his therapist and speaks of how narratives always work towards filling in the absences left in memorial reconstructions of events of mass violence. The therapist says: 'the victims who died can never tell THEIR side of the story, so it is better not to have any more stories.' To this, Art responds: 'Uh-uh. Samuel Beckett once said: "Every word is like an unnecessary stain on silence and nothingness".' This exchange is followed by a frame in which there is no verbal dialogue. In the next frame Art adds: 'On the other hand, he SAID it.' And the therapist replies: 'He was right. Maybe you can include it in your book.'[14]

Is silence, then, an absence? Is it the other of sound? Or is silence as complicatedly constructed as sound? As I stepped into Gulberg Society with Farooq and Imtiaz, I did not know what I would encounter. But my interpretive sensibilities were acutely heightened.

I had to make meaning of what I would see, hear, feel. In a sense, that my interpretive orientation might well have been an unnecessary stain on the silence and nothingness of the space was not something that I was willing to consider. As a researcher, what I was driven by was an interpretive lust with immense capacity to colonize and violate the silence of the space.

When I went to Gujarat in 2002 as a student volunteer to work at the Shah Alam refugee camp in Ahmedabad and conduct interviews as part of yet another fact-finding team—as one of the many voyeuristic tourists deliciously consuming the trauma of others so that I could live to tell the tale of my human rights exploit—I experienced something that changed my perspective of justice and healing forever. At the end of a very taxing day of recording survivor testimonies, I was waiting for my colleague at the entrance of Shah Alam when I heard the laughter of children coming from within the dargah. In the midst of the injured and maimed, this sounded otherworldly. I followed the sound to the central courtyard of the dargah and saw a huge group of children (many of them orphaned) along with some very energetic members from a group called Play for Peace standing in a circle, holding hands and animatedly singing a song called 'Bajra': about the everyday practice of grinding the *bajra* (millet) to make chapattis at home.

The chorus of so many children laughing and singing together was for that particular moment a magical feeling (Campagna 2018). Their laughter was infectious—everyone around joined the cacophony. The circle marked the formation of a very different kind of community: one joined in sorrow through laughter. In the non-competitive games, the children who made mistakes were never 'out'; rather, they occupied pride of position 'in' the circle to lead the game. The very serious-looking, serious-sounding, serious work that many bourgeoisie volunteers like me were doing looked poorly pretentious in the face of songs and games that could evoke spontaneous laughter in children who had been orphaned, seen their family members brutally raped and killed, or 'disappeared'. I never knew that the power of collective laughter could not only heal but also arrest cycles of violence. This was an equally powerful way to mourn. Despite my privileged position of an outsider, who will eventually go back to safer quarters, playing with the children, and spending those few days in Ahmedabad laughing with them gave me a contingent sense of our shared commitment to mourning in precarious times: be it through crying, or laughter.

Beyond what the legal processes will achieve, while our struggles against state impunity and the spectacular onslaught of neoliberalism continue, we need to think of ways in which we can use the powers of mourning to mobilize political communities of human beings who are joined through shared feelings of loss and vulnerability, to forge ethical relationships that connect us with those whose lives were destroyed: not through sentimentality, but solidarity.[15] Gujarat 2002 is paradigmatic of the brutality that a majoritarian secular democracy is capable of. We cannot undo this truth even if Modi is convicted or the BJP is defeated in the next general elections five years from now. We can only hope to mourn together—in silence and in laughter—and ensure that we never forget. As Jacqueline Rose writes: 'Really to forget something, you have to forget that you have forgotten. You have to be 'forgetful of forgetfulness'' (2004: 7). This will be our lived truth—refracted, inadequate.

Notes

1. Quoted in Mitta 2014: 237.
2. Jasbir Puar, citing David Kazanjian, understands a 'flashpoint' as 'a centripetal turbulence of illumination so powerful that it may blind the past even as it spotlights the present and lights up the future' (Puar 2007: xviii).
3. Wikipedia. 'Gujarat 2002 riots'. Accessible on https://en.wikipedia.org/wiki/2002_Gujarat_riots; last accessed 5 July 2013.
4. Google image search, <www.google.co.in/search?rlz=1C1GCEU_enIN820IN821&tbm=isch&q=gujarat+2002+riots&chips=q:gujarat+2002+riots,online_chips:godhra+riots&usg=AI4_-kTkquaaC0tC4CCfkLDOUnd5JR41Mw&sa=X&ved=0ahUKEwjTt__HnI3fAhVDWisKHXGyBaoQ4lYILygI&biw=1366&bih=626&dpr=1>.
5. Human Rights Watch. 2002. 'We Have No Orders to Save You'. Accessible onwww.hrw.org/reports/2002/india/; last accessed 5 July 2013.
6. In fact, the construction of Godhra as the enraging flashpoint has closed the space to grieve for those who lost their lives in the train fire.

7. For an argument against the normative good of neutrality, see Cole 2016: 2012-2017.
8. For commentary on the relationship between rights, suffering, and witnessing, see Baxi 1985b; Kleinman and Kleinman 1997: 1-24.
9. Many scholarly works have traced the origins of Hindutva ideology to that of European fascism. For illustrations, see Ahmad 2002: 129, Basu et al 1993, Sarkar, Sumit 1993: 163–7, Casolari 2000: 218–28, Casolari 2011, Banaji 2016.
10. *The Times of India*. 2016. 'Full Text of Anil Ambani's Birthday Message to PM Narendra Modi' 20 September. Accessible on https://timesofindia.indiatimes.com/india/Full-text-of-Anil-Ambanis-birthday-message-to-PM-Narendra-Modi/articleshow/54383647.cms; last accessed 5 July 2013.
11. Quoted in Sarkar 2002: 2874. For a reproduction of more such pamphlets, see Kumar 2017.
12. Quoted in Concerned Citizens Tribunal 2002: 27.
13. At the time of writing, a plea by Zakia Jafri against the Special Investigation Team's exoneration of Narendra Modi was expected to be heard by the SC in January 2019. NDTV News Desk. 2018. '2002 Gujarat riots: Top Court Defer's Zakia Jafri's Plea Hearing in Gujarat Riots till January', NDTV. 3 December, 2018. Accessible on https://www.ndtv.com/india-news/2002-gujarat-riots-supreme-court-defers-plea-hearing-of-zakia-jafri-widow-of-ehsan-jafri-in-gujarat-1956956; last accessed 5 July 2013.
14. Quoted in Young 2000: 31.
15. I draw on Judith Butler's work for this articulation. See, Butler 2004; Butler, Gambetti and Sabsay 2016.

6

Professor of Pathos

Upendra Baxi's Minor Jurisprudence*

> The minor [. . .] gets cast aside, overlooked, or forgotten in the interplay of major chords. This is the downside of the minor, but also its strength: that it does not have the full force of a pre-existing status, of a given structure, of a predetermined metric, to keep it alive. It is out of time, untimely, rhythmically inventing its own pulse.
>
> — Erin Manning, *The Minor Gesture* (2016: 1–2)

'Testimonial to a Lack'

What is Upendra Baxi's contribution to jurisprudence in India? If one were to engage in a playful speculation about the ways in which lawyers would answer this question, what might some imaginative responses yield? If you are a practising lawyer—I am not, so this is a hazardous guess—he would be considered a respected legal academic who has written a lot on the constitution and the supreme court, but hopelessly theoretical for a practitioner's use. If you are a judge (am I bordering on contempt?)—his stature would invite the salutation

* Written in 2018 in Sonipat; to mark Baxi's 80th birthday.

'brother', but he would also be considered too much of a polemicist who will tear through the myth of judicial propriety. If you are a practising lawyer of the human rights kind—which also I am not, but can risk a more favourable guess—he is a key figure who extols the power of social action litigation, and has encouraged many law students (who have been either taught by him or have read or heard him) to not go down the path of taking up a corporate law job, and to dedicate themselves to litigating against the impunity with which the state and corporations perpetuate violence against the poor, the despised, and the suffering. If you are an activist (which I have been in a past life with some remaining traces, so can speak with contingent authority), Baxi's own activism offers strategies for how law can be used by lawyers and people's movements for social transformation, while you continue to subject law to ethical interrogation.

If you are a legal academic (which is the skin that I have lived in for a fair bit of time now), he is a Dumbledoresque figure[1] for those few in India who engage in what can broadly be called critical legal scholarship, legal theory on the left, or activist scholarship. This is because within the discipline of law in India, the practice of interdisciplinary, self-reflexive, feminist, and anti-capitalist scholarship that questions orthodoxy and dogmatism, speaks truth to power, and foregrounds the social, continues to be marginalized at best and dismissed as not scholarly enough at worst. For the more doctrinal and analytically oriented amongst us, who I feel are in a majority within Indian law schools and colleges, Baxi's works on the Indian legal system, the SC, rule-of-law in India, and Indian constitutionalism are considered worthy of citation (Baxi 1982; 1985a: xv–151; 2002b: 31–63; 2007a: 7–21). However, his sustained engagements with postmodernism and psychoanalysis (Baxi 2007b), and his intellectual and political self-positioning that defies easy ideological pigeonholing (being equally critical of conservatives, liberals, and progressives), have been a cause for some discomfort (Twining 2009: 197–212).

I have never been taught by Baxi in person, but it wouldn't be an exaggeration to say that I have been a student of his thought and writing for a long time now. I hadn't met him until after completing my first law degree. My interactions with him since that brief first encounter at the Critical Legal Conference in Hyderabad in 2006

(I was able to gather enough courage to go up and say hello and mumble something about the discontents of suffering-talk, right before he got into a car) have been mostly fleeting. Yet, through the years of my law education and afterwards, Baxi has had an indelible presence in the way I have shaped my identities as a feminist, law teacher, and jurisprudent (Sircar 2018: 73–99).

One of the regular ways in which such a presence can be thought of as possible is through reading his works as part of my courses. But I went to ILS Law College in Pune from 1999 to 2004, which hadn't introduced teaching methods like the breed of the national law schools. We were taught courses in a mode in which we did not necessarily read beyond a set textbook (actually borrowed or photocopied notes or flimsy guidebooks) for a subject.[2] I first heard about Baxi and his work from the constitutional law scholar S.P. Sathe, who had taught Baxi while he was pursuing his law degree at the University of Bombay in the early 1960s. A senior professor referring to the work of a former student was in itself a pedagogical gesture that was unprecedented for me. Sathe had offered a fond introduction to his work—Baxi was teaching at the University of Warwick at that time and had just published *The Future of Human Rights* (2002a)—calling it something akin to essential and dense (these are my forgetful approximations).

During a lecture on judicial activism, on which Sathe has written a lot (2003), he referred us to Baxi's now classic article 'Taking Suffering Seriously' (1985b). The article wasn't discussed in class in any great detail except for some remarks about what was at stake in shifting the language of judicial activism from 'public' to 'social'. My attempts at trying to find the article online failed. It was available behind the paywall of a journal database, and I had no institutional access. For me, though, that the word 'suffering' was invoked in the context of learning the law—a positive doctrine considered so devoid of emotion that it becomes indistinguishable from a normative *doxa*—left a subliminal impression whose import I would come to realize only later.[3]

The second instance when Baxi's name came up in class was during my law of crimes course. This was a reference to 'An Open Letter to the Chief Justice of India' that Baxi had co-authored in 1979 with three other law professors to register a protest against the SC's acquittal of the accused in what has come to be known as the Mathura rape case. Again, this was a mere reference in class. What struck me was the action involved—the collective writing of a letter addressed directly to the chief justice as a way of demonstrating public dissent as lawyers within the bounds of the constitution's mandate. I found the 'Open Letter' in the pages of a *Supreme Court Cases* volume in the library (Baxi et al. 1979). It was unlike any piece of legal writing that I had read in law college. Instead of legalese, the language was imbued with outrage. It was a passionate piece of writing that taught its readers about the larger context of patriarchal and caste oppression within which practices of adjudication and justice delivery operated. This might sound too obvious a connection—but it was more than revelatory for me as a law student, and tragically requires repeated emphasis to many of the students to whom I've been teaching law over the past decade. Those were the fledgling days of my political consciousness taking shape, and reading more of Baxi's writings—it was (and continues to be) an exciting struggle working through his language—opened up a whole new way to imagine the law, and re-imagine my role as a lawyer beyond litigating or working with a firm. Learning that activism and writing could very well be worthy pursuits that I could use my legal training for was what led me to doing what I have done so far.[4]

The 'Open Letter', although co-authored, bore the hallmark of a distinctive voice in which Baxi wrote that I have come to identify him with—what might be called a voice of pathos—one that distinguishes him from any other legal academic in India, especially among his contemporaries. Pathos, in everyday terms, can be understood as the practice of emotional appeal through language. It is a mode of address that lends aesthetic intensity to the tragedy of human suffering when conveyed to an audience. Pathos constitutes not only the content of speech, text, or image, but also a style: the tone, the use of vocabulary, the deployment of metaphors, the form of delivery. Pathos, though, is not completely synonymous with emotion. While emotion is understood to be connected to the faculty of the mind which interprets experiences to offer socially intelligible responses, pathos is 'intense emotion involving the whole body' (Rabaté 2016: 8) that generates 'affective relationalities' (Arif 2017: 22). It breaks down logocentric dualities like mind/body, reason/sentiment, strength/

vulnerability, public/private, lawful/lawless (Harrison 2018), to produce 'exalted passion'(Rabaté 2016: 8). Baxi's writings—strongly aligned with a decolonial and debrahminizing commitment (Mani 2005; Mignolo and Walsh 2018)—are embedded in pathos as well as kindling pathos in the reader.

If I had to answer the question that I opened this piece with, my response would be that Baxi's single most important contribution to jurisprudence in India has been to infuse legal scholarship with pathos—the pathos of suffering, resistance, responsibility, and care. An apocryphal reading of Baxi's work might make us consider his passionate heft as a sentimental inflection, but it will not necessarily lead us to consider this as a jurisprudence (G. Simpson 2015: 3–29). It might be well accepted that Baxi writes with pathos, but does that pathos constitute a jurisprudence?[5] If we understand jurisprudence as 'a practice, a craft, and a virtue: a way of attending to and taking responsibility for the full range of techniques by which [lawyers] [...] make the world amenable to judgement' (Parker 2015: 39), then pathos would be inseparable from 'the *phronesis* of *jus* [...], law's consciousness and conscience' (Douzinas and Gearey 2005: 3, emphasis in original).

However, if we take the apocryph seriously (Manderson 2001: 27–59), in Baxi's jurisprudence we will find an equally rigorous attachment to the prosaic, procedural, political, and poetic in law—it is a rare demonstration that combines the material with the metaphysical. However, a plain reading of Baxi might not make us see this—which is why I have heard evaluations like 'abstract' or 'polemical' with reference to his work from many students and colleagues. Which is also why Baxi will not necessarily feature in the core syllabus of a jurisprudence or constitutional law course in India, unless perhaps as a supplementary reading. He might still be part of the law and social transformation or human rights law course, or the 'Open Letter' might feature in a criminal law course's module on rape—given the direct connect one would make between the subject and the content of his writings, but not because of the aesthetics of the writing and the emotional investments and ethical imperatives that are conveyed through the voice of the author.[6]

So, in many ways, there seems to be a strange contradiction emerging: Baxi's pathos endeavours to unmask law's violence and silence about the suffering of those on the margins (even as he has offered ways of working with law); and in turn, Baxi's pathos has become marginal to the teaching and learning of jurisprudence in India. Indian legal education is marked by a simultaneous presence and absence of Baxi. His work is acclaimed for its rigorous content, but not necessarily for its innovative forms. While his politics is contingently celebrated, his aesthetics is considered removed from jurisprudential insight. I don't intend to overstate this form/content divide—but it is the task of paying attention to their relationship in Baxi's style of writing that I wish to undertake in this chapter.[7] To mark B.R. Ambedkar's centenary year, in 1995, Baxi had lamented how the 'Indian social science landscape has disarticulated Babasaheb Ambedkar by studious theoretical silence' (Baxi 1995: 122–49). My contention is that legal research and teaching in India has extended a similar theoretical silence towards the aesthetics in and of Baxi's jurisprudence.[8]

Pathos is discernible in the major jurisprudential themes of suffering and violence in the lives of subaltern peoples that Baxi has written about, and is well known for. That is a corpus that I don't need to restate for readers acquainted with his work. In this chapter, I intend to offer some fragments of what I would call Baxi's 'minor jurisprudence' (McVeigh 2015: 499–511; Antaki 2017: 54–75). Minor would not necessarily mean the opposite of major, or lesser and insignificant. A plain language approximation might mean it to be the subtext that comes to the fore only when you look for pathos on the margins of Baxi's writings, in his marginal writings, or read between the lines of his major works. They will show a consistent engagement with an ethic of responsibility exercised in the practice of jurisprudential knowledge production and holding the office of the jurisprudent (Dorsett and McVeigh 2012: 471–93; McVeigh 2014: 471–91, 2015: 499–511). As feminist law professors Amita Dhanda and Archana Parashar, whose own works have been strongly influenced by Baxi's, have written:

> 'While the knowledge and power nexus is now well established, it is equally important to make explicit the nexus of power and responsibility. Legal scholars who theorize the law have the power to constitute valid legal knowledge. Necessarily, they ought to take responsibility for the consequences that flow from their theories' (Dhanda and Parashar 2009: xii).

As I will indicate in what follows, the normative call in this quote is already embodied in Baxi's minor jurisprudence and can provide insights into a practice of jurisprudence that can interrogate the status of modern law as the 'state's emissary' (Baxi 1992: 247–64), or a stooge of the powerful, along with a self-reflexive account of the jurisprudent's own entanglements with networks of power and privilege (Baxi 1992: 254).[9]

Minor Affects

The expression 'minor jurisprudence' draws on what French philosophers Gilles Deleuze and Felix Guattari have called 'minor literature' (1983: 13–33). I had first encountered their names in a not-so-well-known 1991 piece by Baxi titled 'Complicity and Struggle: Theory and Society', which offered an impassioned provocation: the 'complicitous relation of social theory with the noological Indian state' (1991: 21).[10] Following up on that reference inaugurated for me a rival trajectory in the French intellectual tradition with a strong psychoanalytic bent that added more layers to Michel Foucault's theorization of power and government (Schönher 2015: 1–12).

In this section, I will do two things: first, offer a brief understanding of why I have chosen to use the idea of minor jurisprudence to think about Baxi's work. Second, I will illustrate Baxi's minor jurisprudence as a practice of 'affective labour' (Hardt 1999: 89–100)—care work that takes 'immaterial' forms (Lazzarato 2006: 133–46) in nurturing 'socially engaged theoretical labourers' who will be able to interrogate their own complicity in 'the charmed circle of cognitive entrepreneurs operating grids of globalized knowledge systems' (Baxi 1995: 19–20).

Two key characteristics of minor literature are: first, 'everything in them is political' and, second, 'everything takes on a collective value' (Guattari and Deleuze 1986: 17). As Laurie and Khan point out (2017: 3):

> 'minor literatures should not form canons anchored to Masters. […] The minor is not the achievement of individual heroes: it describes a multiplicity. Minor literatures make visible all the collective forces required for liberalism to produce its myths of the autonomous individual. For this reason, there is no moral hierarchy between minor and major works.'

Minor jurisprudence,[11] thus, displaces canonical understandings of law that are traced back almost singularly to Euro-American traditions comprising the works of all white men. Yet, in offering an anti-colonial perspective, minor jurisprudence will not engage in a nativist counter-position that again favours specific individuals or civilizations as the sole repositories of southern legal knowledge. In making visible the machinations of the collective forces in sovereignty, constitutions, rights, and citizenship, minor jurisprudence reveals how the production of the autonomous individual is intrinsic to 'state formative practices' under liberalism and imperialism (Baxi 1999–2000: 1,183–1210). Minor jurisprudence foregrounds the possibility of a co-habitation of a multitude of laws that do not work with a foundational law of authority like Kelsen's '*Grundnorm*' (1967: 8) or Hart's 'Rule of Recognition' (2012). Minor jurisprudence is not a romantic category of resistance to the hegemonic laws of colonialism, apartheid, occupation, capitalism, racism, casteism, patriarchy, or heteronormativity, but an active and ethical practice of legal scholarship that repeatedly challenges, in the words of Peter Goodrich, 'the dominance of any singular system of legal norms' and 'neither aspires nor pretends to be the only law or universal jurisprudence' (1996: 2).

We can see such a working of minor jurisprudence in Baxi's argument in favour of a distinct 'postcolonial legality' that challenges 'epistemic legal racism' while at the same time troubling the idea of the postcolonial itself as 'a hegemonic term of art' (Baxi 2012: 178, 1999–2000: 1,185). Baxi has described constitutions as a 'will to stateness', which is a 'totalizing formation' in which legal recognition of communities and rights postures as the *telos* of justice-seeking enterprises within liberalism (2002b: 32). Alongside, he has also kept alive a 'dark hope' (Shulman 2007) in the Constitution of India and by extension the SC. This is what can be called Baxi's faith in 'demosprudence': 'judicial review process and power that enhances life under a constitutional democracy' (Baxi 2014a: 6). In a similar vein, while on the one hand he has called out the neoliberal co-optation and 'repressive' potential of human rights ('trade-related market-friendly human rights'), he has also re-imagined human rights futures that 'engage in a discourse of suffering that moves the world' (Twining 2009; Baxi 1998: 125–69). Baxi's philosophical interlocutors—from Gandhi to Marx to Ambedkar to Gramsci to Foucault to Derrida to

Rawls to Sen to Nussbaum—demonstrate a committed attempt to not eulogize any singular heroic figure, but to acknowledge a multitudinous bricolage of traditions, which is constituted also by his learnings from the struggles of people's movements. In his approach to legal research and teaching, while Baxi has found a home in what he has called the 'hedonist approach' of 'rebellious pedagogies', he has also sounded a note of caution about the production of exclusionist 'elite theories' by a new generation of law institutes and scholars whose claim to criticality lie in berating doctrinal legal analysis, but not foregrounding their complicity with structures of oppression in the way higher education in general and in law in particular is being privatized and depoliticized in India (Baxi 1990, 2007c).

If postcolonial subjectivity is characterized by what Gayatri Chakravorty Spivak has called a condition of a 'double-bind' or 'learning to live with contradictory instructions' (2012: 3), Baxi's work has been a performative embodiment of that. At the heart of this double-bind lies pathos. As Baxi has commented on pedagogy, research, and scholarship in India:

> [...] our espousal of transformative causes has not kept pace with the need to renovate our practices of theoretical labour... I have a feeling, at least for myself, that much of our social engagement does not inform our academic being. Even if there is a grain of truth in this perception, we must acknowledge the 'germ gnawing at the heart of conviction.' And this should goad us, perhaps to proceed beyond the merger of heroic activism with tearful accountability. (1991: 26)

Thus, the task of pathos in Baxi's minor jurisprudence, as I read it, is one of affective labour: a form of unrecognized work that engages in an ethic of care and responsibility but does not carry exchange value in material terms of being considered legal knowledge. Feminists have long characterized women's domestic work as caregivers, and professional work as sex workers, as affective or immaterial labour because it remains unrecognized as legitimate work, resulting in the exacerbation of gendered exploitation under capitalism (Federici 2012; Ghosh 2009; Kotiswaran 2011). Drawing on the work of Michael Hardt, affective labour can be understood as 'the labor of human contact and interaction, which involves the production and manipulation of affects' (Oksala 2016: 284). Under neoliberal conditions of production, affective labour does not remain restricted to the private sphere alone. Johanna Oksala writes: 'As the marketization and commodification of everyday life expands, people have increasingly come to rely on the affective services that they buy and that they used to receive from their families and communities. [...] Affective labor is increasingly outsourced, and the domestic, private realm is marketized' (2016: 284). The affective labour of Baxi's minor jurisprudence stands unrecognized because it offers gestures of care and responsibility that fall outside of the conventional interpretive frames through which most legal scholarship is written and read in India. As long as they pertain to theorizing law with a capital L, works can claim to qualify as jurisprudential. There is a strong inflection of an instrumental orientation in such practices of reading and writing jurisprudence in the Indian legal academy, where training is directed to turning students into technocrats who will serve the demands of an industrious New India.

Considering the affective labour invested in Baxi's minor jurisprudence gains particular significance in times of the consolidation of the academic–military–industrial complex that individuates academic labour, rewards intellectual depoliticization, managerializes academic relationships through metric-based evaluations, and securitizes university spaces (Weizman 2006: 53–77; Doyle 2015; Collini 2017; Azad et al. 2017). This trend has been particularly acute in the discipline of law globally for many decades (Thornton 2012), and as Baxi has pointed out time and again in the case of post-liberalization legal education in India (Baxi 1976: 1–33, 1996, 2007: 3–21).

Reparatively Reading Baxi

In this section, I will offer some illustrations of Baxi's minor jurisprudence by reading three particular forms of writings which don't get counted as part of his jurisprudential oeuvre: his lesser-known works in the field of law, acknowledgements and footnotes that appear on the margins of major works, and tributes written by him on the passing of his mentors and comrades. My choice of the selected references has to do particularly with how these writings have helped me think through my own work as a teacher of law, and scholar. I do not offer a chronological or comprehensive overview because a claim of that nature in itself will render the idea of minor jurisprudence redundant.

The fragmented nature of my survey is motivated by a practice of what Eve Kosofsky Sedgwick has called 'reparative reading' (2003: 123–51): reading 'texts and semiotic practices [...] in terms of their empowering, productive as well as renewing potential to promote semantic innovation, personal healing and social change' (Roder 2014: 58–9). Further, reparative reading can be understood as

> 'a mode of critical theory that embraces the "privilege of unknowing" and that provides theorists, readers, and scholars with a way to think about texts that does not always already, even before reading, imagine a potential outcome—a possible reading, indeed, that does not imagine a potential as even necessary' (Allan 2016).

Reparative reading, thus, enables an attachment with the text through the foregrounding of interpretive vulnerability rather than interpretive supremacy.[12] The register of vulnerability invokes pathos in the way a reader cares for a text and its author, and in that ethic of care lies the task of affective labour.

In 1990, at the dawn of India's liberalization era, Baxi wrote a short, contemplative essay titled 'Teaching as Provocation' that compellingly foretold how the privatization of higher education in India would solidify knowledge as a 'Brahmanic preserve' and reduce the 'teacher–taught' relation into one between 'producers' and 'consumers' of knowledge' (1990: 154). The piece was a frank insight into Baxi's teaching philosophy, and since the time of my discovery of it, it has remained with me as a manifesto that has inspired my own pedagogical pursuits. I teach this piece as part of my jurisprudence course to emphasize that jurisprudence is not just a pre-existing and distant corpus of knowledge to be mastered, but whose appreciation and reception are intrinsically connected to the ethical imperatives attended to in its teaching (and learning). Despite its brevity, this is a piece with enormous depth. I will hold on some key thoughts from it here as an illustration of Baxi's minor jurisprudence of legal pedagogy.

Drawing from his teaching experience at the University of Sydney (which was his first teaching job after completing his doctorate in the US), Baxi suggests 'a profound inversion of roles' to unsettle the hierarchical structure and ideology through which knowledge is arranged within a classroom (1990: 152). This inversion requires that 'the teacher has to be taught and the taught in turn teaches something to the teacher, the receivers of knowledge are the givers and the givers receivers' (1990: 152). The jurisprudential lesson in this for me lies in its critique of authority as embodied in the figure of the teacher. The call for collaboration between the teacher and students in a classroom is an acknowledgement of the teacher's 'scholarly finitude' (1990: 155). This acknowledgement is not a tacit one, but what Baxi calls a 'confessional activity': 'Every time I bite at the fruit of knowledge, I have to say, I realize the core of my ignorance' (1990: 154). The confession is not metaphorical. In response to the question 'What are you good for?' that Baxi was asked by his students, he replied: '"Do not merely look at what I say; look at *what I do with what I say*." I simply cannot carry conviction about what I say to young minds unless they see that I mean what I say about the rule of law, human rights, human dignity' (1990: 154, emphasis mine). This quote sets up Baxi's own struggle with knowing and doing, or praxis: 'we [...] are the bearers of the very modes of repression we seek to combat through scholarship' (1994: 56). Teaching as an exhibition of the prowess of knowledge is a demonstration of 'specialization' that, according to Baxi, 'reinforces the authority of the knowledge makers and givers' (1990: 155). In this, praxis becomes Baxi's life practice for subjecting knowledge practices to an ethical interrogation for the role they play in reproducing the 'tyranny, injustice and exploitation enacted before our own eyes even as we "teach" and "learn"' (1990: 154).

It is this 'dichotomy between discourse and praxis' in Indian social sciences that prompted Baxi in 1987 to 'an interrogation of the wildfire spread of women's studies in India' (Baxi 1994: 69). As the chairperson of the Indian Council for Social Science Research Committee on Women's Studies, Baxi had raised concerns about how the institutionalization of women's studies in Indian universities can lead to it becoming a depoliticized specialization. As he wrote: 'Suffering women are our true social scientists, not we for whom *their* suffering provides material for nurturing our careers and building institutions focused on "women's studies"' (1994: 59, emphasis in original).

Since its inception in the mid-1970s, born in the wake of the historic 1974 *Towards Equality* report on the status of women in

India (Committee on the Status of Women in India 2011), women's studies has emerged as a critical interdisciplinary field that combines research, pedagogy, and activism, with close ties to women's movements in India (John 2008a: 1–22). Alongside my law education, I had completed a postgraduate certificate from the Women's Studies Centre at Pune University.[13] Under the tutelage of feminist sociologist Sharmila Rege, this course trained me in feminist theory and thought from socialist and anti-caste perspectives, and introduced me to a new vocabulary of politics and scholarship to engage with both the teaching and learning of jurisprudence.[14] So, when I read Baxi's concerns many years after its publication, it seemed premature, a little alarmist, and the tone carried a tinge of what might today be called 'mansplaining' (Solnit 2015). Expressing what I read as doubt laced with humour, Baxi himself noted that with the piece he had aimed at 'shocking sisters', and admitted in an endnote that the questions raised by him were met with 'appropriate silence' by the women scholars who were pioneering women's studies at that time (1994: 68, 69). Contrary to Baxi's position of doubt, it is because of the critical nature of the feminist scholarship being produced by women's studies centres at public universities that there have been repeated attempts by the University Grants Commission to rein them in—once by trying to rechristen them as Women and Family Studies Centres, and more recently through a threat of ending funding (Rajalakshmi 2003; Phadke 2017).

However, a reparative reading allows me to appreciate a broader political motivation behind Baxi's interrogation that becomes relevant for our current times. His caution offers two lessons that speak to the pursuit of 'emancipatory knowledge' in the neoliberal university (1994: 68). First, his position can be read as one about the problematic consequences of institutionalizing movement politics into academic disciplines of expertise that end up severing critique from collective action.[15] Second, a related argument against reducing the experiences of the suffering of others into discourses of academic specialization for a select few is his concern with what can be called academic ventriloquism: potential for violent appropriation that research continues to perform by capitalizing on the voices of the subaltern and then marketing it for consumption as critical scholarship (Kleinman and Kleinman 1996: 1; Wolfe 1997: 57; Sircar and

Dutta 2012: 333). This has, in fact, been a sustained concern for Baxi with regard to the relationship between scholarly expertise and social transformation: 'there is no prospect for an empowering sphere of studies and action within the existing conceptions of uni- and multi-disciplinarism. [...] Versatility, not mere specialization, is what the birth of emancipatory knowledge calls forth [...] at no stage can it become authentic without praxis' (Baxi 1994: 67–8).

This observation has also found amplification in his concerns with the teaching of law as a specialist field, with particular regard to post-liberalization legal education in India which saw the burgeoning of the five-year LLB programme and the growth of the national law school prototypes. As Baxi asserts: 'most "encultured" law products of the National Law School prototypes now serve better the causes of globalized lawyering than the future of human rights in a globalizing India' (2007c: 17). I have a palpable sense of this through my experience of teaching law in India in times of neoliberalism and Hindutva at a university built on money from a steel company known for its exploitation of adivasis and their lands (Pati 2012; Chandrasekhar 2017), obsessed with publication metrics and global rankings as primary markers of scholarly excellence, and with little regard for issues related to access, diversity, and the well-being of its inhabitants in students, faculty, administrative staff, and labourers.

Building on the eleventh thesis of Marx's 'Theses on Feuerbach' first published in 1888,[16] praxis for Baxi brings together knowing (interpretation) and doing (transformation) in many ways. A minor jurisprudential dimension of this can be seen at the margins of some of his texts. When being trained as lawyers, seldom are we taught to look at the acknowledgements section of a book, or the footnotes of a major work as constitutive of the philosophical orientation of the jurisprudent, or at how citational practices reproduce knowledge hegemonies (Ahmed 2014). These components remain mostly extraneous to the work in question and are understood merely as functional conventions, unless being mined for data retrieval or for questioning veracity.

In the acknowledgements section of many of his books, Baxi has remained attentive to the domestic economies of affective labour and the experiences of subaltern suffering and struggles that enable and inspire him to produce his scholarship. In *The Crisis of the Indian*

Legal System, learning from an argument by Australian feminist Anne Summers, Baxi had commented on how the gesture of dedicating a book to one's wife is a manifestation of patriarchy and sexism (1982: xiii). The same is repeated in *Human Rights in a Posthuman World* (2007b: xvi). The wording of two key portions in the acknowledgements in *The Future of Human Rights* carries important minor jurisprudential insights:

> While conventional protocols require acknowledgement of my authorship of this work, it remains a composite creation. The heavily silent burdens of the labour of this writing have been graciously as ever borne by my wife Prema.... I need to say that the work in your hand owes, in many ways beyond traditional labours of authorial acknowledgement, to the *real authors*. If there is anything creative to this work, it owes to three decades old association with social action struggle for the human rights of subordinated peoples at diverse sites, within and outside India and in particular to the heroic struggle of over 200,000 women, children and men afflicted by 47 tonnes of MIC, in the Union Carbide orchestrated largest archetypal peacetime industrial disaster. From them, and the geographies of injustice constituted by the 'organized irresponsibility' and 'organized impunity' of global corporations, I have learnt more about human violation and suffering than the work in your hands can possibly ever convey. I accordingly also dedicate this work to the *suffering of the just*, by no means an abstract 'category'. (Baxi 2006b: xi–xii, emphasis in original)

In a similar vein, in a footnote to Chapter 1 in the same book, as an apologia for his use of the word 'human', Baxi wrote:

> 'I use the term "human" as an act of communicational courtesy. Human stands marked by the presence of man, and person by a "son". My preferred non-sexist version is, therefore, a combination of the first letters of both words: "huper". I await the day when the word "huper" will replace the word "human"' (2006b: 1).

As a practice of pathos, the sharing of authorship with a people's movement, acknowledging the contradiction in dedicating a book to one's partner, and explaining the patriarchal structuring and limitations in the English language, are crucial to a critique of authority in jurisprudence. If we read these as Baxi's affective labour, they offer a training in reading with care and responsibility that make it difficult to respond to acknowledgements and footnotes with 'facile gestures' (Foucault 1988: 152), and reformulate the writing of jurisprudence as 'above all theory which is reflective about the positioning of subjects in the construction of knowledge' (Davies 2002: 22).

An articulation of the scholar's self-positioning in the practices of the production of knowledge also 'creates specific relationalities that generate assemblies of social relations' (Arif 2017: 20). The above instances have pointed at Baxi's acknowledgement of his affective ties with his wife and his engagement with subaltern peoples' struggles. A deep account of such relationalities can also be found in the many tributes that Baxi has written about his mentors and comrades on their passing.[17]

When I had heard about Baxi from S.P. Sathe in the early 2000s, I had no inkling of the fact that as a student at the University of Bombay, Baxi had 'rebelled against [Sathe's] ways of teaching' in class (Baxi 2006a: 3,356). This I learnt on reading 'Adieu, Satyaranjan Sathe', Baxi's tribute to his former teacher. As Baxi recalled:

> Of course, he was outraged at my interlocution of his pedagogic authority. However, what eventually mattered for both of us were the ways which Satyaranjan converted this contestation into a resource for vastly improved methods of law teaching and his reiterated public acknowledgement of this episode as providing further lessons and messages for innovating critical pedagogy. In thus continually recalling with warm affection my acts of rebellion, Satyaranjan thus sought to nourish *dialogical*, rather than *authoritarian*, mode of intergenerational transmission of knowledges. This, I believe, constitutes an enduring Sathe legacy. (2006a: 3,356, emphasis in original)

The sole-surviving signatory to the 'Open Letter', Baxi delivered the First Lotika Sarkar Memorial Lecture in 2014, titled 'Unlearning the Law with Lotika Sarkar'. In a tribute laced with humour, sadness, and gratitude, Baxi said:

> [...] as her students they first learnt the two, and true, meanings of academic freedom: the freedom to teach and the freedom to learn. She emphasized the latter with students and the former with Deans and Heads! And Lot encouraged the students to learn the law as they wished; for her, the syllabus never cast in stone was but a

> mere opportunity to *co-learn*... In a sense I was her student...(Baxi 2014b: 2, emphasis in original)

Both tributes are not hagiographical, but rather what can be called jurisographical: an account of the 'duties that attach to the persona of jurisographer [...] to take care of the many forms and sources of writing of *jurisprudence* the jurisographer inherits' (Genovese 2016: 37, emphasis in original). In keeping alive the legacies of Sathe and Sarkar and Baxi's inheritances of them, the tributes continue a dialogue infused with disagreements, reminiscences, revisits, and absences. They mark an exemplary demonstration of a minor 'jurisprudence of generosity' (Van Marle 2007: 194).

A Tragic Celebration?

The festschrift is a curious artefact and event of academic writing. It honours the work of a veteran scholar (on most occasions a man)[18] at a particular time in her life through the self-aggrandizement of the contributors. It curates a community of inheritors who stake claim to a legacy of (waning?) greatness. The community shares the inherited glory through the individual's attachment to the repertoire of the honoured scholar, and yet each member of the community competes for authentic proximity as the most deserving inheritor. The pieces that constitute the festschrift maintain fidelity to the thoughts of the scholar being honoured, while bringing in subjective insights (both as valorization and disagreements) into her life and works. It claims coherence of convention, but remains inconsistent in treatment (Lewis 1996; Schleicher 2001; Taggart 2002: 227–52).

There are two motivational questions that ought to be responded to while putting together a festschrift. These are, 'Why Baxi?' and 'Why Now?' The first one is the less controversial of the two. The massive influence of Baxi's work in jurisprudence in India and globally, and also on social theory in general, is more or less settled. There might be a debate about the nature of the influence, but few would disagree that he is a towering figure in Indian (critical) legal scholarship. The second question can have an easy answer, and then a very difficult one. The year 2018 marked Baxi's 80th birthday—a worthy occasion to honour the person, his life, and works. That's the easy and happy response. Baxi's life's work has continuously made us confront the 'dark times' that we have been living with, inheriting, and bequeathing (Arendt 1968; Rose 2013). In trying to answer 'why now?', a confrontation with this dark side cannot be wished away. In both honouring Baxi and confronting the horrors of human suffering that his life's work bears witness to, this festschrift becomes at once a celebration and a tragedy. This sense of tragedy is further exacerbated in the banality of violence that we see around us, and live with, even as we honour Baxi.

In the dual characterization of this festschrift as a tragic celebration, I am struggling with a set of contradictions. What does it mean to read Baxi's minor jurisprudence in a volume honouring him as a major figure in Indian jurisprudence? In casting myself as a successor of the Baxian legacy, might I be (unwillingly) reifying of the law of the father? As Austin Sarat writes: 'fatherhood is one term through which law is mythologized and through which fantasies and anxieties about law are expressed' (2000: 9). The festschrift form lends itself to an 'agonistic intimacy' (B.Singh 2011: 430) between my fantasy of staking claim to Baxi's legacy, and my anxieties about mythologizing him. It is a performance of a citational captivity—you are meant to repeat references to the (male) persona of scholarly prowess that you are honouring, even as you desist deification. A '*citational relation*', points out Sara Ahmed, 'is often paternal' (Ahmed 2014, emphasis in original). In attending to Baxi's minor jurisprudence, thus, I as the reader, and Baxi as the author, are both rendered fractured,[19] joined through a relationship of transversal vulnerability (Butler et al. 2016) that is trying hard to disavow paranoid fraternity and embrace an 'ethic of listening' (Lipari 2009: 44; Baxi 1991: 21). I wouldn't like to romanticize and exceptionalize Baxi's minor jurisprudence; yet in his practice of 'ordinary ethics' (Das 2012: 133), he emerges as an extraordinary figure of wisdom and foresight.

Baxi's own negotiations with this authority–vulnerability continuum has been expressed thus: 'how is it that *power* of some people becomes the *fate* of innumerable others?' (Baxi 1991: 21, emphasis in original). All of Baxi's writing, teaching, and activism has been a struggle with finding answers to this question, taking seriously the ethical imperative related to authorizing oneself to be able to ask and answer this question, and thinking about the repeating conditions that offer no escape from the tragedy of this question. This struggle features in the pathos with which Baxi's writings have engaged a range of events and issues, from aboriginal land rights in Australia to the Emergency to the Bhopal gas leak, violence against women, modern gulags, the war on and of terror, the Gujarat pogrom, caste atrocity, human rights, to name just a few.

My attempt in this chapter has been to reparatively read the minor gestures in Baxi's jurisprudence. These gestures, of which I have offered a fragmented survey, can provide affective resources that can help us, at the least, to narrate accounts of the failure that the co-habitation of celebration and tragedy—a 'negative moment'—presents (Mbembe 2015). Upendra Baxi's minor jurisprudence can teach us the responsibilities that are incumbent upon us as jurisprudents in these times of extreme flux: one marked by a perverse coexistence of acute precarity and spectacular affluence. Baxi's minor jurisprudence can train legal academics to be affective labourers and reparative readers who, instead of appropriating the vulnerability of the suffering and claiming interpretive supremacy, will build relationships through their shared experiences of vulnerability.

I will force an 'inconcludable' end on this essay with a quote by Baxi that infuses pathos in these pathetic times (Baxi 2002b: 54). For those of us who teach law and are struggling with our own double-binds between knowing and doing, complicity and contamination, celebration and tragedy, this can be a talisman:

> 'For me, being a teacher in India is to be a deeply fractured, deeply wounded being, constantly in throes of transition, forever being evicted from utopias and yet, forbidden by history from desisting from struggles here and now for whatever "justice" against injustice' (Baxi 1990: 158).

Notes

1. It so happened that I was watching the Harry Potter series of films during the time of writing this piece. The character of Albus Dumbledore, the headmaster of the Hogwarts School of Witchcraft and Wizardry, seemed like an apposite fictional embodiment of Baxi—at once sagacious and pragmatic, caring and responsible, scholarly and activist. Dumbledore, as the creator of the series

J. K. Rowling had revealed, was also queer. Baxi remains a vintage figure in Indian legal scholarship whose commitment to practices of queering jurisprudence have been unprecedented and inspirational. Here, I understand queering as a method of 'reading for difference rather than dominance' (Gibson-Graham 2006: xxxi–xxxii); see generally Knutsen (2006: 197–212).

2. During my years at ILS Law College, learning the law (and its many conflicting meanings) was owed more to my interactions with the diversity of the student population, which comprised a large number from rural Maharashtra. ILS was certainly less cosmopolitan than the neighbouring Symbiosis Law School, and non-elite compared to the national law schools elsewhere in India. One of the key learnings in such a scenario for me was the revelation of a false relationship between cosmopolitanism, progressivism, and modernity. While the national law schools claimed to have modernized legal education in India, such modernization was accompanied by a class and caste homogenization of the student populace. S.P. Sathe was a strong critic of the national law school proposition of the Bar Council of India of which Baxi, in its initial days, was a proponent (see Sathe 1974: 1,643–5). For a recent analysis of the diversity quotient at Bengaluru's National Law School of India University, see C. Jain et al. (2018: 72–8).
3. I wonder whether I should credit Sathe or Baxi for this invocation. Maybe both.
4. Alongside Baxi, I had begun reading feminist legal works that also strongly influenced my political consciousness. Such references were also introduced to me by Sathe. See Sircar, Kapur, and Cossman (2016: 133–63).
5. On jurisprudence's long-standing uneasy relationship with passion, and its vicissitudes in emotion, see Bandes (2001); Nussbaum (2013).
6. This observation is not an empirically deduced one. I am basing this claim through a survey of course manuals for some of the mentioned subjects that are taught at the Jindal Global Law School. My hunch is, however, that it would possibly be the case in other law schools as well in some varying degrees. There is generally a tendency to avoid teaching literature that gets referred to as 'theory heavy' or 'too interdisciplinary' in law schools in India. This theory aversion is both promoted by faculty and administration, as well as demanded by students in a legal education scenario where technocratic training is considered the hallmark of excellence. Such a training also generates an understanding of law as a body of knowledge devoid of ethics and emotion. See generally Kennedy (2011: 257–82).

7. For a sophisticated demonstration of such an engagement with the form and style of Duncan Kennedy's work, see Nesiah (2014: 640–8).
8. For an illustration of this, see Kannabiran and Singh (2008). This book, which brings together a well-known group of feminist and critical legal scholars and activists, is dedicated to Upendra Baxi. My reading of the introduction makes clear that that the engagement with Baxi's work is limited to its politics. Two recent exceptions are Hasan Khan (2016: 2,061–79) and Debolina Dutta (2018: 181–202). Hasan Khan uses the aesthetics of disasters and Dutta locates Baxi using the aesthetics of relationships. While these works read Baxi using an aesthetic orientation, they do not necessarily read for the aesthetic in Baxi's jurisprudence.
9. In this context, Baxi had used the expression 'auto-critique' as a way to foreground his disagreements with his own positions, and revising them in the light of new insights and inspiration. The small corpus of writings on law that I have published, and my orientation towards critical jurisprudence, has been one that aims to take auto-critique seriously as an ethical method in scholarly knowledge production. On this see Davies (2002: 7–26); Sircar (2013: 527–73).
10. Drawing on the work of Deleuze and Guattari, Baxi writes: 'Noology is distinct from ideology and describes ways in which the modern state, with all its carnal and bloody nature of orders of desire which constitute the fantasy of *imperium*, provides and inspires the "very images of thought"' (Baxi 1991: 21, emphasis in original).
11. Minor jurisprudence itself does not have a settled definition. While I have distilled it for my purposes in this chapter, for an expansive discussion, see generally Tomlins (2017).
12. For discussions on the limitations on the practice of interpretation in art and law, its arrogant assumptions and violent consequences, see generally Sontag (1966: 3–14) and Cover (1986: 1601–29).
13. Now called the Savitribai Phule Pune University.
14. In this regard I have been inspired by Rege's piece "Education as *Trutiya Ratna*: Towards Phule-Ambedkarite Feminist Pedagogical Practice" (2010: 88–98).
15. For resonances of similar arguments see Douzinas (2005: 47–69); Chibber (2006: 357–87); Fraser (2013a).
16. 'The philosophers have only interpreted the world, in various ways; the point is to change it' (Marx 2002).
17. Debolina Dutta's doctoral research on the production of feminist jurisprudence in India (completed at the Melbourne Law School) directed me to the relational dimensions of Baxi's scholarship.

18. A search on Google Scholar for the word 'festschrift' throws up pages after pages of references to volumes in honour of male academics. See https://scholar.google.co.in/scholar?hl=en&as sdt=0%2C5&q=festschrift&btnG=
19. Baxi's vulnerability in age and health took on a corporeal dimension when he suffered a stroke a few years back. As he said in an interview: 'We went through a very, very bad time. It's my second life. Thanks to my wife and children, their constant care and nurture allowed the resumption of normal life. I know concretely now how much caregivers have to sacrifice. I know how difficult life could be. I could not do almost anything by myself. I lost languages, handwriting, computer and mechanical memory, some physical movements; had to undergo a lot of physiotherapy and movement' (Baxi 2016).

7

The Conduct of Critique

Jurisdictional Account of a Feminist Journey*

> To live a feminist life is to make everything into something that is questionable. The question of how to live a feminist life is alive as a question as well as being a life question.
>
> — Sara Ahmed, *Living a Feminist Life* (2017: 2)

Boring into Stuckness

The experience of starting to write this piece was boring. The activity of trying to provide an account of my journey as a male feminist jurisprudent felt taxing. Was there really this moment in my academic and political life when something happened and I turned feminist? Without an origin story, can I even begin? Isn't my desire for an origin story a reification of reproductive heteronormativity where I am trying to lay claim to a paternity of sorts to my feminist story? If I am unable to curate a story that offers an authoritative enough account of my relationship with feminism, is this exercise even worth

* Written through 2015—17 in Kolkata, Melbourne, and Sonipat; as a stocktaking of a decade of teaching as a feminist legal scholar.

pursuing? My inability to find such a moment made me feel stuck. Was I genuinely stuck, or was this a reflection of a male anxiety that my claim to being a feminist will risk exposure, and I will be judged to be lacking. Reading Laurent Berlant offered some direction. She describes this condition in the process of writing as a 'performance of stuckness':

> It is a record of where we got stuck on a question for long enough to do some research and write out the whole knot until the original passion and curiosity that made us want to try to say something about something got so detailed, buried, encrypted, and diluted that the energetic and risk-taking impulse became sealed and delivered in the form of a defense against thinking any more about it. Along the way, something might have happened to the scene the question stood for: or not (Berlant 2014).

And then I thought, have I actually been stuck for long enough to even legitimately perform stuckness? The impetus then was to begin narrating a journey, in the hope that I would at some point arrive at stuckness, and that would possibly be a good place to be. My lawyer-self had to step in and play a role too. Margaret Davies's characterization of jurisprudence as 'boring' provided a good dose of lubrication (2015: 1–4). That I felt the experience of writing this piece was boring could be read otherwise. Davies, counter-intuitively, speaks of jurisprudence as a boring philosophy, in that it seeks to bore: 'to dig, to probe under the surface' (2015: 4). The surface here is my academic skin of a male feminist jurisprudent. My boring journey is in fact more of a scratching exploration, and I will possibly get stuck prematurely in this piece, without digging deep enough. This incompleteness, I hope, never offers closure.

The Conduct of Critique

The volume for which this essay was written was themed 'Men Doing Feminism'.[1] It is a framing that can be read as celebratory, as well as contradictory. Depending on what strand of feminism one subscribes to, it might mark the moment of triumph for feminism that it now has converted-men on board, or it might be that fatalistic moment of defeat where feminism has now been infiltrated, co-opted and colonized by men. The framing can even sound like Capitalists Doing Communism, or Fundamentalists Doing Secularism, or their equally ironic inverted avatars. This continuous double-play of possibility and limitation, of glee and caution, is what feminism has meant for me—and here goes the laundry list—as a practising-heterosexual,[2] married, middle class, and upper-caste man. For me, feminism has been a site of inspirational contradictions, or what David Shulman, albeit in a different context, has beautifully termed 'dark hope' (Shulman 2007).

The word 'men' in the title of the theme can be read not merely as a signifier of a conservative biologism (Fausto-Sterling 1987, 2000, 2012). Although I carry some discomfort in the connection that the theme might suggest between identity and ideology, I cannot deny the deep ideological and material performance of privilege that I embody and enact as a cis-gendered man doing feminism. This embodiment and enactment of contradictions, being the recipient of privileges of this hetero–patriarchal–bourgeois–*savarna* social order, and at the same time being embedded in struggles against that very order, is what learning from and living with feminism has meant for me.

'Doing', another word in the theme, is of much significance in this regard. To *do* feminism for me is the training in a certain kind of conduct—not in the instrumentalist sense of etiquette, civility, or good behaviour (what gets pathetically referred to as chivalry), but the practice of an ethic of responsibility (Spivak 1994: 19–64), not responsibilization (Butler and Athanasiou 2013: 104–25). This distinction is crucial to the practice of feminism by men, especially at a time when the emergence of 'Feminism Lite' (Loewenstein 2014) has attained the status of self-congratulatory commonsense and 'Hashtag Feminism' (Loza 2014) has become the lingua franca of ostensibly progressive public engagement on social media as well as in the academy.

Responsibilization privileges privatized conduct of political correctness as a form of self-governance that is incentivized by the promise of membership in the patronage markets of progressive and sexist men, or to draw on Rebecca Solnit, into the 'mansplaining' club (2014: 1–16). For me, an ethic of responsibility is not only a cerebral idea but also a corporeal practice that takes seriously the limits of my authority to practise critique as a male feminist legal scholar. Thus, I'm not so much concerned with the capacity question: are men capable of being feminists? Rather, I am interested in the quotidian and relational concerns that animate the practice of feminism by men. What does it mean for a man to *conduct* oneself as a feminist?[3] It is this question that I will reflect on in this essay—from what Paul Cilliers would call a 'modest position' (Cilliers 2005: 256)—fully aware that as a man, waxing eloquent on being a feminist in many ways can be a self-serving exercise that can very well perpetuate a troubling binary between good and bad masculinities, and good and bad feminists. Which is why, I will not treat feminism as a virtue that men who identify themselves as such and practise it possess. I will think of feminism as a 'sweaty concept' (Ahmed 2017: 12–13) that repeatedly trains me in ways of making sense of the world and living in it by taking embodiment seriously and cautions me that the deployment of self-reflexivity and intersectionality as methods of critical (legal) inquiry might not always be enough (Davies 2002: 7–26).

My reflections can emerge from a wide trajectory of experiences—my childhood, my homes and relationships, my material accumulations and affects, my sexual lives, and my aesthetic and political life, both public and private, academic and activist.[4] For the purposes of this chapter I will draw on some experiences from my life in the academy where I encountered Feminism(s) with capital Fs, institutionalized within the university space.[5] Primary in this account is my over-a-decade-long training as a lawyer and jurisprudent, and my vexed and intimate relationship with the law, which I have both contempt for, and at the same time have maintained fidelity with, at least in disciplinary terms.

'Law' and 'feminism' have had a shared and continuing history of desire and derision, much like my relationship with them. Even while exposing law's misogynist foundations, and active complicity in the perpetuation of hetero-patriarchal orders, feminism has continued to repose faith in the law for challenging those very orders. Consequently, we have sometimes seen law successfully respond to feminisms' calls, and on many occasions feminism getting depoliticized, privatized, and sometimes even turned into a force of oppression (Behrendt 1993: 27–44; Doezema 2005), due to its intimacies with the legalism of the state, the neoliberal market (Fraser 2013),[6] religious fundamentalism (K. Menon 2009), and even left politics (Brown and Halley 2002a).

To *do* feminism means an acknowledgement of these entanglements, and taking responsibility for the consequences of choosing to or our inability to unentangle some of these in our conduct. Thus, to *conduct* oneself as feminist would require living with both feminism's potentials and limits. As a feminist and a jurisprudent, I am responsible for the feminisms I ally with and the laws that I align with, and take on an ethical obligation to care for them, account for their failures, and take responsibility for my inheritances and futures. In thinking with the ideas of failures, futures, and inheritances, my reflections as a male feminist jurisprudent in this chapter take the form of a jurisdictional auto-critique about feminism's relationship with law, which by extension is a comment on my relationship with both law and feminism.

I have deliberately chosen to write using a tentative autobiographical voice (Kaplan 1998: 208–16), fully aware of the critique (J. Scott 1991: 773–97) and defence (Oksala 2014: 388–403) of the idea of experience in feminist and critical theory. This imperative of grounding scholarship by accounting for an author's subjectivity—even if it is fragmented, hybridized, and nearly impossible (Butler 2005)—is inspired by its rich precedence in feminist legal scholarship (Williams 1992; Adjin-Tettey, et al. 2008: 5–38; Behrendt 2009: 71–85). Using this mode of writing serves two purposes for me. First, it enables me to break away from the tradition of the ostensibly neutral voice of authority that characterizes most male legal scholarship, even when critical. Second, it affords me the opportunity to put my own feminist voice of male authority under scrutiny. As Stuart Hall has written: 'Autobiography is usually thought of as seizing the authority of authenticity. But in order not to be authoritative, I've got to speak autobiographically' (Hall1992: 277). Even in symbolic terms, I feel that such a methodological move gains particular significance at a time when the neoliberal and neocolonial (Smith 1999) networks through which a lot of feminist legal scholarship is produced and published (Craig, Turcotte, and Coombe 2011) end up reinforcing the very hegemonic orders such scholarship of solidarity aims to challenge (Land 2015).

Of Failures: Thinking Jurisdictionally

An idea from within the traditions of critical legal theory that has been deeply instructive for me, especially in thinking about the idea of failure, is 'jurisdiction'. On the face of it jurisdiction might seem like a concept of positivist law concerned only with explicit statutory commands of 'which law applies to what and where'. However, a growing body of Antipodean legal scholarship (Mussawir 2011; Barr 2016), that draws on indigenous legal traditions (Black 2010; Watson 2016), has been theorizing jurisdiction to understand it as 'the voice or idiom of law', through which we can arrive at an understanding of 'lawfulness—of what it means to belong to and live with law' (Dorsett & McVeigh 2012: 5–6). As Shaunnagh Dorsett and Shaun McVeigh note: 'If jurisdictional thinking teaches us anything about the contemporary forms and idioms of law it is that the critical engagement of law takes place not just at the level of ideas or practice, but also at the level of conduct' (2012: 6).

Jurisdiction in the philosophical register calls to attention the fact that there can be no authority without limits, and that to conduct oneself lawfully means to acknowledge those limits, and also to take responsibility for the legal authority that we inherit, embody, and the relationships that we are embedded in within those limits. Jurisdictional thinking, thus, is about thinking of feminist critique as lawful conduct, one with a sense of location and the knowledge of limits that not only recognizes privilege, but also accounts for its complicities and failures. Here, law is not banished as the discourse of oppression, or feminism hailed as the discourse of emancipation, but they are understood as relational forms of life, in 'agonistic intimacy',[7] and sharing a 'difficult solidarity',[8] that can engender an ethic of responsibility and offer lessons for a training in the making of lawful feminist selves. Thinking jurisdictionally about feminism helps me make sense of my academic and activist travels, across institutions and intellectual traditions, sovereign and disciplinary borders, and of course across many feminisms. It has enabled me to understand these travels not only as border crossings, but also as 'encounters' (Pahuja 2013: 63–98), between feminisms and laws, between laws, and between feminisms.

I had not developed such an understanding of jurisdiction, let alone feminism, as a law student in the late 1990s. At that time,

I understood jurisdiction 'as the most technical and prosaic form of legal authority' (Dorsett & McVeigh 2012: 4). It was difficult to identify the misogyny written into almost every law that I studied, because the proliferating density of legalese had normalized it, and yet there were no pedagogical interventions to point that out for those of us being trained in the law. Knowledge of law gave me and students in my cohort—who had come of age in the shadow of India's economic liberalization—a sense of power that owes its origins to the sexist, classist, and racist foundations of the common law (Douzinas and Gearey 2005: 259–302; Watson 2002: 253–69). That same rationality seemed to augur well for the propaganda of progress, ably buttressed by the law, that public life was then getting suffused with in India (Sircar 2012: 527–3).

When I began my law education in 1999, the first common law standard with which I got acquainted was that of the 'Reasonable Man'. This mythical masculine standard applied across civil and criminal laws almost at the cost of completely invisibilizing women (Ramanathan 1999: 33). When it came to studying the Indian Penal Code (IPC), the woman was hypervisibilized as a victim, stripped of the ability to consent, and could be rescued by the law only if she was 'respectable' (Agnes 1995; Kumari 1999: 139; Kannabiran & Kannabiran 2002). In family law, similarly, women did find substantial recognition, only to be reduced to being carriers of culture and religion, relegated to the regressive roles of the 'good' wife in marriage, denied access to property, and treated as chattel (Agnes 2001). Constitutional law provided me with the tools of equality and non-discrimination to challenge this misogyny, but these hallowed constitutional ideas were founded on principles of formal equality, and sought protectionist measures to secure women's rights (Kapur and Cossman 1993: 1).

Around this time, I remember studying an upper-year optional course in our (Bar Council of India– [BCI–] approved) syllabus with an unwieldy name: women and law and law relating to the child. This course taught us the contents and provisions of a whole range of landmark judgements and legislations in India that were broadly concerned with the welfare (not rights) of women and children. This was, by itself, a worthy learning objective. However, by equating women and children as objects of conjoined vulnerabilities, discussions in this course infantilized women and thus considered them to be existentially in need of protection and saving by the law, not from it. In doing this, the pedagogical imperative of the course reinforced, rather than questioned, 'familial ideology' (Kapur and Cossman 1996: 87–172), which is at the foundation of the 'feminized' vulnerabilities that we were taught that the law had the capacity to alleviate. Not surprisingly, the words 'patriarchy' or 'feminism' were not uttered even once in class, let alone 'gender'.[9]

There was a growing sense of unease among some students about these laws, especially given the fact that law was taught to us as if it was engraved dictum. It was at this time that I encountered feminism for the first time through a man who was a feminist. The constitutional law scholar S.P. Sathe, at my alma mater the ILS Law College in Pune, introduced this idea called Feminism with which we could legitimately talk about the failures of the law and the judiciary in upholding what he would call 'gender justice' in his writings (Sathe 1993). Sathe encouraged us to not only critique laws, but also judgements, and consider the antecedents of the judge in evaluating the nature of the decision. While teaching us about the Emergency, he would continuously tell us that even the constitution was not above critique. In fact, he emphasized that even women judges could deliver gender-discriminatory decisions. That a feminist critique of law was being done by a man dispelled the myth that only women could be feminists, or that feminism was only about women. Sathe foundationally altered my understanding of constitutional equality by exposing the sham that formal equality can be, despite the fact that he was a strong secular supporter of the Uniform Civil Code.

I had also been introduced to Marxist theories of law at that time (Pashukanis 1987; U. Baxi 1993; Chimni 1999: 337–49), and felt that like communism, feminism was also a method to think about justice and rights of the marginalized; a method that legal theory lacked. Class and gender were the lenses through which the systems of injustice in patriarchy and capitalism, and law's collusion with them, were revealed, and could be challenged. Despite their uneasy alliance (Hartman 1979: 1–33; MacKinnon 1989) feminism was more than a mere philosophy for interpreting the world. It seemed like a more powerful tool than Marxism with which the world could indeed be changed. Not having read Marx in the original at that time made me feel inadequate, especially in Marxist circles, which happened to comprise mostly men. However, that was never the case with feminism, because as Gayatri Spivak points out, unlike Marxism, feminism doesn't 'have a named book at the origin' (2012: 123). Feminism, as thought and politics, was certainly more accessible than Marxism for me; and more importantly, while I always heard feminists acknowledge class in their analysis of gender, the converse was seldom the case, especially with male Marxists.

My belief that as a man I did not have to be apologetic about being a feminist, and that questioning of self-privilege was fundamental to feminist conduct, was further strengthened when I read the works of another feminist man: Upendra Baxi, who had also been Sathe's student at the Government Law College in Bombay in the 1960s. Baxi was one of the four law professors who wrote the historic 1979 Open Letter to the Chief Justice of India, in the light of the Supreme Court's acquittal of the accused in the Mathura rape case,[10] which was arguably the precipitating event that consolidated what today is called the Indian Women's Movement. I will share a quirkily profound footnote from the opening chapter of his 2002 book *The Future of Human Rights* that has had a lasting influence on my feminist thinking. It brought home the role that language, and legal language in particular, plays in the perpetuation of patriarchy. As an apologia for his use of the word 'human', Baxi wrote:

> 'I use the term "human" as an act of communicational courtesy. Human stands marked by the presence of man, and person by a "son". My preferred non-sexist version is, therefore, a combination of the first letters of both words: "huper". I await the day when the word "huper" will replace the word "human"' (2002a: 1).

Yet, even in the most courteous of circles, Sathe and Baxi are not known as feminist legal scholars. As men their claim to fame has been as constitutional scholars or legal theorists—universalist descriptors that avoid any particularized identitarian or ideological pigeonholing. As men they could afford to sometimes invoke feminism in their scholarship (especially when they had to write on issues related to women and gender), and otherwise not. As middle-class, upper-caste men in a male-dominated legal academy, they had materially very little at stake with regard to their use or non-use of feminism.[11]

Going back to the 'Open Letter', interestingly, despite the presence of two prominent women feminist law professors as signatories, in the conclusion to the letter, all the signatories referred to themselves collectively as 'lawmen'. On a different occasion, I had heard Uma Chakravarty once trenchantly comment at a seminar in Delhi that even among declaredly feminist heterosexual academic couples, it would always be the case that the man would work on caste and the woman on gender. On point, Lisa Duggan makes this astute observation about 'heteronormativity in the left academy':

> Have you noticed? The way that so many left academic couples divide up the intellectual and political world in their scholarship and institutional alliances? So many of the straight-identified men analyze the dynamics of class, and sometimes race, but leave gender and sexuality out. As a set-aside agenda of sorts for the women and queers to undertake. The female partners of these men often (not always) address gender and sexuality, usually along with class and race (though again, not always). It's kind of like the primary responsibility for housework—there's a double day for the feminized, who also legitimate the guys. Who can say he's not a feminist, not a queer ally, if his consort and/or close comrades take care of that for him? (2015)

Such are the neat gendered divisions of intellectual labour!

I don't know about the domestic economies of labour within the Sathe and Baxi households. Though a speculative question, it is necessary to ask: for both of them to have carried out their successful public scholarly life as male feminist thinkers, what kind of domestic labour was being carried out, and by whom, in their private lives? This is not a question directed specifically at them, but to point at the fault lines that all male leftist academics like me, who call themselves feminist, need to confront and are obligated to take responsibility for with regard to our work. As a feminist man, calling out the sexism of the law and its language might just not be enough for acknowledging the intellectual and familial inheritances that have enabled us to be feminist and do feminism. In fact, Baxi had made a powerful self-reflexive gesture in this regard, with particular reference to his philosophy of teaching law. In response to a question from his students—'what are you good for?'—he had replied: 'Do not merely look at what I say; look at what I do with what I say. I simply cannot carry conviction about what I say to young minds unless they see that I mean what I say about the rule of law, human rights, human dignity' (U. Baxi 1990: 154). And by extension, I can add, feminism.

For me, to think jurisdictionally about 'men doing feminism' has, thus, been a way to think about feminist speech and action as co-constitutive practices. Doing feminism is not only about how sophisticatedly we use feminist theory in our scholarship and teaching, but also, and more importantly, the methods—the conduct—that we bring to bear on the scholarship we produce and the knowledge we share with students, colleagues, comrades, friends, families, and lovers. The question of conduct, however, is also about the conduct of feminism itself, as an active form of knowledge, its relational lives, and its journeys and mutations across jurisdictions.

It is important to acknowledge that Sathe and Baxi, along with their women feminist colleagues Lotika Sarkar and Vasudha Dhagamwar, have contributed to the training of some of India's most important women feminist legal scholars. It was through Sathe's teaching and scholarship that I was introduced to the rich tradition of feminist legal writing in India: Flavia Agnes, Nandita Haksar, Archana Parashar, Kalpana Kannabiran, and Ratna Kapur, among others, who, over the years, have compellingly demonstrated how law has been an active and constituent element in sustaining women's subordination in India, and what feminist legal scholarship and activism can do to challenge law's misogyny. Even while critiquing the law, each of these scholar-activists has offered provocative feminist visions of how to think creatively with and against the law. Their feminisms have taught me that we cannot give up law to the state or religion—and now increasingly to the market.

If Sathe and Baxi had set me off on my feminist journey as a man, and taught me how feminism could both reveal and challenge the sexist limits of the law, it was two women feminists—Ratna Kapur and Sharmila Rege—who taught me to recognize and challenge the statist and casteist limits of feminism.

Kapur, in particular, has had a very strong influence on my feminist thinking, because it was in her work that sexuality, agency, and pleasure entered the feminist legal frame that had until then been occupied primarily by gender and violence (Kapur and Cossman 1996: 87–172; Kapur 2005). That law had to be re-conceptualized outside of the liberal rights framework, that feminists had to rethink how activism for law reform reified conservative sexual morality, that feminism had to think of sexual rights and not just of sexual wrongs, and that feminism had to start thinking of sex not just as a site of violence, but also of pleasure and agency, were revelatory ideas. Kapur also offered postcolonial feminist critiques of international human rights law to expose its colonial foundations, thus fracturing the romantic notion of feminist global sisterhood that I had much faith in. It is because of her scholarship, and an opportunity to work with her in 2002 at the Centre for Feminist Legal Research in New Delhi, that I got to know about the sex workers' movement in India which motivated me to get involved with the activism of the Durbar Mahila Samanwaya Committee (DMSC) in Kolkata (Sircar and Dutta 2011: 333–49).

Kapur has been a sex-positive feminist and a supporter of the right *to* sex work. Her scholarship opened up a way to understand feminism that was hitherto unknown to me. Until then I understood feminism to be a discourse that enabled me to recognize the limits of the law, but now the limits within feminism started coming to the fore. That the sex workers' struggles for the right to work with dignity in India and across the world had very little support from feminists, which still continues to be the case, is part of a history of feminism's failures (Murthy and Seshu 2014). Not only sex work, but as pointed out by Nivedita Menon, the Indian women's movement has also had a very uneasy relationship with lesbianism (N. Menon 2007: 23). Kapur's theorizing of the 'sexual subaltern' (2005) was what set the stage for my encounter with queer theory, and deepened my engagement with the politics of the sexual rights movement in India (Sircar 2017: 1–36).

If Kapur enabled me to see the failures of feminist legal scholarship and activism in India, which broadly carried a combination of liberal and radical feminist proclivities, it is my disciplinary crossover and encounter with women's studies that enabled me to see the failure of sex-positive feminisms' engagement with caste in India. As a student of Sharmila Rege at the University of Pune's Krantijyoti Savitribai Phule Women's Studies Centre (KSPWSC) in 2003, I learned about feminist traditions that were rooted in the struggles of the anti-caste movement in India, and in Maharashtra in particular. Much before she wrote *Against the Madness of Manu* (2013), Rege introduced Ambedkar to her students as not just an anti-caste, but also a feminist thinker. Reading Ambedkar, Jyotiba and Savitribai Phule, Tarabai Shinde, and many other male and female Dalit and anti-caste thinkers alerted me to my scandalous silence, as well as that of both feminism and law on caste, in pedagogy, scholarship, and politics. The idea of self-reflexivity that I had inherited from feminism until then seemed so hollow, so superficial, that it made me conveniently avert an acknowledgement of my upper-caste status. As if thinking of myself as a secular feminist had washed away my caste privilege.

Even as I held on to Kapur's sex-positive feminism, I wondered why in her writings on sex work, or even in her writings on secularism and her critique of the Hindu Right (Cossmanand Kapur 1999), had caste never featured. I have also wondered if one can conversely question Dalit feminism of harking back to radical feminism in talking about violence against Dalit women, of yet again reposing faith in the law, and foreclosing the space to talk about sexuality and pleasure especially in the context of sex work that many Dalit feminists understand as systemic perpetuation of caste oppression. I wouldn't know of others, but Rege's feminist scholarship, while foregrounding caste, has also spoken of women's pleasure and its patriarchal appropriation (1995: 23–38), and has come out in strong defence of homosexuality by exposing the Indian Left's homophobia (1996: 1,359–60).

Yet, I have kept wondering, in line with a question that I would continuously ask myself: how have Kapur and Rege accounted for their subject positions as upper-caste scholars in their own feminist conduct? Rege provided some understanding of this in her political and methodological adoption of what she called a 'dalit feminist standpoint': 'A transformation from "their cause" to "our cause" is feasible for subjectivities can be transformed. By this we do not argue that non-dalit feminists can "speak as" or "for" the dalit feminists but they can "reinvent" themselves as dalit feminists. Such a position therefore avoids the narrow alley of direct experience based "authenticity" and narrow "identity politics"' (Rege 1998: 39–46). Despite opening up the possibility for taking up a 'feminist standpoint' as it were, feminist scholarship, and feminist legal scholarship in much greater measure, for me, has inadequately responded to the question about male feminist subjectivity, except for pointing at the limits and perils of lines of enquiry that invoke 'experience' and 'authenticity'. How have I taken responsibility for these contradictory feminist inheritances in my conduct as a male feminist jurisprudent?

In response, I want to share an exchange with Sharmila from that time which has left a deep impression on me and continues to carry a talismanic quality in my teaching life as a feminist. As a human rights educator and youth worker, I had approached her with a proposal to offer short workshops on law and sexuality for students at the KSPWSC. The programme was being supported by a local NGO. In a considered email she wrote: 'I have been quite upset with "survival" issues that a majority of students coming to the university are facing and do not find any NGO effort addressing this. I find most of the themes [in your workshop outline] assuming a middle class urban student—while I see in my classroom at least 50% who have had no access to English and the cultural capital that goes with it—there is a need to think through these issues and this has been troubling me a lot.' At that time the import of her concern didn't dawn on me; in fact, I even considered her response to be slightly conservative and on the lines of those who consider sexuality to be a bourgeois issue. The workshops did not take place.

A year after that I began teaching a course on gender, law, and citizenship at the KSPWSC and confronted the reality of what Sharmila had expressed in the email. That teaching experience, one which sealed my decision to pursue full-time academic work, was the most challenging that I had ever undertaken. A majority of the students in my class, most of them women, were first-generation undergraduates, from some of the most rural parts of Maharashtra, and Marathi was the language they were most comfortable in. Many were Dalit. Despite the pressures of joining a so-called professional course that might have made them more job-worthy, they were committed to pursuing women's studies. The course material that I had put together was entirely in English. At the end of the first class a group came over to me and said that they would not be able to go through the course, but they really wanted to do it. They offered a suggestion: that I take separate classes in Hindi for them (since I did not speak Marathi). Not that my Hindi was much better, but I said yes. Through the rest of the semester we met both for the classes taught in English (they wanted to learn as much from those), as well as additional classes that I tried hard to teach in Hindi.

Never before, and never since then, have I experienced collaborative learning in this way. While I tried to explain concepts in Hindi, for which my vocabulary was woefully inadequate, the students contributed to building a Marathi word bank for key feminist legal ideas and theories. They helped me find the words, we debated and disagreed. I fumbled, they were lost at times; but we persisted. As a group assignment for the course, the students translated into Marathi the texts of the Universal Declaration of Human Rights and the Convention on the Elimination of All Forms of Discrimination Against Women, a practice which was in line with a massive project that the KSPWSC had taken on to translate key feminist writings from English to Marathi. It is possibly too romantic of me to expect that such a sense of feminist community and kinship can be rekindled whenever I teach—but there was indeed something about the material conditions of 'survival issues' that enabled such a collaboration. Sharmila and her colleagues tried to build these structures of feminist care within the university. Systemically, the neoliberal university (which works as a corporation that treats the student as client and the teacher as a service provider), is built to destroy ideas of collaboration, community, and kinship—its primary aim is to incentivize excellence through individuation and responsibilization.

Of Futures: Taking a Break?

Failure can be a moment of both painful paralysis and intense inspiration. Taking responsibility for failure is germane to an ethical practice of transformative politics and scholarship (Halberstam 2011). My travels to a geographical and intellectual jurisdiction outside of India took me to the University of Toronto in 2008. At this time my work focused primarily on queer sexualities—particularly sex workers' and LGBT rights—and the two conceptual repositories of knowledge and politics that I had were those of feminism and Marxism, with all their fractures and friendships. Despite the fact that feminism had begun to feel slightly inadequate (much less than Marxism though) in theorizing sexuality—as I realized on reading Gayle Rubin (2011:

137–81)—I held on to it, not only for loyalty's sake, but also because it was the manifesto that I lived by.

Brenda Cossman, my teacher in Toronto, pushed me to think of what it might mean to take a break from feminism. Cossman for long has been engaging with colleagues across other North American law schools in asking the question: 'Is feminist theory enough?' (Cossman et al. 2003: 601–37). This was indeed a paralysing question for me. I would have to answer the same question that I had asked of Sathe and Baxi: am I able to take a break from feminism because I am a man, and do not have high stakes beyond a materially inconsequential compromise?

That irresponsibility towards a certain kind of 'paranoid structuralism' (Kennedy 1991: 75–116) in (mostly radical) feminist thinking can be politically productive was something that I discovered through Janet Halley's *Split Decisions* (Halley 2006a). Halley argues that 'taking a break from feminism' is a good thing to do because feminism has now begun to walk the corridors of power. According to her, feminism today, in active collusion with law and technologies of global governance (Halley et al. 2006b: 335–423), is no longer about making possible an emancipatory future. In many ways it keeps in place the very identities, binaries, and power structures it claims to challenge, but to do that it uses the same vocabulary of transformation that it was founded upon. Halley, of course, borrows from North American queer theory's anti-identitarian critique to argue that 'identity is not the core truth and safe zone of authenticity and authority posited by our most widely shared assumptions about identity politics; rather, identity may be part of the problem' (2000: 42).

Although aware of feminism's limitations, taking a break initially sounded flippant to me, as if I was now bored of it and wanted to go cherry picking in the theory bazaar. It felt like an irresponsible act, especially for feminist men, who do not have high stakes beyond a materially inconsequential compromise if they choose to take a break from feminism. Yet, Halley's proposition was very inviting. Albeit not beyond critique (Cossman et al. 2003: 601–37; Otto 2007: 345–52), reading Halley seemed to have momentarily put to rest my troubles with being a feminist man. I did not have to always have an explanation for how I could be a feminist or a queerist (if a word like that exists) despite not possessing the authentic 'experience' of identifying as woman or queer, a disqualification that has been pointed out to me many a time within feminist (but not queer) academic and activist circles.

And yet, even if I could think of taking a break from feminism, I could never think of a feminist 'self' devoid of experience; one without historical consciousness (Genovese 2013: 41–57). Even at the cost of valorizing experience and forcing a theory–practice binary, I continue to unsuccessfully grapple with the question: does theorizing become the queer-feminist academic's privilege whereas identity politics remains the drudgery of the materially disenfranchised woman/queer? Isn't it telling that the 'taking a break from feminism' project in North America—of which I have been a part as one of its many Southern interlocutors—has primarily been a white enterprise that remains conspiratorially silent about First Nations' sovereignty in settler-colonial states? Can 'taking a break' imply a convenient academic mirage to avoid taking responsibility for both feminist and queer theory's complicities with colonialism and capitalism? (McCluskey 2009: 115–34; Morgensen 2011).

That 'taking a break' or queer feminism's anti-identitarian turn could be a way to imagine other futures is inspirational, and it is an unsettling inspiration that I would like to live with. An inspiration that does not let the excitement of the future blind us to the darkness of our failures. A darkness that is not only in the past tense, but in the here and now. A darkness that will also accompany us into the future.

Undoing

Some years ago, in the anonymous feedback to a course called law and social hierarchies that I had taught at Jindal Global Law School (JGLS), a student wrote: 'too much feminism'. More recently, while teaching a course on critical approaches to jurisprudence, a bright male student came up after class and earnestly asked: 'for how much more time will we carry on with feminism? When will it end? Are we not going to do anything else in this course?' I must admit that I was elated despite the tone to criticism. On another occasion, during the same course a student asked in class which critical approach to jurisprudence was my favourite. Even before I could answer, another student shouted out: 'feminism!' I returned a smile, satisfied that it had turned out to be obvious to them. Would I read this as an achievement? Not entirely, because the mythical moral heft that I am bestowed with because of being perceived as a mild-mannered feminist man (oh, he's so sensitive!), might not, in fact, be extended to a female feminist faculty who calls out sexism more confrontationally and with far more acuity than me (oh, she's so aggressive!).

Still, feminism is one excess—along with my fatness—that I would take pride in proliferating as a man. This gains particular significance where I've seen even very critically oriented male students who tend to pay more attention to the modules on Marx or Foucault, but feel bored at best, and frustrated at worst, when discussing feminist jurisprudence. It is also difficult to remain agnostic to such responses from students because it speaks of a much larger institutional culture of intellectual sexism in the legal discipline where, in the teaching of so-called 'hard' law subjects, feminist jurisprudence and feminist legal theory continue to be considered merely an add-on (Thornton 1998: 171). This pervasive sentiment is institutionally perpetuated, and as Pratiksha Baxi has argued, it has reduced feminist jurisprudence to merely a 'perspective' rather than recognizing its 'epistemic challenge' to the foundations of legal theory and legal education in India (2008: 81).

Yet, if I had to write a feedback on my conduct as a feminist man—both inside and outside the legal academy—would I be able to say that I practise 'too much feminism'? Perhaps not.

It is imperative for male feminist academics to start thinking about undoing feminism as scholarship, to understand doing as conduct,[12] taking seriously the fact that it is not enough that I call myself a feminist man, or write using feminist theoretical tools, or with sound arguments about why men ought to be feminists. Feminism is not only about what I write and the kind of politics I bring to my research, writing, and teaching, but also about the material, relational, and embodied practices of knowledge production and circulation that I participate in.

Is my scholarly conduct collaborative, or does it reinforce privatized ownership of intellectual ideas that do not acknowledge and share its inheritances? How do I acknowledge the traditions and inheritances that have made me a feminist? In footnotes to academic papers that get published in journals behind prohibitively expensive paywalls? What are my citation practices? Do I engender the classroom space and yet practise my masculine authoritative self as the teacher? How do I account for the sexual and gendered economies of labour in my marriage that enable me to be a man doing feminism? As a feminist man, how do I account for the institutions of heterosexual marriage and the neoliberal academy that I inhabit and draw power and privilege from?

I can have smart answers to these questions because both law and feminism within the neoliberal academy increasingly work, under the garb of criticality, in a technocratic problem-solving mode that I have been trained well in (Thornton 2012). But, these theoretically sound, well-argued answers will have little to say about how, as a man, I *do* my feminism. The brief academic journey that I have charted might have much to say about my scholarly feminist inheritances, but it says very little about how I *do* feminism. Because doing feminism cannot possibly be entirely reduced to writing or research. It is not possible for jurisprudence or feminist scholarship to make intelligible what men (or women) *do* when they *do* feminism, and how they *do* it. As a man doing feminism, that is a jurisdictional limitation of critical scholarship (the aporia of praxis) and my legal academic career's investments in it, which I ought to acknowledge and take responsibility for (Cornell 1992).

A Slow and Struggling Afterthought

On re-reading the last paragraph in the preceding section, it seems to me that I rushed into finishing the piece. I found the questions that I had posed (both in this chapter and in the preceding ones) difficult to answer. I wanted to overcome the difficulty by ending the piece (and the book), because it had to be brought to a close. In law, arriving at the judgement by resolving the 'hard case' is the mark of good (or, masculine) jurisprudence (Rackley 2005: 213–32). My conclusion as judgement signifies a resolution, even if indefinite. The feminist in me was left feeling dissatisfied. I could have returned to revise and update that last paragraph. The process of figuring out how to address my difficulty was slow. It was too late to make more changes. Thus, this afterthought. An equally inadequate appendage.

I want to take the idea of the afterthought as a form of feral feminist conduct that enables us to return, ruminate, and stray without fear and apology, after an imposed closure. After *we* impose a closure. Such a conduct is of particular significance for me as a feminist jurisprudent because of the primacy put on the ideas of speed and transformation in feminist legal reform projects; and the instrumental ends (conviction, compensation, incarceration) that characterize the practice of adjudication. Governmental, judicial, and institutional delays and apathy when it comes to questions of gender and its intersectionalities ought to be questioned, no doubt, especially at a time where the violence being directed at marginalized women's and gender non-conforming bodies has mutated into a macabre concoction of spectacular and numbing visibility, and tacit and normalized brutality (Dutta andSircar 2013: 293–306). But I've been sensing a growing prejudice attached to the idea of slowness, particularly in the realms of agenda- and funding- driven feminist activism and research in a hyper-mediatized age (Berg and Seeber 2016).

Slowness sometimes does find place in our feminist legal frames of meaning making. The word 'struggle', much more than 'difficulty', is what offers hospitality to the idea of being slow, contemplative, and acknowledges 'the value of silence' (Eng 2002: 85–94). So what is the difference between struggle and difficulty? Creating an affective hierarchy between the two is unhelpful. However, it might be worth recognizing that there is a certain kind of romance attached to the former. Does difficulty not sound feminist enough? Or is it feminism's Marxist hangover that attaches us to struggle more strongly? But doing feminism is difficult and that difficulty is lived through struggle. Or am I merely expressing academic vanity?

A similar pairing of terms poses another quandary. As I considered whether to write this afterthought or not, I kept wondering if I am getting late with meeting the deadline, or have I been too slow in thinking about a good conclusion? Do they carry the same valence? What determines which expression we use to describe our feminist limitations to keep up with patriarchal/capitalist/racist/colonial/secular time? Or do we use it to describe, sometimes deride aporia? In a way, these concerns have emerged from my experience of writing the afterthought: have I been very slow, or too late in completing it? It might be both. Lateness, it seems, carries with it a pejorative sense of sloth—slowness, on the other hand, carries a floaty sensation of abandon. Both do not merit appreciation in the deeply toxic masculine culture of the neoliberal academy.

Interestingly, difficulty and/or struggle has a connection with lateness and/or slowness. If it was not for the protracted lateness or slowness of feminist experiences, will anything ever qualify as a difficulty or a struggle?

Notes

1. The framing of the theme as such corresponds with the title of an edited collection from 1998, in which authors from a range of identitarian and ideological positions self-reflexively engaged with the possibilities and perils of 'men doing feminism' (Digby 1998).
2. Many kindred colleagues have often misread this particular description that I have been using for a while now. It generally gets understood as my way of claiming legitimacy as a heterosexual person who researches and writes on queerness. In my mind this has nothing to do with claiming legitimacy—because I am not writing with the intention of being judged by anyone—though that might be a consequence over which I wish to have no control. By using practising-heterosexual, I make a queering gesture that does two things: first, it complicates the relationship between sexual behaviour and identity, and second, it unsettles the naturalness attached to heterosexuality by calling it out to be a historically contingent and socially constructed act. For a discussion on this see Sircar (2008: 10).
3. For the conceptual relationship between 'doing' and 'conduct', I draw on Debolina Dutta's doctoral research on the politics of feminist jurisprudential knowledge production and how this is a material practice of self-making tied to a time and place. For some allusions to this argument, see Dutta (2016b: 186–201).
4. In this chapter I do not offer an account of my personal or familial locations where I also (try) to live feminist lives. This decision was not an easy one. I feel vulnerable and scared to do so, especially because of the relational accounts I will have to share, and that I still do not have the courage to deal with the consequences such accounts might have for me and the people involved. This leaves me in a state of a double-bind. While I see the problem with not making the personal political in my account here as a betrayal of sorts, I hope that this account will offer a counter-intuitive possibility of making the political, personal.

5. The privileging of my academic journey is not to de-prioritize what I have learnt from my activist engagements. Academics and activism are not mutually exclusive domains of feminism for me, but for the purposes of understanding a particular kind of trajectory feminism in the university has taken and how that has shaped my journey, I focus on what I have learnt in the academy. For one account of my activist engagements with feminism, see Sircar (2010).
6. For an anticolonial counter to Fraser, see Bhandar and DaSilva (2013).
7. I borrow this expression from Bhrigupati Singh who has used it in a different context (Singh 2011: 430–50).
8. This was Trina Nileena Banerjee's characterization of the 'men doing feminism in India' project.
9. For a distribution of courses in a five-year law programme at ILS Law College, Pune, see http://209.190.24.122:8080/display/academics/.5-yr+BA,LLB+course+details. In 2008, many years after I had passed out of law school, a subject called gender justice and feminist jurisprudence was included by the BCI as an optional course under the constitutional law group. See http://www.barcouncilofindia.org/wp-content/uploads/2010/05/BCIRulePartIV.pdf.
10. The other signatories to the letter were Lotika Sarkar, Vasudha Dhagamwar, and Raghunath Kelkar. For a reproduction of the letter, see John (2008b: 267).
11. Between the two, Baxi of course has produced a much more rigorous and sustained body of feminist scholarship. For some representative works, see Baxi (1994b: 168–80, 1994a: 67–88, 1999: 275–90).
12. I do not mean to suggest that I had no inkling of the 'conduct' question prior to this. My exchanges with colleagues and teachers at the Melbourne Law School—particularly Sundhya Pahuja, Shaun McVeigh, Ann Genovese, Claire Opperman, and Debolina Dutta—have offered me a language to speak about it from within the disciplinary location of law.

Consolidated Bibliography

Case Law and Legislation

Additional District Magistrate, Jabalpur vs S Shukla, 1976. SCR 172 India.

Almitra H. Patel and another vs Union of India, 2000. 2 Supreme Court Cases 16.

Armed Forces (Special Powers) Act, No. 28 of 1958.

BALCO Employees Union vs Union of India, 2002, 2 SCC 343.

Bhautik Vijaykumar Bhatt vs Central Board of Film Certifi cation, 23 September 2014. Accessible on http://indiankanoon.org/doc/36425680/; last accessed 5 July 2019.

Central Bureau of Investigation vs Sakru Mahagu and Others, Criminal Confirmation Case No 4/2008.

Charan Lal Sahu vs Union of India, AIR 1990 SC 1480.

Contempt of Courts Act, No. 70 of 1971, India Code.

Chhattishgarh Vishesh Jan Suraksha Adhiniyam, No. 14 of 2006, India Code.

Government of India Act, 1935 (UK), 25 & 26 Geo V, c 42.

I.C. Golaknath and Others vs State of Punjab and Others, 1967 AIR 1643.

Kartar Singh vs. State of Punjab, 1994 Supreme Court Cases (3) 539.

Kesavananda Bharathi vs State of Kerala, 1973 4 SCC 225.

Koushal vs Naz Foundation, 2014 1 SCC 1 (India).

Maneka Gandhi vs Union of India, 1978 AIR 597.

Minerva Mills Limited and others vs Union of India and Others, 1980 AIR 1789.

N.D. Jayal vs Union of India, 2003 7 SCALE 54.

Naga People's Human Rights Movement vs Union of India, Writ Petition (Civil) No. 5328/80, 9229-30/82, Civil Appeal Nos. 721/85, 722/85, 723/85, 724/85, 2173-76/91, 2551/91 and Writ Petitions (C) NOS. 13644-45/84 S.C.

Nandini Sundar and Others vs State of Chattisgargh, Writ Petition (Civil) No 250 of 2007 (India).

Narmada Bachao Andolan vs Union of India and Others, 2000 10 SCC 664.

National Legal Services Authority vs Union of India, AIR 2014 SC 1863.

National Rural Employment Guarantee Act, No. 42 of 2005, India Code.

Naz Foundation vs Government of Delhi, 2009 111 DRJ 1 (DB).

Naz Foundation vs Government of NCT of Delhi and Others, WP(C) No.7455/2001(2009).

Obergefell vs Hodges, 2015 135 S. Ct. 2584.

Olga Tellis and Others vs Bombay Municipal Corporation and Others, AIR 1986 SC 180.

People's Union for Civil Liberties vs Union of India, AIR 2004 SC 256.

Prevention of Terrorism Act, 2002, No. 15 of 2002, India Code.

Protection of Women from Domestic Violence Act, No. 43 of 2005, India Code.

Ramdeo Chauhan and Rajnath Chauhan vs Bani Kant Das Ors, 2009 No. 1378 (review petition).

Right of Children to Free and Compulsory Education Act, No. 35 of 2009, India Code.

Right to Information Act, No. 22 of 2005, India Code.

T.N. Godavaraman vs Union of India and Others, 2008 9 Supreme Court Cases 711.

T.N. Rangarajan vs Govt of Tamil Nadu and Others, 2003 SLP Case No. 429.

Tata Housing Development Committee vs Goa Foundation, 2003 7 SCALE 54.

Terrorist Activities and Disruptive Activities (Prevention) Act, No. 28 of 1987, India Code.

The Constitution (Forty-fourth Amendment) Act, No. 88 of 1978, India Code.

The Constitution of India, 1950.

The Scheduled Tribes and Other Traditional Forest Dwellers (Recognition of Forest Rights) Act, 2006, No. 2 of 2007, India Code.

Union Carbide Corporation vs Union of India and Others, etc., 1989 SCALE (1) 380 (India).

Union of India vs Azadi Bachao Andolan, 2003 8 SCALE 287.

Zahira Habibulla H. Sheikh vs State of Gujarat, 12 April 2004. Accessible on http://indiankanoon.org/doc/1067991/; last accessed 5 July 2019.

Zahira Habibulla Sheikh and Another v. State of Gujarat and Others, Appeal (crl.) 446-449 of 2004 (12 April 2004). Accessible on https://indiankanoon.org/doc/105430/; last accessed 5 July 2019.

Offline Academic and Activist Sources

Abbas, Hoveyda and Ranajay Kumar. 2012. *Political Theory*. New Delhi: Pearson.

Adjin-Tettey, Elizabeth, Gillian Calder, Angela Cameron, Maneesha Deckha, Rebecca Johnson, Hester Lessard, Maureen Maloney, and Margot Young. 2008. 'Postcard From the Edge (of Empire)'. *Social and Legal Studies* 17(1): 5–38.

Agamben, Giorgio (trans. by Kevin Attell). 2005. *State of Exception*. Chicago: University of Chicago Press.

Agnes, Flavia. 1995. State, Gender and the Rhetoric of Law Reform. Research Centre for Women's Studies, SNDT University, Mumbai.

———. 2001. *Law and Gender Inequality: The Politics of Women's Rights in India*. New Delhi: Oxford University Press.

Aguilera, Pilar, Ricardo Fredes, and Ariel Dorfman. 2006. *Chile: The Other September 11: An Anthology of Reflections on the 1973 Coup*. Melbourne: Ocean Press.

Ahmad, Aijaz. 2002. *Lineages of the Present. Ideology and Politics in Contemporary South Asia*. London: Verso.

Ahmad, Irfan. 2017. 'In Conversation with an Ordinary Indian: Kaliyuga, War, End of the Word and Hindutva'. *Journal of Religious and Political Practice* 3(1-2): 57.

Ahmed, Sara. 2017. *Living a Feminist Life*. Durham: Duke University Press.

Ambedkar, Bhimrao Ramji. 2014. *Annihilation of Caste: The Annotated Critical Edition*. New Delhi: Navayana.

———. 1940. *Pakistan or The Partition of India*. Bombay: Thackers Publishers.

Anand, Dibyesh. 2011. *Hindu Nationalism in India and the Politics of Fear*. New York: Palgrave Macmillan.

Anandan, Sujata. 2014. *Samrat: How the Shiv Sena Changed Mumbai Forever*. New Delhi: HarperCollins.

Antaki, Mark. 2017. 'Making Sense of Minor Jurisprudence'. *Law Text Culture* 21: 54–75.

Appadurai, Arjun. 1996. *Modernity at Large: Cultural Dimensions of Globalization*. Minneapolis: University of Minnesota Press.

Arendt, Hannah. 1968. *Men in Dark Times*. New York: Harvest.

Arif, Yasmeen. 2015. 'The Audacity of Method'. *Economic and Political Weekly* 50(1) 53.

Arif, Yasmeen. 2017. *Life, Emergent: The Social in the Afterlives of Violence* Hyderabad: Orient BlackSwan.

Arondekar, Anjali. 2010. 'Time's Corpus: On Sexuality, Historiography and the Indian Penal Code', in William J. Spurlin, Jarrod Hayes, and Margaret R. Higonnet (eds), in *Comparatively Queer: Interrogating Identities Across Time and Culture*. New York: Palgrave McMillan.

———. 2009. *For the Record: On Sexuality and The Colonial Archive in India.* Durham: Duke University Press.

Assman, Jan. 1997. *Moses the Egyptian. The Memory of Egypt in Western Monotheism.* Cambridge: Harvard University Press.

Ayyub, Rana. 2016. *Gujarat Files: Anatomy of a Cover Up.*

Azad, Rohit et al. (eds). 2017. *What the Nation Really Needs to Know: The JNU Nationalism Lectures.* New Delhi: HarperCollins.

Bacchetta, Paola. 1999. 'When the (Hindu) Nation Exiles its Queers'. *Social Text*, Vol. 61: 141–66.

Balagopal, K. 2000. 'A Tangled Web: Subdivision of SC Reservations in AP', *Economic and Political Weekly*, 35(13): 1,075– 81.

———2002. 'Reflections on Gujarat Pradesh of Hindu Rashtra'. *Economic and Political Weekly* 37(22): 2117.

Banaji, Jairus (ed.). 2016. *Fascism: Essays on Europe and India* (Three Essays Collective).

Bandes, Susan A. (ed.). 2001. *The Passions of Law.* New York: New York University Press.

Banerjee, Sumanta. 2000. *Dangerous Outcaste: The Prostitute in Nineteenth Century Bengal.* Kolkata: Seagull Books.

———. 1984. *India's Simmering Revolution: The Naxalite Uprising.* London: Zed Books.

Barnett, Hilaire. 1998. *Introduction to Feminist Jurisprudence.* London: Cavendish Publishing Limited.

Barr, Olivia. 2016. *A Jurisprudence of Movement: Common Law, Walking, Unsettling Place.* New York: Routledge.

Basu, Anustup. 2010. *Bollywood in the Age of New Media. The Geo-Televisual Aesthetic.* Edinburgh: Edinburgh University Press .

Basu, Tapan, Pradip Datta, Sumit Sarkar, Tanika Sarkar, and Sambuddha Sen. 1993. *Khaki Shorts Saffron Flags.* Hyderabad: Orient Longman.

Baxi, Pratiksha. 2008. 'Feminist Contributions to the Sociology of Law: A Review'. *Economic and Political Weekly* 43(43): 79–81.

Baxi, Upendra. 1976. 'Notes Towards a Socially Relevant Legal Education: A Working Paper for the UGC Regional Workshop in Law 1975–6'. *Journal of the Bar Council of India* 5(1–3): 1–33

Baxi, Upendra, Lotika Sarkar, Vasudha Dhagamwar, and Raghunath Kelkar. 1979. 'An Open Letter to the Chief Justice of India', 4 SCC (Jour) 17.

Baxi, Upendra. 1982. *The Crisis of the Indian Legal System*. New Delhi: Vikas.

———. 1985a. *Courage, Craft and Contention: The Indian Supreme Court in the Eighties*. Bombay: N.M. Tripathi.

———. 1985b. 'Taking Suffering Seriously'. *Third World Legal Studies* 4(6): 107–32.

———. 1990. 'Teaching as Provocation', in Amrik Singh (ed.), *On Being a Teacher*, pp. 150–8. New Delhi: Konark Publishers.

———. 1991. 'Complicity and Struggle: Theory and Society'. *Social Scientist*, October–November 19(10/11): 19–26.

———. 1992. '"The State's Emissary": The Place of Law in Subaltern Studies', in Partha Chatterjee and Gyanendra Pandey (eds), *Subaltern Studies VII*, pp. 247–64. New Delhi: Oxford University Press.

———. 1993. *Marx, Law and Justice*. Bombay: N.M Tripati.

———. 1994a. *Inhuman Wrongs and Human Rights: Unconventional Essays*. New Delhi: Har Anand Publications.

———. 1994b. 'On Being a Woman', in *Mambrino's Helmet: Human Rights for a Changing World*, pp. 168–80. New Delhi: Har-Anand Publications.

———. 1994c. 'Violence Against Women in the Labyrinth of the Law', in *Inhuman Wrongs and Human Rights: Unconventional Essays*, pp. 67–88. New Delhi: Har-Anand Publications.

———. 1995. 'Emancipation as Justice: Babasaheb Ambedkar's Legacy and Vision', in Upendra Baxi and Bhikhu Parekh (eds), *Crisis and Change in Contemporary India*, New Delhi: Sage.

———. 1996. *On Judicial Activism, Legal Education and Research in a Globalising India: Annual Capital Foundation Lecture*. New Delhi: Capital Foundation Society.

———. 1998. 'Voices of Suffering and the Future of Human Rights'. *Translational Law and Contemporary Problems* 8: 125–69.

———. 1999. 'From Human Rights to the Right to be a Woman', in Amita Dhanda and Archana Parasher (eds), *Engendering Law: Essays in Honour of Lotika Sarkar*, pp. 275–90. Lucknow: Eastern Book Company.

———. 1999–2000. 'Constitutionalism as a Site of State Formative Practices'. *Cardozo Law Review* (21): 1,183–210.

———. 2002a. *The Future of Human Rights*. New Delhi: Oxford University Press.

———. 2002b. 'The (Im)possibility of Constitutional Justice: Seismographic Notes on Indian Constitutionalism', in Zoya Hasan, E. Sridharan, and R.

Sudarshan (eds), *India's Living Constitution: Ideas, Practices, Controversies*, pp. 31–63. New Delhi: Permanent Black.
———. 2002c. Preface, in S.P. Sathe, *Judicial Activism in India: Transgressing Borders and Enforcing Limits*, pp. xvi–xvii. New Delhi: Oxford University Press.
———. 2003. 'Memory and Rightlessness: 15th J.P. Naik Memorial Lecture'. Centre for Women's Development Studies.
———. 2006a. '*Adieu*, Satyaranjan Sathe'. *Economic and Political Weekly*, 5–11 August 41(31): 3,356.
———. 2006b. *The Future of Human Rights*, 2nd Edition, pp. xi–xii, 1. New Delhi: Oxford University Press.
———. 2006c. 'Structural Adjustment of Judicial Activism'. Inaugural Lecture, West Bengal National Academy of Juridical Sciences, Kolkata.
———. 2007a. 'The Rule of Law in India'. *SUR: The International Journal on Human Rights* 6(4): 7–21.
———. 2007b. *Human Rights in a Posthuman World: Critical Essays.* New Delhi: Oxford University Press.
———. 2007c. 'Enculturing Law? Some Unphilosophic Remarks', in Mathew John and Sitharaman Kakarala (eds), *Enculturing Law: New Agendas for Legal Pedagogy*, pp. 3–21. New Delhi: Tulika Books.
———. 2008. 'Outline of a "Theory of Practice" of Indian Constitutionalism', in Rajeev Bhargava (ed.), *Politics and Ethics of the Indian Constitution*, pp.92. New Delhi: Oxford University Press.
———. 2012. 'Postcolonial Legality: A Postscript from India'. *Verfassung und Recht in Ubersee/ Law and Politics in Africa, Asia and Latin America* 45(2): 178–94.
———. 2014a. 'Demosprudence versus Jurisprudence: The Indian Judicial Experience in the Context of Comparative Constitutional Studies'. *Macquarie Law Journal* (14): 3–23.
Bayat, A. 2010. *Life as Politics: How Ordinary People Change the Middle East.* Amsterdam: University of Amsterdam Press.
Behrendt, Larissa. 1993. 'Aboroginal Women and the While Lies of the Feminist Movement: Implications for Aboriginal Women in Rights Discourse'. *Australian Feminist Law Journal* 1(1): 27–44.
———. 2009. 'Home: The Importance of Place to the Dispossessed', *South Atlantic Quarterly*, 108(1): 71–85.
Ben-Dor, Oren. 2011. 'Introduction. Standing Before the Gates of the Law?', in Oren Ben-Dor (ed.), *Law and Art: Justice, Ethics and Aesthetics*, pp. 1–30. Oxford: Routledge.
Berg, Maggie and Barbara Seeber. 2016. *The Slow Professor: Challenging the Culture of Speed in the Academy.* Toronto: University of Toronto Press.

Berger, John. 1976. *A Painter of Our Time*. London: Writers and Readers Publishing Cooperative.

Berlant, Lauren (ed.). 2004. *Compassion: The Culture and Politics of an Emotion*. New York: Routledge.

Bhaba, Jaqueline. 2002. 'Internationalist Gatekeepers?: The Tension Between Asylum Advocacy and Human Rights'. *Harvard Human Rights Journal* (15): 155, 162.

Bhagat, Chetan. 2008. *3 Mistakes of My Life*. New Delhi: Rupa Publications.

Bhargava, Rajeev (ed.). 2008. *Politics and Ethics of the Indian Constitution.* New Delhi: Oxford University Press.

Bhaskaran, Suparna. 2002. 'The Politics of Penetration: Section 377 of the Indian Penal Code', in Ruth Vanita (ed.), *Queering India: Same-Sex Love and Eroticism in Indian Culture and Society*, pp. 15–29. New York: Routledge.

Bhowmik, Someswar. 2009. *Cinema and Censorship: The Politics of Control in India.* Hyderabad: Orient Blackswan.

———. 2004. 'Misplaced Priorities and Class Bias of the Judiciary'. *Economic and Political Weekly* 44(14): 32–7.

———. 2009. 'Supreme Court and PIL: Changing Perspectives Under Liberalisation'. *Economic and Political Weekly* 39 (18): 1770–4

Black, C.F. 2010. *The Land is the Source of the Law: A Dialogic Encounter with Indigenous Jurisprudence*. New York: Routledge.

Bobbio, Tommaso. 2013. 'Never-Ending Modi: *Hindutva* and Gujarati Neoliberalism as Prelude to All-India Premiership?'. *Focaal:Journal of Global and Historical Anthropology* (67): 123–34.

Bortolotti, L. 2014. *Irrationality*. Cambridge: Polity Press.

Bowring, John. 1843. *The Works of Jeremy Bentham* Vol. IV, pp. 316. Edinburgh: Tait.

Brown, Wendy. 1995. *States of Injury: Power and Freedom in Late Modernity.* Princeton: Princeton University Press.

Brown, Wendy and Janey Halley (eds). 2002. *Left Legalism/Left Critique.* Durham: Duke University Press.

Buchanan, Ruth and Rebecca Johnson. 2009. 'Strange Encounters: Exploring Law and Film in the Affective Register'. *Studies in Law, Politics and Society* 46: 33–60.

Butler, Judith. 2004. *Precarious Life: The Powers of Mourning and Violence.* London: Verso

Butler, Judith and Athena Athanasiou. 2013. *Dispossession: The Performative in the Political.* Cambridge: Polity Press.

Butler, Judith. 2005. *Giving an Account of Oneself.* New York: Fordham University Press.

Butler, Judith, Zeynep Gambetti, and Leticia Sabsey (eds). 2016. *Vulnerability in Resistance*. Durham: Duke University Press.

Campagna, Federico. 2018. *Technic and Magic. The Construction of Reality*. London: Bloomsbury.

Casolari, Marzia. 2000. 'Hindutva's Foreign Tie-Ups in the 1930s: Archival Evidence'. *Economic and Political Weekly* 35(4):218-28.

———. 2011. *In the Shade of the Swastika: The Ambiguous Relationship Between Indian Nationalism and Nazi-Fascism*. Bologna: I Libri di Emil.

Chacko, Priya and Peter Mayer. 2014. 'The Modi Lahar (Wave) in the 2014 Indian National Election: A Critical Realignment?'. *Australian Journal of Political Science* 49(3): 518– 28.

Chadha, Kalyanee and Anandam P. Kavoori. 2008. 'Exoticized, Marginalized, Demonized: The Muslim "Other" in Indian Cinema', in Anandam P. Kavoori and Aswin Punathambekar (eds), *Global Bollywood*, pp. 131–45. New York: New York University Press.

Chakrabarty, Dipesh. 1992. 'Postcoloniality and the Artifice of History: Who Speaks for 'Indian' Pasts?'. *Representations* 37(1): 8.

———. 2000. *Provincializing Europe: Postcolonial Thought and Historical Difference*. Princeton: Princeton University Press.

Chandoke, Neera. 2012. 'Modi's Gujarat and Its Little Illusions'. *Economic and Political Weekly* 47(49): 10–11.

Chatterjee, Moyukh. 2017. 'The Impunity Effect: Majoritarian Rule, Everyday Legality, and State Formation in India'. *American Ethnologist* 44(1): 118.

Chatterjee, Partha. 1999. 'The Nationalist Resolution of the Women's Question', in Kumkum Sangari and Sudesh Vaid (eds), *Recasting Women: Essays in Indian Colonial History*, pp. 233. New Brunswick: Rutgers University Press.

——— (ed.). 1997. *State and Politics in India*. New Delhi: Oxford University Press.

———. 2004. *The Politics of the Governed: Reflections on Popular Politics in Most of the World.* New York: Columbia University Press.

Chaturvedi, Vinayak. 2010. 'Rethinking Knowledge with Action: V.D. Savarkar, the Bhagawad Gita, and Histories of Warfare'. *Modern Intellectual History* 7(2): 417–35.

Chaudhuri, Amit. 2014. *Telling Tales: Selected Writings 1993-2013*, New Delhi: Penguin.

Cherabandaraju. 2009. 'Right', in Sumanta Banerjee (ed), *Thema Book of Naxalite Poetry*, pp. 56. Kolkata: Thema.

Chibber, Vivek. 2006. 'On the Decline of Class Analysis in South Asian Studies'. *Critical Asian Studies* 38(4): 357–87.

Chimni, B.S. 1999. 'Marxism and International Law: A Contemporary Analysis'. *Economic and Political Weekly* 34(6): 337–49.

Cixous, Hélène and Mireille Calle-Gruber. 1997. *Hélène Cixous, Rootprints: Memory and Life Writing* (trans. Eric Prenowitz). London: Routledge.

Cole, Teju. 2016. 'Against Neutrality', in Teju Cole, *Known and Strange Things*, pp. 212–7. New York: Penguin Books.

Collini, Stefan. 2017. *Speaking of Universities*. London: Verso.

Comaroff, Jean and John L. Comaroff. 2006. 'Law and Disorder in the Postcolony: An Introduction', in Jean Comaroff and John L. Comaroff (eds), *Law and Disorder in the Postcolony*, pp. 1–56. Chicago: University of Chicago Press.

———. 2009. 'Reflections on the Anthropology of Law, Governance and Sovreignty', in Franz von Benda-Beckman, Keebet von Benda-Beckman, and Julia Eckert (eds), *Rules of Law and Laws of Ruling: On the Governance of Law*, pp. 33. Surrey: Ashgate.

Committee on the Status of Women in India. 2011. *Towards Equality* (introduced by Kumud Sharma and K.P. Sujaya). New Delhi: Pearson Education.

Cornell, Drucilla. 1992. *The Philosophy of the Limit*. New York: Routledge.

Cossman, Brenda. 2000. 'Canadian Same Sex Relationship Recognition and the contradictory nature of legal victories'. *Cleveland State Law Review* 48: 49–59.

———. et al. 2003. Gender, Sexuality, and Power: Is Feminist Theory Enough?. *Columbia Journal of Gender & Law* 12(3): 601–37.

———. and Ratna Kapur. 2001. *Secularism's Last Sigh?. Hindutva and the (Mis)rule of Law*. New Delhi: Oxford University Press.

———. 2007. *Sexual Citizens: The Legal and Cultural Regulation of Sex and Belonging*. Palo Alto: Stanford University Press.

Cover, Robert. 1983. 'Nomos and Narrative'.*Yale Law Journal* 97: 4–68.

———. 1986. 'Violence and the Word'. *Yale Law Journal* 95(1601): 601.

———. 1995. 'Violence and the Word', in Martha Minow, Michael Ryan, and Austin Sarat (eds), *Narrative, Violence, and the Law: The Essays of Robert Cover*, pp. 203–38. Ann Arbor: University of Michigan Press.

Cubilie, Anne. 2005. *Women Witnessing Terror: Testimony and the Cultural Politics of Rights*. New York: Fordham University Press.

D'Souza, Radha. 2005. 'The "Third World" and Socio-Legal Studies: Neo-Liberalism and Lessons from India's Legal Innovations'. *Social & Legal Studies* 14(4): 488.

Daly, Kerry. 2003. 'Family Theory Versus the Theory Families Live By'. *Journal of Marriage and Family*, November 65(4): 771–84.

Das, Veena. 1995. *Critical Events: An Anthropological Perspective on Contemporary India*. New Delhi: Oxford University Press.

———. 2012. 'Ordinary Ethics', in Didier Fassin (ed.), *A Companion to Moral Anthropology*, pp. 133–49. Oxford: Wiley-Blackwell.

Dave, Naisargi. 2012. *Queer Activism in India: A Story in the Anthropology of Ethics*. Durham: Duke University Press.

Davies, Margaret. 2002. 'Ethics and Methodology in Legal Theory a (Personal) Research Anti-Manifesto'. *Law Text Culture* 6(7): 7–26.

———. 2008. *Asking the Law Question* (3rd edition). Sydney: Thomson Reuters.

———. 2015. *Asking the Law Question.* Sydney: Thomson Reuters.

———. 2017. *Law Unlimited: Materialism, Pluralism, and Legal Theory.* London: Routledge.

Davis, Donald R. Jr.. 2010. *The Spirit of Hindu Law*. Oxford: Oxford University Press.

Debord, G. 1983. *Society of the Spectacle*. Detroit: Black and Red.

Deleuze, Gilles and Felix Guattari. 1983. 'What is a Minor Literature?', *Mississippi Review*, Winter/Spring. 11(3): 13–33.

———. 1986. *Kafka. Toward a Minor Literature*. Minneapolis: University of Minnesota Press.

Derrida, Jacques (trans. by Barbara Johnson). 1981. *Dissemination*. London: The Athlone Press.

———. 1972. 'Structure, Sign, and Play in the Discourse of the Human Sciences', in Richard Macksey and Eugenio Donato (eds), *The Structuralist Controversy*. Baltimore: The Johns Hopkins University Press.

——— (trans. by Alan Bass). 1978. 'Ellipsis', in Jacques Derrida, *Writing and Difference*, pp. 294. Chicago: University of Chicago Press.

———. 1992. 'Force of Law: The 'Mystical Foundations of Authority', in Drucilla Cornell, Michel Rosenfeld, and David Gray Carlson (eds), *Deconstruction and the Possibility of Justice*, pp. 3–67. New York: Routledge.

Desai, A.H. and S. Muralidhar. 2000. 'Public Interest Litigation: Potential and Problems', in B.N. Kirpal et al (eds), *Supreme But Not Infallible: Essays in Honour of the Supreme Court of India*, pp. 161. New Delhi: Oxford University Press.

Desai, Darshan. 2004 .'Massacres and the Media: A Field Reporter Looks Back on Gujarat 2002', in *Sarai Reader 04: Crisis/Media*, (Sarai, CSDS, 2004) 228–234.

Desai, Radhika. 2004. *Slouching Towards Ayodhya: From Congress to Hindutva in Indian Politics*. Gururgram: Three Essays Collective.

Deshpande, Satish. 2004. *Contemporary India: A Sociological View*, pp. 2. New Delhi: Penguin Books.

Devi, Mahasveta (trans. by Gayatri Chakravorty Spivak). 1981. 'Draupadi'. *Critical Inquiry* 8(2): 381–402.

Dhanda, Amita & Archana Parashar (eds). 2009. *Decolonisation of Legal Knowledge: Whose Responsibility?*. Routledge: New Delhi.

———. 2009. 'Decolonisation of Legal Knowledge: Whose Responsibility?', in Amita Dhanda and Archana Parashar (eds), *Decolonisation of Legal Knowledge*. New Delhi: Routledge.

Dhavan, Rajeev. 2003. 'Justice, Justice and the Best Bakery Case'. *India International Centre Quarterly* 30(2): 1–11.

———. 2008. *Publish and Be Damned: Censorship and Intolerance in India*. New Delhi: Tulika Books.

Dhawan, Nikita. 2012. 'Hegemonic Listening and Subversive Silences: Ethical-Political Imperatives'. *Critical Studies* (36): 47–60.

———. 2013. 'The Empire Prays Back: Religion, Secularity and Queer Critique'. *boundary 2*, 2(2): 191.

Digby, Tom (ed). 1998. *Men Doing Feminism*. New York: Routledge.

Dillon, Brian. 2017. *Essayism*. London: Fitzcarraldo Editions.

Dirlik, Arif. 2014. 'Developmentalism: A Critique'. *Interventions: International Journal of Postcolonial Studies* 16(1): 30–48.

Doezema, J. 2010. *Sex Slaves and Discourse Masters: The Construction of Trafficking*. New York: Zed Books.

Doniger, Wendy and Brian K Smith. 1991. *The Laws of Manu*. London: Penguin Books.

Dorsett, Shaunnagh and Shaun McVeigh. 2012. *Jurisdiction*. Oxford: Routledge.

Douzinas, Costas. 2005. 'Oubliez Critique'. *Law and Critique* (16): 47–69.

Douzinas, Costas and Adam Gearey. 2005. *Critical Jurisprudence*. Oxford: Hart Publishing.

Douzinas, Costas and Lynda Nead. 1999. 'Introduction', in Castas Douzinas and Lynda Nead (eds), *Law and the Image: The Authority of Art and the Aesthetics of Law*, pp. 1–18. Chicago: University of Chicago Press.

Doyle, Jennifer. 2015. *Campus Sex, Campus Security*. South Pasadena: Semiotexte.

Duggan, Lisa and José Esteban Muñoz. 2009. 'Hope and Hopelessness: A Dialogue'. *Women & Performance: A Journal of Feminist Theory* (19): 275–83.

Duggan, Lisa. 2002. 'The New Homonormativity: The Sexual Politics of Neoliberalism', in Russ Castronovo and Dana D. Nelson (eds), *Materializing Democracy: Toward A Revitalized Cultural Politics*, pp. 175. Durham: Duke University Press.

Duncan, Nigel. 2011. 'Addressing Emotions in Preparing Ethical Lawyers', in Paul Maharg and Caroline Maughan (eds), *Affect and Legal*

Education: Emotion in Learning and Teaching the Law, pp. 257– 82. Surrey: Ashgate.

Dutta, Ani. 2016. 'Gatekeeping Transgender', *Raiot*. Accessible on http://raiot.in/gatekeeping-transgender/; last accessed 5 July 2019.

Dutta, Aniruddha. 2015. 'Contradictory Tendencies: The Supreme Court's NALSA Judgment on Transgender Recognition and Rights'. *Journal of Indian Law & Society* (5): 225.

———. 2013. 'Digitizing the National Imaginary: Technology and Hybridization in Hindi Film Songs of the Post-liberalization Period', in K. Moti Gokulsingh and Wimal Dissanayake (eds), *Routledge Handbook of Indian Cinemas*, pp. 231–45. Oxford: Routledge.

Dutta, Debolina. 2016a. 'A Story of the Open Letter'. Paper Presented at 'Provocations III: Feminist Experiences of Law', Melbourne Law School, 27–8 October.

———. 2016b. 'Rethinking Care and Economic Justice with Third World Sex Workers', in Wendy Harcourt (ed.), *The Palgrave Handbook of Gender and Development*, pp. 186–201. London: Palgrave Macmillan.

———. 2018. 'A Story of the Open Letter'. *Jindal Global Law Review* 9(2): 181–202.

Dutta, Debolina and Oishik Sircar. 2008. 'From Sex Worker to Entertainment Worker: Strategic Politics of DMSC', *Sephis*, April, 4(3): 3. Accessible on http://sephisemagazine.org/issues/volume_4_3.pdf; last accessed 5 July 2019 .

———. 2013. 'India's Winter of Discontent: Some Feminist Dilemmas in the Wake of a Rape'. *Feminist Studies* 39(1): 293–306.

Eng, David L. 2002. 'The Value of Silence'. *Theatre Journal* 54(1): 85–94.

Engineer, Asghar Ali (ed). 2003. *The Gujarat Carnage*. Hyderabad: Orient Longman.

Farasat, Warisha and Prita Jha. 2016. *Splintered Justice: Living the Horror of Mass Communal Violence in Bhagalpur and Gujarat*. Gurgaon: Three Essays Collective.

Farmer, Victoria L. 1996. 'Mass Media: Images, Mobilization, and Communalism', in David Ludden (ed), *Contesting the Nation: Religion, Community, and the Politics of Democracy in India*, pp. 98–118. Philadelphia: University of Pennsylvania Press.

Fausto-Sterling, Anne. 1987. *Myths of Gender: Biological Theories about Women and Men*. New York: Basic Books.

———. 2000. *Sexing the Body: Gender politics and the construction of sexuality*. New York: Basic Books.

———. 2012. *Sex/Gender: Biology in a Social World*. New York: Routledge.

Federici, Silvia. 2012. *Revolution at Point Zero: Housework, Reproduction, and Feminist Struggle*. Oakland: PM Press.

Felman, Shoshana. 2002. *The Juridical Unconscious. Trials and Traumas in the Twentieth Century*. Cambridge: Harvard University Press.

Figueira, M. Dorothy. 2002. *Aryans, Jews, Brahmins: Theorizing Authority through Myths of Identity.* New York: SUNY Press.

Fitzpatrick, Peter. 1992. *The Mythology of Modern Law*. London: Routledge.

———. 2012. 'Reading Slowly: The Law of Literature and the Literature of Law', in Ruth Buchanan, Stewart Motha, and Sundhya Pahuja (eds), *Reading Modern Law: Critical Methodologies and Sovereign Formations*, pp. 193–210. London: Routledge.

Flood, Catharine and Gavin Grindon (eds). 2014. *Disobedient Objects*. London: V&A Publishing.

Foucault, Michel, Hubert L. Dreyfus, and Paul Rabinow. 1983. 'Afterword: On the Genealogy of Ethics: An Overview of Work in Progress', in Hubert L. Dreyfus and Paul Rabinow, *Michel Foucault: Beyond Structuralism and Hermeneutics*, pp. 229–52. Chicago: University of Chicago Press.

Foucault, Michel (trans. by Alan Sheridan et al). 1988. 'Practicing Criticism', in L.D. Kritzman (ed.), *Politics, Philosophy, Culture: Interviews and Other Writings, 1977–1984*, pp. 152–8. New York: Routledge.

———. 1991. 'Governmentality', in Graham Burchell, Colin Gordon, and Peter Miller (eds), *The Foucault Effect. Studies in Governmentality*', pp. 87–104. Chicago: University of Chicago Press.

———. 1994. 'La Philosophie Analytique de la Politique', in Daniel Defert et François Ewald (eds), in *3 Dits et Écrits. 1954–1988*, pp. 534, 540–1. Paris: Éditions Gallimard.

———. 2012. *Discipline and Punish: The Birth of the Prison*. New York: Knopf Doubleday.

Fraser, Nancy. 2013. *Fortunes of Feminism: From State-managed Capitalism to Neoliberal Crisis.* London: Verso.

Front Line. 2016. *Annual Report 2016*. Dublin: International Foundation for the Protection of Human Rights Defenders.

Fuller, C.J. and Haripriya Narasimhan. 2014. *Tamil Brahmans: The Making of a Middle-Class Caste*. Chicago: University of Chicago Press.

Galanter, Marc. 1993. 'Making Law Work for the Oppressed', *The Other Side*, March, III(2): 7.

Gandhi, Leela. 2006. *Affective Communities: Anticolonial Thought, Fin-De-Siècle Radicalism, and the Politics of Friendship*. Durham: Duke University Press.

Ganti, Tejaswini. 2013. *Bollywood: A Guide to Popular Hindi Cinema*. New York: Routledge.

Gauri, V. 2009. *Public Interest Litigation in India: Overreaching or Underachieving?* pp. 16, Policy Research Working Paper 5109. World Bank, New York.

Geertz, Clifford. 1983. *Local Knowledge: Further Essays in Interpretive Anthropology*.New York: Basic Books.

George, Susan. 2003. 'Globalizing Rights?', in Matthew J. Gibney (ed.), *Globalizing Rights*, pp. 15. Oxford: Oxford University Press.

Genovese, Ann. 2013. 'Inheriting and Inhabiting the Pleasures and Duties of Our Own Existence: The Second Sex and Feminist Jurisprudence', *Australian Feminist Law Journal*, 38(1): 41–57.

———. 2016. 'About Libraries: A Jurisographer's Notes on Lives Lived with Law (in London and Sydney),' *Law Text Culture* 20 :37.

Ghassem-Fachandi, Parvis. 2012. *Pogrom in Gujarat: Hindu Nationalism and Anti-Muslim Violence in India*. Princeton: Princeton University Press.

Ghosh, Amitav. 2008. *The Shadow Lines*. New Delhi: Penguin Books.

Ghosh, Jayati. 2009. *Never Done and Poorly Paid: Women's Work in Globalising India*. New Delhi: Women Unlimited.

Gibson-Graham, J.K. 2006. *A Postcapitalist Politics*. Minneapolis: University of Minnesota Press.

Goldoni, Marco and Michael A. Wilkinson. 2018. 'The Material Constitution', *Modern Law Review* 81(4): 569.

Goodman, Ryan. 2001. 'Beyond the Enforcement Principle: Sodomy Laws, Social Norms and Social Panoptics', *California Law Review*, 89(643): 651–3.

Goodrich, Peter. 1995. *Oedipus Lex: Psychoanalysis, History, Law*. Berkeley: University of California Press.

———. 1996. *Law in the Courts of Love: Literature and Other Minor Jurisprudences*. Oxford: Routledge.

———. Winter 1998. 'Law by Other Means', *Cardozo Studies in Law and Literature*, 10(2): 111–6.

———. 2014. *Legal Emblems and the Art of Law: Obiter Depicta as the Vision of Governance*. Cambridge: Cambridge University Press.

Gopalakrishnan, Shankar. 2006. *Neoliberalism and Hindutva: Fascism, Free Markets and the Restructuring of Indian Capitalism*. New Delhi: Aakar Books.

Gregor, A. James. 2006. *The Search of Neofascism: The Use and Abuse of Social Science*. Cambridge: Cambridge University Press.

Grover, Sonja. 2005. 'Advocacy by Children as a Causal Factor in Promoting Resilience'. *Childhood* 12(4):527–38.

Grover, Vrinda. 2002. 'The Elusive Quest for Justice: Delhi 1984 to Gujarat 2002', in Siddharth Varadarajan (ed.), *Gujarat: The Making of a Tragedy*, pp. 355–88. New Delhi: Penguin Books.

Guattari, Felix and Gilles Deleuze (trans. by Dana Polan). 1986. *Kafka: Toward a Minor Literature*, pp. 17. Minneapolis: University of Minnesota Press

Guha, Ranajit. 1996. 'The Small Voice of History', in Shahid Amin and Dipesh Chakrabarty (eds), *Subaltern Studies IX. Writings on South Asian History and Society*, pp. 1–12. New Delhi: Oxford University Press.

Gupta, Akhil. 2012. *Red Tape: Bureaucracy, Structural Violence, and Poverty in India*. Durham: Duke University Press.

Gupta, Charu. 2009. 'Hindu Women, Muslim Men: Love Jihad and Conversions', *Economic and Political Weekly*, 44(51): 13–5.

Gupta, Dipankar. 2011. *Justice Before Reconciliation: Negotiating a 'New Normal' in Post-Riot Mumbai and Ahmedabad*. New Delhi: Routledge.

Guru, Gopal and Sundar Sarukkai. 2012. *The Cracked Mirror: An Indian Debate on Experience and Theory*. New Delhi: Oxford University Press.

Halberstam, Judith. 2011. *The Queer Art of Failure*. Durham: Duke University Press.

Halbwachs, Maurice. 1992. *On Collective Memory*. Translated with an introduction by Lewis A. Coser. Chicago: University of Chicago Press.

Hall, Stuart. 1992. 'Cultural Studies and its Theoretical Legacies,' in Lawrence Grossberg, Cary Nelson, and Paula Treichler (ed.), *Cultural Studies*, pp. 277–86. New York and London: Routledge.

Hall, Stuart (ed.). 2009. *Cultural Representations and Signifying Practices*. London: SAGE.

Halley, Janet. 2000. 'Like Race Arguments', in Judith Butler, John Guillory, and Kendall Thomas (eds), *What's Left of Theory? New Work on the Politics of Literary Theory*, pp.40–74. New York: Routledge.

———. 2006a. *Split Decisions: How and Why to take a Break from Feminism*. Princeton: Princeton University Press.

Halley, Janet et al. 2006b. 'From the International to the Local in Feminist Legal Responses to Rape, Prostitution/Sex Work and Sex Trafficking: Four Studies in Contemporary Governance Feminism', *Harvard Journal of Law and Gender*, 29(2): 335–423.

Hanna Bridget, Ward Morehouse and Satinath Sarangi. 2005. *The Bhopal Reader: Remembering Twenty Years of the World's Worst Industrial Disaster*. Goa: The Other India Press.

Hardt, Michael. 1999. 'Affective Labor'. *boundary 2*, 26(1): 89–100.

Hardt, Michael. and Antonio. Negri. 2000. *Empire*. Boston: Harvard University Press.

Haritaworn, Jin, Tamsila Tauqir, and Esra Erdem. 2009. 'Gay Imperialism: Gender and Sexuality Discourse in the "War on Terror"', in Adi Kuntsman and Esperanza Miyake (eds), *Out of Place: Interrogating Silences in Queerness/ Raciality*. New York: Raw Nerve Books Ltd.

Hart, H.L.A. 2012. *The Concept of Law*. Oxford: Oxford University Press.

Hartman, Heidi I. 1979. 'The Unhappy Marriage of Marxism and Feminism: Towards a More Progressive Union', *Capital & Class*, 3(2): 1–33.

Hasan, Zoya et al (eds.). 2004. *India's Living Constitution: Ideas, Practices, Controversies*. New Delhi: Permanent Black.

Hasan Khan, Adil. 2016. 'International Lawyers in the Aftermath of Disasters: Inheriting from Radhabinod Pal and Upendra Baxi', *Third World Quarterly* 37(11): 2,061–79.

Hirway, Indira. 2014. Amita Shah and Ghanshyam Shah (eds), *Growth or Development: Which Way Is Gujarat Going?*. New Delhi: Oxford University Press.

Hoenig, Patrick and Navsharan Singh (eds). 2015. *Landscapes of Fear: Understanding Impunity in India*. New Delhi: Zubaan.

Höijer, Birgitta. 2004. 'The Discourse of Global Compassion: The Audience and Media Reporting of Human Suffering', *Media Culture Society* 26(4): 513–31.

Holland, Patricia. 2004. *Picturing Childhood: The Myth of the Child in Popular Imagery*. New York: I.B. Tauris.

hooks, bell. 1991. 'Theory as Liberatory Practice', (1991) *Yale Journal of Law and Feminism* Vol. 4, pp. 1-12.

Human Rights Watch Report. 2008. *These Fellows Must be Eliminated: Relentless Violence and Impunity in Manipur*. Accessible on http://www.hrw.org/reports/2008/09/29/these-fellows-must-be-eliminated; last accessed 5 July 2019.

Hussain, Nasser. 2006. *The Jurisprudence of Emergency: Colonialism and the Rule of Law*. Ann Arbor: University of Michigan Press.

Hussain, Nasser. 2007. 'Hyperlegality', *New Criminal Law Review: An International and Interdisciplinary Journal*, 10 (4): 514.

International Initiative for Justice in Gujarat. *Threatened Existence: A Feminist Analysis of the Genocide in Gujarat*, Mumbai 2003.

International Human Rights and Conflict Resolution Clinic (IHRCRC), *When Justice Becomes the Victim: The Quest for Justice after the 2002 Violence in Gujarat* (Stanford Law School, 2014).

Iyer, Sriya and Anand Shrivastava. 2018. 'Religious Riots and Electoral Politics in India' 131 *Journal of Development Economics* 104.

Jackman, Michael Connors and Nishant Upadhyay. 2014. 'Pinkwatching Israel, Whitewashing Canada: Queer (Settler) Politics and Indigenous Colonization in Canada', *Women's Studies Quarterly* 42(195): 200–1.

Jaffrelot, Christophe and Charlotte Thomas. 2012. 'Facing Ghettoisation in Riot City', in Laurent Gayer and Christophe Jaffrelot (eds), pp. 43–81. *Muslims in Indian Cities: Trajectories of Marginalisation*. London: Hurst.

Jaffrelot, Christophe. 2015. 'What "Gujarat Model"? Growth Without Development—and With Socio-political Polarisation', *South Asia: Journal of South Asian Studies*, 38(4): 820–38.

———. 2005a. *The Sangh Parivar: A Reader*. New Delhi: Oxford University Press.

———. 2005b. *Dr Ambedkar and Untouchability: Analysing and Fighting Caste*. London: Hurst & Company.

Jaffrey, Zia. 1996. *The Invisibles: A Tale of the Eunuchs of India*. New York: Pantheon.

Jain, Anuja. 2010. '"Beaming It Live": 24 Hour Television News, the Spectator and the Spectacle of the 2002 Gujarat Carnage', *South Asian Popular Culture*, 8(2): 163–79.

Jain, Chirayu et al. 2018. 'Accessibility and Inclusivity at National Law School', *Economic and Political Weekly*, 6 Januray, 51(1): 72–8.

Jasbir, Puar. 2007. *Terrorist Assemblages: Homonationalism In Queer Times*. Durham: Duke University Press.

Jay, Martin. 2003. *Refractions of Violence*. New York: Routledge.

Jha, D.N. 2009. *The Myth of The Holy Cow*. New Delhi: Navayana.

John, Mary E. 2008a. 'Introduction', in Mary E. John (ed.), *Women's Studies in India: A Reader*, pp. 1–22. New Delhi: Penguin Books.

John, Mary E. (ed). 2008b. *Women's Studies in India: A Reader*, pp. 267. New Delhi: Penguin Books.

Johnson, J. 2011. "The Arithmetic of Compassion': Rethinking the Politics of Photography'. *British Journal of Political Science 41*(3): 621–43.

Josh, Bhagwan. 2018. 'Partition and the Rise of Hindutva Movement in Contemporary India' 76 *Revista Canaria de Estudios Ingleses* 175.

Joshi, Priya. 2015. *Bollywood's India: A Public Fantasy*. New York: Columbia University Press.

Kabeer, Nasreen Munni. 2002. 'Playback Time', *Film Comment* 38(3): 42.

Kandasamy, Meena. 2010. *Ms Military*, pp. 28–9. New Delhi: Navayana Publishing.

Kannabiran, Kalpana and Vasanth Kannabiran. 2002. *De-eroticizing Assault: Essays on Modesty, Honour and Power.* Kolkata: Stree.

Kannabiran, Kalpana. 2012. *Tools of Justice: Non-Discrimination and the Indian Constitution*. New Delhi: Routledge.

———. 2015. 'Storytelling in the Time of Hate: Deciphering Law(s) through Literature'. *Economic and Political Weekly* 50(2): 76–83.

——— (ed.). 2016. *Violence Studies*. New Delhi: Oxford University Press.

Kannabiran, Kalpana and Ranbir Singh (eds). 2008. *Challenging the Rule(s) of Law: Colonialism, Criminology and Human Rights in India.* New Delhi: SAGE.

Kapila, Shruti and Faisal Devji. 2010. 'The Bhagavad Gita and Modern Thought: Introduction', *Modern Intellectual History*, 7(2): 269–73.

Kaplan, Caren. 1998. 'Resisting Autobiography: Out-Law Genres and Transnational Feminist Subjects', in Sidonie Smith and Julia Watson (eds), *Women, Autobiography, Theory: A Reader*, pp. 208–16. Madison: University of Wisconsin Press.

Kapur, Ratna. 1999. '"A Love Song to Our Mongrel Selves": Hybridity, Sexuality and the Law'. *Social & Legal Studies* 8(3): 353.

———. 2000. 'Too Hot to Handle: The Cultural Politics of Fire', *Feminist Review* (64): 53– 64.

———. 2005. *Erotic Justice: Law and the New Politics of Postcolonialism*. Ranikhet: Permanent Black.

———. 2005. 'Travel Plans: Border Crossings and the Rights of Transnational Migrants', *Harvard Human Rights Journal* (18): 107, 128.

———. 2006. 'Normalizing Violence: Transitional Justice and the Gujarat Riots', *Columbia Journal of Gender and Law*, 15(3): 885–927.

———. 2007. 'Faith and the "Good" Liberal: The Construction of Female Sexual Subjectivity in Anti-trafficking Legal Discourse', in V. Munro and C. Stychin (eds), *Sexuality and the Law: Feminist Engagements*, pp. 223–58. Oxford: Routledge-Cavendish.

Kapur, Ratna and Brenda Cossman. 1993. 'On Women, Equality and the Constitution: Through the Looking Glass of Feminism'. *National Law School Journal* (1): 1.

———. 1996. *Subversive Sites: Feminist Engagements with Law in India*. New Delhi: SAGE.

———. 1999. *Secularism's Last Sigh: Hindutva and the (Mis) Rule of Law*. New Delhi: Oxford University Press.

Katz, Cindi. 2004. *Growing Up Global: Economic Restructuring and Children's Everyday Lives*, Minneapolis: University of Minnesota Press.

———. 2008. 'Childhood as Spectacle: Relays of Anxiety and the Reconfiguration of the Child', *Cultural Geographies*, 15(1): 5.

Kaviraj, Sudipta. 2010. *The Imaginary Institution of India: Politics and Ideas*. New York: Columbia University Press.

Kazanjian, David. 2003. *The Colonizing Trick: National Culture and Imperial Citizenship in Early America*. Minneapolis: University of Minnesota Press.

Kelman, Mark. 1987. *A Guide to Critical Legal Studies*. Cambridge: Harvard University Press.

Kelsen, Hans. 1967. *Pure Theory of Law*. Berkeley: University of California Press.

Kempadoo, Kamala (ed.). 2005. *Trafficking and Prostitution Reconsidered: New Perspectives on Migration, Sex Work, and Human Rights*. Boulder: Paradigm Publishers.

Kennedy, Duncan. 1982. 'Legal Education and the Reproduction of Hierarchy', *Journal of Legal Education*, 32(4): 591-615.

———. 1991. 'A Semiotics of Legal Argument', *Syracuse Law Review*, 42(75): 75–116.

———. 2002. 'The Critique of Rights in Critical Legal Studies', in Wendy Brown and Janet Halley (eds), *Left Legalism/Left Critique*, pp. 178–228 . Durham: Duke University Press.

Kenny, Paul D. 2017. *Populism and Patronage: Why Populists Win Elections in India, Asia, and Beyond*. Oxford: Oxford University Press.

Kerruish, Valerie. 1992. *Jurisprudence as Ideology*. London: Routledge.

Khanna, H.R. 2008. *Making of India's Constitution*. Lucknow: Eastern Book Company.

Khosla, Madhav. 2010. 'Making Social Rights Conditional: Lessons from India', *International Journal of Constitutional Law*, 8(4): 739–65.

Klein, Naomi. 2007. *Shock Doctrine: The Rise of Disaster Capitalism*. New York: Penguin Books.

Kleinman, Arthur and Joan Kleinman. 1996. 'The Appeal of Experience; The Dismay of Images: Cultural Appropriations of Suffering in Our Times', *Daedalus*, Winter, 125(1): 1–23.

———. 1997. 'The Appeal of Experience; The Dismay of Images: Cultural Appropriations of Suffering in Our Times', in Kleinman, A. et al (eds), *Social Suffering*, pp. 1–24. Berkeley: University of California Press.

Knutsen, Torbjorn L. 2006. 'Dumbledore's Pedagogy: Knowledge and Virtue at Hogwarts', in Daniel H. Nexon and Iver B. Neumann (eds), *Harry Potter and International Relations*, pp. 197–212. Oxford: Rowman and Littlefield.

Kotiswaran, Prabha. 2011. *Dangerous Sex, Invisible Labour: Sex Work and the Law in India*, Princeton: Princeton University Press.

Kumar, Megha. 2017. *Communalism and Sexual Violence: Ahmedabad Since 1969*. New Delhi: Tulika.

Kumar, Sanjay. 2002. 'Gujarat Assembly Elections 2002: Analysing the Verdict', *Economic and Political Weekly*, 38(4): 270–75.

Kumari, Ved. 1999. 'Gender Analysis of the Indian Penal Code', in Amita Dhanda and Archana Parashar (eds), *Engendering Law: Essays in Honour of Lotika Sarkar*, pp. 139. Lucknow: Eastern Book Company.

Kundera, Milan (Trans. from French by Linda Asher). 2005. *The Art of the Novel*. London: Faber and Faber.

Krishna, Sankaran. 1994. 'Cartographic Anxieties: Mapping the Body Politic in India', *Alternatives: Global, Local, Political*, Fall 1994, 19 (4): 507–21.

Land, Clare. 2015. *Decolonizing Solidarity: Dilemmas and Directions for Supporters of Indigenous Struggles*. London: Zed Books.

Laurie, Timothy and Rimi Khan. 2017. 'The Concept of Minority for the Study of Culture', *Continuum: Journal of Media and Communication Studies*, 31 (1): 1–12.

Lazzarato, Maurizio. 2006. 'Immaterial Labor', in Paolo Virno and Michael Hardt (eds), *Radical Thought in Italy: A Potential Politics*, pp. 133–46. Minneapolis: University of Minnesota Press.

Liang, Lawrence. 2005. 'Cinematic Citizenship and the Illegal City', *Inter Asia Cultural Studies*, 6(3): 366–85.

Lipari, Lisbeth. 2009. 'Listening Otherwise: The Voice of Ethics', *International Journal of Listening*, 23(1): 44–59.

Lothspeich, Pamela. 2007. 'The *Kaliyug* of Modernity in Surendra Verma's *Draupadi*', in Malashri Lal and Suktara Paul Kumar (eds), *Interpreting Homes in South Asian Literature*. New Delhi: Pearson, 159

MacKinnon, Catharine A. 1989. *Toward a Feminist Theory of the State*. Cambridge: Harvard University Press.

Mahadevia, Darshini. 2007. 'A City with Many Borders: Beyond Ghettoisation in Ahmedabad' in Annapurna Shaw (ed.), *Indian Cities in Transition*. Hyderabad: Orient Longman, 341–89.

Malik, Iftikhar Haider. 2005. *Jihad, Hindutva, and the Taliban: South Asia at the Crossroads*. Oxford University Press.

Mamdani, Mahmood. 2004. *Good Muslim, Bad Muslim: America, The Cold War, and the Roots of Terror*. New York: Doubleday.

Mandal, Saptarshi. 2009. 'Right to Privacy' in Naz Foundation: A Counter-Heteronormative Critique, *NUJS Law Review* 2: 525-540.

Mander, Harsh. 2009. *Fear and Forgiveness: The Aftermath of Massacre*, pp. 48. New Delhi: Penguin Books.

Manderson, Desmond. 2001. 'Apocryphal Jurisprudence', *Australian Journal of Legal Philosophy* (26): 27–59.

Mani, Braj Ranjan. 2005. *Debrahminising History: Dominance and Resistance in Indian Society*. New Delhi: Manohar Publishers.

Manning, Erin. 2016. *The Minor Gesture*. Durham: Duke University Press.

Manto, Saadat Hasan (trans. by Khalid Hasan). 2008. 'The New Constitution', in Khalid Hasan (ed.). *Bitter Fruit: The Very Best of Saadat Hasan Manto*. New Delhi: Penguin Books.

Marle, Karin Van. 2003. 'Law's Time, Particularity and Slowness', *South African Journal on Human Rights*, (19): 239.

———. 2013. 'Liminal Landscape: Law, Literature and Landscape in Post-Apartheid South Africa', in Karin Van Marle and Stewart Motha (eds), *Genres of Critique: Law, Aesthetics and Liminality*. Stellenbosch: SUN Press.

Marx, Karl. 1978. 'On the Jewish Question', in R.C. Tucker (ed.), *The Marx-Engels Reader*, pp. 45. New York: Norton.

Mazumdar, Ranjani. 2007. *Bombay Cinema. An Archive of the City*. Minneapolis: University of Minnesota Press.

Mazzarella, W. 2003. *Shoveling Smoke: Advertising and Globalization in Contemporary India*. Durham: Duke University Press.

———. 2003. *Shovelling Smoke: Advertising and Globalization in Contemporary India*, pp. 68. Durham: Duke University Press.

———. 2013. *Censorium: Cinema and the Open Edge of Mass Publicity*. Durham: Duke University Press.

Mbembe, Achille. 2003. 'Necropolitics'. *Public Culture* 15(1): 11–40.

———. 1992. 'Provisional Notes on the Postcolony'. *Africa: Journal of the International African Institute* 62(1): 3–37.

McCluskey, Martha. 2009. 'How Queer Theory Makes Neoliberalism Sexy', in Martha Fineman, Jack E. Jackson, and Adam P. Romero (eds), *Feminist and Queer Legal Theory: Intimate Encounters, Uncomfortable Conversations*, pp. 115–34. Farnham: Ashgate.

McMaster, Don. 2002. 'White Australia to Tampa: The Politics of Fear', *Dialogue* (21): 3.

McVeigh, Shaun. 2014. 'Law As (More or Less) Itself: On Some Not Very Reflective Elements of Law', *UC Irvine Law Review*, (4): 471–91.

———. 2015. 'Afterword: Office and Conduct of the Minor Jurisprudence', *UC Irvine Law Review*, (5): 499–511.

Mehrotra, Deepti Priya. 2009. *Burning Bright: Irom Sharmila and the Struggle for Peace in Manipur*. New Delhi: Penguin Books.

Mehta, Uday Singh. 1999. *Liberalism and Empire: A Study in Nineteenth-Century British Liberal Thought*. Chicago: University of Chicago Press.

Menke, Christophe. 2010. 'Law and Violence', *Law and Literature*, Spring, 22(1): 1–17.

Menon, Dilip. 2006. *The Blindness of Insight: Essays on Caste in Modern India*. New Delhi: Navayana.

Menon, Kalyani Devaki. 2009. *Everyday Nationalism: Women of the Hindu Right in India*. Pennsylvania: University of Pennsylvania Press.

Menon, Meena. 2011. *Riots and After in Mumbai: Chronicles of Truth and Reconciliation*. New Delhi: SAGE.

Menon, Nivedita. 2004. *Recovering Subversion: Feminist Politics Beyond the Law*. Ranikhet: Permanent Black.

———. 2007. 'Outing Heteronormativity: Nation, Citizen, Feminist Disruptions', in Nivedita Menon (ed.), *Sexualities*, pp.23. New Delhi: Women Unlimited.

———. 2008. 'Citizenship and the Passive Revolution: Interpreting the First Amendment', in Rajeev Bhargava (ed.), *Politics and Ethics of the Indian Constitution*, pp. 189–210. New Delhi: Oxford University Press.

Menon-Sen, Kalyani and Gautam Bhan. 2008. *Swept Off the Map: Surviving Eviction and Resettlement in Delhi*. New Delhi: Yoda Press.

Mignolo, Walter D. and Catherine E. Walsh. 2018. *On Decoloniality: Concepts, Analytics, Praxis*. Durham: Duke University Press.

Mill, John Stuart. 2002. *On Liberty*. New York: Dover Publications.

Mishra, Shalini, Shivani Chaudhry, and Miloon Kothari. 2012. 'The 2010 Commonwealth Games: Whose Wealth? Whose Commons?', Housing and Land Rights Network, South Asia Regional Programme, Habitat International Coalition, New Delhi.

Mishra, Vijay Mishra. 2002. *Bollywood Cinema: Temples of Desire*. New York: Routledge.

Mitta, Manoj and H.M. Phoolka. 2008. *When a Tree Shook: The 1984 Carnage and its Aftermath*. New Delhi: Roli Books.

Mitta, Manoj. 2014. *Modi & Godhra: The Fiction of Fact-Finding*. New Delhi: HarperCollins.

Mohanty, C.T. 2003. *Feminism Without Borders: Decolonizing Theory, Practicing Solidarity*. Durham: Duke University Press.

Morgensen, Scott L. 2011. *Spaces Between Us: Queer Settler Colonialism and Indigenous Decolonization*. Minneapolis: University of Minnesota Press.

Mufti, Aamir R. 2000. 'A Greater Story Writer than God: Genre, Gender and Minority in Late Colonial India', in Partha Chatterjee and Pradeep Jeganathan (eds), *Subaltern Studies XI: Community, Gender and Violence*, pp. 21. New Delhi: Permanent Black and Ravi Dayal Publisher.

Mukherjee, Rudrangshu. 2018. *Twilight Falls on Liberalism*. New Delhi: Aleph.

Muldoon, A. 2009. *Empire, Politics and the Creation of the 1935 India Act: Last Act of the Raj*, Surrey: Ashgate.

Murthy, Laxmi and Meena Seshu (eds). 2014. *The Business of Sex*. New Delhi: Zubaan.

Mussawir, Edward. 2011. *Jurisdiction in Deleuze: The Expression and Representation of Law*. New York: Routledge.

Nainar, Vahida and Saumya Uma (eds). 2013. *Pursuing Elusive Justice: Mass Crimes in India and Relevance of International Standards*. New Delhi: Oxford University Press.

Nanda, Meera. 2007. 'Secularism without Secularisation: Reflections on God and Politics in US and India'. *Economic and Political Weekly* 42(1): 39.

Nanda, Meera. 2009. *The God Market: How Globalization Is Making India More Hindu*. New York: Monthly Review Press.

Nandy, Ashis. 1995. 'An Anti-Secularist Manifesto', *India International Centre Quarterly*, 22(1): 35–64.

———. 1999. 'Introduction: Indian Popular Cinema as a Slum's Eye View of Politics', in Ashis Nandy (ed.), *The Secret Politics of Our Desires: Innocence, Culpability and Indian Popular Cinema*. London: Zed Books.

Narayan, Badri. 2009. *Fascinating Hindutva: Saffron Politics and Dalit Mobilisation*. New Delhi: SAGE.

Narayan, Uma. 1997. *Dislocating Cultures: Identities, Traditions and Third World Women*. New York: Routledge.

Nesiah, Vasuki. 2014. 'Sexy Dressing, Gender and Legal Theory: A Style of Political Engagement', *Transnational Legal Theory* 5(4): 640–8.

Noorani, A. G. 2017. *Destruction of the Babri Masjid: A National Dishonour*. New Delhi: Tulika Books.

Nussbaum, Martha. 2007. *The Clash Within: Democracy, Religious Violence and India's Future*. Cambridge: Harvard University Press.

———. 2013. *Political Emotions: Why Love Matters for Justice*. Cambridge: Harvard University Press.

Ohm, Britta. 2010. 'Forgetting to Remember: The Privatisation of the Public, the Economisation of Hindutva, and the Medialisation of Genocide', in Shakuntala Banaji (ed.), *South Asian Media Cultures: Audiences, Representations, Contexts*, pp. 123–44. London: Anthem Press.

Oksala, Johanna. 2014. 'In Defense of Experience', *Hypatia* 29(2): 388–403.

———. 2016. 'Affective Labour and Feminist Politics', *Signs: Journal of Women in Culture and Society* 41(2): 281–303.

Olick, Jeffrey K., Vered Vinitzky-Seroussi, and Daniel Levy. 2011. 'Introduction', in Jeffrey K. Olick, Vered Vinitzky-Seroussi, and Daniel Levy (eds), *The Collective Memory Reader*, pp. 3–62. Oxford: Oxford University Press.

Olick, Jeffrey K. 2007. *The Politics of Regret: On Collective Memory and Historical Responsibility*. New York: Routledge.

Orford, Anne. 2012. 'In Praise of Description', *Leiden Journal of International Law*, (25): 609–25.

Otto, Dianne. 2007. 'The Gastronomics of TWAIL's Feminist Flavourings: Some Lunch-Time Offerings', *International Community Law Review*, 9(4): 345–52.

Pahuja, Sundhya. 2013. 'Laws of Encounter: A Jurisdictional Account of International Law', *London Review of International Law*, 1(1): 63–98.

Pandey, Gyanendra. 2002. *Remembering Partititon: Violence, Nationalism and History in India*. New Delhi: Cambridge University Press.

Parker, James E.K. 2015. *Acoustic Jurisprudence: Listening to the Trial of Simon Bikindi*, pp. 39. New York: Oxford University Press.

Pashukanis, Evgeny. 1987. *Law and Marxism: A General Theory.* London: Pluto Press.

People's Union for Civil Liberties. 2001. *Human Rights Violations Against Sexual Minorities in India: A PUCL-K Fact-Finding Report About Bangalore*. Karnataka.

Philippopoulos-Mihalopoulos, Andreas. 2013. 'Atmospheres of Law: Senses, Affects, Lawscapes', *Emotion, Space and Society* (7): 35–44.

Pinker, Steven. 2011. *Better Angels of Our Nature: A History of Violence and Humanity.* New York: Penguin Books.

Pinker, Steven. 2018. *Enlightenment Now: The Case for Reason, Science, Humanism and Progress.* New York: Penguin Books.

Prabhupada, A.C. Bhaktivedanta Swami. 1983. *Bhagavad-Gita As It Is.* Bombay: The Bhaktivedanta Book Trust.

Prasad, Madhava M. 2008. 'Surviving Bollywood', in Anandam P. Kavoori and Aswin Punathambekar (eds), *Global Bollywood*, pp. 41–51. New York: New York University Press.

———. 1998. *Ideology of the Hindi Film: A Historical Construction*. New Delhi: Oxford University Press.

Puar, Jasbir. 2007. *Terrorist Assemblages: Homonationalism in Queer Times.* Durham: Duke University Press.

———. 2011. 'Citation and Censorship: The Politics of Talking about the Sexual Politics of Israel', *Feminist Legal Studies* 19(2): 133.

———. 2017. *The Right to Maim: Debility, Capacity, Disability*. Durham: Duke University Press.

Pugliese, Joseph. 2002. 'Penal Asylum: Refugees, Ethics, Hospitality'. *Borderlands* 1(1).

Puri, Jyoti. 2016. Sexual States: Governance And The Struggle To Decriminalize Homosexuality In India. Durham: Duke University Press.

Rabaté, Jean-Michel. 2016. *The Pathos of Distance: Affects of the Moderns*, pp. 8. New York: Bloomsbury.

Rackley, Erika. 2005. 'When Hercules Met the Happy Prince: Re-imagining the Judge'. *Texas Wesleyan Law Review* 12(1): 213–32.

Rajadhyaksha, Ashish. 2008. 'The 'Bollywodization' of the Indian Cinema: Cultural Nationalism in a Global Arena', in Anandam P. Kavoori and Aswin Punathambekar (eds), *Global Bollywood*, pp. 17–40. New York: New York University Press.

Rajagopal, Arvind. 2001. *Politics After Television: Hindu Nationalism and the Reshaping of the Public in India*. Cambridge: Cambridge University Press.

Rajagopal, Balakrishnan. 2007. 'Pro-Human Rights But Anti-Poor? A Critical Evaluation of the Indian Supreme Court from a Social Movement Perspective'. *Human Rights Review* 8(3): 180.

Ramanathan, Usha. 1999. 'Images (1920–1950) Reasonable Man, Reasonable Woman and Reasonable Expectations', in Amita Dhanda and Archana Parashar (eds), *Engendering Law: Essays in Honour of Lotika Sarkar*, pp. 33. Lucknow: Eastern Book Company.

Rao, Anupama and Saurabh Dube (eds). 2013. *Crime Through Time*. New Delhi: Oxford University Press.

Rao, Rahul. 2014. 'Queer Questions'. *International Feminist Journal of Politics* (16): 199.

———. 2015. 'Global Homocapitalism'. *Radical Philosophy* (194): 38.

Raz, Joseph. 1974. 'Kelsen's Theory of the Basic Norm'. *American Journal of Jurisprudence* 19(1): 94.

Reddy, Gayatri. 2005. *With Respect to Sex: Negotiating Hijra Identity in South India*. Chicago: Chicago University Press.

Rege, Sharmila. 1995. 'The Hegemonic Appropriation of Sexuality: The Case of the Lavani Performers of Maharashtra'. *Contributions to Indian Sociology* 29(1–2): 23–38.

———. 1996. 'Homophobia in the Name of Marxism'. *Economic and Political Weekly* 31(22): 1,359–60.

———. 1998. 'Dalit Women Talk Differently: A Critique of "Difference" and Towards a Dalit Feminist Standpoint Position'. *Economic and Political Weekly* 33(44): 39–46.

———. 2010. 'Education as *Trutiya Ratna*: Towards Phule-Ambedkarite Feminist Pedagogical Practice'. *Economic and Political Weekly*, October 45(44–5): 88–98.

———. 2013. *Against the Madness of Manu: B.R Ambedkar's Writings on Brahmanical Patriarchy*. New Delhi: Navayana.

Robinson, Shirleene (ed.). 2008. *Homophobia: An Australian History*. Federation Press.

Roder, Katrin. 2014. 'Reparative Reading, Post-structuralist Hermeneutics and T. S. Eliot's *Four Quartets*'. *Anglia* 132(1): 58–9.

Rose, Jacqueline. 2004. *On Not Being Able to Sleep: Psychoanalysis and the Modern World*. London: Vintage.

———. 2013. *Women in Dark Times*. London: Bloomsbury.

Roy, Arundhati. 2011. *Broken Republic: Three Essays*. London: Penguin Books.

———. 2017. *The Ministry of Utmost Happiness*. New Delhi: Penguin Books.

———. 2019. *My Seditious Heart: Collected Non-Fiction*. New Delhi: Penguin Books.

Rubin, Gayle S. 2011. *Deviations: A Gayle Rubin Reader*, pp. 137–81. Durham: Duke University Press.

Sadgopal, Anil. 2010. 'Right to Education vs. Right to Education Act'. *Social Scientist* 38(9–12): 17.

Samaddar, Ranabir. 2007. *The Materiality of Politics: The Technologies of Rule*, Vol. I. London: Anthem Press.

———. 2007. *The Materiality of Politics: The Technologies of Rule*, Vol. II. London: Anthem Press.

———. 2015. 'Beyond the Frame of Practical Reason: The Indian Evidence Act and Its Performative Life'. *Diogenes* 60 (3–4): 58–73.

Sarat, Austin. 2000. 'Imagining the Law of the Father: Loss, Dread, and Mourning in "The Sweet Hereafter"'. *Law & Society Review* 34(1): 3–46.

———. 2011. 'What Popular Culture Does For, and To, Law: An Introduction', in Austin Sarat (ed.), *Imagining Legality: Where Law Meets Popular Culture*, pp. 1–21. Alabama: The University of Alabama Press.

Sarat, Austin, Lawrence Douglas, and Martha Merrill Umphrey. 2005. 'On Film and Law: Broadening the Focus', in Austin Sarat, Lawrence Douglas, and Martha Merrill Umphrey (eds), *Law on the Screen*, pp. 1–26. Stanford: Stanford University Press.

Sarkar, Sumit. 1993. 'The Fascism of the Sangh Parivar'. *Economic and Political Weekly* 28(5): 163–7.

Sarkar, Tanika. 2002. 'Semiotics of Terror: Muslim Women and Children in Hindu Rashtra'. *Economic and Political Weekly* 37(28): 2872–6.

Sathe, S.P. 1974. 'Is a National Law School Necessary?'. *Economic and Political Weekly* 28 September, 9(39): 1,643–5.

———. 1993. *Towards Gender Justice*, Research Centre for Women's Studies, SNDT University, Bombay.

———. 2002. *Judicial Activism in India: Transgressing Borders and Enforcing Limits*. New Delhi: Oxford University Press.

———. 2003. *Judicial Activism in India: Transgressing Borders and Enforcing Limits*, 2nd edition. New Delhi: Oxford University Press.

Saul, Ben. 2012. 'Dark Justice: On Australia's Indefinite Detention of Refugees on Security Grounds Under International Human Rights Law'. *Melbourne Journal of International Law* (13): 685.

Schleicher, David. 2013. 'From Here All-The-Way-Down, or How to Write a Festschrift Piece'. *Tulsa Law Review* (48): 401–25.

Schmitt, Carl (trans. by George Schwab). 2005. *Political Theology: Four Chapters on the Concept of Sovereignty*. Chicago: University of Chicago Press.

Scott, David. 1995. 'Colonial Governmentality'. *Social Text* (43): 191–220.

Scott, Joan. 1991. 'The Evidence of Experience'. *Critical Inquiry* 17(4): 773–97.

Sedgwick, Eve Kosofsky. 2003. *Touching Feeling: Affect, Pedagogy, Performativity*. Durham: Duke University Press.

Sen, Amartya. 2006. *Identity and Violence: The Illusion of Destiny*, pp. 20. New York: W.W. Norton & Company.

Sen, Ronojoy. 2010. *Articles of Faith: Religion, Secularism, and the Indian Supreme Court*. New Delhi: Oxford University Press.

Sen, S. 2009. 'Das Kapital', in Sumanta Banerjee (ed.), *Thema Book of Naxalite Poetry*, pp. 72. Kolkata: Thema.

Sen, Satadru. 2015. 'Fascism without Fascists? A Comparative Look at Hindutva and Zionism'. *South Asia: Journal of South Asian Studies* 38(4): 690.

Setalvad, Teesta. 2013. 'The Importance of Zakia Jafri's Petition'. *Economic and Political Weekly* 48(21): 10–13.

———. 2017. *Foot Soldier of the Constitution: A Memoir*. New Delhi: LeftWord.

Seuffert, Nan. 2015. 'Sexual Minorities and the Proliferation of Regulation in Australia's Asylum Seeker Detention Camps'. *Law Text Culture* (19): 39–83.

Seymour, David M. 2004. 'Film and Law: In Search of a Critical Method', in Leslie J. Moran, Emma Sandon, Elena Loizidou, and Ian Christie (eds), *Law's Moving Image*, pp. 107–20. London: The Glass House Press.

Shah, Amrita. 2015. *Ahmedabad: A City in the World*. New Delhi: Bloomsbury.

Shah, Svati. 2006. 'Producing the Spectacle of Kamathipura: The Politics of Red Light Visibility in Mumbai'. *Cultural Dynamics* 18(3): 269–92.

Shani, Ornit. 2007. *Communalism, Caste and Hindu Nationalism: The Violence in Gujarat*. Cambridge: Cambridge University Press.

Shankar, Shylashree. and Pratap Bhanu Mehta. 2008. 'Courts and Socioeconomic Rights in India', in Varun Gauri and Daniel M. Brinks (eds), *Courting Social Justice: Judicial Enforcement of Social and Economic Rights in the Developing World*, pp. 147. Cambridge: Cambridge University Press.

Sharma, Arvind. 2002. 'On Hindu, Hindustān, Hinduism and Hindutva'. *Numen* 49(1): 1–36.

Sheikh, Danish. 2013. 'The Road to Decriminalization: Litigating India's Anti-Sodomy Law'. *Yale Human Rights and Development Journal* (16): 104–32.

Sheikh, Narmeen. 2007. *The Present as History: Critical Perspectives on Global Power*. New York: Columbia University Press.

Sherwin, Richard K. 2005. 'Anti-Oedipus, Lynch: Initiatory Rites and the Ordeal of Justice', in Austin Sarat, Lawrence Douglas, and Martha Merrill Umphrey (eds), *Law on the Screen*, pp. 106–52. Stanford: Stanford University Press.

———. 2011. *Visualizing Law in the Age of Digital Baroque: Arabesques and Entanglements*. Oxford: Routledge.

Shklar, Judith N. 1964. *Legalism: Law, Morals and Political Trials*. Cambridge: Harvard University Press.

Silbey, Jessica. 2014. 'Persuasive Visions: Film and Memory'. *Law, Culture and the Humanities* 10(1): 24–42.

Shulman, David. 2007. *Dark Hope: Working for Peace in Israel and Palestine*. Chicago: University of Chicago Press.

Simpson, Edward. 2006. 'The State of Gujarat and the Men without Souls'. *Critique of Anthropology* (26): 331–48.

Simpson, Gerry. 2015. 'The Sentimental Life of International Law'. *London Review of International Law* 3(1): 3–29.

Singh, Bhrigupati. 2011. 'Agonistic Intimacy and Moral Aspiration in Popular Hinduism: A Study in the Political Theology of the Neighbor'. *American Ethnologist* 38(3): 430–50.

Singh, M.P. and Surya Deva. 2005. 'The Constitution of India: Symbol of Unity in Diversity'. *Jahrbuch des of entlichen Rechts der Gegenwart* (*Yearbook of Public Law*, Germany) (53): 649–86.

Singh, M.P. 2001. *V.N. Shukla's Constitution of India*, pp. 175. Lucknow: Eastern Book Company.

Singh, Pritam. 2005. 'Hindu Bias in India's Secular Constitution: Probing Flaws in the Instruments of Government'. *Third World Quarterly* 26(6): 909–26.

Singh, Ujjwal Kumar. 2007. *The State, Democracy and Anti-terror Laws in India*. New Delhi: SAGE.

Sircar, Oishik. 2008. 'Questions of Visibility'. *In Plainspeak* (2): 10–17.

———. 2009. 'The Fallacy of Equality: "Anti-Citizens", Sexual Justice and the Law in India', in Ashok Agrwaal and Bharat Bushan (eds), *Justice and Law: The Limits of the Deliverables of Law, Vol. II: State of Justice in India: Issues of Social Justice*, pp. 210. New Delhi: SAGE.

———. 2010. *Sexing Spaces of Emancipation: The Politics and Poetics of Sexuality within the World Social Forum Process*, Critical Engagement Occasional Paper 9, Critical Action Centre in Movement, New Delhi.

———. 2011. 'Some Paradoxes of Human Rights: Fragmented Refractions in Neoliberal Times'. *Journal of Indian Law & Society* (2): 182–228.

———. 2012. 'Spectacles of Emancipation: Reading Rights Differently in India's Legal Discourse'. *Osgoode Hall Law Journal* 49(3): 527.

———. 2013a. 'Spectacles of Emancipation: Reading Rights Differently in India's Legal Discourse'. *Osgoode Hall Law Journal* 49(3): 527–73.

———. 2015. 'Doing and Undoing Feminism: A Jurisdictional Journey'. *Economic and Political Weekly* 50(20): 44–7.

———. 2017. 'New Queer Politics in the New India: Notes on Failure and Stuckness in a Negative Moment'. *Unbound: Harvard Journal of the Legal Left* (11): 1–36.

———. 2018. 'Doing and Undoing Feminism: A Jurisdictional Journey', in Romit Chowdhury and Zaid Al Baset (eds), *Men and Feminism in India*, pp. 73–99. New Delhi: Routledge.

Sircar, Oishik and Debolina Dutta. 2012. 'Beyond Compassion: Children of Sex Workers in Kolkata's Sonagachi'. *Childhood* 18(3): 333–49.

Sircar, Oishik and Dipika Jain. 2012. 'New Intimacies/Old Desires: Law, Culture and Queer Politics in Neoliberal Times'. *Jindal Global Law Review* 4(1): 1–2.

Sircar, Oishik and Dipika Jain. 2017. 'Of Powerful Feelings and Facile Gestures', in Oishik Sircar & Dipika Jain (eds), *New Intimacies, Old Desires: Law, Culture and Queer Politics in Neoliberal Times*. New Delhi: Zubaan.

Sircar, Oishik, Ratna Kapur, and Brenda Cossman. 2016. 'The Fraught Terrain of Law and Feminism: 20 Years of Subversive Sites'. *Socio-Legal Review* 21(1): 133–63.

Slattery, Kate. 2003. 'Drowning Not Waving: The "Children Overboard" Event and Australia's Fear of the Other'. *Media International Australia* (109): 93.

Smith, Linda Tuhiwai. 1999. *Decolonizing Methodologies: Research and Indigenous Peoples.* London: Zed Books.

Solnit, Rebecca. 2014. *Men Explain Things to Me and Other Essays*. London: Granta.

Sontag, Susan. 1966. *Against Interpretation and Other Essays.* New York: Picador.

———. 2007. *At the Same Time: Essays and Speeches.* New York: Farrar, Straus, and Giroux.

Sood, Nikita. 2012. *Liberalization, Hindu Nationalism and The State: A Biography of Gujarat.* New Delhi: Oxford University Press.

Spivak, Gayatri Chakravorty. 1993. *Outside in the Teaching Machine.* New York: Routledge.

———.1994. 'Responsibility'. *boundary 2,* 21(3): 19–64.

———. 2012. *An Aesthetic Education in the Era of Globalization*. Cambridge: Harvard University Press.

———. 1998. 'Can the Subaltern Speak?', in Cary Nelson and Lawrence Grossberg (eds), *Marxism and The Interpretation of Culture,* pp. 271–314. Urbana: University of Illinois Press.

———. 2012. *An Aesthetic Education in the Era of Globalization*. Cambridge: Harvard University Press.

———. 2012. 'Culture: Situating Feminism', in *An Aesthetic Education in the Era of Globalization*, pp. 123. Cambridge: Harvard University Press.

———. 'Translator's Preface', in Jacques Derrida, *Of Grammatology*. New Delhi: Motilal Banarsidass Publishers.

Spodek, Howard. 2010. 'In the Hindutva Laboratory: Pogroms and Politics in Gujarat, 2002'. *Modern Asian Studies* 44(2): 349–99.

———. 2011. *Ahmedabad: Shock City of Twentieth-Century India*. Bloomington: Indiana University Press.

Sundar, Nandini. 2016. *The Burning Forest: India's War in Bastar*. New Delhi: Juggernaut.

Sud, Atul (ed.). 2012. *Poverty Amidst Prosperity; Essays on the Trajectory of Development in Gujarat*. New Delhi: Aakar Books.

Taggart, Michael. 2002. 'Gardens or Graveyards of Scholarship? Festschriften in the Literature of the Common Law'. *Oxford Journal of Legal Studies* 22(2): 227–52.

Taylor, McComas. 2014. 'Hindu Activism and Academic Censorship in India'. *South Asia: Journal of South Asian Studies* (37): 717.

Tellis, Ashley. 2012. 'Disrupting the Dinner Table: Rethinking the "Queer Movement" in Contemporary India'. *Jindal Global Law Review* 4(1): 142–56.

Tellis, Ashley and Sruti Bala (eds). 2015. *The Global Trajectories of Queerness: Rethinking Same-Sex Politics in the Global South*. Amsterdam: Brill Rodopi.

Teltumbde, Anand. 2010. *The Persistence of Caste: The Khairlanji Murders and India's Hidden Apartheid*. New Delhi: Navayana.

———. 2016. 'Modi's Faux Pas on Ambedkar'. *Economic and Political Weekly* 51(16): 23.

———. 2018. *Republic of Caste: Thinking Equality in the Time of Neoliberal Hindutva*. New Delhi: Navayana.

Thobani, Sunera. 2014. 'Performing Terror, Mediating Religion: Indian Cinema and the Politics of National Belonging'. *International Journal of Communication* (8): 483–505.

Thornton, Margaret. 1998. 'The Development of Feminist Jurisprudence'. *Legal Education Review* 9(2): 171.

———. 2012. *Privatizing the Public University: The Case of Law*. New York: Routledge.

Tomlins, Christopher (ed.). 2017. 'Law As… Minor Jurisprudence in Historical Key'. *Law Text Culture* (21).

Toner, Anne. 2015. *Ellipsis in English Literature: Signs of Omission*. Cambridge: Cambridge University Press.

Triggs, Gillian. 2014. *The Forgotten Children: National Inquiry into Children in Immigration Detention*. Sydney: Australian Human Rights Commission.

Tripathi, Salil. 1997. 'Sarasvati Unleashed'. *Index on Censorship* 26(6): 90–1.

Twining, William (ed.). 2009. *Human Rights, Southern Voices: Francis Deng, Abdullahi An-Na'im, Yash Ghai and Upendra Baxi*. Cambridge: Cambridge University Press.

Uberoi, Patricia. 2006. *Freedom and Destiny: Gender, Family and Popular Culture in India*. New Delhi: Oxford University Press.

Udayakumar, S. P. 1997. 'Historicizing Myth and Mythologizing History: The "Ram Temple" Drama'. *Social Scientist* 25(7–8): 11.

———. 2005. *'Presenting' the Past: Anxious History and Ancient Future in Hindutva India*. Westport: Praeger.

Vaid, Minnie. 2011. *A Doctor to Defend: The Binayak Sen Story*. New Delhi: Rajpal & Sons.

Van Marle, Karin. 2007. 'Laughter, Refusal, Friendship: Thoughts on a "Jurisprudence of Generosity"'. *Stellenbosch Law Review* (1): 194–206.

———. 2013. 'Liminal Landscape: Law, Literature and Landscape in Post-apartheid South Africa', in Karin Van Marle and Stewart Motha (eds), *Genres of Critique: Law, Aesthetics and Liminality*, pp. 109–22. Stellenbosch: African Sun Media.

Vashist, Latika and Jyoti Dogra Sood (eds). 2020. *Rethinking Law and Violence*. New Delhi: Oxford University Press.

Vanita, Ruth and Saleem Kidwai (eds). 2000. *Same Sex Love in India: Readings From Literature And History*. New York: Palgrave Macmillan.

Varadarajan, Siddharth (ed.). 2002. *Gujarat: The Making of a Tragedy*. New Delhi: Penguin Books.

Varughese, Anil Mathew. 2014. 'Globalization and Culture Wars: The Case of India', in Richard Sandbrook and Ali Burak Güven (eds), *Civilizing Globalization: A Survivor's Guide*, pp. 93–108. Albany: SUNY Press.

Vasudevan, Ravi. 2012. 'Aesthetics and Politics in Popular Cinema', in Vasudha Dalmia and Rashmi Sadana (eds), *The Cambridge Companion to Modern Indian Culture*, pp. 233. Cambridge: Cambridge University Press.

Verma, Preeti (ed.). 2004. *The Terror of POTA and Other Security Legislation in India*. New Delhi: Human Rights Law Network.

Virdi, Jyotika. 2003. *The Cinematic ImagiNation: Indian Popular Films as Social History*. New Jersey: Rutgers University Press.

Vissman, Cornelia. 2008. 'Image and Law—A Troubled Relationship'. *Parallax* 14(4): 1–9.

Visvanathan, Shiv and Teesta Setalvad. 2014. 'Narratives of Vulnerability and Violence: Retelling the Gujarat Riots', in Anique Hommels, Jessica

Mesman, and Wiebe E. Bijker (eds), *Vulnerability in Technological Cultures: New Directions in Research and Governance*, pp. 109–30. Cambridg: MIT Press.

Wariavwalla, Bharat. 2000. 'Religion and Nationalism in India: Ram the God of the Hindu Nation'. *Round Table: Commonwealth Journal of International Affairs* 89(357) :593.

Weizman, Eyal. 2006. 'Lethal Theory'. *Log*, Winter/ Spring (7): 53–77.

Williams, Patricia J. 1992. *The Alchemy of Race and Rights: Diary of a Law Professor.* Cambridge: Harvard University Press.

Williams, Raymond. 1988. *Keywords: A Vocabulary of Culture and Society.* London: Fontana Press.

———. 2001. *The Long Revolution.* Peterborough: Broadview Press.

Woodward, Kathleen. 2004. "Calculating Compassion," in Lauren Berlant (ed.), *Compassion: The Cultures and Politics of an Emotion*, pp. 59-86. New York: Routledge.

Wolfe, Patrick. 1997. 'Should the Subaltern Dream? "Australian Aborigines" and the Problem of Ethnographic Ventriloquism', in S.C. Humphreys (ed.), *Cultures of Scholarship*, pp. 57–94. Ann Arbor: The University of Michigan Press.

Yagnik, Achyut and Suchitra Sheth. 2005. *The Shaping of Modern Gujarat: Plurality, Hindutva, and Beyond.* New Delhi: Penguin Books.

Young, Alison. 1997. 'Murder in the Eyes of the Law', *Studies in Law, Politics and Society*, (17): 31–58.

Young, James E. 2000. *At Memory's Edge: After-Images of the Holocaust in Contemporary Art and Architecture.* New Haven: Yale University Press.

Yue, Audrey. 2008. 'Same-Sex Migration in Australia: From Interdependency to Intimacy'. *GLQ: Journal of Lesbian and Gay Studies* (14): 239.

———. 2014. 'Queer Asian Australian Migration Stories: Intimate Archives Big and Small'. *Sinister Wisdom: A Multicultural Lesbian Literary & Art Journal* (94): 114.

Online and Media Sources

Agarwal, Vibhuti. 2013. 'The Ishrat Jahan Case, An Explainer'. *The Wall Street Journal* blog. Accessible on http://blogs.wsj.com/indiarealtime/2013/07/05/the-ishrat-jahan-case-an-explainer/; last accessed 5 July 2019.

Agence France-Presse (AFP). 2016. Hindu Sena celebrates Trump's victory in US presidential election, *Hindustan Times*, 9 November. Accesssible on http://www.hindustantimes.com/india-news/hindu-sena-celebrates-trump-s-victory-inus-presidential-election/story-z4Dk-WJRITC06cvDnfyUemJ.html; last accessed 5 July 2019.

Ahmad, Tufail. 2017. 'Abrahamic Hindutva: The Religious Fundamentalism That Is a Threat to India's Tolerant and Pluralist Civilisational Order', *Firstpost*, 18 July. Accessible on https://www.firstpost.com/india/abrahamic-hindutva-the-religious-fundamentalism-that-is-a-threat-to-indias-tolerant-and-pluralist-civilisational-order-2-3825669.html; last accessed 5 July 2019.

Ahmed, Sara. 2014. 'White Men', *Feministkilljoys*, 4 November. Accessible on https://feministkilljoys.com/2014/11/04/white-men/; last accessed 5 July 2019.

Allan, Jonathan A. 2016. 'The Paranoid Anus', *Zed Books* blog, 9 August. Accessible on https://www.zedbooks.net/blog/posts/the-paranoid-anus/; last accessed 5 July 2019.

Ambedkar, Bhimrao Ramji. 1940. *Pakistan or the Partition of India*. Accessible on http://www.columbia.edu/itc/mealac/pritchett/00ambedkar/ambedkar_partition/; last accessed 5 July 2019.

Amnesty International. 2012. *A Decade On from the Gujarat Riots, an Overwhelming Majority of Victims Await Justice in India*, April. Accessible on http://www.amnesty.org/en/library/asset/ASA20/006/2012/en/e77dabb7-151f-410e-93c9-68513bd3eebc/asa200062012en.html, last accessed 5 July 2019.

Ashraf, Ajaz. 2015. 'Ban Triple Talaq and Abolish Muslim Personal Law Board, Says Former Minorities Commission Chairman', *Scroll*. Accessible on http://scroll.in/article/724902/ban-triple-talaq-and-abolish-muslim-personal-law-board-says-former-minorities-commission-chairman; last accessed 5 July 2019.

Associated Press. 2006. 'Dutch Immigrants Must Watch Racy Film'. Fox News. Accessible on http://www.foxnews.com/story/2006/03/16/dutch-immigrants-must-watch-racy-film.html, last accessed 5 July 2013.

Badgett, Mary Virginia Lee. 2014. 'The Economic Cost of Homphobia and the Exclusion of LGBT People: A Case Study of India', World Bank. Accessible on https://www.worldbank.org/content/dam/Worldbank/document/SAR/economic-costs-homophobia-lgbt-exlusion-india.pdf, last accessed 5 July 2019.

Bal, Hartosh Singh. 2018. 'Spare Me the Good Hindu: The Hindu vs Hindutva Battle Is Meaningless in Shaping Our Politics', *Caravan*, 6 July. Accessible on <http://www.caravanmagazine.in/politics/hindu-vs-hindutva-battle-meaningless-in-shaping-our-politics; last accessed 5 July 2019.

Baxi, Pratiksha: 2013. 'Suresh Koushal vs Naz Foundation', *Kafila*. Accessible on http://kafila.org/2013/12/16/suresh-koushal-v-naz-foundation-pratiksha-baxi/; last accessed 5 July 2019.

Baxi, Upendra. 2014b. 'Unlearning the Law with Lotika Sarkar'. The 1st Lotika Sarkar Memorial Lecture, Campus Law Centre, University of Delhi, 22 February, pp. 2, 12 Accessible on https://www.academia.edu/8360054/2014._Unlearning_the_Law_with_Lotika_Sarkar; last accessed 5 July 2019.

———. 2016. 'In This Democracy, We Must Not Distrust or Suspect Dissent, or Disagree with It'. Interview with Upendra Baxi, *Caravan*, 24 April. Accessible on https://caravanmagazine.in/vantage/democracy-must-not-distrust-suspect-dissent-disagree; last accessed 5 July 2019.

2002. 'Bhopal Activists Freed', BBC News. Accessible on http://news.bbc.co.uk/2/hi/south_asia/2513883.stm;last accessed 5 July 2019.

Berlant, Lauren. 2014. 'Sitting On a Plane, a Mule', *Berfois*. Accessible on http://www.berfrois.com/2014/12/lauren-berlant-flies/; last accessed 5 July 2019.

Bhattacharya, Sayan. 2015. 'The Cool Queers', *Kindle*. Accessible on http://kindlemag.in/cool-queers/; last accessed 5 July 2019.

Bhattacharya, Stuti. 2014. 'Photo Essay–Delhi Pride Parade 2014', *Inpec Magazine*. Accessible on http://inpecmagazine.com/2014/12/07/photo-essay-delhi-pride-parade-2014/;last accessed 5 July 2019.

Bhusan, Prashant. 2001. 'Judges in Their Own Cause-I', *The Hindu*. Accessible on http://www.hindu.com/2001/09/04/stories/05042524.htm; last accessed 5 July 2019.

———. 2006. 'The Judiciary: Cutting Edge of a Predator State', *Countercurrents.org*. Accessible on http://www.countercurrents.org/hr-bhushan071206.htm; last accessed 5 July 2019.

Borges, Andre. 2015. 'This Guy's Mom Wanted to Find Him a Husband, So She Placed India's First Gay "Groom Wanted" Ad', *Buzzfeed*. Accessible on http://www.buzzfeed.com/andreborges/first-gay-matrimonial-groom-wanted-ad#.erywMDn6W; last accessed 5 July 2019.

Boyce, Paul and Aniruddha Dutta. 2013. 'Vulnerability of Gay and Transgender Indians Goes Way Beyond Section 377'. *The Conversation*. Accessible on https://theconversation.com/vulnerability-of-gay-and-transgender-indians-goes-way-beyond-section-377-21392; last accessed 5 July 2019.

2014. '"India First" Should be Govt's Religion and "Constitution" Its Holy Book': Narendra Modi, *Business Standard*. Accessible on http://www.business-standard.com/video-gallery/general/india-first-should-be-govt-s-religion-and-constitution-its-holy-book-narendra-modi-3442/

india-first-should-be-govt-s-religion-and-constitution-its-holy-book-narendra-modi-6767.htm; last accessed 5 July 2019.

Chakraborty, Mridula Nath. 2015. 'Same-Sex and Other Desires: Asian Diversity in the Face of Australian Decadence', *Southern Crossings*. Accessible on http://southerncrossings.com.au/arts-and-culture/same-sex-and-other-desires-asian-diversity-in-the-face-of-australian-decadence/; last accessed 5 July 2019.

Chandrasekhar, Aruna. 2017. 'A Successful Protest Against a Chhattisgarh Mine Highlights the Failure of India's Coal Auctions', *The Wire*, 10 October. Accessible on https://thewire.in/175055/chhattisgarh-mine-protest-coal-auctions/; last accessed 5 July 2019.

Choksi, Mansi. 2014. 'Narendra Modi's Shame: Muslim Survivors of the Gujarat Riots are Still Suffering', Vice News, *Vice*. Accessible on https://news.vice.com/article/narendra-modis-shame-muslim-survivors-of-the-gujarat-riots-are-still-suffering; last accessed 5 July 2019.

Citizen's Initiative. 2002. *The Survivors Speak: How has the Gujarat Massacre Affected Minority Women*. Outlook. Accessible on http://www.outlookindia.com/article.aspx?215433; last accessed 5 July 2019.

Cole, Daniel H., Aurelian Craiutu. 2018. 'The Many Deaths of Liberalism', *Aeon*, 28 June. Accessible on https://aeon.co/essays/reports-of-the-demise-of-liberalism-are-greatly-exaggerated; last accessed 5 July 2019.

Concerned Citizens Tribunal. 2002. 'Crime Against Humanity', *Sabrang*. Accessible on http://www.sabrang.com/tribunal/index.html; last accessed 5 July 2019.

Concerned Citizens Tribunal. 2002. *Crimes Against Humanity: An Enquiry into the Carnage in Gujarat, Vol. 1*, Mumbai: Citizens for Justice and Peace. Accessible on: https://www.sabrang.com/tribunal/tribunal1.pdf; last accessed 5 July 2019.

Corbet, Deanne, 2006. 'Testing the Limits of Tolerance', *Deutsche Welle (DW)*. Accessible on http://dw.de/p/87cC; last accessed 5 July 2019.

Craig, Carys J., Joseph F. Turcotte, and Rosemary J. Coombe. 2011. 'What's Feminist About Open Access? A Relational Approach to Copyright in the Academy', *Feminists@law* 1(1). Accessible on http://journals.kent.ac.uk/index.php/feministsatlaw/article/view/7/54; last accessed 5 July 2019.

Crenshaw, Kimberlé. Facebook 2015. Accessible on https://www.facebook.com/kimberle.crenshaw/posts/10153367636743851?fref=nf); last accessed 5 July 2019.

Dalrymple, William, 2014. 'Narendra Modi: Man of the Masses', *New Statesman*. Accessible on http://www.newstatesman.com/politics/2014/05/narendra-modi-man-masses; last accessed 5 July 2019.

Dayal, John. 2015. '300 Days: Documenting Sangh Hate and Communal Violence Under the Modi Regime: Interim Report'. Accessible on https://www.sabrang.com/news/2015/ReportModi300days.pdf; last accessed 5 July 2019.

Debroy, Bibek. 2012. 'Why State Emblem "Satyameva Jayate" Has Vanished Both Literally & Symbolically', *Economic Times*, 4 June. Accessible on https://economictimes.indiatimes.com/opinion/et-commentary/why-state-emblem-satyameva-jayate-has-vanished-both-literally-symbolically/articleshow/13794181.cms; last accessed 5 July 2019.

Dembowski, Hans. 2009. 'Academic Freedom Only for the Online Avatar? Calcutta High Court Puts Limits on Sociological Debate'. Paper presented at 1st LASSNet Conference, Jawaharlal Nehru University, New Delhi, 10 January. Accessible on http://www.lassnet.org/2009/readings/dembowski2008academic-freedom.pdf; last accessed 5 July 2019.

Dey, A. 2009. 'Government the Biggest Litigant in the State', *Times News Network*. Accessible on http://articles.timesofindia.indiatimes.com/2009-02-10/jaipur/28004985_1_cases-biggest-litigant-lawyers; last accessed 5 July 2019.

Duggan, Lisa. 2015. 'He Does Class and Race, She Does Gender and Sexuality (And Class and Race): Heteronormativity in the Left Academy', *Bullybloggers*. Accessible on https://bullybloggers.wordpress.com/2015/04/04/he-does-class-and-race-she-does-gender-and-sexuality-and-class-and-race-heteronormativity-in-the-left-academy/; last accessed 5 July 2019.

Express News Service. 2015. 'India Votes Against Gay Rights for UN Employees', *The Indian Express*. Accessible on http://indianexpress.com/article/india/india-others/india-votes-against-gay-rights-for-un-employees/; last accessed 5 July 2019.

Faleiro, Sonia. 2006. 'The willing who want it legalised', *Tehelka*. Accessible on: www.tehelka.com/story_main18.asp?filename=Cr052006The_willing.asp; last accessed 5 July 2019.

Fernandes, Jason Keith. 2009. 'The Dilemma after the Decision: Stray thoughts after Gay Liberation', *Notes of an Itinerant Mendicant*. Accessible on http://dervishnotes.blogspot.com/2009/08/dilemma-after-decision-strays-thoughts.html; last accessed on 5 July 2019.

FP Staff. 2013a. 'BJP Will Not Support "Unnatural" Homosexuality: Rajnath Singh', *Firstpost*. Accessible on http://www.firstpost.com/politics/bjp-will-not-support-unnatural-homosexuality-rajnath-singh-1286933.html; last accessed 5 July 2019.

FP Politics. 2013b. 'Here It Comes: An Apology from Modi for Gujarat Riots', *Firstpost*. Accessible on http://www.firstpost.com/politics/here-it-comes-an-apology-from-modi-for-gujarat-riots-680400.html; last accessed 5 July 2019.

Flock, Elizabeth. 2009. 'The Law Breaker', *Business*. Accessible on http://business.in.com/printcontent/8082; last accessed 5 July 2019.

First Post Politics. 2015. 'Gowda Flip-flops on Scrapping Sec 377, Swamy Says Homosexuality a "Genetic Disorder"', *Firstpost*. Accessible on http://www.firstpost.com/politics/kabhi-haan-kabhi-naa-gowda-flip-flops-on-scrapping-sec-377-swamy-says-homosexuality-a-genetic-disorder-2318852.html; last accessed 5 July 2019.

Fraser, Nancy. 2013b. 'How Feminism became Capitalism's Handmaiden–and How to Reclaim It', *The Guardian*. Accessible on http://www.theguardian.com/commentisfree/2013/oct/14/feminism-capitalist-handmaiden-neoliberal; last accessed 5 July 2019.

Gahlot, Mandakini. 2015. 'High-Risk Behaviour', *Caravan*. Accessible on http://www.caravanmagazine.in/reportage/government-apathy-india-aids-programme; last accessed 5 July 2019.

Gayen S. 2005. 'Letters to editor: Nightmares on celluloid'. *The Telegraph*, 1 March. Accessible on https://www.telegraphindia.com/opinion/letters-to-editor-15-03-2005/cid/1022371; last accessed 5 July 2019.

Ghufran, Iram. 2013. 'No Redemption Without Justice', *Outlook*. Accessible on http://www.outlookindia.com/article/no-redemption-without-justice/284592; last accessed 5 July 2019.

Grant, Kelly. 2012. 'Group That Dare Not Speak Its Name to March in Toronto's Pride Parade Anyway', *The Globe and Mail*. Accessible on http://www.theglobeandmail.com/news/toronto/group-that-dare-not-speak-its-name-to-march-in-torontos-pride-parade-anyway/article4189686; last accessed 5 July 2019.

Greenpeace Press Release. 2005. 'Bhopal Activists Brutally Assaulted and Arrested for Demanding Clean Drinking Water', 19 May. Accessible on http://www.greenpeace.org/india/press/releases/bhopal-activists-brutally-assa; last accessed 5 July 2019.

Gupte, Manisha. et al. 2007. *In the Name of Rescue: A Report of the Fact Finding Committee Investigation into the Molestation/ Rape of a Minor Girl by a Decoy Customer in Uttamnagar, Miraj, Maharashtra*, 12 May 2006. Accessible on http://web.nswp.org/pdf/20070512-MirajFactFindingReport.pdf; last accessed 5 July 2019.

Haider, Suhasini. 2015. 'India Vote at U.N. Not Anti-gay, Explains Government', *The Hindu*. Accessible on http://www.thehindu.com/news/national/india-vote-at-un-not-antigay-explains-government/article7032970.ece; last accessed 5 July 2019.

Halberstam, Jack. 2012. 'Failure and the Future of Queer Studies', *Bullybloggers*. Accessible on http://bullybloggers.wordpress.com/2012/04/02/bullybloggers-on-failure-and-the-future-of-queer-studies; last accessed 5 July 2019.

Harrison, Michael. 2018. '"Logocentrism", The Chicago School of Media Theory: Keywords'. Accessible on https://lucian.uchicago.edu/blogs/mediatheory/keywords/logocentrism/; last accessed 5 July 2019.

Hazra, Indrajit. 2012. 'The Forgotten Man', *Hindustan Times*. Accessible on http://www.hindustantimes.com/indrajithazra/the-forgotten-man/article1-820381.aspx; last accessed 5 July 2019.

HT Correspondent. 2013. 'Modi Gets Relief in 2002 Riots, Tweets "Truth Alone Triumphs"; Zakia Jafri Says Won't Give Up', *Hindustan Times*. Accessible on http://www.hindustantimes.com/india-news/modi-gets-relief-in-2002-riots-tweets-truth-alone-triumphs-zakia-jafri-says-won-t-give-up/article1-1166526.aspx; last accessed 5 July 2019.

Human Rights Watch Report. 2002. *We Have No Orders to Save You*. Accessible on http://www.hrw.org/reports/2002/india/; last accessed 5 July 2019.

Inani, Rohit. 2015. 'Mother Posts India's First Gay Marriage Advert to Seek Groom for Her Son', *Time*. Accessible on http://time.com/3891962/india-gay-homosexual-lgbt-rights-marriage-advert/; last accessed 5 July 2019.

'Indian Politics Under Modi', *Social Text*. Accessible on http://socialtext-journal.org/periscope_topic/indian-politics-under-modi/; last accessed 5 July 2019.

IndiaSpend Team. 2015. 'Despots, Religious Extremists: Company India Keeps on Gay Rights', *IndiaSpend*. Accessible on http://www.indiaspend.com/special-reports/despots-religious-extremists-company-india-keeps-on-gay-rights-88767; last accessed 5 July 2019.

Iyer, Harish. 2015. Twitter. Accessible on https://twitter.com/hiyer/status/600601846722334720?ref_src=twsrc%5Etfw; last accessed 5 July 2019.

Jain Nair, Rupam. 2015. 'Zakia Jafri Fights Narendra Modi in "Final" Court Battle Over Deadly Riots', *Reuters*, 22 September. Accessible on http://in.reuters.com/article/narendramodi-zakia-ehsanteesta-riots-idINKCN0RL2G720150922; last accessed 5 July 2019.

Jaffrelot, Christophe. 2008. 'Hindu Nationalism and the (Not So Easy) Art of Being Outraged: The *Ram Setu* Controversy' 2 *South Asia Multidisciplinary Academic Journal* (online). Accessible on https://journals.openedition.org/samaj/1372; last accessed 5 July 2019.

———. 2012. 'Gujarat 2002: What Justice for the Victims?', *Economic and Political Weekly*, 47(8): 77–89.

Janmohamed, Zahir. 2013. 'Kai Po Che and the Reduction of 2002', *Kafila*. Accessible on http://kafila.org/2013/03/02/kai-po-che-and-the-reduction-of-2002-zahir-janmohamed/; last accessed 5 July 2019.

Johari, Aarefa. 2015. 'At Delhi Pride March, Jaitley's Support for Gay Rights Draws Both Bouquets and Brickbats', *Scroll*. Accessible on http://scroll.

in/article/772467/at-delhi-pride-march-jaitleys-support-for-gay-rights-draws-both-bouquets-and-brickbats; last accessed 5 July 2019.

John, Arshu. 2017. 'The Professional Fortunes of Cops, Bureaucrats and SIT Members Associated with the 2002 Godhra Investigation', *Caravan*, 22 September. Accessible on http://www.caravanmagazine.in/vantage/postings-cops-bureaucrats-sit-members-godhra-2002-investigation; last accessed 5 July 2019.

Johri, Aarefa. 2015. 'I Was Sick of the Hateful Climate in Gujarat: Judge Explains Why He Quit after the Riots', *Scroll*, 7 August. Accessible on https://scroll.in/article/746832/i-was-sick-of-the-hateful-climate-in-gujarat-judge-explains-why-he-quit-after-the-riots; last accessed 5 July 2019.

Johri, Vikram. 2016a. 'India's First Lesbian Ad is Actually Wonderful', *Daily O*. Accessible on http://www.dailyo.in/lifestyle/myntra-anouk-ad-bold-is-beautiful-lesbians/story/1/4243.html; last accessed 5 July 2019.

———. 2016b. 'I am a Gay Indian Man and Still Lean To the Right. Here's Why', *Scroll*. Accessible on http://scroll.in/article/816569/i-am-a-gay-indian-man-and-still-lean-to-the-right-heres-why; last accessed 5 July 2019.

Katakam, Anupama. 2012. 'A Decade of Shame', *Frontline*. Accessible on http://www.frontline.in/static/html/fl2904/stories/20120309290400400.htm; last accessed 5 July 2019.

Katyal, Akhil. 2015. 'The Homo Pathetic', *Readings*. Accessible on http://akhilkatyal.blogspot.com.au/2015/01/the-homo-pathetic.html; last accessed 5 July 2019.

Khan, Ayesha. 2004. 'In Best Bakery City, They are Lining Up To Watch *Dev*'s Aaliya', *The Indian Express*. Accessible on http://expressindia.indianexpress.com/news/fullstory.php?newsid=32798; last accessed 5 July 2019.

Krishnan, Vidya. 2016. 'Diluted HIV Bill Leaves Activists Shocked', *The Hindu*. Accessible on http://www.thehindu.com/todays-paper/tp-national/Diluted-HIV-Bill-leaves-activists-shocked/article16673389.ece; last accessed 5 July 2019.

Kumar, Pramod G. 2014. 'RSS softens stand of homosexuality: Will BJP scrap Sec. 377?', *Firstpost*. Accessible on http://www.firstpost.com/politics/rss-softens-stand-on-homosexuality-will-bjp-scrap-section-377-1546469.html; last accessed 5 July 2019.

Kumara, K. and K. Jones. 2008. 'India: Supreme Court Judge Advocates "Animal Rights" for Alleged Terrorists', *World Socialist Website*. Accessible on http://www.wsws.org/articles/2009/feb2009/indi-f20.shtml; last accessed 5 July 2019.

Lenin, Vladimir Ilyich. 1999. 'What Is To Be Done? Burning Questions for Our Movement', *Marxists Internet Archive*. Accessible on https://www.marxists.org/archive/lenin/works/1901/witbd/; last accessed 5 July 2019.

Lewis, Ricki. 1996. 'Festschriften Honor Exceptional Scientific Careers, Scholarly Influences', *The Scientist*, 2 September. Accessible on https://www.the-scientist.com/?articles.view/articleNo/18041/title/Festschriften-Honor-Exceptional-Scientific-Careers-Scholarly-Influences/; last accessed 5 July 2019.

Liang, Lawrence. 2016. 'Jana Gana Mana and the Danger of Passing Sentiment as Law', *The Wire*. Accessible on http://thewire.in/83606/jana-gana-mana-dangers-passing-sentiment-law/; last accessed 5 July 2019.

Loewenstein, Anthony. 2014. '" Feminism Lite" Is Letting Down the Women Who Need It the Most', *The Guardian*. Accessible on https://www.theguardian.com/commentisfree/2014/oct/28/feminism-lite-is-letting-down-the-women-who-need-it-the-most; last accessed 5 July 2019.

Loza, Susana. 2014. 'Hashtag Feminism, #SolidarityIsForWhiteWomen, and the Other #FemFuture', *Ada: A Journal of Gender, New Media, and Technology*, Issue 5. Accessible on http://adanewmedia.org/2014/07/issue5-loza/; last accessed 5 July 2019.

Mahapatra, D. 2008. 'Dissenter Judge during Emergency Forgotten', Times News Network 2008. Accessible on http://articles.timesofindia.indiatimes.com/2008-03-03/india/27760185_1_fundamental-rights-constitution-judgment/2; last accessed 5 July 2019.

Manayath, Nithin. 2013. 'Why Marriage Equality May Not Be That Equal', *Tehelka*. Accessible on http://old.tehelka.com/why-marriage-equality-may-not-be-that-equal/; last accessed 5 July 2019.

Mander, Harsh . 2017. 'Where Are India's Dissenting Hindus?' *The Wire*, 12 April. Accessible on https://thewire.in/123008/india-hindutva-narendra-modi-rss-muslims/; last accessed 5 July 2019.

Marx, Karl. 2002. 'Theses on Feuerbach', Marxists.org. Accessible on https://www.marxists.org/archive/marx/works/1845/theses/theses.htm; last accessed 5 July 2019.

Mazumdar, Ranjani . 2003. 'The Bombay Film Poster', *Seminar*. Accessible on http://www.india-seminar.com/2003/525/525%20ranjani%20mazumdar.htm; last accessed 5 July 2019.

Mbembe, Achille. 2015. *Decolonizing Knowledge and the Question of the Archive*, University of Witwatersrand. Accessible on http://wiser.wits.ac.za/system/files/Achille%20Mbembe%20-%20Decolonizing%20Knowledge%20and%20the%20Question%20of%20the%20Archive.pdf; last accessed 5 July 2019.

Menon, Madhavi. 2015. 'Outrage over India's Vote Against Benefits To Same-Sex Couples Because of Homophilia or Islamophobia?', *The Economic Times*. Accesible on http://economictimes.indiatimes.com/magazines/panache/outrage-over-indias-vote-against-benefits-to-same-sex-couples-because-of-homophilia-or-islamophobia/articleshow/46807937.cms; last accessed 5 July 2019.

Menon, Parvathi. 2004. 'Censoring Freedom', *Frontline*. Accessible on http://www.frontline.in/static/html/fl2117/stories/20040827003210300.htm; last accessed 5 July 2019.

Mikdashi, Maya. 2011. 'Gay Rights as Human Rights: Pinkwashing Homonationalism', *Jadaliyya*. Accessible on http://www.jadaliyya.com/pages/index/3560/gay-rights-as-human-rights_pinkwashing-homonationa; last accessed 5 July 2019.

Mishra, M. 2010. 'Aligargh Muslim University Professor Suspended for Being Gay', Times News Network, 18 February. Accessible on http://articles.timesofindia.indiatimes.com/2010-02-18/india/28118769_1_shrinivas-ramchandra-siras-rickshaw-puller-amu-campus; last accessed 5 July 2019.

Misra, R. K. 2015. 'Judge Who Convicted Modi's Minister in Riots Case Now Fears for Her Family', *Wire,* 23 July. Accessible on https://thewire.in/law/judge-who-convicted-modis-minister-in-riots-case-now-fears-for-her-family; last accessed 5 July 2019.

Modi, Narendra. 2002. 'Should We Run Relief Camps? Open Child Producing Centres?', *Outlook,* 30 September. Accessible on http://www.outlookindia.com/article/should-we-run-relief-camps-open-child-producing-centres/217398; last accessed 5 July 2019.

Mohan, Lalit. 2015. 'Gita in School: Religious Text or Philosophical Treatise?', *The Times of India*. Accessible on http://timesofindia.indiatimes.com/india/Gita-in-school-Religious-text-or-philosophical-treatise/articleshow/46180717.cms; last accessed 5 July 2019.

Mukherjee, Debashree. 2013. 'No Time For Grieving', *Outlook*. Accessible on http://www.outlookindia.com/article/no-time-for-grieving/284593; last accessed 5 July 2019.

Myntra. 2015. 'Anouk: Bold is Beautiful – The Visit', YouTube. Accessible on https://www.youtube.com/watch?v=Ef27m5ocK6Q; last accessed 5 July 2019.

Narrain, Siddharth. 2013. 'Policing Hijras', *Infochange Agenda,* March. Accessible on http://infochangeindia.org/agenda/access-to-justice/policing-hijras.html; last accessed 5 July 2019.

Nashrulla, Tasneem. 2013. '15 Heartening Ways Indian Brands and Bollywood Stars are Fighting for LGBT Rights', *Buzzfeed*. Accessible on http://www.

buzzfeed.com/tasneemnashrulla/15-heartening-ways-indian-brands-and-bollywood-are-fighting#.cbzG39enB; last accessed 5 July 2019.

———. 2013. 'Activists Plan 'Global Day of Rage' To Fight For India's LGBT Community', *Buzzfeed*. Accessible on http://www.buzzfeed.com/tasneemnashrulla/activists-plan-global-day-of-rage-to-fight-for-indias-lgbt-c#.cvKL2bax0; last accessed 5 July 2019.

Noorani, A. G. 2017. 'Modi and Zionism', *Frontline*, 4 August. Accessible on https://www.frontline.in/the-nation/modi-amp-zionism/article9774462.ece; Last Accessed 5 July 2019.

Nundy, Karuna. 2010. 'A Traffic Accident in Bhopal', *The Hindu*. Accessible on http://www.thehindu.com/opinion/op-ed/article450106.ece; last accessed 5 July 2019.

Nussbaum, Martha. 2004. 'Body of the Nation. Why Women were Mutilated in Gujarat', *Boston Review*. Accessible on http://bostonreview.net/martha-nussbaum-women-mutilated-gujarat; last accessed 5 July 2019.

Open Letters. The *New York Times*. Accessible on http://www.nytimes.com/packages/pdf/international/open_letter.pdf; last accessed 5 July 2019.

Pandya, Haresh. 2004. 'Govind Nihalani's Dev in Trouble', *Rediff India Abroad*. Accessible on http://www.rediff.com/movies/2004/jun/16dev.htm; last accessed 5 July 2019.

Patel, Aakar. 2013. 'Riot Act', *Caravan*. Accessible on http://www.caravan-magazine.in/perspectives/riot-act; last accessed 5 July 2019.

Pati, Bibhuti. 2012. 'Steel Plant Bludgeons Tribals in a Brutal Barter', *Tehelka*, 25 February, 9(8). Accessible on http://old.tehelka.com/steel-plant-bludgeons-tribals-in-a-brutal-barter/ last accessed 5 July 2019.

Pawar, Yogesh. 2013. 'Supreme Court Judgment on Section 377 Has Put the Clock Back By 150 Years: Gay Rights Activists', *Daily News & Analysis* (*DNA*). Accessible on http://www.dnaindia.com/india/report-supreme-court-judgment-on-section-377-has-turned-the-clock-back-by-150-years-gay-rights-activists-1933608; last accessed 5 July 2019.

Phadke, Shilpa. 2017. 'Why is the Government Threatened by Women's Studies Centres in Indian Universities?', *The Indian Express*, 15 June. Accessible on http://indianexpress.com/article/education/why-is-the-government-threatened-by-womens-studies-centres-in-indian-universities/; last accessed 5 July 2019.

Pisharoty, Sangeeta Barooah. 2013. 'It Is Like Reversing the Motion of the Earth', *The Hindu*. Accessible on http://www.thehindu.com/features/metroplus/society/it-is-like-reversing-the-motion-of-the-earth/article5483306.ece; last accessed 5 July 2019.

Press Trust of India. 2010. Supreme Court Snubs Govt. for Raising Naxal Bogey Against Rights Activists', *The Hindu*. Accessible on http://beta.

thehindu.com/news/national/article11511.ece; last accessed 5 July 2019.

———. 2014. Second FIR against Amit Shah for Muzaffarnagar 'Revenge' speech, *Live Mint*, April 6. Accessible on http://www.livemint.com/HomePage/bAa6OEGxWGs2k1TRcXr8hL/Amit-Shah-booked-for-revenge-speech-under-ECscrutiny.html; last accessed 5 July 2019.

———. 2014. 'Government Should Protect Gay Rights: Harsh Vardhan', *The Hindu*. Accessible on http://www.thehindu.com/news/national/government-should-protect-gay-rights-harsh-vardhan/article6220869.ece; last accessed 5 July 2019.

———. 2014. 'Ban Ki-moon to attend Vibrant Gujarat Summit – 2015', *The Economic Times*, 20 December. Accessible on https://economictimes.indiatimes.com/news/politics-and-nation/ban-ki-moon-to-attend-vibrant-gujarat-summit-2015/articleshow/45414391.cms?from=mdr; last accessed 5 July 2019.

———. 2015. 'Shashi Tharoor's Bill to Decriminalize Homosexuality Defeated in Lok Sabha', *The Indian Express*. Accessible on http://indianexpress.com/article/india/india-news-india/shashi-tharoors-bill-to-decriminalise-homosexuality-defeated-in-ls/; last accessed 5 July 2019.

Puar, Jasbir. 2010. 'Israel's Gay Propaganda War', *The Guardian*. Accessible on http://www.theguardian.com/commentisfree/2010/jul/01/israels-gay-propaganda-war; last accessed 5 July 2019.

Rajagopal, Arvind. 2011. 'Urban Segregation and the Special Political Zone in Ahmedabad: An Emerging Paradigm for Religio-political Violence'(Article 5), *South Asia Multidisciplinary Academic Journal* (online) . Accessible on https://journals.openedition.org/samaj/3285; last accessed 5 July 2019.

Rajalakshmi, T.K. 2003. 'Shifting Emphasis', *Frontline*, October. Accessible on http://www.frontline.in/static/html/fl2020/stories/20031010002108100.htm; last accessed 5 July 2019.

Rajkumar, Chemkuri Azad. 2010. 'A Last Note to a Neo-Colonialist', *Outlook*. Accessible on http://www.outlookindia.com/article.aspx?266164; last accessed 5 July 2019.

Ramanathan, Usha. 2002. 'Of Judicial Power', Frontline. Accessible on http://www.frontlineonnet.com/fl1906/19060300.htm; last accessed 5 July 2019.

Rehman, Teresa. 2011. 'Gaga Over Anna, Mute Over Irom Sharmila', *The Hoot* 2011. Accessible on http://www.thehoot.org/web/home/story.php?storyid=5468&pg=1&mod=1&sectionld=19&sectionname=ISSUES%201N%20MEDIA; last accessed 5 July 2019.

———. 2012. 'Why I Screamed, Rape Us, Take Our Flesh,' *The Shillong Times*. Accessible on https://theshillongtimes.com/2012/02/28/why-i-screamed-rape-us-take-our-flesh/; last accessed 5 July 2019.

Robinson, Nic. 2010. 'Hard to Reach', *Frontline*. Accessible on http://www.hindu.com/thehindu/fline/fl2703/stories/20100212270304600.htm; last accessed 5 July 2019.

Rognstrand, Andrea. 2014. 'Escaping India's Anti-Gay Laws: "Coming to Australia is the Runaway Plan"', *SameSame*. Accessible on http://www.samesame.com.au/features/10901/Escaping-Indias-anti-gay-laws-Coming-to-Australia-is-the-run-away-plan; last accessed 5 July 2019.

Ross, Colvin and Sruthi Gottipati. 2013. 'Interview with BJP Leader Narendra Modi', *Reuters*. Accessible on http://blogs.reuters.com/india/2013/07/12/interview-with-bjp-leader-narendra-modi/; last accessed 5 July 2019.

Roy, Arundhati. 1999. 'The Greater Common Good', *Outlook*. Accessible on http://www.outlookindia.com/article.aspx?207509; last accessed 5 July 2019.

———. 2009. 'Mr Chidambaram's War', *Outlook*. Accessible on http://www.outlookindia.com/article/mr-chidambarams-war/262519; last accessed 5 July 2019.

———. 2015. 'I Am Returning My Award Because I'm Ashamed of What's Happening in India', *The Guardian*. Accessible on http://www.theguardian.com/commentisfree/2015/nov/06/returning-award-ashamed-india-arundhati-roy; last accessed 5 July 2019.

The Hindu Staff. 2013. '"Ruling Regressive", Say Gay Rights Activists', *The Hindu*. Accessible on http://www.thehindu.com/todays-paper/tp-national/ruling-regressive-say-gay-rights-activists/article5449868.ece; last accessed 5 July 2019.

Sahni, Diksha. 2012. 'Ansari and the Anatomy of Fear', *The Wall Street Journal*. Accessible on http://blogs.wsj.com/indiarealtime/2012/02/28/picture-focus-ansari-and-the-anatomy-of-fear/; last accessed 5 July 2019.

Sarkar, Urvashi. 2010. 'Mystery Shrouds Death of AMU Professor', *The Hindu*. Accessible on http://www.thehindu.com/news/national/article391265.ece; last accessed 5 July 2019.

Schönher, Mathias. 2015. 'Deleuze, a Split with Foucault', *Le Foucaldien*, pp. 1–12. Accessible on https://foucaldien.net/articles/abstract/10.16995/lefou.8/; last accessed 5 July 2019.

Scroll Staff. 2015. India Stood with Iran, Saudi and Pakistan in Failed Attempt To Block Benefits for Gay UN Staffers', *Scroll*. Accessible on http://scroll.in/article/716131/india-stood-with-iran-saudi-and-pakistan-in-failed-attempt-to-block-benefits-for-gay-un-staffers; last accessed 5 July 2019.

Seervai, Shanoor. 2014. 'Who's Behind the Transgender Video on Seatbelt Safety', *The Wall Street Journal*. Accessible on http://blogs.wsj.com/

indiarealtime/2014/05/13/whos-behind-the-transgender-video-on-seat-belt-safety-2/; last accessed 5 July 2019.

Seetha. 2006. 'Turf Tussle–Judicial Pronouncements Have Ranged from the Divine to the Comical', *The Telegraph*. Accessible on http://www.telegraphindia.com/1061224/asp/insight/story_7168959.asp; last accessed 5 July 2019.

Sen, Jahnavi. 2016. 'Gulberg Society Verdict: Of 24 Convicted, 11 Imprisoned for Life; Timeline of Events', *The Wire*, 17 June. Accessible on https://thewire.in/communalism/gulberg-society-2002-gujarat-ehsan-jafri-verdict; last accessed 5 July 2019.

Sengupta, Somini. 2009. 'Attack on Women at an Indian Bar Intensifies a Clash of Cultures', The *New York Times*. Accessible on <http://www.nytimes.com/2009/02/09/world/asia/09india.html?_r=0; last accessed 5 July 2019.

Setalvad, Teesta. 2013. 'Contours of a Conspiracy', *Frontline*, 17 May. Accessible on www.frontline.in/cover-story/contours-of-a-conspiracy/article4660251.ece; last accessed 5 July 2019.

Sethi, A. 2012. 'Activists Shocked at Gallantry Award for Chhattisgarh Cop', *The Hindu*. Accessible on http://www.thehindu.com/news/national/article2834675.ece; last accessed 5 July 2019.

Sharma, Mansi. 2009. 'State of the Nation Survey: Homosexuality Still a Taboo', CNN-IBN Live. Accessible on http://www.ibnlive.com/news/india/sotn-homosexuality-322354.html; last accessed 5 July 2019.

Shukla, Stuti. 2014. 'Mixed Response to Cong Promise to Decriminalize Homosexuality,' *The Indian Express*. Accessible on http://indianexpress.com/article/cities/mumbai/mixed-response-to-cong-promise-to-decriminalise-homosexuality/; last accessed 5 July 2019.

Simons, M. 1993. 'The Sex Marker: Scourge on the World's Children', The *New York Times*, April 9. Accessible on http://www.nytimes.com/1993/04/09/world/the-sex-market-scourge-on-the-world-s-children.html; last accessed 5 July 2019.

Singh, Bhrigupati. 2002. 'One Week in Aman Chowk', *Seminar* 517. Accessible on available at: https://india-seminar.com/2002/517/517%20comment.htm; last accessed 5 July 2019.

Sircar, Oishik. 2012. 'Homonationalism: Queer Tales of Queer Prides', *Academia*. Accessible on academia.edu/5547147/Homonationalism_Queer_Tales_of_Queer_Prides; last accessed 5 July 2019.

———. 2013b. 'Coffee Shops, Cricket and a Pogrom', *InfoChange*. Accessible on http://infochangeindia.org/human-rights/rights-and-resistance/coffee-shops-cricket-and-a-pogrom.html; last accessed 5 July 2019.

———. 2013c. 'How Do We Remember Gujarat 2002?' *Infochange*. Accessible on http://infochangeindia.org/human-rights/rights-and-resistance/how-do-we-remember-gujarat-2002.html; last accessed 5 July 2019.

———. 2013d. 'Of Complicity and Contamination in the Neoliberal Academy', *Kafila*. Accessible on https://kafila.online/2013/01/30/of-complicity-and-contamination-in-the-neoliberal-academy-oishik-sircar/; last accessed 5 July 2019.

———. 2014. 'Desire against Desire', *In Plainspeak*, June 1. Accessible on https://www.tarshi.net/inplainspeak/issue-in-focus-desire-against-desire/; last accessed 5 July 2019.

———. 2014. 'Desire against Desire', *In Plainspeak*. Accessible on http://www.tarshi.net/inplainspeak/issue-in-focus-desire-against-desire/; last accessed 10 July 2020.

Special Correspondent. 2009. 'I Was Warned Against Deposing: Sreekumar', *The Hindu*. Accessible on http://www.thehindu.com/news/national/article5896.ece; last accessed 5 July 2019.

———. 2013. 'Ruling regressive, say gay rights activists', *The Hindu*, 12 December. Accessible on http://www.thehindu.com/todays-paper/tp-national/ruling-regressive-say-gay-rightsactivists/article5449868.ece; last accessed 5 July 2019.

Speed News Desk. 2016. 'If You Care about Gay Rights, You Must Read Justice A. P. Shah's Lowdown on Sec. 377', *Catch News*. Accessible on http://www.catchnews.com/national-news/if-you-care-about-gay-rights-you-must-read-justice-ap-shah-s-lowdown-on-sec-377-lgbtq-supreme-court-delhi-high-court-1454418692.html; last accessed 5 July 2019.

Tasneem, Nashrulla. 2013. 'Activists Plan 'Global Day of Rage' To Fight For India's LGBT Community', *Buzzfeed*. Available on http://www.buzzfeed.com/tasneemnashrulla/activists-plan-global-day-of-rage-to-fight-for-indias-lgbt-c#.cvKL2bax0; last accessed 5 July 2019.

Tehelka Staff. 2007. 'The Truth: Gujarat 2002', *Tehelka*. Accessible on https://web.archive.org/web/20130511203516/http://archive.tehelka.com/story_main35.asp?filename=Ne031107gujrat_sec.asp; last accessed 5 July 2019.

Tellis, Ashley. 2010. 'Nothing to Celebrate About 377', *DNA*. Accessible on http://www.dnaindia.com/lifestyle/comment_nothing-to-celebrate-about-section-377_1401765; last accessed 5 July 2019.

Times News Network. 2011. 'Judiciary Shouldn't Undermine Executive: PM', *Times News Network*. Accessible on http://articles.timesofindia.indiatimes.com/2011-02-07/india/28377720_1_judiciary-justice-kapadia-democracy; last accessed 5 July 2019.

———. 2012. 'Gujarat IPS Officer Sanjeev Bhatt Who Took On Narendra Modi Arrested', *The Times of India*. Accessible on http://timesofindia.indiatimes.com/india/Gujarat-IPS-officer-Sanjeev-Bhatt-who-took-on-Narendra-Modi-arrested/articleshow/10191519.cms; last accessed 5 July 2019.

———. 2013. 'A Great Day for Prejudice and Inhumanity: Vikram Seth', *The Times of India*. Accessible on http://timesofindia.indiatimes.com/india/A-great-day-for-prejudice-and-inhumanity-Vikram-Seth/articleshow/27231344.cms; last accessed 5 July 2019.

The Times of India. 2013. 'PIL against Kai Po Che for "Biased" Portrayal of Gujarat Riots', *The Times of India*. Accessible on http://articles.timesofindia.indiatimes.com/2013-05-03/news-interviews/39007874_1_po-che-the-3-mistakes-hindi-film; last accessed 5 July 2019.

UN Human Rights Office. *Free and Equal*. Accessible on https://www.unfe.org/en/actions/the-welcome; last accessed 5 July 2019.

Vasuki Nesiah. 2014. '"The Law, this violent thing": Dissident Memory and Democratic Futures', *Groundviews* 2 February. Accessible on https://groundviews.org/2014/02/02/the-law-this-violent-thing-dissident-memory-and-democratic-futures/; last accessed 5 July 2019.

Venkatesan, J. 2008. 'Supreme Court Disapproves of arming Salwa Judum', *The Hindu*. Accessible on http://hindu.com/2008/04/01/stories/2008040161000100.htm; last accessed 5 July 2019.

———. 2011a. 'Our Republic Must Not Kill Its Own Children: Supreme Court', *The Hindu*. Accessible on http://www.thehindu.com/news/nationalarticle 1092489.ece; last accessed 5 July 2019.

———. 2011b. 'SPOs Ban Will Apply Only in Chhattisgarh: Court', *The Hindu*. Accessible on http://www.thehindu.com/news/national/article2639134.ece?css=print>; last accessed 5 July 2019.

Vishwanath, Apurva and Dhamini Ratnam. 2016. 'Supreme Court Refers Section 377 Petition to Chief Justice', *Livemint*. Accessible on http://www.livemint.com/Politics/oWL6utUghmgS0pOPsEoyYM/Supreme-Court-says-chief-justice-to-decide-on-Section-377-ap.html; last accessed 5 July 2019.

Visual Sources

Born into Brothels. 2004 Directed by Zana Brisky and Ross Kaufmann. USA: Think Film.

Kapoor, Abhishek. 2013. *Kai Po Che*. UTV Motion Pictures.

Nihalani, Govind. 2004. *Dev*. Eros Entertainment.

Selling of Innocents. 1996. Directed by Ruchira Gupta. Associated Producers Ltd.

UN Human Rights. 2014. 'The Welcome', YouTube. Accessible on https://www.youtube.com/watch?v=lihVCIFamb0; last accessed 5 July 2019.

V with U. 2014. *The Seatbelt Crew.* YouTube. Accessible on https://www.youtube.com/watch?v=ET-egGfzHeQ; last accessed 5 July 2019.

Dutta, Debolina and Oishik Sircar. 2011. *We are Foot Soldiers.* Public Service Broadcasting Trust.

Index

About the Author

Oishik Sircar is associate professor at Jindal Global Law School, Sonepat, visiting fellow at University of Technology Sydney Law School, and associate member, Institute for International Law and the Humanities, Melbourne Law School. Oishik is the co-editor of *New Intimacies, Old Desires: Law, Culture and Queer Politics in Neoliberal Times* (2017), and the co-director of the documentary film *We Are Foot Soldiers* (2010).

